The *Mayaguez* Crisis, Mission Command, and Civil-Military Relations

D1716765

The *Mayaguez* Crisis, Mission Command, and Civil-Military Relations

CHRISTOPHER J. LAMB

Joint History Office
Office of the Chairman of the Joint Chiefs of Staff
Washington, DC - 2018

This book was reviewed by the appropriate US government departments and agencies and cleared for public release. It is a publication of the Office of the Chairman of the Joint Chiefs of Staff, but its contents are the sole responsibility of the author and do not represent the official position of the chairman or the Joint Chiefs of Staff, the Department of Defense, or the US government.

First edition 2018

Library of Congress Cataloging-in-Publication Data

Names: Lamb, Christopher J. (Christopher Jon), 1955- author.
Title: The Mayaguez Crisis, mission command, and civil-military relations / Christopher J. Lamb.
Description: First edition. | Washington, DC : Office of the Chairman of the Joint Chiefs of Staff, 2018. | Includes bibliographical references and index.
ISubjects: LCSH: Mayaguez Incident, 1975. | United States--Foreign

relations--1974-1977--Decision making. | Crisis management in government--United States--Case studies. | Civil-military relations--United States--Case studies. | United States--Foreign relations--Cambodia. | Cambodia--Foreign relations--United States.

To the members of the US armed forces who served
during the *Mayaguez* crisis, and to those who similarly have been
called upon in the past, or who will be in the future.

What I fear is not the enemy's strategy,
but our own mistakes.

—Thucydides,
The History of the Peloponnesian War

Contents

List of Illustrations x

Foreword xi

Preface xiii

Key Figures in the *Mayaguez* Crisis xix

Abbreviations. xxiii

Introduction 1

Part I: Crisis Behaviors

    1. Day One: Monday, May 12 11

    2. Day Two: Tuesday, May 13 19

    3. Day Three: Wednesday, May 14 35

    4. Day Four: Thursday, May 15 57

Part II: Crisis Explanations

    5. Critical Crisis Decisions. 69

    6. Explaining Decisions, Behaviors, and Outcomes. 105

    7. Refining the Explanation: Rationality, Bureaucracy, and Beliefs 137

    8. Findings, Issues, and Prescriptions. 165

Conclusion 213

Notes. 219

Map Credits 273

Index 275

Illustrations

Maps

Mainland Southeast Asia 3

Local Area Map 12

Locations of US Air Bases in Thailand 20

Command and Control Communications, May 14–15, 1975 38

Planned Tang Island and *Mayaguez* Actions, 0600, May 15, 1975 44

Tang Island: Khmer Rouge Defensive Positions, 6:20 a.m. 45

Tang Island: Situation 7:00 a.m. 47

Marine Forces on Tang Island after First Wave 58

Tang Island: Situation 4:00 p.m. 62

Operations against SS *Mayaguez* and Koh Tang 81

Figures

1. Key Events and Decisions 75

2. Military Chain of Command in 1975 199

Photographs follow page 136.

Foreword

═══════════════════════════

On May 12, 1975—only two weeks after the fall of Saigon and the collapse of South Vietnam—Cambodian Khmer Rouge forces boarded and seized the US merchant vessel SS *Mayaguez* in international waters and took its crew hostage. This unprovoked challenge to American power was a major test of Gerald R. Ford's presidency and an international crisis with significant consequences for the United States and its allies.

Ford himself considered the *Mayaguez* crisis the "tensest moments" of his entire presidency. From Monday, May 12, through Thursday, May 15, the president and his advisors deliberated on the best course of action and struggled to manage the rapidly evolving crisis. During this time, the National Security Council convened four times for over five hours of meetings; this is the only time a president ever directly managed a crisis through the National Security Council. The episode was also the first test of the 1973 War Powers Act, which requires the president to notify Congress within forty-eight hours of committing US forces to military action.

Although the crew of *Mayaguez* was returned safely, forty-one servicemen lost their lives during the rescue mission, and over fifty were wounded. The decisions made during the crisis have often been misconstrued—the story behind the decision making and the operations is confusing and sometimes conflicting. Even though multiple books and studies have been written about the crisis, and a plethora of unclassified and declassified sources are available on the subject, to date none of them have adequately explained what US leaders hoped to accomplish and why the crisis unfolded the way it did.

Christopher J. Lamb sets out to remedy this in *The* Mayaguez *Crisis, Mission Command, and Civil-Military Relations*. Dr. Lamb is a distinguished research fellow in the Center for Strategic Research at the Institute for National Strategic Studies at National Defense University. His earlier book on the incident, *Belief Systems and Decision Making in the* Mayaguez *Crisis*, was published by the University of Florida Press in 1989.

He has published widely on international relations, the US national security system, and defense policy and strategy. He holds a doctorate in international relations from Georgetown University; his dissertation was on the *Mayaguez* crisis.

This publication has been reviewed and approved for publication by the Department of Defense. It is an official publication of the Joint History Office, but the views expressed are those of the author and do not necessarily represent those the Joint Chiefs of Staff or the Department of Defense.

—David B. Crist, PhD
Executive Director
Joint History and Research Office

Preface

Even though the *Mayaguez* crisis took place almost forty-five years ago, it remains an item of interest to many, including Department of Defense leaders. Not long ago, former secretary of defense Robert M. Gates cited the *Mayaguez* incident as an example of our inability to anticipate the nature and location of our future military engagements.[1] More recently, the chairman of the Joint Chiefs of Staff, Marine General Joseph F. Dunford Jr., told a graduating class of the United States Air Force Academy that the *Mayaguez* crisis illustrated the enduring truth that "the primary difference between success and failure on and off the battlefield has historically been about the human, not the hardware."[2] He related the example of Richard C. Brims, a 1971 Air Force Academy graduate, who risked everything to extract Marines from a heavily defended island during the *Mayaguez* operations. With eleven of fourteen available helicopters already put out of action by enemy fire, Brims persisted in trying to land and finally succeeded, holding his position under fire until twenty-seven Marines were loaded so that he could carry them to safety.

Although the *Mayaguez* is an example of the courage and fortitude of American servicemen,[3] for most it also remains—as Senator John S. McCain III once observed in his own speech to Air Force Academy graduates[4]—an enduring symbol of what can go wrong in the planning and execution of military operations, and even a metaphor for military tragedy and the Vietnam War as a whole.[5] Other conclusions and lessons continue to be extracted from the *Mayaguez* crisis by scholars and pundits, including the belief that it terminated a nascent effort to learn the true lessons of Vietnam,[6] and worse, that it effectively ended the Vietnam War with a lie, which many believe is how the war began.[7] Some of the variance in opinions about the *Mayaguez* is explained by the commentators' differing beliefs, values, and priorities, but widespread confusion about what happened and why it happened also plays a role.

This point was brought home to me in January 2015 when Commander Richard B. Hughes, USNR, paid a visit to my office at National Defense University to discuss the

Mayaguez. He had researched the event for a war college class and wanted to compare his findings with my research. Thirty years ago I devoted five years of study to the *Mayaguez* crisis, writing my master's thesis and doctoral dissertation on the topic. I never expected to write about it again and fully anticipated my findings would some-day be eclipsed by new scholarship. Among other things, my requests for interviews with Henry A. Kissinger, the national security advisor and secretary of state during the crisis, and James R. Schlesinger, the secretary of defense at the time, had not been granted. I reasoned they would someday have their say on the matter and that archived materials about the crisis would eventually be declassified, enabling scholars to refine or revise conclusions.

Over the years, these and other primary and secondary sources gradually emerged, producing an astonishing amount of new information about decision making during the crisis. In 1993 Lucien S. Vandenbroucke more fully revealed the tension between the White House and the Department of Defense over the sinking of Cambodian patrol boats during the crisis. As more information became available, other details of crisis behavior were illuminated. In 2008 I had a chance to familiarize myself with the bur-geoning literature on the *Mayaguez* while researching a short case study on the topic for the Project on National Security Reform. However, it was not until Commander Hughes showed me the full range of documentation and literature on the *Mayaguez* that I came to appreciate just how much new primary information on the crisis was available and how many books and articles had examined that new data. The more I considered these new sources, the more surprised I was to discover how little the new data had contributed to a clear, consensus explanation for US behavior during the crisis.

This book began as an attempt to fathom how so much valuable descriptive mate-rial could confuse rather than advance a compelling explanation for US behavior. I wanted to see if a careful examination of all available documentation could clarify what happened during the crisis and, more importantly, sharpen the explanation for why it happened. Along the way, I uncovered some new sources, including Army General John A. Wickham Jr.'s notes during his service as the military assistant to Secretary of Defense Schlesinger. General Wickham also graciously consented to an interview. Others helped me find additional sources of major import, including Joseph E. Davis of the Veterans of Foreign Wars' Washington office and Mokie Pratt Porter, the director of communications for the Vietnam Veterans of America, who helped me obtain a copy of the telltale Schlesinger interview in *Veteran* magazine. In examining such revealing materials, I came to believe the mysterious *Mayaguez* crisis still has important lessons to teach us about defense, foreign affairs, and national security policy. Leaders at National Defense University agreed, and I am thankful they afforded me the opportunity to do this study.

In short, that is how I ended up returning to the *Mayaguez* as a research topic thirty years later, something I never expected. A peer review by my talented colleague T. X. Hammes led to a recommendation to separate the academic argument about social science methodology from the findings on defense policy and national security issues. It pays to follow T. X.'s advice, as it does to follow his research more generally. Consequently, there is an article titled "The *Mayaguez* Crisis: Correcting 30 Years of Scholarship"[8] in the spring 2018 issue of the Academy of Political Science journal *Political Science Quarterly*. Readers interested in methodology and academic analysis will find the article more helpful than this book, which is aimed more narrowly at the defense and national security community. I must thank Marylena Mantas, the managing editor of *Political Science Quarterly*, for all her assistance and courtesy and the journal's anonymous reviewers for their comments and insights, all of which improved the article I submitted for their consideration. *Political Science Quarterly* also granted permission for us to use a timeline chart submitted with the article. I also appreciated the helpful comments from Colonel Susan Bryant, USA (Ret.), another colleague who reviewed an early draft of the manuscript.

I owe a deep debt of gratitude to the many librarians and archivists who did so much to facilitate the research effort, beginning with National Defense University's own reference librarian, Karen Cooper, who was unusually tenacious in helping track down obscure, decades-old documentation. I greatly appreciate her dedicated assistance, which was typical of the type of support we receive from our librarians. Karen's colleague, Mary Bowser, repeatedly intervened to assist my extended use of key sources, trusting they would eventually be returned. Archivists at the Air Force Historical Research Agency were also uniformly helpful and diligent, particularly Samuel Shearin, who persisted until he could track down internal CINCPAC documents and oral interviews with personnel who served during the crisis. Lynn Gamma and Sylvester Jackson Jr. also assisted in this regard. Archivist Laurie Varenhorst was most kind in sharing copies of documents on the *Mayaguez* crisis from Clemson University's special collection of Senator Strom Thurmond materials.

Obtaining graphics was a major challenge that was made much easier by the kind willingness of many other authors and publishers who granted us permission to use their photographs and illustrations. Colonel Ralph F. Wetterhahn, USAF (Ret.), kindly allowed us to use his insightful battle maps from his book *The Last Battle: The* Mayaguez *Incident and the End of the Vietnam War*. I admire Colonel Wetterhahn, who is notable among the authors investigating the military operations during the *Mayaguez* crisis for having traveled to Cambodia to find and interview Cambodian personnel involved in the fighting. W. W. Norton & Company and Osprey Publishing allowed us to use graphics from books they published: Roy Rowan's *The Four Days of Mayaguez* and Clayton K. S. Chun's *The Last Boarding Party: The USMC and the SS* Mayaguez *1975*, respectively.

Two active-duty sailors during the *Mayaguez* operation shared photos they took during the crisis. Wayne K. Stewart served on board the USS *Wilson*, and Mike Chan served on board the USS *Holt*. Both took many amazing photographs during the military operations and are still producing great photography. We appreciate their quick assistance and permission to use their photographs. Elizabeth Druga, an archivist at the Gerald R. Ford Presidential Library and Museum, provided us with all the photographic archives from the White House during the crisis. She was extremely helpful in getting the high-resolution photographs from the Ford Library approved and ready for use in this book under tight time constraints.

Dr. Bill Eliason, our editor at National Defense University Press, kindly reached out to help secure the assistance of Juliette Kelsey Chagnon, the managing editor at *Air Force Magazine*, and Mike Tsukamoto, the magazine's photo editor. They provided many of the photographs used in this book. Hill Goodspeed, historian at the National Naval Aviation Museum, and Susan Todd Brook, the senior acquisitions editor at the Naval Institute Press, also helped us locate photos and granted permission for their use, as did Dr. Doug Lantry and Brett Stolle from the National Museum of the US Air Force. Technical Sergeant Shawn Nickel, USAF, went out of his way to obtain a high-resolution photo of Knife-22, which now resides at Hurlburt Field. Romondo Davis repeatedly helped us track down photos taken on the USS *Coral Sea*. I also want to recognize the exceedingly helpful cooperation of the Koh Tang/*Mayaguez* Veterans Organization, particularly Fred B. Morris and Don Raatz, for assisting our search for photographers and approving our use of photographs from their website.

Finally, I want to acknowledge the support of David B. Crist, the director of the Joint History Office. This book would not have seen the light of day without his conviction that it made a worthy contribution to understanding an important military operation. I especially appreciate the many hours his sharp-eyed editor, Shawn H. Vreeland, spent laboring over the manuscript and working to put it in the most presentable form. He certainly deserves great credit for the superb craftsmanship evident in the final product. Collectively, David, Shawn, and I want to express our admiration for the talents of Jamie Harvey, who led the book design effort at the Government Publishing Office. I would also like to thank Rob Kocher for his expertise in redrawing and adapting the maps.

As this long list of acknowledgements suggests, the book is really a collective effort. Perhaps the only singular credit I should claim for the work is any errors or omissions the reader finds. Those, to be sure, are my responsibility. Readers inclined to share their observations, corrections, or clarifications can email me at lambc@ndu.edu.

I close these prefatory remarks with an expression of appreciation for all the members of the national security community who serve overseas, especially those who serve in the military, and particularly those who served during the *Mayaguez* crisis. On a personal note, it is impossible to study the *Mayaguez* without thinking time and again of the servicemen sent into combat during the crisis, and especially of the three young Marines inadvertently left behind. Their service and sacrifices underscore the stakes involved when foreign powers seize American citizens and US leaders must decide whether to risk a small minority of citizens on behalf of the longer-term interests of the entire community.[9]

What I now appreciate, much better than thirty years ago when I first studied the *Mayaguez* crisis, is how frequently national security leaders have to decide between prioritizing the welfare of a small group of citizens or the broader national interests as a whole. This difficult choice arises not only when hostages are seized by foreign powers, but tacitly every time diplomats, intelligence personnel, other national security officials, and especially military personnel are sent beyond the bounds of our own body politic and its laws and authorities. These personnel constantly accept risks on behalf of the larger community.

While dedicating a memorial plaque to the veterans of the *Mayaguez* operations in 1996, Senator McCain said it would "commemorate the sacrifice of Americans— comrades and friends to some; heroes to us all—who lived, fought and died for the honor of a free people."[10] The senator's tribute more accurately depicts why the United States used military force during the crisis than most books and articles on the topic. My hope is that this book will honor the sacrifice of those who participated in the *Mayaguez* operations, and the service of all those we send into danger overseas, by improving our understanding of decision making during the crisis and its implications for the mission command concept and civil-military relations.

Key Figures in the *Mayaguez* Crisis

In Washington, DC

General George S. Brown, USAF	Chairman of the Joint Chiefs of Staff, 1974–78
Philip W. Buchen	White House Counsel, 1975–77
William P. Clements Jr.	Deputy Secretary of Defense, 1973–77
William E. Colby	Director of the Central Intelligence, 1973–76
General Robert E. Cushman Jr.	Commandant of the Marine Corps, 1972–75
Gerald R. Ford	President of the United States, 1974–77
Robert T. Hartmann	Counselor to President Ford, 1974–77
William G. Hyland	Director of the Bureau of Intelligence and Research, Department of State, 1974–75
Robert S. Ingersoll	Deputy Secretary of State, 1974–76
General David C. Jones	Acting Chairman of the Joint Chiefs of Staff, 1975
David H. Kennerly	White House photographer, 1974–77
Henry A. Kissinger	National Security Advisor, 1969–75/ Secretary of State, 1973–77
Joseph Laitin	Assistant Secretary of Defense for Public Affairs, 1975
Major Robert C. "Bud" McFarlane, USMC	Scowcroft's assistant
Ronald H. "Ron" Nessen	White House Press Secretary, 1974–77

Lieutenant General John W. Pauly, USAF	Assistant to the Chairman of the Joint Chiefs of Staff, 1974–75
Nelson A. Rockefeller	Vice President of the United States, 1974–77
Donald H. Rumsfeld	White House Chief of Staff, 1974–75
John A. Scali	US ambassador to the United Nations, 1973–75
James R. Schlesinger	Secretary of Defense, 1973–75
Lieutenant General Brent Scowcroft, USAF	Deputy National Security Advisor, 1973–75
Joseph J. Sisco	Under Secretary of State for Political Affairs, 1974–76
William Lloyd Stearman	National Security Council staff member, 1971–76
Kurt J. Waldheim	United Nations Secretary-General, 1972–81
Major General John A. Wickham Jr., USA	Schlesinger's military assistant, 1973–75

In the military chain of command

Lieutenant Colonel Randall W. Austin, USMC	Battalion landing team assault commander
Lieutenant General John L. Burns, USAF	On-scene commander/commander of US Support Activities Group and the Seventh Air Force
Second Lieutenant Michael A. Cicere, USMC	
Rear Admiral R. P. Coogan	USS *Coral Sea*
Admiral Noel A. M. Gayler	Commander in Chief, US Pacific Command, 1972–76
Admiral James L. Holloway III	Chief of Naval Operations, 1974–78
Major General Ira A. "Jim" Hunt	Lieutenant General Burns's deputy

Colonel John M. Johnson, USMC   Ground force commander

First Lieutenant James D.
"Dick" Keith, USMC

Second Lieutenant James
McDaniel, USMC

Vice Admiral George P. Steele   Commander, Seventh Fleet, 1973–75

Lieutenant General Ray B. Sitton, USAF   Director of Operations, Joint Chiefs of Staff, 1974–76

Brigadier General Charles E. Word, USAF   Deputy Director of Operations, National Military Command Center, 1974–75

Other

Charles T. Miller   Captain of the *Mayaguez*

Abbreviations

CIA	Central Intelligence Agency
CINCPAC	commander in chief, Pacific Command
COMUSSAG/7AF	commander of US Support Activities Group and Seventh Air Force
DIA	Defense Intelligence Agency
DoD	Department of Defense
FBIS	Foreign Broadcast Information Service (Central Intelligence Agency)
GAO	US General Accounting Office
INR	Bureau of Intelligence and Research (Department of State)
IPAC	Pacific Command's intelligence center
JCS	Joint Chiefs of Staff
NMCC	National Military Command Center
NSA	National Security Agency
NSC	National Security Council
PRC	People's Republic of China
TACAIR	tactical air
UN	United Nations
USSAG	US Support Activities Group

Introduction

The last battle of the Vietnam War[1] and the "tensest moments" of Gerald R. Ford's presidency[2] began off the coast of Cambodia on May 12, 1975. A commercial US-registered ship, the SS *Mayaguez*, was commandeered by Cambodian forces while en route from Hong Kong to a port in southern Thailand. The incident sparked immediate concerns for National Security Advisor and Secretary of State Henry A. Kissinger. Throughout early 1975, Kissinger and President Ford had been doing their best to convince Congress to approve aid to support the tottering regimes in South Vietnam and Cambodia. Both men lobbied Capitol Hill hard, repeatedly warning in speeches that American credibility would suffer a grievous wound if the United States did not support its allies in Indochina. Lobbying efforts by lower-ranking officials such as Philip C. Habib, the assistant secretary of state for East Asian and Pacific affairs, had little effect, so the president appealed to a joint session of Congress on April 10. Kissinger met with congressional committees the following week.

Ford and Kissinger warned that not propping up Vietnam would signal friend and foe alike that the United States had weakened and was no longer reliable. Ford argued, "We want our friends to know that we will stand by them, and we want any potential adversaries to know that we will stand up to them."[3] Kissinger insisted, "The United States cannot pursue a policy of selective credibility. We cannot abandon friends in one part of the world without jeopardizing the security of friends everywhere." He also declared, "A reduction of American influence in key areas can have disastrous consequences. How other nations perceive us is thus a matter of major consequence." Kissinger's statements also reveal a "premonition of doom"—his conviction that the fall of Southeast Asia would invariably engender a time of testing for the United States.

But it was all to no avail: Congress had had enough of the Vietnam War and refused to provide any more assistance. Phnom Penh and Saigon fell to Communist forces in April, forcing the evacuation of US forces and creating hundreds of thousands of refugees. In the weeks leading up to the seizure of the *Mayaguez*, Kissinger,

Ford, and Defense Secretary James R. Schlesinger had managed these evacuations intensively. They also did their best to limit the geostrategic fallout from the loss of Indochina by signaling to international observers that US reversals in Southeast Asia should not be misread as weakness or lack of resolve. Ford and Kissinger were particularly active, making speeches, giving interviews and answering questions in news conferences. They consistently made three points, arguing that Americans had a moral obligation not to abandon their longtime friends and allies, that it was imperative for Congress and the executive branch to work together in forging a new national unity on geopolitics, and that failure to do these things would invariably have negative strategic consequences.

In this context, it was probably inevitable that US leaders would attach more than ordinary significance to the news that Cambodian gunboats had seized the *Mayaguez*. They quickly decided to dispatch US airplanes to monitor the situation and direct other US forces to the area. US pilots warned and then sank Cambodian gunboats in an attempt to quarantine the *Mayaguez* from Tang Island (also known as Koh Tang; *koh* means "island" in the Khmer language) where US leaders believed some crew members were being held. Eventually the Cambodians decided to release the ship's crew. Just as they were about to do so, US forces launched operations to retake the *Mayaguez*, assault Tang Island, and conduct airstrikes against the mainland. The island assault was nearly disastrous: Cambodian forces downed most of the US helicopters and inflicted numerous casualties. However, all the members of the *Mayaguez* crew who had been released just prior to the assault were recovered unharmed.

A large majority of Americans responded to the return of the crew with relief and regarded the use of force with approval. An apparently successful operation was welcome news in the aftermath of the depressing withdrawal of US forces from Indochina. Yet questions about US motives and the way the crisis was managed quickly arose. The military operations cost the lives of forty-one servicemen. Fifty more were wounded in the effort to rescue the thirty-nine crew members of the *Mayaguez*.[4] Ten of the eleven helicopters used in the mission were damaged or destroyed. No crew members were on the island that was assaulted. Instead, they had been held captive near the Cambodian mainland and released just prior to the Marine assault. As these and other details became available, Congress decided to investigate the handling of the incident. The resultant report raised issues about US motives, the adequacy of intelligence, and missed diplomatic opportunities but could not provide a definitive explanation for US behavior.

Since then a number of books have contributed to a better understanding of what happened during the crisis, both on the scene in Cambodia and during the

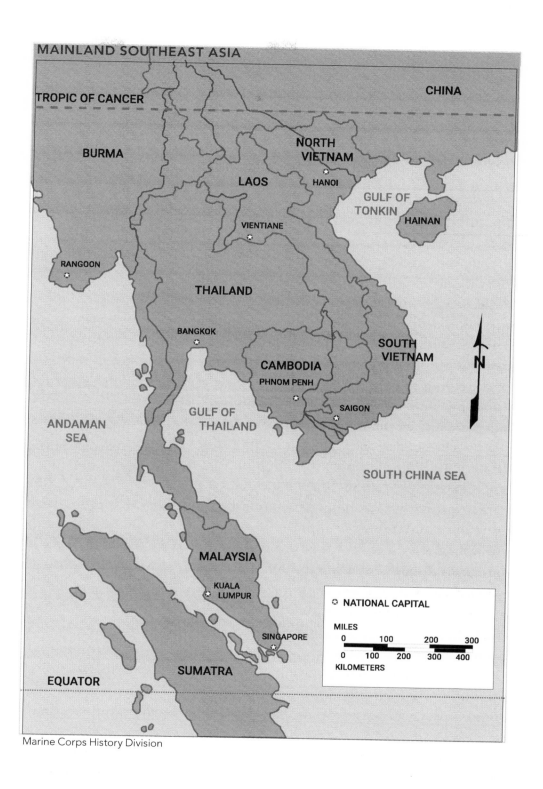

MAINLAND SOUTHEAST ASIA

TROPIC OF CANCER

CHINA

BURMA

NORTH
VIETNAM

LAOS

HANOI

GULF OF
TONKIN

HAINAN

VIENTIANE

RANGOON

THAILAND

BANGKOK

SOUTH
VIETNAM

CAMBODIA

PHNOM PENH

ANDAMAN
SEA

GULF OF
THAILAND

SAIGON

SOUTH CHINA SEA

N

MALAYSIA

KUALA
LUMPUR

SINGAPORE

NATIONAL CAPITAL

MILES

0   100   200   300

0   100   200   300   400

KILOMETERS

SUMATRA

EQUATOR

Marine Corps History Division

decision-making process in Washington.[5] Over the years researchers interviewed an increasing number of senior US leaders involved in the episode, many of whom have also published memoirs.[6] In addition, an astonishing amount of primary information—much of it previously classified—has been released. On the whole, and with the notable exception of the Cuban missile crisis,[7] it is doubtful there are many other major US foreign policy events as well documented as the *Mayaguez* crisis.[8]

For instance, researchers now know the president's whereabouts on a minute-by-minute basis during the crisis, what was said in all the National Security Council (NSC) meetings where the president made his major decisions, and what was said during telephone calls and conversations between key leaders, including the president and his senior advisors. Moreover, there are numerous primary sources available, such as all the intelligence community communications during the crisis, all the oral and written Department of Defense orders, the most important diplomatic communications, the conversations held during Kissinger's staff meeting on the first day of the crisis, the content of NSC staff products, and memorandums of conversation in the Oval Office between the central figures. There is no dearth of secondary sources either. The memoirs of numerous major and minor White House officials who provide their impressions of decision making during the crisis have been published, as have in-depth interviews with key leaders, including President Ford, who gave two detailed interviews immediately following the crisis. For an operational perspective, there are declassified military histories that chart the military decision-making process between the Pentagon and forces in the field, and numerous accounts written by military officers who commanded and conducted the military operations. In addition to the above materials (which represent only a portion of those available), I was also able to obtain for this book a declassified copy of the minute-by-minute notes from the military assistant to Secretary of Defense Schlesinger (Major General John A. Wickham Jr., USA), who recorded Schlesinger's phone and meeting conversations.

Surprisingly, despite the copious amount of data available, scholars have not reached a consensus as to what happened and why. Thirty years ago I argued the US response to the seizure of the *Mayaguez* "was a hasty, risky, ill-conceived action not commensurate with publicly stated objectives." Today there is a consensus on this point. All agree that US military operations narrowly avoided disaster,[9] but there is no corresponding agreement on why the United States behaved as it did. The event is still explained as a rescue mission, a principled defense of freedom of the seas, an exercise in realpolitik with the United States acting to preserve its reputation for protecting its interests, a political gambit by President Ford to enhance his political fortunes, and a national spasm of violence reflecting the collective frustration felt from the debacle suffered in Vietnam.[10]

A compelling explanation for the crisis must resolve numerous inconsistencies that arise between asserted motives and actual behaviors. With respect to the quick decision by US leaders to use force, the following questions must be answered. If it was a principled defense of freedom of the seas, why did the Marines launch a risky invasion of Tang Island instead of just recovering the ship? If it was a rescue mission, why did the United States sink the gunboats leaving Tang, which ran the clear risk of killing those who needed to be rescued? If the United States was reinforcing its reputation for protecting its interests, why did it conduct hasty military operations that ran the risk of embarrassing failure? If Ford was trying to enhance his political fortunes, why did he act so precipitously, increasing the risks to operations that almost ended in disaster? If it was an emotional spasm of violence reflecting the frustration from the debacle suffered in Vietnam, why were B-52s not used as initially planned?

As for the Cambodians, most commentators seem to believe local commanders seized the ship and the nascent central government never managed to catch up and respond effectively. But if the Cambodians were just innocent bystanders, why did they make determined efforts to transport the crew to the mainland despite US diplomatic warnings and warning fire from military aircraft? On the other hand, if they were not innocent bystanders and had nefarious motives, why did they give up the crew so easily?

Scholarship over the past several decades has not really answered such questions. The increasingly detailed information available about crisis decision making has been used to provide rich descriptions of the crisis that obscure, rather than illuminate, the most important explanatory factors. As more information became available, explanations for US behavior became more diffuse and idiosyncratic. Worse, some elements of what was once well understood about the crisis were lost. Thus the motives for US behavior remain contested and widely misunderstood, and the significance of the crisis is also often underestimated. This is as unnecessary as it is unfortunate and unsatisfactory. It is unnecessary because the data overwhelmingly demonstrate that one variable accounts for all US behavior with great consistency. It is unsatisfactory because not distinguishing between competing explanatory variables and their efficacy hinders progress toward cumulative knowledge.

The purpose of this study is to rectify these shortfalls by correcting some key descriptive omissions and errors, and to provide a compelling explanation for US behavior based on all available evidence. There are excellent descriptive accounts of the crisis, but they all suffer from a few notable errors or omissions. After accurately describing what happened during the crisis, particularly during the four days of decision making by leaders in Washington, it is much easier to analyze the critical decisions that determined the outcome of the crisis. Once decision making in the *Mayaguez* crisis is well described and explained, it is useful as a valuable case study for policy analysis.

The incident has been dismissed as a mere "historical footnote," but this reflects a poor understanding of the significant issues raised by the crisis, including what decision makers thought was at stake, the organizational mechanism used to manage the crisis, and the insights that can be generated from a close examination of the roles played by key leaders during the crisis. Properly understood, the *Mayaguez* incident can be used to illustrate a number of important policy issues and to impart important lessons for senior defense leaders and policy makers.

For example, the *Mayaguez* crisis offers a fascinating case study in national security decision making. It was the first test of the War Powers Act,* was a major stimulus for defense reform, and is widely considered a metaphor for the entire US experience in Vietnam, especially given the way the incident was managed and its outcome. The incident also has attracted interest because of some unique features, reportedly being the only time US forces fought the Khmer Rouge and the first time Marines had made a ship-to-ship boarding of a hostile vessel since the Civil War.[11]

Of greater significance is the fact that the *Mayaguez* crisis was the only time in history when a president directly managed a crisis through the NSC,[12] which met four times for five and a quarter hours of deliberations and decision making.[13] From Monday, May 12, through Thursday, May 15, the president and his senior advisors struggled to control the crisis precipitated by the news that Cambodian forces had seized the *Mayaguez*. Ford announced he would personally manage the crisis, and he made most major decisions on how to do that in those meetings rather than during informal gatherings of key subordinates or by authorizing a subordinate group to exercise oversight on an ongoing basis. There was near unanimity on objectives, but not on how to achieve them. The extent to which cabinet officials used their positions to control implementation of presidential decisions to obtain preferred outcomes has not been fully appreciated. In the end, Ford fired Schlesinger for insubordination but without clearly understanding where Schlesinger was actually guilty of insubordination or

---

*The War Powers Act is a law passed in 1973 that requires the president to notify Congress within forty-eight hours of committing US armed forces to military action. It prohibits the use of armed forces for more than sixty days (and allows another thirty days for purposes of withdrawing the forces) without congressional authorization or a declaration of war. Of the many reports submitted by presidents in accordance with reporting requirements in the War Powers Act, the *Mayaguez* crisis is the only case where the president cited Section 4(a)(1), which triggers a sixty-day withdrawal requirement.

how Schlesinger's decisions benefited him. In contrast, Ford either was unaware of, or overlooked, Kissinger's decision to withhold information from the NSC in order to make military operations more likely.

For these and other reasons the *Mayaguez* crisis had a negative impact on civil-military relations that deserves more scrutiny than it has received. It is also possible to extract useful lessons about command and control of US forces more generally by examining the incident. These and other leadership and policy issues are discussed in the concluding section of this book.

PART I

Crisis Behaviors

CHAPTER 1

Day One | Monday, May 12

ews of the *Mayaguez* seizure reached Washington about two hours after the fact. The US embassy in Jakarta alerted the National Military Command Center (NMCC) at the Pentagon and other addresses around 5:12 a.m., and Deputy National Security Advisor Brent Scowcroft heard about the incident fifteen minutes later.* Noting the reports were of uncertain validity, he waited until his 7 a.m. intelligence briefing to inform President Ford.[1] Cabinet officials learned of the event in their morning briefings or staff meetings.

The Department of State's intelligence organization (the Bureau of Intelligence and Research, or INR) was the only element of the intelligence community to include the seizure in its morning summary, and National Security Advisor and Secretary of State Henry Kissinger was the only senior leader who immediately reacted to the news with great alarm. He demanded to know why the president had not been notified and why nothing had been done in response. He ordered an immediate investigation of those issues. William G. Hyland, who headed INR, asked what could be done given that the Cambodians already had the crew in custody. Kissinger responded angrily, saying he was not the chief of naval operations and was not sure what the military options were. But he added, "I know you damned well cannot let Cambodia capture a ship a hundred miles at sea and do nothing."[2] Given Kissinger's angst, Hyland made a point of keeping Secretary Kissinger and other key State Department leaders well informed over the next several days.[3]

When Kissinger and Scowcroft met with President Ford at 9:15 a.m. for their morning meeting, they discussed the *Mayaguez*. Kissinger impressed upon the president the gravity of the situation, and it was agreed that Ford should convene an NSC meeting around noon to examine options. Ford told Scowcroft to inform the NSC attendees that he would personally take charge of the crisis, which he said "is what the American people expect."[4]

---

*Local Cambodian time was eleven hours ahead of Washington, DC, but befitting the discussion of US decisions, all times mentioned in this book are eastern standard time unless otherwise noted.

Not long after this meeting, Ford told his press secretary, Ronald H. "Ron" Nessen, about the seizure. He surprised Nessen by asking him whether he would "go in there and bomb the Cambodian boat and take a chance of the Americans being killed? Would you send helicopters in there? Would you mine every harbor in Cambodia?"[5] Ford's questions suggest he was already mulling over the risks of using military force.

At the midday NSC meeting the likely motive for Cambodian behavior was immediately raised by William E. Colby, the director of the Central Intelligence Agency (CIA). He noted the islands near the site of the *Mayaguez* seizure were coveted and contested by Vietnam and Cambodia because of underlying oil fields. Secretary of Defense James Schlesinger speculated Cambodian behavior might be a "bureaucratic misjudgment" or might reflect their determination to underscore their sovereignty over the islands and protect them from the Vietnamese, which would explain why they had already seized Panamanian and Philippine ships. Later in the conversation, after the NSC members had been discussing military options, Deputy Secretary of Defense William P. Clements Jr. again reminded everyone that it was important to remember the seizure was likely "an in-house spat" over control of up to one or one and a half million barrels of oil.[6] The president responded, "That is interesting, but it does not solve our problem," and opined that strong public and private communications and turning around the aircraft carrier USS *Coral Sea* were in order.

The fact that the United States did not have a lot of military assets near the scene and would not for a day or two constrained any immediate decisions to use force. One misconception also influenced the discussion of military options. It was assumed that the Cambodians had probably succeeded in taking the ship and crew to the mainland port of Kompong Som (also called Sihanoukville).[7] Thus, when Schlesinger initially outlined a range of possible military options for the president, they were reactive and punitive, ranging from seizing Cambodian assets, assembling forces, taking an island hostage, or mounting a blockade. Kissinger also raised the idea of seizing Cambodian shipping or mining their harbors, and later Schlesinger offered the possibility of sinking the Cambodian navy.

In the NSC meeting Kissinger noted that pursuing multiple American objectives—for example, recovering the ship and demonstrating American strength—could militate against one another. He was particularly leery of getting into negotiations with the Cambodians for fear of appearing weak. Multiple sources assert Kissinger strongly argued in this first NSC meeting that international perceptions of American power and will were at stake.[8] However, the meeting minutes indicate it was Vice President Nelson A. Rockefeller who, after politely asking the president's permission to speak, insisted that "this will be seen as a test case" and "judged in South Korea." He mentioned the USS *Pueblo*, the US spy ship and its crew that were seized by the North Koreans in 1968 and held for a humiliating eleven months before the crew was released (see sidebar). He stated bluntly:

> I think a violent response is in order. The world should know that we will act and that we will act quickly. We should have an immediate response in terms of action. I do not know if we have any targets that we can strike, but we should certainly consider this. If they get any hostages, this can go on forever.[9]

Schlesinger responded by noting the Cambodians already had hostages: the thirty-nine crew members. Rockefeller, not dissuaded, said action was required. Ford said he was inclined to agree, observing they needed to get the *Coral Sea* on the way to the scene and have mines ready. He promised, "We will take action." Rockefeller later opined that turning the carrier around was not "action" and that "unless the Cambodians are hurt, this pattern [i.e., of wanton provocation] will not be broken." He advocated bombing with planes based in Thailand. Kissinger agreed with Rockefeller and wanted to "give the impression that we are not to be trifled with." He mentioned the possibility of using B-52 bombers from Guam or aircraft from the carrier, which would not require approval from Thailand or the Philippines. But he also said more than once that it "should not look as though we want to pop somebody" and that "we should know what we are doing." He wanted to know what military assets would be required to seize an island, retake the ship and crew, and take or mine Kompong Som. The meeting ended after general agreement on the need for strong public and private statements demanding the release of the ship and crew and more information about military options from the Pentagon.

After the meeting, Kissinger called Schlesinger at the Pentagon. He told Schlesinger that Ford had not yet decided on the specifics of how to respond and that he wanted to share his thinking with Schlesinger. "I'm not in favor of bombing," Kissinger said. "Once done it is over." He was thinking more along the lines of entering Kompong Som

The *Pueblo* Incident

In January 1968, the United States endured a humiliating experience when North Korea seized the USS *Pueblo*—a ship equipped for electronic surveillance—in international waters. The *Pueblo*'s captain, Commander Lloyd M. Bucher, maneuvered for two hours to prevent the North Koreans from boarding while frantically calling for assistance that never arrived. After the North Koreans opened fire, killing one member of the *Pueblo*'s eighty-three-man crew and wounding several others, Bucher gave up the ship and its highly classified materials. The crew was imprisoned for almost a year, enduring frequent beatings, torture, and a subsistence diet. The North Koreans flaunted their confessions as spies.

One account of the *Pueblo* incident claims that the American response turned on the argument of then–Secretary of Defense Clark M. Clifford, who suggested that his colleagues stop asking, "What have we got to hit them with?" Clifford said if they decided their prime objective was to reassert the principle of freedom of the seas, or teach the North Koreans a lesson, well, so be it. But he believed the prime objective should be the safe return of the crew, and a military response was inappropriate for that objective.[10]

Gerald Ford, a congressman at the time, called US options "very, very limited." A Gallup poll taken at the time of the *Pueblo*'s capture indicated that a majority of Americans not only preferred the use of force to secure the return of the *Pueblo* and its crew, but they expected it to lead to war.[11]

harbor and seizing the ship, and perhaps the island at the same time. But, he said, "My experience in Indochina is to do more rather than enough." Schlesinger noted that seizing the mainland port would require congressional support and that there would be casualties and domestic political fallout. Kissinger concluded by saying he "didn't think we should take any small actions" and should at least plan for seizing the harbor, ship, or an island. He wanted to "plan it well and get prepared rather than [taking] some piddling measures."[12]

Kissinger also ordered a complete clampdown on State Department briefings of newsmen. He said he wanted "to let diplomacy run its course." In reality, Kissinger was cooperating with the president's political advisors who wanted it known that Ford personally had taken command of the crisis. Accordingly, Kissinger kept his previously scheduled event in Kansas City and flew off to Missouri that afternoon. While his plane was in the air, the White House announced the seizure of the ship. The president called it an "act of piracy" and demanded its immediate release, promising the most serious consequences if the Cambodians did otherwise. Several hours after this public threat, Deputy Secretary of State Robert S. Ingersoll tried to pass the same dire warning to a representative of the liaison office of the People's Republic of China who was asked to deliver the message to Cambodian authorities. The Chinese representative refused to even hear the content of the message.[13] Similarly, in Beijing the Chinese foreign ministry said the relevant official was not available to accept the message but that it could be dropped off in the ministry's mail room. That happened, but later the ministry returned the document saying it was not in a position to pass the message to Cambodian authorities. In contrast, an officer at the Cambodian embassy in Beijing accepted the message for his country and said he would transmit it. However, the Cambodians also returned the message to the US liaison office without any note of explanation other than having stamped the original envelope with "return to sender." The timing of the Cambodian return of the US message inclined the US representatives in Beijing to speculate that China and Cambodia had coordinated their responses.[14]

Meanwhile, Pentagon leaders ordered the *Coral Sea* and her escorts, which were about to transit Indonesia's Lombok Strait on the way to Australia, to turn back and head for Cambodia. Pentagon senior leaders also settled in to develop the range of military options requested by the president. Schlesinger supervised a debate between the Navy and the acting chairman of the Joint Chiefs of Staff, Air Force General David C. Jones, on options.[15] Schlesinger preferred using carrier aircraft rather than Air Force B-52s because they would be more accurate and involve less collateral and political damage—presumably the Navy's sentiment as well. Thereafter, Admiral Noel A. M. Gayler, commander in chief of US Pacific Command (CINCPAC), who happened to then be in Washington rather than at his headquarters in Honolulu, worked out a basic plan at the Pentagon with a few of his staff and others from the Joint Chiefs' staff.[16] Gayler's plans were reviewed by Jones, who then discussed them with Schlesinger before reviewing them with the NSC.[17]

It was during this initial planning that the first of many misunderstandings between the Pentagon and the White House arose. About halfway through the first NSC meeting, Jones suggested "that we get our contingency plans together as soon as possible and start assembling a task force," and Ford closed the meeting saying he looked forward to seeing the Pentagon's options. Somehow Scowcroft and the NSC staff had the impression that the plans would be produced quickly and reviewed in another NSC meeting later that same day. The Pentagon thought the situation was too fluid for that. No US forces were in the vicinity, given Kissinger's prohibition against using Thai-based military assets. He insisted on this in the first NSC meeting after Jones mentioned launching helicopters to take a Cambodian island. Schlesinger reminded him that their ongoing reconnaissance flights originated in Thailand. Kissinger thought reconnaissance was acceptable but not other military operations.[18] With no assets on hand and the location of the *Mayaguez* uncertain, Jones was reluctant to offer premature options based on inadequate information. Thus, no options paper was provided to the White House on Monday afternoon, which disappointed the NSC staff.[19] In the next NSC meeting after nascent options were reviewed orally, the president made a point of asking for "next steps written in sequence as to when they can take place."

General Jones's concern about the fluidity of the situation proved prescient. That evening, shortly after 9:30 p.m., the Pentagon called Scowcroft with some good news. With daylight emerging in the Gulf of Thailand, a US reconnaissance plane had located the *Mayaguez* and two accompanying Cambodian patrol boats not far from where the seizure had taken place near Poulo Wai island. Contrary to assumptions, the *Mayaguez* had not been taken to the mainland port of Kompong Som. It was still possible, perhaps, to isolate the ship from the mainland. Scowcroft discussed this briefly with President Ford.[20] Then, with the situation apparently stabilized, he left for home. Less than an hour later (10:15 p.m.) Scowcroft's assistant, Marine Major Robert C. "Bud" McFarlane, called Scowcroft with more news. The *Mayaguez* was moving again in the direction of Kompong Som, its assumed destination, and could be there within six hours. Scowcroft immediately returned to the White House, where he contacted Major General John Wickham, Schlesinger's assistant. Alarmed about the potential for another *Pueblo*, Scowcroft asked if there was still time for US aircraft to prevent the *Mayaguez* from reaching the mainland. Wickham said he would find out and call back. Scowcroft and McFarlane settled in to wait for Wickham's news. It was the beginning of what would prove to be a long night for both men.

CHAPTER 2

Day Two | Tuesday, May 13

Wickham called Scowcroft back around 1:00 a.m. and told him Thai-based F-4 fighters could reach the ship in time and were being loaded for that mission. Scowcroft told Wickham to launch the aircraft while he sought presidential permission for the interdiction. Scowcroft made this decision despite Kissinger's earlier injunction against operating out of Thailand. He then called Ford, who approved his action. It turned out US decision makers had more time than they knew. Captain Charles T. Miller of the *Mayaguez* had convinced the Cambodians that Kompong Som harbor was not deep enough to take his ship.[1] Not long thereafter US intelligence intercepted a Cambodian communication indicating local Cambodian authorities had been told that "the American prisoners were to be moved to Tang Island,"[2] a narrow three-mile-long island about thirty miles southeast of Kompong Som. It took time for this intercept to be translated and evaluated.[3] Meanwhile the prevailing assumption was that the Cambodians would try to get the *Mayaguez* to a mainland port.

Knowing none of this, and having been led to believe the *Mayaguez* was as little as fifteen minutes from Kompong Som,[4] Scowcroft called Ford again at 2:23 a.m. He was upset that slow communications might have precluded the opportunity to successfully interdict the ship and prevent a repeat of the *Pueblo* debacle. Dispirited, he told Ford he didn't think there was time for an intercept but felt they needed to try. The president agreed to aerial interdiction but emphatically cautioned Scowcroft that the plane should not sink the *Mayaguez*, which Scowcroft agreed would be disastrous. Just a few minutes later, Scowcroft received news that the *Mayaguez* was actually anchored off of Tang Island and relayed this news to the president.[5] Later, US P-3 reconnaissance aircraft reported that at least some of the crew apparently had been transferred to Tang Island on small boats.[6]

Shortly before 6 a.m. Ford called Schlesinger. The two men had a long conversation.[7] Ford reinforced the concern Scowcroft had shared with Wickham: preventing a repeat of the *Pueblo* ordeal. He ordered Schlesinger to quarantine the *Mayaguez* and in effect, its crew, by making sure that no Cambodian vessels moved between Tang Island and the mainland. Schlesinger passed the president's orders through the chain of command to Air Force Lieutenant General John J. Burns. General Burns was the on-scene commander for directing and coordinating the operations. He commanded the several thousand airmen and Marines still in Thailand as part of US Support Activities Group (USSAG) and the Seventh Air Force. He and his staff operated from his headquarters at a US Air Force base in Nakhon Phanom, located in the northeast corner of the country near Thailand's border with Laos.

LOCATIONS OF US AIR BASES IN THAILAND

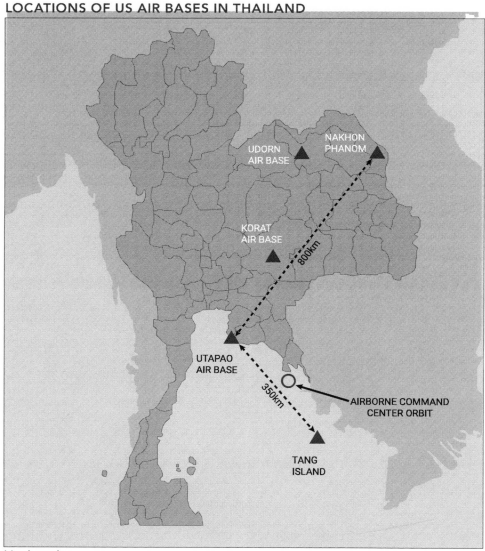

Map by author

The exact wording of the orders passed to Burns was noteworthy:

It is desired that we isolate island of Kas Tang [*sic*] by turning boats away that are approaching the island or by turning back any boats that attempt to leave and give evidence of heading for the mainland. Gunfire across the bow is one method that can be used. In view of the direct communications contact with the on-scene commander, immediate report on any movements should be available to Washington. Therefore, the decision to fire on or sink any boats resides in Washington. It is particularly important to get maximum information on any outgoing boat to determine if there are Americans aboard and to report such when requesting authority to sink. Although this will be difficult to accomplish, deck loading will probably be required on the small boats as they did in taking personnel, believed to be Americans, from the ship to the island.[8]

These unusually specific instructions from Schlesinger demonstrated great concern with a carefully modulated use of force.[9] Conversing with General Wickham early that morning, Schlesinger also made the point that it was important to sequence actions so that punitive strikes followed the release of the crew and seizure of the ship. "When it is all through," he said, "we should sink the PT boats" and "pulverize the KC [Khmer Communists]." He also noted that if the crew had been taken to the island, it would have to be seized as well.[10]

Just before 7 a.m. Ford called Schlesinger again. He was disturbed by the inaccuracy of the reports on the ship's location. Schlesinger explained it had stopped at a second island about twenty-five miles from the mainland. He also explained the Pentagon wanted to use riot control agents to discourage the ship from moving. "By all means," Ford replied. Ford emphasized he wanted to be kept "fully informed" and invited Schlesinger to let him know if another NSC meeting would be helpful. Schlesinger said the location of the ship was the critical issue. Knowing it was not in Kompong Som, the Pentagon needed to revise its options paper. The one thing he asked Ford's help on was operating out of Thailand. In the previous NSC meeting, Kissinger had said that was out of bounds, but Schlesinger believed that unless US forces had that latitude they would "lose the ship." Despite having already approved Scowcroft's action to launch F-4s from Thailand, Ford seemed unsure of how to respond. He noted Kissinger had said the cost of flying out of Thailand would be a forced withdrawal of American forces from the country within thirty days. He told Schlesinger to "proceed as you are unless I call back." Not long thereafter Scowcroft called back on behalf of Ford and said the Pentagon was free to mobilize and make available all the troops it could and move them to Thailand.[11] Clearly it had been decided that Thai sensitivities would not be allowed to impinge upon military operations.

Scowcroft met that morning with Ford, but without Kissinger, who was in Missouri. The two men agreed that with the *Mayaguez* resting off Tang Island, thirty-four miles from the mainland, it should be possible to prevent the Cambodians from moving the ship and crew. They also agreed another NSC meeting should be convened. Scowcroft called Wickham to tell him about the meeting and inform him that the president wanted an update and a discussion on military options.

In preparation for the next NSC meeting, Schlesinger met with the operations deputies from all the service branches (they are the flag officers who execute the decisions the service chiefs make). Schlesinger communicated the urgency felt by senior leaders and told acting Chairman Jones and the other senior military staff he was "inclined to use Marines at first light."[12] He had the Pentagon staff prepare a memorandum to the president outlining military options.[13] It argued that as long as the *Mayaguez* could be stopped from entering the mainland harbors, the primary US objective should be to recover the ship and crew "by eliminating unfriendly escorts" and boarding the *Mayaguez* once US naval assets arrived in the area. The memo noted there were indications the crew had been moved to Tang Island, in which case a helicopter assault of Marines on the island could be made. In the event the ship reached a mainland harbor, much more force would be needed to mine or seize a port, or blockade the Cambodian coast. The Pentagon options paper also discussed seizing or sinking Cambodian naval and merchant craft in retaliation or even seizing the island of Poulo Wai, which it was believed the Cambodians valued for potential oil production.

The memo's assessment of the pros and cons of alternative courses of action suggested initial Department of Defense preferences. "Minimum use of force" was considered a "pro" and "unfavorable reaction from Congress and US public" a "con." The memo also recommended quick consultations with Congress in light of the War Powers Act, adding "any unilateral action which generates too much congressional and public antipathy could create the notion that we as a government are unable to act forcefully to protect our interests." Schlesinger insisted on this key point throughout the crisis, to the point that he was misunderstood and mischaracterized as not favoring the use of punitive force. This depiction of military options from the Pentagon illustrates that Schlesinger, like Kissinger, had arrived at some conclusions early on concerning how he wanted to manage the crisis.

Also that morning there were some indications that Cambodia might be interested in a diplomatic resolution to the crisis. The Defense Intelligence Agency (DIA) requested information from the State Department's INR on a news broadcast reporting that the

Mayaguez would be released after Cambodia received "US apologies and the return of Khmer aircraft that were flown to Thailand." Thinking ahead about communicating with the Cambodians, DIA shot a query to the National Security Agency (NSA) about its ability to enter the Khmer communications net to transmit messages to Khmer leadership.[14]

At 10:22 the president convened the second NSC meeting. Colby updated the group on the situation and the belief that some of the crew had been transferred to Tang Island. He noted the Cambodians had fired on US surveillance aircraft and also remarked on their recent ruthless execution of seven Vietnamese crewmen they had captured. Vice President Rockefeller played an active role in the discussion again, criticizing the faulty intelligence about the ship's location for having misled decision makers about the possibility of preventing the ship from being taken into the harbor. President Ford echoed the vice president, registering his concern about delayed and inaccurate information. He said he was "very concerned" and emphasized that "we must have the information immediately. There must be the quickest possible communication to me."[15]

General Jones tried to reassure the group that the Pentagon now had firm orders to quarantine the ship and crew from the mainland, but he said they had to be careful about how the ship would be dissuaded or ultimately disabled if it tried to move. "We cannot guarantee that we could stop it, but we think that there is a good chance that we could keep it from going into the harbor without sinking it." With respect to rescuing the crew on the island, Schlesinger noted the inherent risk, but he thought a dominant force along with Khmer language speakers who could communicate an ultimatum might do the trick:

> The danger for the Americans on the island is that we do not know what the Cambodians would do. I think there is less danger if we have the dominant force. We will have Cambodians on the choppers who will be able to say that we can take the island unless they give us the Americans or the foreigners. This message would be bull-horned from the choppers at a time when we are ready to act.[16]

Rockefeller again took up his and Kissinger's theme that perceptions of American credibility were the paramount concern.[17] However, he was leery of an island assault and instead echoed Schlesinger's preference for sinking Cambodian naval assets:

> I do not think the freighter is the issue. The issue is how we respond. Many are watching us, in Korea and elsewhere. The big question is whether or not we look silly. I think we need to respond quickly. The longer we wait, the more time they have to get ready. Why not sink their boats until they move? Once they have got hostages, they can twist our tails for months to come, and if you

go ashore, we may lose more Marines trying to land than the Americans who were on the boat originally. Why not just sink their ships until they respond?[18]

Schlesinger agreed but thought the sequence of military actions was important. He proposed first retaking the ship and crew and then "attacking and sinking the Cambodian Navy . . . in order to maximize the punishment." Schlesinger pointed out that sinking their ships as a matter of priority "might precipitate sinking of the freighter and jeopardize getting the Americans out." Rockefeller had more faith in the ability of a resolute response to intimidate the Cambodians, reiterating his earlier observation that the Communists would press on until they hit a "steel" resolve. Listening to the debate, Ford asked Scowcroft what he thought. Scowcroft agreed with Schlesinger that it made sense to get the ship first before assaulting the island. Rockefeller again insisted that "the longer we take, the worse it gets," arguing for a strong and fast response.

Ford ordered aircraft to quarantine the island, both incoming and outgoing traffic. With respect to timing, he asked Pentagon leaders when US forces would arrive and could be committed to action. The meeting ended with general agreement on the need for better information about the possible timing of military operations to retake the ship and storm the island. The most notable decision in the meeting was Ford's repetition of his early morning orders that the *Mayaguez* and crew be isolated from the mainland. He told the Pentagon to do it with minimum force, not necessarily sinking the boats but dissuading them from moving. Because Schlesinger had told the forces in the field to be ready for precisely that, and to be on the lookout for crewmembers huddled on deck, the NSC meeting essentially served to reinforce existing orders.

Immediately following the NSC meeting, Ford met with some congressmen on other issues, during which he said to Representative Joseph D. "Joe" Waggoner (D-LA) that "I've got a tough decision to make on the ship." The comment suggested Ford was mulling over the inherent difficulty of preventing boat movement without endangering the ship and crew, a concern he acknowledged in his memoirs.[19]

A little later, during a meeting on domestic policy issues, the president stepped away to make a call to Kissinger in Missouri. Perhaps the president had heard that Senator Robert C. Byrd (D-WV) had suggested giving the Cambodians a forty-eight-hour deadline, or perhaps he had been thinking more about Schlesinger's comment that US forces would broadcast an ultimatum message in the Khmer language via bullhorns when assaulting Tang Island.[20] In any case, Ford wanted Kissinger's thoughts about setting a deadline for the Cambodians to release the *Mayaguez*—a position favored by some of Ford's advisors. An ultimatum had already been drafted by the DIA and sent out by the Joint Chiefs of Staff (JCS) to field commands with the caveat that the message might be changed and that if it were approved, an "execute" message would follow. The ultimatum was to be read over international distress frequencies and channels the Cambodians were known to be monitoring. The key line in the ultimatum read, "If the Cambodian authorities do not announce by 10:00 this morning their intention to release all crew members unconditionally and immediately, the Cambodian authorities will be fully responsible for the further consequences." Kissinger told Ford he did not support the ultimatum.

During his trip Kissinger was kept informed by Scowcroft and received situation reports from his Department of State staff. One report related the anger expressed by Thailand's prime minister, Kukrit Pramoj, over the use of his country as a staging area for operations related to the *Mayaguez*. The US charge d'affaires advised Kissinger that the United States should "play by the rules" or otherwise lose a great deal of Thai cooperation. Kissinger was not concerned about the Thais and in general was upbeat. He told newsmen he had participated in one NSC meeting and received a full report on another, and he had "the impression that the government is fully united on the course that needs to be taken." To the newsmen, he seemed in high spirits:

> Kissinger, who had seemed morose since the ignominious US evacuations of Phnom Penh and Saigon, appeared to have regained his old ebullience. In Kansas City he pounded the podium with booming enthusiasm and proclaimed: "The United States will not accept harassment of its ships in international sea lanes." In private, too, he seemed remarkably buoyant. Asked by *Time* correspondent Strobe Talbott when he foresaw the incident ending, he smiled and said: "I know your magazine's deadline. I think we can meet it."[21]

Back in Washington, Ford spoke with Schlesinger about an hour after his conversation with Kissinger about the ultimatum. Ford said there would be another NSC meeting at 10 p.m., and he wanted to see the various military options in writing.[22] He reiterated his instructions on the quarantine of the island and also specified how the ship was to be prevented from moving with carefully escalated force if the Cambodians attempted to take it to the mainland. He wanted the military options "in black and white." The president was surprised to learn the 1,000 Marines had not yet moved from Okinawa, saying he thought they were going to Utapao, Thailand. Seemingly confused as to whether he was missing something, he promised to call Schlesinger back on that issue.

Ford then met with Scowcroft for clarification, and Scowcroft quickly passed Ford's instructions to Wickham at 2 p.m. Scowcroft emphasized that if the ship moved it should be "interdicted with as little force as possible" and that the president would make the decisions on each escalation of force, "step by step."[23] These instructions were fully consistent with what the Pentagon had already told the on-scene commander, but the White House did not seem reassured about the matter. Scowcroft said the president wanted a coordinated assault on the island and the ship and that he had approved moving Marines from Okinawa to Thailand. Scowcroft also told Wickham that the vice president had talked Ford into bombing the Kompong Som and Phnom Penh airports as part of the island assault[24] and that this should be added to the military options being prepared for the next NSC meeting. Scowcroft closed with an odd request, saying White House lawyers needed a copy of the execute orders on interdicting the Cambodian boats.

The official orders for the Marines to deploy went out about an hour later. More guidance on the discriminate, escalating use of force against the *Mayaguez* if it began moving went out in a "flash" message (i.e., one conveying extreme urgency) two hours after that. Consistent with Schlesinger's earlier guidance, this message was again extremely detailed, specifying the amount and type of force to be used should the ship be towed without the crew or if operating "under her own steam" with the crew. The types of force ranged from warning shots across the bow and riot control agents; to selective disabling fires; to, as a final resort, gunfire directed at the bridge of the ship. The message underscored extremely tight control of lethal options against any Cambodian naval craft or mainland targets:

> The international implications of this operation make restraint imperative. Complete command and control must be maintained by COMUSSAG/7AF [commander of USSAG and Seventh Air Force (i.e., Burns)], who will be acting upon direction from the National Military Command Center. . . . Expenditure of ordnance will be in strict accordance with the ROE [rules of engagement] included in this SSI [standing signal instruction]. Ordnance expenditures will be restricted to forward firing ordnance (i.e. 7.62mm, 20mm, 40mm, 2.75[-inch] forward firing aircraft rockets) employed to impede attempts to move the boarded ship and its escorts to an unfriendly port (fire only alongside the boat or across the bows). Fire will not be directed toward the vessels or against shore targets unless specifically authorized by COMUSSAG/7AF.[25]

COMUSSAG/7AF was General Burns, the on-scene commander, and consistent with previous guidance, he had to have authorization from the NMCC before planes could expend any ordnance.[26]

Just after 6 p.m. Schlesinger called Ford with news that one of the small boats had left the island, and Ford reiterated any boats leaving should be sunk.[27] Schlesinger also gave the president the tragic news that twenty-three US personnel had died in a helicopter crash. Air Force troops from the 56th Security Police Squadron[28] were being positioned as an emergency assault force at Utapao in case Marines could not arrive quickly enough.[29] One of the helicopters crashed, killing all eighteen security police and its five-man crew, a tragic reminder to all concerned of the inherent risk involved in any military operations.[30]

Meanwhile, some minor political and diplomatic signaling took place on the evening of the thirteenth. The under secretary of state for political affairs, Joseph J. Sisco, learned that Deng Xiaoping burst into laughter in Paris when asked about Beijing's reaction if the United States intervened to recover the *Mayaguez*. "If the United States intervenes, there is nothing we can do," he said.[31] He also told reporters he was not aware of China's alleged role as intermediary in diplomatic negotiations between the United States and Cambodia. Shortly after that report a discreet inquiry was sent out from the CIA notifying personnel in Thailand that it would be "most helpful" to have prompt reporting on the host country reaction to US Marines taking "limited military action against Koh Tang Island."[32] Also that evening, White House staff began notifying selected members of Congress about the military measures being used to quarantine the *Mayaguez* and her crew from the Cambodian mainland and to keep Cambodian reinforcements from reaching Tang Island.

Then began several hours of rapid decision making that would determine the outcome of the crisis. For three hours, orders from the president would be sidestepped, questioned, delayed, and eventually thwarted in an act of insubordination that greatly angered the White House but saved the lives of the crew and arguably the president's reputation. The sequence began with the chairman of the JCS's assistant, Lieutenant General John Pauly, USAF, discussing with General Wickham the fact that several boats had departed Tang Island and were apparently headed toward the mainland. US planes had used riot control agents and two of the boats had turned back, but a third was continuing. Wickham immediately called Scowcroft with this information at 8:11 p.m., adding that one of the three boats had sunk. Scowcroft and Ford discussed the situation while Wickham and Schlesinger did the same (at 8:12 p.m.). Schlesinger told Wickham to "destroy it," before leaving to get ready for his late night NSC meeting at the White House.[33] Ford and Scowcroft reached the same conclusion. "If they can't stop it any other way, we have no choice but to destroy it," Scowcroft said. Ford agreed:

Ford: I think we have no choice.

Scowcroft: It is obvious they know what we want.

Ford: No, I think you should. If we don't do it, it is an indication of some considerable weakness.

Scowcroft: No question about it.

Ford: I think we should just give it to them.

Scowcroft: To show them we mean business.

Ford: I am glad they got the first two. I think we ought to take the action on the third one.

Scowcroft: Thank you, Sir.[34]

Scowcroft called Wickham back at 8:14 p.m. and told him the president said the boat had to be stopped: "If they can't do it any other way, it has to be destroyed." Alarmed, Wickham responded, "We may lose the thing here in the next few minutes."[35]

According to Wickham, despite the order to sink the boat, he deferred.[36] Wickham discussed the issue with General Pauly. They were both listening in on pilot commentary from cockpits. A P-3 reconnaissance aircraft first reported the "fishing boat with possible Caucasians huddled in the bow."[37] A large group of about forty people on deck was unusual. The gunboats had no personnel visible on deck. Other aircraft were asked to take a close look and determine if the people were, in fact, the *Mayaguez*'s crew. A pilot took a pass and said "the ten to twelve up on the fo'c'sle appear to be Caucasian."[38] Wickham and Pauly agreed the pilot should take another look and wanted to know if the others on deck were "Caucasian" as well. But that pilot had to peel off because of fuel depletion, and so another pilot went in to try to confirm all forty or so people on deck—a group similar to the *Mayaguez* crew in number—were Caucasian. Apparently those on the back of the boat were harder to see, so it was not clear whether they were Caucasians or not. In any case, the two generals conferred and said, "Do not shoot."[39]

An A-7 trying to deter the vessels had set fire to a Cambodian patrol boat, which eventually sank. Pauly confirmed the sinking of the patrol boat with Wickham at 8:31 after several calls discussing its status. The pilot's observation that the fishing boat might hold Caucasians arrived at the Pentagon at 8:45.[40] However, trying to determine how many of the people on deck were Caucasians took time, and it was not until 9:48 p.m. that Wickham called Scowcroft back to seek presidential approval for attempting to disable the boat:

Wickham: We have got one of these little boats five miles off Kampong Som. No aircraft around with RCA [riot control agents]. They have expended [them]. Pilot reports a group of what looks like Caucasians huddled on the bow. He made several passes. The pilot thinks he could probably disable it by hitting it in the rear. Can we get Presidential approval?

Scowcroft: Do you need it? He's already . . .

Wickham: Well, now we have a question as to the identity of the people on the bow. Do we want to stop them and possibly sink the boat? Why don't you run it by the President? I have an open line to them and you can get right back to me.[41]

Scowcroft called the president at 9:50 to get approval for firing on the boat that might contain the *Mayaguez*'s crew members. The pilot's confidence gave Scowcroft and Ford an option other than just sinking the boat or letting it escape to the mainland:

S [Scowcroft]: We have just had a report that on one of the boats which is five miles off Kompong Som there may be some Caucasians held in the front. The pilot thinks he can stop it without sinking it.

P [Ford]: Right. As I understand it, one fled and got to another island and then we sank the one and the third one is the one you are discussing.

S: Yeah.

P: Well, I don't think we have any choice.

S: If they get the Americans to the mainland they have hostages and . . .

P: We have to predicate all these actions on the possibility of losing Americans.

S: I will have them ask the pilot to do his best to stop it without sinking it.

P: I think that is right. I will be over there in about 15 minutes.[42]

Scowcroft called Wickham back at 9:54 and said, "Go ahead, John. Have the pilot to disable it, and not to sink it."[43] Schlesinger returned to see Wickham, most likely to get an update before heading to the White House for the third NSC meeting.[44] Wickham told him the boat was five miles from the mainland with uncertain passengers aboard, but the pilot was saying he thought he could disable the boat without injuring them. Schlesinger told Wickham to pass the news to Scowcroft, requesting the president's approval for such a risky endeavor, which he did at 9:56 p.m. Schlesinger then left for the White House.

Schlesinger had called Scowcroft earlier to tell him his thinking on the timing of military operations. During that call he had suggested that since Kissinger was coming back to Washington late, it might be better to have the NSC meeting the following morning. Apparently Schlesinger was not anxious to have another NSC meeting. However, Scowcroft and Ford, believing the Pentagon was chary of using force to sink the Cambodian patrol boats, wanted the meeting. They decided to hold the NSC meeting late enough to accommodate Kissinger's arrival,[45] a point they had agreed upon in their 9:50 telephone conversation. During that same conversation Scowcroft told Ford the Pentagon's option paper would be available by then.

At 10:00 p.m. Scowcroft took another call from Wickham. This time Wickham was asking for the president's permission to have the pilot disable the boat that possibly contained the *Mayaguez* crew. Scowcroft told him to go ahead. But when Wickham called Pauly to pass this authorization along, Pauly had news for Wickham. The pilot was now reporting that the forty-foot boat could have as many as thirty to forty people on board, with eight or so in the bow. Either the pilot, Pauly, Wickham, or all three concluded it was too risky to try to disable the boat by shooting off its rudder. Too much was at stake, and there was no available search and rescue capability for survivors if the boat was inadvertently sunk. Pauly also reported two high-speed boats were coming from Kompong Som toward the fishing boat. After speaking with Ford at 10:30, Scowcroft called Wickham back. Hearing the news about the two high-speed boats, he told Wickham to have them sunk. Wickham agreed to do so but asked Scowcroft to inform Schlesinger when he got to the White House that this action had been ordered.

Meanwhile the NSC members took their seats, and the third NSC meeting began at 10:40 p.m. The president bypassed the usual update from Colby and instead asked Scowcroft to summarize the current situation with the fishing vessel. Ford then observed that if the boat got to the mainland, "and we have done the other things we are contemplating, there will not be much opportunity for them anyway." The president seemed to anticipate that the Khmer regime would retaliate for US military action by killing the crew. Kissinger interjected with another, perhaps worse, possibility: that the Cambodians would "hold them for bargaining" purposes. Schlesinger's rejoinder was, "I would think that avoiding bargaining chips is less of an objective than not being in a position where the Cambodians can say that the F-4's killed our own men." This was the crux of the issue, and the president asked what his advisers recommended.

Schlesinger was for sinking the Cambodian patrol boats but for only using riot control agents on the vessel with the possible *Mayaguez* crew members. Kissinger dithered and then reluctantly agreed with Schlesinger, saying, "We will take a beating if we kill the Americans." But, he told Ford, "At the same time, we must understand that we cannot negotiate for them once they are on the mainland. If you are willing to take that position, then I think we can let them go." The important thing, Kissinger said, was that the crew not "become bargaining chips."

Scowcroft observed that they already had sunk a boat, implying the decision to run the risk of harming the crew had already been made. Schlesinger responded that the boat "did not have Caucasians on it," which prompted Kissinger to observe that could not be known with certainty. The exchange opened the floodgates of White House frustration about the Pentagon not having sunk boats automatically as ordered. Tactfully, no one from the Department of Defense observed the repeated White House orders for a carefully modulated use of force or that, when the Pentagon presented options for degrees of force applied to the boat with Caucasians, the White House had decided in favor of dissuasion rather than just sinking it.

In any case, after discussing whether the Pentagon was implementing presidential orders with alacrity, Ford decided to "reluctantly agree with Jim [Schlesinger] and Henry [Kissinger]" and try further dissuasion rather than sinking the boat that might contain the *Mayaguez*'s crew. He ordered that riot control agents, but not lethal force, be used in an attempt to turn the boat around. Scowcroft left the meeting to pass those orders to the Pentagon, which relayed them down the chain of command to forces in the field. Later, testimony from the captain and crew of the *Mayaguez* revealed how harrowing it was to be on the receiving end of the dissuasion. A circling AC-130 Spectre gunship, temporarily directing the other air elements, had F-111s drop 2,000-pound bombs a mile in front of the boats, and when that failed to stop their progress, drop the same ordnance again, only a half mile off their bows, "which is just about the edge of a 2,000-pounder's blast range." This caused some gunboats to turn back, but not the fishing boat and its escort. Then,

> even after Spectre raked the water ahead with a dazzling display of firepower, the boats kept going. Finally, Spectre had had enough. He had been taking 40-mm fire regularly from the patrol craft so, with JCS authorization, Spectre directed a flight of A-7s . . . to attack. The patrol craft sank so fast the RF-4s in the area missed getting pictures of it. . . .

Later, Captain Miller would describe what happened next: "We were bombed a hundred times by our jets. Ten foot forward of our bow light. Rockets and machine gun fire. You have to give our pilots credit. They can thread the eye of needle from a mile away. They did everything that was possible without blowing us out of the water to try to get this boat to turn around and take us back to the ship."

The crew—Thai fishermen who were also captives—tried several times to turn away from the onslaught. The Cambodians forced them to press on. "When they [the aircraft] saw it wasn't going to work," said Miller, "two jets overflew the boat from bow to stern about seven feet above us and tear-gassed us."[46]

As it turned out, the Cambodians were not dissuaded by the gas either, and the boat continued on to the mainland along with what decision makers would later learn was the entire crew of the *Mayaguez*. Once it entered the territorial waters of Cambodia and began to mix with coastal traffic, US planes, which were not authorized to overfly the mainland, abandoned their attempts to track the vessel.

Having decided the fate of the fishing boat, the NSC members then agreed to go ahead and sink the Cambodian patrol boats, even though it was acknowledged they could be carrying Americans. Confused, Counselor to the President John O. Marsh Jr. asked about the possibility of the other boats containing Americans. Kissinger clarified, "The pilot should sink them. He should destroy the boats and not send situation reports." As Kissinger later explained,

> We were sliding into a position in which much of the President's time and the NSC's was taken up with decisions about the movement of individual small boats eight thousand miles away. To avoid this, Ford ordered the destruction of all the boats near Koh Tang, squelching attempts to return to a case-by-case consideration.[47]

The president agreed with Kissinger, stating near the end of the meeting, "I think we should sink any boats that can be used to try to move the Americans." Around midnight Scowcroft again left the meeting to call Wickham with the orders to sink four Cambodian patrol boats near the island. Accounts differ, but most agree that three Cambodian gunboats were immediately sunk and another four damaged.

Back in the NSC meeting, the risk involved in seizing Tang Island was being discussed. It was clear to the NSC members that taking Tang before all possible US forces were assembled carried higher risks. The group weighed the risks of alternative scenarios, assessing the arrival of various assets and their impact on risk. Schlesinger framed the issue by saying 270 Marines "in all probability" could take the island given the estimate of 100 Cambodian defenders, but said the Pentagon "would prefer to land with 1,000." For some reason Schlesinger was using the estimate of Cambodian defenders on Tang Island from Pacific Command's intelligence center (IPAC) rather than DIA's larger estimate of 150 to 200 heavily armed troops. When Colby asked if the 270 Marines could not "protect themselves" while waiting for the next wave, General Jones reminded him, "We have nothing to confirm the exact force on that island." Colby's concern was that the Cambodians might execute crew members. While noting "this is not my business," he nonetheless weighed in repeatedly in favor of moving faster, worrying "if they take reprisals, it would be very difficult for us."

Kissinger agreed there were advantages to speed. However, with the risk of humiliating hostage negotiations negated by the decision to sink boat traffic, he emphasized the risks of using insufficient force. He wanted a "more reliable force." Ford at one point summarized the debate, saying, "In other words, the time you gain in this cycle is not worth the gamble." Schlesinger, Kissinger, and Jones all agreed on that point, so the president abandoned the idea of early operations on the fourteenth. The issue then became whether a one- or two-day delay was the better course of action. More than once Kissinger noted he was not competent to assess the military risks of seizing Tang with a smaller Marine force, essentially inviting an intervention from General Jones that never came. After some discussion on the military and political pros and cons of waiting one as opposed to two days, the president ruled forces should be prepared to go within twenty-four hours but reserved the final decision on that issue for the next NSC meeting.

The group also considered the advantages and disadvantages of using B-52 strikes against the mainland versus aircraft from the *Coral Sea*. Schlesinger argued, "B-52's are a red flag on the Hill [Capitol Hill]. Moreover, they bomb a very large box and they are not so accurate. They might generate a lot of casualties outside the exact areas that we would want to hit." Kissinger worried that waiting for the *Coral Sea* entailed another daylong delay, but then White House Chief of Staff and former Navy pilot Donald H. Rumsfeld observed that the aircraft could launch from the aircraft carrier while it was still a good distance away. The debate over overwhelming force (B-52s) versus more discriminate punitive attacks (carrier aircraft) was confused at times by interventions from lesser participants who assumed the purpose of the military operations was to rescue the crew. For example, Deputy Secretary of Defense Clements said:

> I hate to have us lose sight of our objectives in this case. Those objectives are to get the Americans and the ship. If we want to punish people, that's another thing. I think that dropping a lot of bombs on the mainland will not help us with the release of the Americans.[48]

The president cut off this line of reasoning: "I think we have to assume that the Americans were taken from the island and that some were killed. This is tragic, but I think that we have to assume that it happened." He then asked, "Does anybody disagree?" and no one did.

With the punitive nature of the operations agreed upon, the question arose as to the amount of punishment. Whereas some like Schlesinger and White House Counsel Philip W. Buchen were concerned about reactions from Congress, Kissinger and Rockefeller preferred disproportionate force. Kissinger argued that if only a degree of force commensurate with the provocation was used, there would be no disadvantage to challenging the United States at every opportunity. He considered it helpful to prove that the president was willing to ignore congressional concerns. "In fact," he said, "some domestic cost is to our advantage in demonstrating the seriousness with which we view this kind of challenge." Kissinger emphasized they needed to "impress the Koreans and the Chinese." His points led to a discussion of worthwhile targets and how to justify attacking the mainland, which is how the meeting ended.

CHAPTER 3

Day Three | Wednesday, May 14

N ot long after those attending the third NSC meeting dispersed around 12:30 a.m., an intercepted Cambodian communication indicated a possible desire on the part of Cambodian authorities to seek a political solution. INR alerted the director of the *Mayaguez* working group to this development at 1:20 a.m. as well as Secretary Kissinger's personal assistant and the White House Situation Room. An hour later Defense Secretary Schlesinger requested copies of all Cambodian intercepts. Apparently he was just as interested in what the Cambodians were up to as INR was. INR renewed its request to NSA for verification of the report later that morning (shortly after 8 a.m.). NSA promised a quick response, but it took another eight hours before the agency responded that it was "unable to clarify the information."[1]

Just before 5 a.m. an unusual message arrived in the Department of State from the US embassy in Tehran. The subject line was "Chinese Embassy Tehran Believes *Mayaguez* to be Freed Soon."[2] The Pakistani first secretary had told an American diplomat that a senior Chinese embassy official in Tehran said China was "embarrassed" by the Cambodian seizure of the *Mayaguez* and expected it to be released soon. The report was credible insofar as the Chinese source knew and shared the fact that the US liaison office in Beijing had called on the Chinese Ministry of Foreign Affairs about the *Mayaguez*. The Chinese source commented that China was using its influence with the Khmer Rouge to seek the early release of the ship.[3] State Department officials also learned that morning that China's Ministry of Foreign Affairs had returned the US message for Cambodia, saying the Cambodians had refused to accept it.

Scowcroft met with Ford early on the morning of the fourteenth as was their usual practice, but there was not much news other than that the headwinds delaying the *Coral Sea* had abated. After Scowcroft and the CIA briefer provided their morning updates to the president, Rumsfeld slipped into the Oval Office to share his views privately on the *Mayaguez* crisis. He had prepared a memo on the best options, which he gave to the president. The main point he made was that Ford should not use B-52s "since they were associated with damage inflicted across Vietnam and had caused negative reactions in the region and in America." Instead, the former aircraft-carrier pilot thought it made more sense to use aircraft from the *Coral Sea* because they could strike with greater precision and reduce potential civilian casualties.[4]

Rumsfeld was followed by Scowcroft and Kissinger, who met with Ford several times that morning. During one such meeting Kissinger took a phone call from Under Secretary Joseph Sisco just before 10 a.m. that demonstrated Kissinger's subordinates understood he was not looking for a diplomatic solution to the crisis. Sisco advised Kissinger to contact the United Nations (UN) for help in securing the release of the *Mayaguez* but emphasized the outreach would just be for appearances' sake:

> For public relations reasons only, why don't we go through the cosmetic motions by writing a letter to the UN and send it to the Security Council protesting the seizure on the high seas. It will help us with the Congress when we get to military action. Why don't we also try to get the Secretary General? I know nothing will come from this.[5]

Reassurances notwithstanding, Kissinger was leery, responding that they already had communicated through the Chinese. But Sisco persisted, saying, "We can't lose a thing by it." Kissinger gave Sisco permission to prepare a communication for his review. Meanwhile, Scowcroft called General Wickham at 10:30 to ensure Schlesinger would have the required mainland bombing options ready for the final NSC meeting later that day, including the pros and cons of using B-52s as opposed to carrier aircraft. His call was followed by one from McFarlane, who told Wickham the White House needed regular situation reports directly from the NMCC. The White House was not going to allow the Pentagon to control information flow. Wickham complied and arranged for the reports.[6]

After the call from Scowcroft, General Jones and Schlesinger discussed the military options. They reached agreement on two critically important points: the use of airpower and the risks the Marines were running. It was agreed that the *Coral Sea*'s forty-eight tactical aircraft were not really good for destroying runways. However, Schlesinger voiced strong opposition to use of B-52s because they were indiscriminate and ill-suited for their targets, arguing "any use would have to be on political grounds." He wanted any attacks on the mainland to be "surgical." The two Pentagon leaders agreed the *Coral Sea* aircraft should avoid the two ships in the harbor of unknown registry. Instead they would be given an "armed recce mission" to find other, more relevant water and shore targets.[7]

As for the Marine assault, it appears from Wickham's notes on the meeting that both men expected some "preparation" of the landing zone by tactical aircraft and continuous air cover for the Marines thereafter. Schlesinger cautioned that care should be taken to avoid collateral damage when preparing the landing zone. The point was made that the commandant of the Marine Corps, General Robert E. Cushman Jr., "had no concern about securing the assault area," but he noted it would take time to do the clearing operation.[8] They would wait for the insertion of the second wave of Marines before moving out for the clearing operation. When there were 600 Marines ashore they would have a commanding force that could be withdrawn safely the following day. Broadcasting directly into the Khmer radio network to issue an ultimatum or other demands was also discussed.

Later that morning Ford, Kissinger, and Scowcroft met with the visiting prime minister of the Netherlands, Johannes den Uyl. Afterwards, Kissinger and Scowcroft stayed on to further discuss their preoccupation: the *Mayaguez*. Kissinger hedged on whether to use the B-52s, but he wanted to reinforce presidential resolve in favor of a forceful response. He encouraged the president to favor a larger military operation, telling him he "should take out the port" and that he would "take as much heat for a big strike as for a small strike."[9] Kissinger then left the Oval Office briefly to make a call to Sisco. He had been thinking about Sisco's recommended outreach to the UN. "Joe," he asked, "can we just send that letter to the Secretary General and not to the President of the Security Council?" Sisco agreed, saying he would make it public so that it "looks like a serious attempt."[10] Kissinger directed him to go ahead. Sisco moved quickly. Within the hour the US ambassador to the UN, John A. Scali, delivered a request for assistance to UN Secretary-General Kurt J. Waldheim that noted the United States reserved the right to act in self-defense in accordance with Article 51 of the UN Charter.

While Ford, Kissinger, and Scowcroft were meeting in the White House to discuss how they could get the results they wanted from the Pentagon, military leaders were meeting in the Pentagon to decide how they would rule on the all-important question of military risk in the next NSC meeting. The Joint Chiefs agreed that another day to coordinate the disparate forces arriving on the scene would be useful and provide a higher assurance of success. However, given countervailing risks associated with delay, the Chiefs decided not to insist on more time.

About the same time, the news media were also showing a marked interest in risk assessment. Reporters grilled Nessen at his noon press briefing. Before Nessen could make his first announcement, reporters pounced on him, demanding to know if he could confirm the Associated Press report that US warplanes had attacked three

Cambodian vessels. In the middle of the news conference, Nessen was handed a statement by Pentagon spokesman Joseph Laitin that said "the Cambodians appeared to be attempting to move US captive crewmen from the ship to the mainland" and that after firing warning shots to dissuade them, "three Cambodian patrol craft were destroyed and about four others were damaged and immobilized. One boat succeeded in reaching Kompong Som." Reporters wanted to know whether any American crewmen were on the Cambodian patrol craft being attacked. Nessen dodged the questions as best he could, saying he had no further information.[11] That afternoon the Senate Foreign Relations Committee joined the fray, unanimously adopting a resolution supporting the president's attempt to resolve the crisis with diplomacy and calling upon Cambodia to release the crew.

General Burns finalized his plan for the military operations at 1:30 p.m. on the fourteenth. Burns and his staff, operating from his headquarters in Nakhon Phanom near Thailand's northeast border with Laos, created the plan with input from the Navy and Marine Corps. The Air Force helicopters and Marines assembling to retake the *Mayaguez* and its crew were 800 miles to the southwest of Burns's headquarters at the US Air Force base in Utapao, Thailand, located on the coast not far from Bangkok (see map on page 20). An orbiting EC-130 aircraft outfitted for airborne command and control would link the communications of the dispersed commanders and forces.

General Burns authorized close air support of the Marines assaulting Tang Island and tactical aircraft and naval gunfire strikes to destroy all Cambodian small naval craft within twenty-five nautical miles of Tang Island, Paulo Wai, Kompong Som, and Ream (excluding Vietnamese territory). He emphasized that

> all forces must be aware of the fact that the primary purpose for conducting ground operations is to secure the safe release of US/third-country national prisoners [several of the crewmen were not US citizens]. Actions which will unduly jeopardize this objective are to be avoided.[12]

Somewhat incongruously, Burns also authorized the use of the largest conventional bomb in the US inventory (the 15,000-pound BLU-82) to clear a landing zone on the island. His plan would be reviewed in detail during the fourth NSC meeting, which began just before 4 p.m. that afternoon and went on for almost two hours.[13]

The final NSC meeting began with Colby telling the participants that the Cambodians had apparently transported at least some of the crew from Tang Island to the mainland, putting them ashore at Kompong Som port around 11 p.m. the previous night (Washington time). He thought the determined attempt to get some crew to the mainland indicated the Cambodians appreciated their value "as bargaining chips."[14] After Colby reported on crew location, Cambodian strength, and disposition of Cambodian patrol craft not yet sunk by US planes, Kissinger suddenly changed the direction of the conversation. "Why are we not sinking the boats?" he asked, apparently referring to those remaining. This set off a discussion of the missions that US forces had been assigned. Kissinger clarified through questioning that the US warships on the scene— the USS *Henry B. Wilson* (a guided-missile destroyer) and the USS *Harold E. Holt* (a destroyer escort)—were not blockading the island and interdicting boat traffic. The president fumed that he had the impression the *Holt* would station itself between the island and mainland to prevent Cambodian naval traffic between the two, saying, "I am amazed at this." General Jones explained the ships were over the horizon to avoid tipping the Cambodians to the possibility of pending military operations, but the president's skepticism about Pentagon compliance with his expectations was evident.[15]

After further discussion on Cambodian and US forces, the president asked the Department of Defense for its recommendations. At Schlesinger's invitation, Jones briefed the group on the seizure of the ship and the island. He began by saying he did not recommend using B-52s, which the Joint Chiefs considered "overkill," and also notably left out aircraft strikes against the mainland. Instead, tactical aircraft would suppress enemy fires. When he finished, the president immediately asked about the *Coral Sea* and B-52s. The general then identified three target sets on the mainland—the airfield at Kompong Som, the naval port, and the regular port—saying there was not much to hit at the airfield or the naval port. There were targets at the regular port, however, including eight fast patrol craft and some buildings and other facilities. The president asked whether the breakwater could be destroyed by B-52s, and Jones said it would be difficult. He also asked about the comparative impact of B-52s and the carrier aircraft, and Jones said the former would generate more damage to the runway and port but also result in collateral damage.

Having heard General Jones's recommendation, timing was discussed and Jones noted the need "to get the order out as soon as possible." The president agreed on the need to launch both operations as quickly as possible, and Admiral James L. Holloway,[16] the chief of naval operations, said it would be "at first light." Jones agreed but said that "may be a moot question." When the president asked about the departure of the Marines in helicopters, Jones said it should be "within an hour." The president noted they already were forty minutes behind schedule, but instead of seizing the opportunity to argue for another day's delay, Jones responded: "They should still make it." Holloway then left the meeting at 4:45 to pass along instructions for the military operations.

The NSC meeting then turned to the issue of strikes on the mainland. General Jones raised the idea of issuing an ultimatum to the Cambodians before striking mainland targets with either B-52s or carrier aircraft.[17] The president ultimately decided in favor of carrier strikes, noting later in the meeting they would be more responsive in terms of timing and would produce less collateral damage and less possible harm to Americans. He specified that once the cyclic operations from the *Coral Sea* began "they should not stop until we tell them." He would let the Pentagon know when he thought the Cambodians had been sufficiently punished.

Concerning the ultimatum, Rumsfeld offered his views on the right way to communicate the ultimatum: privately, with specificity, and via a diplomatic effort. Kissinger then told the group about his initiative to contact the UN secretary-general but said he thought it would be too complicated to try to issue ultimatums to the Cambodians by way of Beijing. Schlesinger asked about a local ultimatum (presumably from the Marines to the Cambodians on the island who might be holding crew members). Kissinger said he would not object to that, but the ultimatum should not delay mainland strikes, which they had agreed they would say were necessary to protect the Marines. He wanted to "move massively and firmly." He mentioned taking out the one hundred aircraft at Phnom Penh but said, "I do not want to upset people too much."

Buchen was in favor of an ultimatum, saying it "may be the only way to get the Americans out"; later he added, "With an ultimatum, [neutral ships in the harbor] have a chance to get out." He also worried that hitting mainland facilities might risk harm to crew members being held on the mainland. Kissinger responded to Buchen by objecting again to the idea of an ultimatum. Later he would say using bullhorns on the island to relay demands for the release of the crew was okay, but he insisted they should just state the demand and not negotiate. Kissinger countered the proposal for an ultimatum to the Cambodian government by saying they should consider advancing the timetable for airstrikes.

Thus, the conversation segued to a discussion of how to manage the mainland airstrikes. During that discussion, some critical points were made that were later forgotten, contributing to major misunderstandings and presidential ire. In accordance with the earlier agreement with Schlesinger, Jones noted that carrier aircraft would be armed with precision-guided munitions and that the first wave would be "armed reconnaissance." Admiral Holloway elaborated, saying the first wave "will hit targets connected with the operation" (i.e., Cambodian assets that theoretically could interfere with Marine operations). "Later waves," Holloway said, "will hit other targets, including the . . . airfield and the ports." He then added that after "the first operation (i.e. wave) the fighters will come back and report." Kissinger then specified that strikes on the mainland should not occur before the *Holt* could retake the *Mayaguez*, presumably to minimize the chance that the Cambodians might sink it in retaliation.

Holloway again left the meeting to pass along the instructions for the airstrikes, which went out at 5:10 p.m. Consistent with what he had explained, the first wave of aircraft were assigned the mission of "armed reconnaissance," that is, "locating and attacking targets of opportunity"—in this case those that might be able to reinforce Cambodian forces on Tang Island. What the execute message that went to forces in the field said in that regard was that "principal targets" for the first wave of armed reconnaissance were "aircraft and military watercraft."[18]

Schlesinger asked if there were any changes to the estimate of Cambodians forces on Tang, and Colby said no. The group also discussed possible casualties.[19] General Jones said it was very hard to estimate, and Schlesinger opined it might be twenty or thirty killed in action. Deputy Secretary Clements noted sooner or later the public would also hear about the twenty-three Air Force personnel killed in the earlier helicopter crash. After Kissinger had to explain again to Buchen why he did not favor an ultimatum before hitting mainland targets, the group discussed whether any Americans were on the island and if so, how many. Kissinger pointed out there was no way to know and that "taking the island if they are not there is easier to explain than failing to take it if they are." Schlesinger agreed that "we have an obligation to get the Americans or to see if they are there."

The meeting ended with a discussion about how to manage "consultation" with Congress and when to notify the public and allies that operations were underway. The possibility of congressmen and senators objecting to the operations was raised, and Kissinger responded that the president "would have to go ahead anyway." The decision was made to brief selected representatives and senators as quickly as possible.

The NSC meeting ended with many participants rushing to prepare for the outreach effort. Just after 6 o'clock, Kissinger and Rumsfeld both popped into the Oval Office for short discussions with Ford on how to manage the discussion with the congressmen and senators, who were arriving around 6:30 p.m. Back in his office, Kissinger received a telephone call from Sisco at 6:16. Sisco told Kissinger he had the deputy secretary with him and all the regional assistant secretaries. They were working out details for notifying US allies, and they wanted Kissinger's approval to send cables to key US posts instead of rounding up foreign ambassadors in Washington. Given concerns about timing, they agreed to do both cables and telephonic notifications, but Kissinger again demonstrated his concern with making a strong impression on other nations:

> **Kissinger:** I want a strong—I don't want a weeping State Department—just say we're trying to rescue the ship and the crew and we are doing military operations on the Island [Tang] and trying to seize the ship and there may be a few associated operations.
> **Sisco:** Yeah, that's all you would say.
> **Kissinger:** Yeah.
> **Sisco:** Sure. And you might add one other point: namely, that we undertook certain diplomatic steps beforehand . . .
> **Kissinger:** Yes, but I do not want to give the impression of super reasonableness.
> **Sisco:** No. All right, that's fine. I'll pass that along.[20]

Ten minutes later the meeting with members of Congress started. Sisco interrupted it to get further guidance. He had a secretary slip in and hand Scowcroft a short message asking for immediate "yes/no" decisions on two issues. Sisco wanted to be sure the military operation had commenced before any diplomatic notifications took place, which Scowcroft could not confirm. Second, he wanted approval to include the Russians and Chinese on the list of countries informed, which Scowcroft confirmed was correct.

The discussion with the congressmen and senators began with President Ford briefing them on the military operations. He covered the basics and justified the strikes against the mainland as necessary to protect the Marines. Kissinger's explanation that all diplomatic means had been exhausted fell flat. The reaction was, as Kissinger later described it, "unenthusiastic" (so much so that he later told Ford he thought the exchange with congressional leaders inclined Schlesinger to scale back the use of force).[21] The very first question posed to the president by House Speaker Carl B. Albert (D-OK) was about endangering the lives of crew. He asked, "Could Americans be on the boats that will be destroyed?" The president said candidly, "There is no way of knowing." Other questions followed about whether we were "just going into Koh Tang shooting," why we could not wait longer before using force, why Cambodia was not given a deadline for compliance, and why the mainland was being bombed. Many also wondered, what next? As House Majority Leader Thomas P. "Tip" O'Neill Jr. (D-MA) later said, "There was a tremendous feeling of uneasiness of where do we go from here if we don't find the crew."[22] There were also concerns expressed about compliance with the War Powers Act. Other questions and comments were more supportive, but overall the reception suggested the likely political reaction to the president's management of the crisis depended on the outcome. Ford ended the meeting by asking the senators and congressmen to join him in a prayer for "the very best" results possible.[23]

* * *

On the other side of the world, US forces hastily prepared for combat and departed Utapao, Thailand. They left shortly after 4 a.m. (local Cambodian time).[24] The Marines were transported by CH-53 Sea Stallion helicopters from the 21st Special Operations Squadron, code-named Knives, and heavily armored HH-53 helicopters (nicknamed "Super Jolly Green Giants") from the 40th Aerospace Rescue and Recovery Squadron, code-named Jollies.[25] Five CH-53s and three HH-53s carried 177 Marines from the 2nd Battalion of the 9th Marine Regiment and three Army linguists to assault Tang Island. Another three HH-53s carried 59 Marines from D Company of the 1st Battalion of the 4th Marine Regiment, along with an Army intelligence officer fluent in Cambodian, an explosive ordnance disposal team, two Navy corpsmen, and Navy and civilian personnel to get the *Mayaguez* under way. Cambodian gunboats observed and fired on the assault force during its 200-plus-mile flight from Utapao over the Gulf of Thailand to Tang Island and the SS *Mayaguez*, located about 33 miles southwest of the Cambodian port of Kompong Som. No damage was done, but it was clear the Cambodians were alert to their presence.

The Cambodians who seized the *Mayaguez* were well armed, so taking the ship was expected to be difficult. The Marines were prepared for a stout defense, booby traps, and even the possibility that the Cambodians might try to scuttle the ship. It was assumed the Marines would pay a high price for retaking the ship.[26] That was not the case. The Marines were deposited on the USS *Holt*, which then was brought alongside the *Mayaguez*. Six armed Cambodians had been observed through binoculars forty minutes earlier, so the *Mayaguez* had been doused with riot control gas to suppress resistance just prior to the *Holt*'s arrival. However, the Marine boarding party, wearing gas masks, was surprised to discover the Cambodians had left the ship unattended. After Marines raised the American flag, sailors prepared the ship for towing. The *Holt* then towed the *Mayaguez* away from the combat zone.

Conversely, US forces were shocked by the Cambodians' ferocious defense of Tang. The Marines were expecting only token resistance from a few irregular Cambodian forces. The assault commander, Lieutenant Colonel Randall W. Austin, and three other officers had scrambled to obtain intelligence about Tang Island, which they found hard to obtain. They managed to get an Army U-21 Ute to inspect the island from the air, but the airplane was restricted by Air Force leaders to an altitude of 6,000 feet, which made it difficult to observe much. However, they were able to see that the island was heavily foliated except for a cleared strip that cut across a small peninsula on the northern tip of the island connecting what appeared to be two harbors. It seemed obvious to Austin and his colleagues that these harbors were the center of any activity on the island.[27] They could also see the *Mayaguez* anchored a mile north of Tang.

Despite the paucity of information collected during his reconnaissance, Austin was assured before departing Utapao that pre-assault strikes to neutralize known antiaircraft sites would be conducted. That did not happen.[28] Austin and his Marines approached Tang Island at dawn in eight helicopters, four from the west and four from the east. A ninth helicopter, one of the three that had carried Marines to the USS *Holt*, also joined the first assault wave. Instead of a "walk-ashore" operation, the Marines flew into the teeth of a defense prepared by numerically superior, better-armed, well-entrenched, and well-disciplined Khmer Rouge soldiers who had recently improved their defenses and were expecting the attack.[29]

Knife-21 and Knife-22 were the first helicopters on the western beach with their loads of Marines, many of whom were fresh out of boot camp and had never seen combat. Shortly after 6 a.m., Knife-21 reached the beach, swung around, and lowered its ramp facing the tree line. As Marines poured onto the beach, the Cambodians unleashed a devastating barrage of direct and indirect fires. Knife-22 aborted its approach and concentrated on providing cover fire for Knife-21, which had been badly damaged and was limping away from the beach. About a mile out to sea, it collapsed in the water. Knife-22 was also badly damaged and struggled back toward Thailand, barely reaching the coast before its pilots made an emergency landing.

Knife-23 and Knife-31 approached the eastern beach. Again the Cambodian defenders waited until the Marines were unloading before firing. Knife-23 was severely hit. It lost an engine and its tail section, falling stricken to the beach. Marines emerged from the wreckage and made it to the tree line, followed by the surviving Air Force crew members. Knife-31 fared even worse. The cockpit took a direct hit from a rocket, and the helicopter burst into flames. It settled in the surf just offshore, taking with it all the Marine radios intended for coordinating close air support. Some of the survivors from Knife-31 attempted to make it ashore and were lost to enemy fire; others, including some badly wounded, used the helicopter to shield their movement as they swam out to sea. A Marine braved enemy fire and was badly burned trying to recover the body of the copilot, Second Lieutenant Richard Vandegeer. Another Marine, the forward air controller, used an Air Force survival radio to call in airstrikes on enemy positions that were trying to kill Knife-31's survivors.

About 8:30 a.m. Jolly-13 made an effort to retrieve the small group from Knife-23 isolated on the eastern beach. By then, an AC-130, code-named Spectre-61, had been sent to support the Marines, and it delivered its first tentative fires in support of Jolly 13: ten 40-mm rounds directed at enemy troops. Jolly-13 landed, taking numerous hits while waiting for the Marines to board, but the Marines were pinned down. Eventually, a fuel tank on Jolly-13 caught fire, and it was forced to depart. The helicopter struggled back to Thailand, where it was declared out of action.

After the devastating results on the eastern beach, all the remaining helicopters were directed toward the western beach where repeated attempts were made to reinforce the Marines already on the ground. Jolly-41, Jolly-42, and Jolly-43 made runs at the beach but had to abort after being damaged by ground fires. Knife-32 finally made it in, discharging thirteen Marines but suffering great damage in the process. A rocket tore a hole in its side and exploded in the passenger compartment as the Marines exited. The helicopter made it back to Utapao but was so badly damaged it would not return to the fight. Jolly-42 made another attempt at insertion and managed to unload twenty-seven Marines, including First Lieutenant James D. "Dick" Keith, who would assume command of the largest group of Marines on the western beach from Second Lieutenant James McDaniel. Although Jolly-42 succeeded in delivering its Marines, it too was so badly damaged it was rendered inoperable after returning to base.

Jolly-43 fared better, finding an undefended portion of the beach south of the main Marine force. It offloaded twenty-nine Marines, including Lieutenant Colonel Austin and his staff who were armed mostly with .45-caliber automatic pistols. Austin tried to coordinate supporting airstrikes before starting to move a mile north and join up with the other Marines. Jolly-41 made five separate insertion attempts, each time forced away by enemy fire. Finally, at about 10 a.m., the helicopter succeeded in unloading twenty-two of its twenty-seven personnel before mortar fire forced it to lift off again. It hovered, prepared to touch down once more, suffered damage from a near miss by a mortar round, and then pulled away as another mortar round exploded where it had just been hovering. Jolly-41's successful insertion of Marines had been facilitated by fire support from Spectre-61, the "AC-130 gunship that provided the first effective air support to the assault force."[30] Nevertheless, the damage Jolly-41 sustained in the process also required its removal from action after it managed to return to Thailand.

The net result of such concentrated enemy fire was that at the end of the invasion's first hour there were only fifty-four Americans on Tang and fourteen of them were dead. At the end of the first planned assault wave, the number of Americans on the island had climbed to more than one hundred and thirty, but eight out of the nine helicopters that participated in the assault had been shot down or otherwise damaged so badly by enemy fire they could no longer be used. Meanwhile, the Marines on Tang were divided into three isolated detachments. Second Lieutenant Michael A. Cicere and twenty Marines were pinned down along with the five crew members of Knife 23 on the east beach. Lieutenant Keith with eighty-two Marines were dug in on the west beach, and the command element under Lieutenant Colonel Austin with a total of twenty-nine Marines was still about a mile further south. The Marines from Knife-31 treading water off the coast of Tang were eventually discovered by the destroyer, USS *Wilson*, which launched a motorboat to retrieve them. The *Wilson*'s sailors suppressed fire from the Cambodians on Tang Island who tried to pick off sailors and Marines during the process.

* * *

While the Marines were for fighting on Tang, feverish diplomatic activity was underway back in the United States. In New York, Secretary-General Waldheim had moved with alacrity. As soon as he received the appeal from Ambassador Scali, he broke off his meeting (which, coincidentally, he was having with UN representatives forced by the Khmer Rouge to leave Cambodia) to contact both the Chinese and the Cambodians. He called the Chinese representative to the UN to his office, and for the Cambodians he used an open channel that had worked for him with an earlier intervention on behalf of foreign evacuees from Phnom Penh.[31] At 7 p.m. the UN issued a statement that the secretary-general was communicating with the Cambodians and that he encouraged all parties to refrain from further use of force. Seven minutes later the Cambodians locally broadcast a message in their own language announcing the release of the ship. It was a long, rambling statement that ended with a reference to the *Mayaguez*:

> Regarding the *Mayaguez* ship, we have no intention of detaining it permanently and we have no desire to stage provocations. We only wanted to know the reason for its coming and to warn it against violating our waters again. This is

why our coast guard seized this ship. Their goal was to examine it, question it and make a report to higher authorities who would then report to the Royal Government so that the Royal Government could itself decide to order it to withdraw from Cambodia's territorial waters and warn it against conducting further espionage and provocative activities. This applies to this *Mayaguez* ship and to any other vessels, like the ship flying Panamanian flags that we released on 9 May 1975. Wishing to provoke no one or to make trouble, adhering to the stand of peace and neutrality, we will release this ship, but we will not allow the US imperialists to violate our territorial waters, provoke incidents in our territorial waters or force us to release their ships whenever they want, by applying threats.[32]

Clearly the Cambodians were cognizant of US threats to use military action. While denying the efficacy of the threats, the Cambodians nonetheless were signaling their willingness to let the ship go. But it took time to receive, translate, and pass along their message to authorities in Washington. The CIA's Foreign Broadcast Information Service (FBIS) notified the Department of State about the broadcast just minutes before 8 p.m., precisely when Sisco was calling Kissinger again to obtain his approval of routine diplomatic communications.

Sisco told Kissinger that Deputy Ingersoll would bring a list of countries being notified to the 8:00 dinner in honor of Dutch Prime Minister Uyl. Kissinger interrupted him to again insist, "I don't [want] some of these usual pansy briefings." Sisco reassured him that State Department veterans like Philip C. Habib were handling the notifications and they were "not pantywaists." Sisco then tried to get Kissinger's quick approval for three diplomatic communications. He offered to read them over the phone or have them hand-delivered by Deputy Secretary Ingersoll, who was about to leave for the Uyl dinner. One was a brief cable to all diplomatic posts so that they would not be in the dark; another was a short telegram for Bangkok so the US ambassador there had "a little guidance." The third initiative was another run at notifying the UN Security Council instead of just the secretary-general. Sisco said it was necessary "because we are using force and we are obligated to tell them we are using force under Article 51," and because "we should do this from a public relations point of view." Instead of approving these diplomatic efforts over the phone, Kissinger told Sisco to send them to the White House for his review.

Fifteen minutes later both Kissinger and Scowcroft learned of the Cambodian broadcast announcing the release of the *Mayaguez*. What transpired next can be pieced together from a careful reading of multiple firsthand accounts that are not always consistent. The president says in his memoirs that he was notified about the broadcast by Scowcroft at 8:15 and that he "told Brent [Scowcroft] to have Schlesinger hold up the first strike until we had a better idea of what was happening." Kissinger in his memoirs agrees that Scowcroft called the Pentagon to hold off the first strike but says that he asked

> Scowcroft to instruct the National Military Command Center that I would be seeking presidential guidance and that I also intended to consult Secretary Schlesinger. Since there was little time left, I suggested that the planes from the *Coral Sea* proceed on course *but drop no ordnance* until the President had made his decision. (emphasis added)[33]

At 8:30 Scowcroft told General Wickham the aircraft from the *Coral Sea* were not to release any ordnance. Simultaneously, the JCS was informing Admiral Gayler "not to use Navy TACAIR [tactical air] for strikes on Kompong Som Harbor." Several minutes later (at 8:32) the JCS clarified for Admiral Gayler that the assault on the island and boarding of the *Mayaguez* could continue. Two minutes after that Gayler was told to "use all possible communications to divert and cancel *CORAL SEA* TACAIR." At 8:44 a flash message from the JCS went out notifying forces in the field that *Coral Sea* strikes against targets in Kompong Som complex were "rescinded repeat rescinded. Cease repeat cease strike operations against targets in Kompong Som complex."

While Scowcroft was on the phone with the Pentagon at 8:30, Kissinger was on the phone with the president discussing the broadcast. Kissinger notes in his memoirs that he could see pros and cons to canceling the airstrikes on the mainland in light of the broadcast, but that in any case, the president was resolute.[34] Ford "would not alter any of his directives, he said, until he was sure of the crew's release." In his memoirs Ford said that Scowcroft called back shortly after 8:30 and they "decided to go ahead with the bombing because we couldn't act on the basis of a radio message that was so imprecise."[35] However, in an interview the president gave immediately following the crisis, he said that he was enjoying the first sips of his martini-on-the-rocks at 8:29 when Kissinger, not Scowcroft, called about the broadcast:

> The secretary [Kissinger] told me that the word had come that they were releasing the ship. And I said to the secretary, "They don't mention the crew," and apparently in the information Henry had, he had not been told or the announcement didn't include the crew. So I said to him, "Proceed as we had agreed, with the air strikes and the full operation."[36]

Schlesinger was on his way to the White House while Scowcroft, Kissinger, and Ford were discussing the broadcast. After arriving, Schlesinger received a call from the Pentagon explaining the cancellation of the first strike. He found Kissinger, who gave him a copy of the FBIS translation of the Radio Phnom Penh broadcast. Fearing the broadcast was just propaganda, Schlesinger argued mainland strikes should continue.[37] Kissinger then called Ford out of the dinner at 8:50 p.m., and the two men informed him of their recommendation, at which time, Kissinger would later claim in his memoirs, "the planes from the *Coral Sea* were still en route."[38] Ford then made a firm decision, saying, "Tell them to go ahead, right now." Scowcroft then called Wickham back—not two minutes later as he had said he would, but twenty-two minutes later, because that is how long it took Kissinger, Schlesinger, and Ford to discuss the issue and for the president to arrive at a definitive decision.

In fact, the planes were over their targets at 8:45, and the flash JCS message rescinding authority for the strike had reached the planes a mere minute earlier. They aborted, dropped their ordnance in the sea, and returned to the carrier. Several people communicated Ford's decision to resume strikes, with sources recording different times for doing so. Scowcroft's assistant, Major McFarlane, could call Wickham with the news that the first wave could go ahead and strike. McFarlane did so at 8:47 p.m. The Pentagon sent a message to its forces a minute later, at 8:48 p.m.: "correction to previous order: First wave of TACAIR from *CORAL SEA* to strike mainland targets. BDA [bomb damage assessment] is to be made and reported to National Military Command Center." Scowcroft reinforced the message McFarlane had delivered, calling Wickham at 8:52 to say the *Coral Sea* strike operations could proceed as originally planned. A verbal order to that effect went out to General Burns, the on-scene commander, at 8:58. Interestingly, the order also noted that Burns had the authority to detour strikes against the mainland to support the Marines if necessary.

While the back and forth occasioned by the Cambodian broadcast complicated the first mainland strike mission, the White House was considering how to get a message back to the Cambodians in response to their broadcast. One NSC staffer, William Lloyd Stearman, who had been in contact with DIA about the ultimatum to be broadcast to the Cambodians, suggested using the broadcast frequencies the Khmer Rouge was using and that NSA was monitoring. Stearman recalled Kissinger thinking this was a great idea but said NSA objected since it considered knowledge of Cambodian frequencies to be classified.[39] If NSA objected, they did so at high levels and directly to the White House because at lower echelons NSA had been collaborating with DIA on preparing the ultimatum for broadcast into the Cambodian radio network.[40]

In any case, broadcasting the US response directly into the Cambodian radio network did not happen, even though Kissinger and the White House spokesman, Nessen, claimed it had and President Ford thought so as well. Nessen told the press the United States had broadcast its response on a radio frequency "we knew would be monitored" in Cambodia. On May 16, the secretary of state agreed, saying the United States took "drastic communications measures" and broadcast the US statement directly into Cambodia.[41] Ford privately told the shah of Iran, who visited the White House on May 15, that "we put a message through their frequencies and over the AP [Associated Press] that we would stop when the crew was released."[42] However, a later congressional investigation found no evidence of a direct broadcast response to Cambodia.

Even as the discussion about how to communicate with the Cambodians was underway, NSA radio intercepts indicated the Cambodians were releasing the crew. An unknown Cambodian source said, "Let the Americans go. We do not want to become prisoners ourselves." While NSA was trying to evaluate the accuracy of the message, intelligence agencies began sharing the news. Admiral Gayler's staff thought this intelligence supported the belief that at least some Americans were still on Tang Island. At 9:15 p.m., INR received the NSA message saying an unidentified Khmer command had said, "Let them take their ship and leave." It was shared with the State Department's working group on the *Mayaguez* crisis.

Whether Kissinger was informed of the intercepts is not known. In his memoirs, he merely notes that "after toying with the idea of breaking into Cambodian communications, we decided that the most expeditious way would be to release a statement to the news services." When Nessen failed to respond quickly enough to Kissinger's request that he come to his office, Kissinger sent Scowcroft to grab Nessen, who took the message and put it out to the press at 9:15 p.m.:

> We have heard [a] radio broadcast that you are prepared to release the S.S. *Mayaguez*. We welcome this development, if true.
>
> As you know, we have seized the ship. As soon as you issue a statement that you are prepared to release the crew members you hold unconditionally and immediately, we will promptly cease military operations.[43]

While Nessen was encouraging the press to file their reports immediately, Kissinger was on the phone with Sisco again. He told Sisco about delivering the message to the Cambodians via the press and keeping up the bombing in the meantime. Sisco responded that he was glad to hear about the outreach through the press because he anticipated criticism on that score:

Sisco: I was going to recommend to you that you take the offensive and take the initiative because the one kind of criticism we would face here is if you guys had waited another hour or two, you know, and all that sort of thing. That's what we will hear so I was going to recommend to you get out and get our side of the story that these guys have had three days to respond. But . . .

Kissinger: That's right.

Sisco: But now this announcement I think meets that particular concern, you see.

Kissinger: Yeah. Okay.

Sisco: All right. Look, I'm going to go out and get a bowl of chili but I'll be back if there's anything you want from Phil [Habib] and me.

Kissinger: Okay, fine. You can send that letter to the Security Council although I just don't see why it can't wait until first thing in the morning.

Sisco: No, it . . . I'll send it now, Mr. Secretary. Take my word for it, get it out.

Kissinger: Why?

Sisco: Simply because you are fulfilling an obligation . . .

Kissinger: Okay, go ahead; send it.

Sisco: . . . and nobody can criticize you.

Kissinger: Okay.

Sisco: Okay.[44]

Within ten minutes Sisco had a message out to Ambassador Scali to deliver the notification to the UN Security Council. By then the Marines had been fighting for almost two hours and were in increasingly desperate straits.

While White House principals waited for more news from Cambodia, they labored through the dinner with Uyl, which by all accounts was an awkward affair. The dinner had been delayed a half hour as the Cambodian broadcast was dealt with, and once under way Ford kept popping out of the black tie affair to receive reports in the usher's office adjoining the state dining room. Scowcroft and Rumsfeld made only token appearances, and Kissinger stayed for only one course. Schlesinger arrived late but stayed until dessert had been served before leaving. Shortly after 10 p.m. Ford ushered the guests to the Red Room for coffee.

While the dinner party had coffee, on the other side of the world the *Mayaguez* crew had been released. The Cambodians sent them toward American forces on the same Thai fishing boat that had carried them to the mainland. They were soon sighted by an American reconnaissance plane. Four minutes after the president bid his guests farewell at the North Portico of the White House, the USS *Wilson* intercepted the fishing boat and took the *Mayaguez* crew on board. Ford then headed for

Kissinger's office in the West Wing for the latest information. At 10:57, while Ford was in Kissinger's office, the second wave of A-6 Intruders and A-7 Corsairs from the *Coral Sea* bombed Ream airfield, destroying seventeen planes, cratering the runway, and flattening the hangar.

Ford returned to the Oval Office at 11 p.m. where he was joined by Kissinger, Scowcroft, and McFarlane, and over the next half hour, by Rumsfeld and other staff. McFarlane, in direct touch with the NMCC as previously arranged with Wickham, already had the news that the entire crew had been safely recovered. He shared this information with the president and his top aides. When Schlesinger called the president from the Pentagon at 11:08 with the news that the crew had been recovered, he said thirty members were on the fishing boat. Thirty was the estimate made by the American reconnaissance plane that first sighted the fishing boat. For some reason Schlesinger had not yet received the more complete report from the *Wilson* that the entire crew was safe. In his memoirs, McFarlane recalled the moment:

> Ford, who already knew from me that the crew was in fact safe in US hands, gave no indication of this to Schlesinger, but thanked him and hung up. Then he let out a loud guffaw. "Schlesinger didn't have a clue as to what was going on," he said, laughing. "He didn't even know the crew had already been recovered." Kissinger, Scowcroft and Rumsfeld joined in his merriment [and] broke into loud laughter. At that moment, David Hume Kennerly, the White House photographer, snapped a picture. Later, press secretary, Ron Nessen, looking for a quote to put under the picture, asked me what the President had said when he heard the crew had been recovered. I told him truthfully that he had reacted with relief and thanked God that they were all safe. The next day, the photograph appeared on the front page of *The New York Times*, the caption indicating it was a shot of the President and his aides reacting to the news that the *Mayaguez* crew had been released.[45]

Schlesinger called Ford back a few minutes later with the update that the entire crew had been rescued, but the merrymaking in the Oval Office at Schlesinger's expense reveals the extent to which the secretary of defense was considered an outsider by the White House at this juncture. Reinforcing that division, the occupants of the Oval Office discovered the Pentagon's press secretary already had "scooped" the White House by announcing the successful recovery of the crew. Nessen and other advisors were furious at the Pentagon, which "from the very beginning of the operation had been leaking information about the *Mayaguez* to reporters" in advance of White House press reports.[46] Nessen recommended the president trump the Pentagon with a live television announcement of the recovery of the ship and crew.

About two minutes after the second call from Schlesinger confirming the entire crew's recovery, the third wave of aircraft from the *Coral Sea* launched. Two A-6s and six A-7s, plus support aircraft, were headed toward Kompong Som and Ream Naval Base. Meanwhile, the news moved up the chain of command that the captain of the *Mayaguez* had informed Navy personnel that his entire crew was accounted for, that they had not been mistreated, and that he had convinced the Cambodian command in Phnom Penh that if they released the ship and crew, US airstrikes would be stopped. In light of this information, Admiral Gayler asked the JCS whether the third wave should continue on course.

This very issue was being debated in the White House by Kissinger and his staff. Stearman argued, "Henry, we got our people back, we got the ship back, why don't we call off the air strikes. Suppose one of our guys gets shot down and we have another prisoner or worse yet somebody gets killed. So, why don't we knock it off?" Kissinger retorted, "We are not going to lose any aircraft."[47] Rumsfeld had a different concern. Given the intention to make a national announcement on live television, he recommended that Ford call Schlesinger back for absolute confirmation that the entire crew had been recovered. Ford did so at 11:45, and Schlesinger assured Ford the news had been confirmed by three different sources. While Ford was on the phone with Schlesinger, Scowcroft asked whether there was any reason for the Pentagon not to disengage. Kissinger said, "No, but tell them to bomb the mainland. Let's look ferocious! Otherwise they will attack us as the ship leaves."[48]

CHAPTER 4

Day Four | Thursday, May 15

ith the benefit of the phone call from the White House, during which Kissinger encouraged the president to continue the mainland strikes, Schlesinger had the instructions necessary to answer Gayler's inquiry as to whether the third wave of aircraft should continue. General Jones discussed the issue with Schlesinger, who confirmed that the third strike should be carried out. Accordingly, five minutes later at 11:50 p.m., the third group of aircraft struck an oil refinery; several buildings, including a barracks complex; and several warehouses.

On Tang Island the Marines were unaware that the *Mayaguez* crew members had been released by the Cambodians. The news that Washington had ordered the termination of military operations was unexpected and incomprehensible to them. The decision effectively stranded the Marines on Tang in dire straits. Austin and other on-scene commanders quickly convinced the chain of command to reverse the order, and the second wave of Marines was allowed to proceed to Tang.[1] Once there they informed Austin that the crew had been released. However, the confusion had delayed the arrival of Marine reinforcements and therefore the amount of time to organize a withdrawal. Even worse, US forces were down to a handful of operational helicopters. The depleted force of five helicopters would only be able to transport 127 Marines.

On the other hand, the recovery of the *Mayaguez* crew meant air and naval fire could support the Marines unconstrained, that is, if the Marines could communicate their locations well enough to effectively direct fires. The two groups of Marines on the western side of the island tried to link up, which precipitated ground fighting every bit as intense as the insertion process. Fortified enemy positions (bunkers and huts) separated the two groups. A small detachment from the northern group moved south to lead Austin's group back to the larger contingent, but it immediately encountered automatic weapons fire and claymore mines. One Marine was killed and a number of others seriously wounded.

Austin and his Marines worked their way north, advancing aggressively into Cambodian fire. They wanted to disguise their weakness and link up with the larger force of Marines to reduce their vulnerability. They succeeded in advancing and picked up captured Khmer Rouge weapons to augment their meager firepower. Visibility in the dense jungle was approximately five to fifteen feet, so the American and Khmer forces were constantly within a few meters of one another. Between periodic rushes by the Khmer soldiers, the fighting was characterized by grenade duels. One Marine patrol working along the rocky shoreline overran a Cambodian log bunker, killing its three defenders. They discovered an abundance of captured US ordnance and a US-made PRC–44 radio tuned to Marine frequencies.

During the intense fighting, the Marines managed to coordinate close air support despite the loss of their UHF radios:

> Keith and the battalion air liaison officer, Capt. Barry Cassidy, improvised a radio relay system whereby information was forwarded on the battalion's tactical frequency to the Airborne Mission Commander . . . who in turn relayed the information to the A-7s and F-4s flying close air support. Even more incredible was that Cassidy was with [Austin's] command element while Keith was with the main force.[2]

This improvised communication linkup and the resultant close air support made a great difference. The gunship Spectre-61's fire support for the Marines thereafter was quite effective at knocking out the enemy bunkers that lay between Austin's southern group and the main body of Marines.[3] The two bodies of Marines finally joined up about noon, just prior to the arrival of the second wave of Marines aboard the five helicopters that were still operable. The reinforcements included Marines from Company E and three 81-mm mortars. Unfortunately, Spectre-61 was leaving to refuel just as the second wave arrived.[4] Knife-52 took a run at the east beach to reinforce Cicere's Marines. A barrage of enemy fire erupted, hitting its fuel tank. Losing fuel and without the capability to refuel in flight, Knife-52 and its complement of twenty-seven Marines turned back to Thailand. They made it as far as the Thai coast before crash-landing close to where Knife-22 had made its emergency landing earlier in the day.[5]

Knife-51 and Jolly-43 also were forced to abort their insertion efforts on the east beach. Offloading on the west beach proved easier because the larger group of Marines on that side of the island had established a small perimeter around the landing zone. Knife-51 was able to discharge nineteen Marines and take aboard five wounded. Jolly-43 inserted twenty-eight Marines and then headed off to refuel. Jolly-11 and Jolly-12 inserted twenty-seven and twenty-six Marines, respectively, bringing the total number to 204 on the west beach.[6] Austin used the additional Marines to expand his perimeter and dig in, not knowing at that point whether they would be remaining overnight.

* * *

Back in Washington, President Ford made his brief televised remarks to the nation announcing the safe recovery of the ship and crew just before 12:30 a.m. Next he spent a few minutes in the Oval Office with Kissinger; Scowcroft; Rumsfeld; and Robert T. Hartmann, the counselor to the president, before returning to his residence, where he took one last call from Schlesinger at 12:35 and then accepted a rare sleeping pill from his personal physician.[7]

After speaking with the president, Schlesinger cancelled the fourth planned airstrike against the Cambodian mainland. Instead, all subsequent *Coral Sea* air missions would be close air support for the Marines on Tang Island. Thus, the fourth wave was redirected toward Tang to support the Marines. However, the Navy planes had not prepped for that mission nor did they have communications with the Marines, so the mission was aborted.[8]

Even after the Marines understood the *Mayaguez* crew had been released, they were unhappy with the decision by Jones and Schlesinger to order a cessation of offensive operations. The Marines had expended precious blood to take the island, and some in their chain of command wanted to complete the mission.[9] Nonetheless, Schlesinger saw no point in continuing the fighting on Tang Island and ordered a withdrawal. "At that point," he recalled later,

> I got some objection from Honolulu [Marine headquarters for Pacific operations], which ran along the lines of, "The Marines have landed and they are going to achieve their military objective!" I had to order the Marines off the island. No point in inflicting additional casualties on the Marines or the Cambodians, for that matter.[10]

For the next eight hours the US forces on the scene worked in harrowing circumstances to extract the Marines while minimizing casualties.

* * *

With orders to disengage, the Marines turned their attention to evacuation, which would turn out to be every bit as harrowing as the insertion. The group isolated on the eastern beach was in constant danger of being overrun. Two attempts to extract these Marines and airmen in midafternoon were abandoned after enemy fire severely damaged Jolly-11 and Jolly-43. Both helicopters flew out to the *Coral Sea*, where they were safely recovered. Maintenance crews quickly patched Jolly-11 back into flying shape. Eventually, using a hose from the ship's galley as a substitute for a new fuel line, they were able to get Jolly-43 reengaged as well.[11] Along with Jolly-12, Knife-51, and newly arrived Jolly-44, there would be a total of five helicopters left to try to evacuate the Marines.

Meanwhile two US Air Force OV-10 forward air control aircraft (Nail-68 and Nail-47), arrived. Major Robert W. Undorf, USAF, in Nail-68 assumed control of close air support operations, which greatly improved as a result. The AC-130's 105-mm cannon provided the most effective supporting fires, but they had to be carefully coordinated given how closely the Cambodians were clinging to Marine positions.[12] Undorf also successfully directed supporting fire from the *Wilson*'s 5-inch gun, which took out several .50-caliber machine guns operating from a partially sunken Cambodian gunboat that had bedeviled US helicopters.[13] Austin would later credit Undorf with turning the tide of battle.[14]

As welcome as the effective close fire support was, darkness was descending. Austin's Marines on the western side of the island might survive overnight, but it was doubtful that Cicere's group would. Consequently, the decision was made to attempt another run at evacuating Cicere's group from the eastern beach. To further augment fire support and rescue personnel from downed aircraft, the *Wilson*'s commander called for volunteers to man the ship's small boat (called a "gig"). Eight volunteers with "brown water navy" experience in Vietnam were dispatched on the gig. Once the gig was on station, some consideration was given to whether it could evacuate personnel from the eastern beach. The gig could take approximately ten men at a time, which meant thirteen or so would have to stay behind and risk being overrun. Cicere requested volunteers. After Marine Staff Sergeant J. Wyatt, Air Force pilot First Lieutenant John P. Lucas, and Marine Lance Corporal A. Louis Ybarra volunteered, all the rest did as well.[15]

As it turned out, the gig was used to support a helicopter evacuation instead. It darted in close to shore and used its mounted M-60 machine guns to distract Khmer soldiers from the incoming helicopters.[16] While Undorf directed supporting fires from Spectre-11, the *Wilson*'s gig, and A-7s and F-4s, Jolly-11 darted in to extract the hard-pressed Marines and airmen. Despite all the cover fire, Jolly-11 took heavy enemy fire. Khmer Rouge tossing hand grenades chased the US servicemen back to the rescue helicopter. They were cut down by helicopter miniguns, an Air Force photographer who joined the fight, and the Marines, who stopped to return fire. Having successfully extracted the survivors of Knife-23, Jolly-11 flew to the *Coral Sea*. A bit later, fearing one Marine had taken shelter in the wreckage of Knife-23, Jolly-12 risked yet another rescue effort. It hovered over the site with a rescue line while Knife-51 provided supporting fire. No Marine emerged from the downed helicopter, so after waiting for several minutes—during which it suffered damage and a crew member was wounded—Jolly-12 departed for the *Coral Sea*. Both Jolly-11 and Jolly-12 sustained so much damage during the evacuation of the eastern beach that they were unable to fly again for the remainder of the operation. US forces were now down to three helicopters—Jolly-43, Jolly-44, and Knife 51—with exhausted crews that had been flying all day.

Also around this time, as light was fading, the decision was made to relieve pressure on the remaining Marines by hitting the Cambodians with a 15,000-pound BLU-82 packed with almost eight tons of high explosive. BLU-82s were the largest nonnuclear bombs in the US arsenal. The use of the BLU-82 had been approved earlier in the operation to cut a landing zone out of the dense forest. Just before operations were launched, Gayler told Burns to put the BLU-82s on launch alert. Now, running out of daylight, helicopters, and patience, Gayler was anxious to alleviate the Marines' increasingly precarious situation. Austin had been notified that the BLU-82 was available, but he never requested its use. As Austin reported on Cambodian pressure and the risk of being overrun during the withdrawal process, Gayler directed Burns to unleash the BLU-82 but to "insure caution" and "stay clear of the Marines and choppers."[17]

A C-130 transport aircraft dropped the BLU-82 on the southern portion of the island, about a thousand yards from the Marines. Presumably Gayler's purpose in using the huge bomb was to display the extent of US firepower and encourage the zealous Cambodians to consider letting the Marines depart the island with minimum interference. Burns later said the bomb was dropped for its "diversionary and inhibiting effect." The blast, which created a small mushroom cloud and tore an area the size of a football field out of the island's dense vegetation, surprised the Marines, ruptured eardrums, blew Nail-68 almost a 1,000 feet higher, and jolted Jolly-11's automatic flight controls off-line.[18] By some accounts, Cambodian activity following the detonation of the BLU-82 was greatly reduced, especially enemy traffic along footpaths.[19] Even so, the Marines requested that the BLU-82 not be used again.[20]

As night fell, Nail-68 ran out of fuel and was replaced by Nail-69, flown by Captain Gregory Wilson. Wilson, who had not trained for night operations, asked Spectre-11 to drop an illumination flare, which briefly sidelined the OV-10 by destroying Wilson's night vision and disorienting him.[21] Meanwhile, the decision to extract the Americans from the western side of Tang surprised the Marines. The relative merits of digging in to remain overnight and evacuating in darkness had been discussed, but the sudden arrival of helicopters was unexpected. Nevertheless, Knife-51 succeeded in picking up forty-one Marines while taking little damage. In the darkness, enemy fires proved much less accurate. Jolly-43 followed on the heels of Knife-51, lifting off with fifty-four Marines, more than double the normal load.[22] Jolly-44 then took its turn, extracting thirty-four. As the Marine perimeter constricted, increasing the distance from the enemy, more supporting fires were called in on the Cambodians. However, the well-disciplined Khmer soldiers countered by moving closer to the evacuating Marines, occupying their abandoned positions. This made the dwindling number of Marines increasingly vulnerable.

Realizing time was running out, Jolly-44, which had barely avoided a midair collision with Jolly-43 in the darkness, opted to offload its Marines on the *Holt* rather than the *Coral Sea* in order to return to the island more rapidly. Without the benefit of its low-light-level television system and operating in total darkness, Jolly-44 attempted to unload its exhausted Marines. After making three passes at the *Holt*, Jolly-44 was talked in slowly by a flight mechanic until the rotors were within two feet of the *Holt*'s superstructure. Then, with the end of the helicopter protruding over the sea, the Marines exited through its front door onto the *Holt*. Jolly-44 immediately returned to the western beach.

In total darkness, the Marines' reduced numbers made their position particularly vulnerable. Austin had departed aboard Knife-51, so Captain James H. Davis was in charge. He feared the last seventy-three Marines were in danger of being overrun. Nail-69 heard the Marine commander observe, "We need to get off the LZ [landing zone] in 15 minutes or we won't get off at all."[23] The Cambodians could not see well either, but it seemed only a matter of time before they realized there were few remaining Marines and that they had moved down to the surf line. Nail-68 had lost radio contact with the Marines, but it flew low over the beach with its lights on, drawing enemy fire and verifying there were still Marines to evacuate.

To the relief of the Marines, Jolly-44 quickly reappeared on the western beach, but darkness made it difficult to find the increasingly small beach, much reduced by high tide. Thanks to a strobe light Davis just happened to have, and which he tossed out in front of the Marine position, Jolly-44 was able to find the Marines.[24] It took off with forty-four Marines and reported there was one more contingent left. One Marine recalls being out about fifty yards from the helicopter extraction point on the dwindling Marine line, and in jungle with foliage so dense there was only about ten feet of visibility. In the pitch dark they could hear the Khmer Rouge but could only detect their locations from muzzle flashes. A gunny sergeant "came around and removed about every other guy as they reduced the perimeter. He then sent a runner around to let us know that the next chopper was it. When the next bird [helicopter] came in, we were to empty the M-60 into the woods and get to the helicopter because it would be the last one out."[25]

That helicopter, Knife-51, returning from the *Coral Sea*, was guided to the landing zone by Nail-69, which circled the beach flashing its landing lights. As it did so it drew enemy fire, which the circling AC-130 then suppressed. With the diverse sources of light, Knife-51 had trouble finding the Marines. But after three failures, Knife-51 went in with all its lights on, which drew intense fire from the Cambodians but enabled it to find the landing zone. Twenty-seven Marines climbed aboard. At the last minute a pararescueman, Technical Sergeant Wayne L. Fisk, left the helicopter and raced to the tree line to make sure no Marines were being left behind. While the vulnerable helicopter hovered, Fisk found two Marines who otherwise would have been left behind. Together they returned to Knife-51, which then departed. Once the extraction was complete, Captain Davis reported that he was "relatively certain" there were no more Marines left on Tang Island.[26]

Despite all the precautions and last-minute checks, and all the previous, selfless acts of heroism to recover bodies and stranded personnel, the unthinkable happened. Amid all the confusion, a three-member Marine machine-gun crew—Gary L. Hall, Joseph N. Hargrove, and Danny G. Marshall—was overlooked, and the body of another Marine was also left behind on the beach.[27] With Marines having been evacuated to Thailand, the *Holt*, and the *Coral Sea*, it took a while to determine any Marines were missing. On board the *Coral Sea*, the Marines discussed plans to return to Tang to retrieve their missing comrades while Rear Admiral R. T. Coogan called for Navy SEALs from Subic Bay to be flown in. On the *Wilson*, volunteers were again requested to man the gig in case it was sent back to the island.[28]

After a platoon from SEAL Team One arrived, Coogan met with the SEAL team commander—Lieutenant (junior grade) R. T. Coulter—Lieutenant Colonel Austin,

Captain Davis, and Gunnery Sergeant Lester McNemar to decide on a course of action. The SEAL commander proposed a night insertion to recover the missing Marines. Marines volunteered to go back in as well. Despite this proposal, Coogan did not want to risk more lives without knowing the Marines were still alive.[29] Coogan asked whether the SEALs could return in daylight after a leaflet drop telling the Cambodians that they just wanted to recover personnel. The leaflets had already been prepared in French and the Khmer language.[30] However, in light of the Khmer behavior over the past few days, the SEAL commander considered that plan unsound.[31] The conversation grew heated as it became clear to the distraught Marines that a search for their compatriots would not be approved.[32] In the end, the decision was made to approach the island and search for any signs of American survivors. The next day aircraft overflew the island electronically scanning for signals, and the *Wilson* cruised off the coast of Tang with all available crew and optical devices scanning the coast for the three Marines. Bullhorns were used to encourage any stranded Marines to attempt evacuation. A few Cambodians, who quickly hid themselves, were observed on the beaches. However, there was no sign of the three Marines.[33]

* * *

The White House was not aware of the three Marines left behind but did understand the evacuation had been hurried, difficult, and confused. When Kissinger and Scowcroft met with Ford at 9:50 on the morning of May 15, they repeated Captain Davis's assessment, telling the president they were "reasonably sure that all the Marines got out." Scowcroft also informed the president that the *Wilson* and *Holt* were continuing to cruise the island trying to observe and communicate with any Marines still on the island. With Marines and airmen in hospitals and bases in Thailand and others scattered over multiple ships heading in different directions, no casualty count was immediately available. In fact, it was five days before an accurate count was completed. Eighteen servicemen—including the three missing Marines—were killed assaulting Tang Island, and almost eighty more suffered wounds. Including the twenty-three personnel lost when the helicopter carrying Air Force security police went down, forty-one servicemen perished altogether. As critics were quick to point out, that tally was one more lost than saved with the return of the *Mayaguez* crew.[34]

PART II

Crisis Explanations

CHAPTER 5

Critical Crisis Decisions

A s has long been noted, the military operations during the *Mayaguez* crisis were fraught with danger. Any number of decisions made during those operations could have made a major impact on what subsequently happened and the casualties suffered by US forces. The difficult decision about whether to stay the night on the island or withdrawal under cover of darkness is a case in point. The USS *Hancock* was on the way with its load of additional helicopters and more Marines, which would have allowed a more orderly withdrawal and could have prevented the loss of the three Marines left behind. On the other hand, more casualties might have been sustained by the small remaining force of Marines on the island as darkness descended—and perhaps they would have been overrun by the more numerous defenders who were pressing close to their perimeter. Few commentators have been inclined to second-guess such decisions.

The same is not true for the decisions made further up the chain of command, however. The key decision makers in Washington have been roundly criticized for their performance, typically with little appreciation for what they thought was at stake and what they were trying to achieve. In an earlier work on the *Mayaguez* crisis, this author argued the key decision makers were Ford, Kissinger, Schlesinger, and Scowcroft. With the rich detail now available about the crisis decision-making process, and depending on how influential behavior is assessed, a case might be made for including some other major participants, particularly Vice President Rockefeller and General Jones, or even for excluding Scowcroft from the set of key leaders. However, for many reasons, I believe the record supports the argument that Ford, Kissinger, Schlesinger, and Scowcroft were the key decision makers.[1] The analysis of critical crisis decisions proceeds on that basis.

Priorities

The paramount objective during the crisis, as Scowcroft later explained, "was to make it clear, to everyone, to our friends, to potential opponents, that notwithstanding the fact that we had just withdrawn from Southeast Asia under fairly ignominious circumstances, if you will, that the United States understood its interests and was prepared to protect them."[2] Schlesinger later said the same thing, acknowledging the primary reason for the use of force was "to make quite clear to all parties that the United States was still an effective force."[3] Although the general goal was to reinforce the US reputation for defending its interests, the main concern in that regard was the Korean Peninsula. As Scowcroft related in 1980, "To the extent that we were looking anywhere specifically, it was primarily probably not Southeast Asia at that time, but at Korea," where the renewal of the long-simmering conflict between the two Koreas was considered a real possibility.[4]

Kissinger emphatically made the case for a demonstrative use of force in his first private meeting with Ford and shortly thereafter in the first NSC meeting. Rockefeller chimed in at this meeting, mentioning the USS *Pueblo*. It was assumed the *Mayaguez*'s crew already had been taken to the mainland, so the analogy to the *Pueblo* was not raised to argue for the need to recover the crew but rather to emphasize that the crisis was a test of American will and a punitive response was imperative. For the rest of the NSC meeting, the decision makers considered a wide range of retaliatory and punitive options.

The *Pueblo* was not Kissinger's preferred historical analogy, however. Instead, he was thinking of the EC-121 incident (see sidebar).[5] He thought the US reaction to the North Korean downing of the US Navy's EC-121 in international airspace with the loss of all thirty-one men was exactly what they should avoid. After returning from Kansas City for the third NSC meeting, he told the security council members, "I remember 1969, when the EC-121 was shot down off Korea. We assembled forces like crazy. But in the end, we did not do anything." To prevent inaction in the case of the *Mayaguez*, Kissinger argued for an aggressive and quick response. Between the third and fourth NSC meetings, he met privately with Ford and encouraged him to be resolute, saying, "This is your first crisis. You should establish a reputation for being too tough to tackle. This is a replay of the EC-121."

The corollary of the decision makers' primary objective—an impressive demonstration of US power and determination to protect interests—was the need to avoid opposite outcomes, namely, a failure to act; a weak response; or worst of all, a humiliation akin to the *Pueblo* experience. Thus, when decision makers learned during the second NSC meeting that there was still a chance to isolate the crew from the mainland, they tailored military operations to include a quarantine and an assault on the island where they thought at least some of the crew were being held. But the ultimate

The EC-121 Incident

On April 14, 1969, the North Koreans shot down a US Navy EC-121 surveillance aircraft, killing all thirty-one servicemen on board.[6] North Korean motivations for the attack have long been disputed. Some have argued it was an accident, and others claim that the North Korean leadership expected military retaliation,[7] which did not occur because the United States was worried that a military response might involve a confrontation with the Soviet Union.

It also has been argued that the Soviet Union's ability to constrain North Korean provocations was less than commonly believed at the time. Cold War documents suggest the Soviets were concerned about North Korean bellicosity, but that North Korea ignored Soviet remonstrations. Instead, they focused on US behavior, period. The North Koreans believed such small acts of aggression as seizing the *Pueblo* in 1968 and downing the EC-121 in 1969 helped establish their reputation for deterrence and kept the United States at bay. Besides, the United States did not respond with military force to the seizure of the *Pueblo*, so the risks of another attack seemed marginal.[8]

In his memoirs, Henry Kissinger agreed with the North Korean assessment that US performance during the EC-121 crisis was weak:

A leisurely process of decision-making creates a presumption in favor of eventual inaction. . . . In a crisis boldness is the safest course. Hesitation encourages the adversary to persevere, maybe even raise the ante. . . . Overall, I judge our conduct in the EC-121 crisis as weak, indecisive and disorganized. . . . I believe we paid for it in many intangible ways, in demoralized friends and emboldened adversaries.[9]

Kissinger was determined to do better during the *Mayaguez* crisis.

priority was a strong demonstration of resolve. From the beginning Kissinger had argued the lives of the *Mayaguez* crew "must unfortunately be a secondary consideration."[10] He later denied this quote, but circumstantial evidence,[11] and the subsequent decisions and behaviors of the key leaders—including Ford, Kissinger, Scowcroft, Schlesinger, and arguably Rockefeller—indicate they all agreed with this assertion.

In discussing risk to the crew, Ford told Scowcroft, "We have to predicate all these actions on the possibility of losing Americans." Schlesinger noted several times that the Cambodians could kill the crew at will, suggesting their ultimate fate was not in the hands of US decision makers. Similarly, Scowcroft made the point in an NSC meeting that boats had already been destroyed that might have carried crew members, thus reinforcing Ford's point that they had already crossed the point of no return on taking such risks. The island assault and the bombing of the mainland were also undertaken despite the obvious dangers posed to the crew.

Beyond the core group of senior decision makers, however, it is true that subordinate leaders, presidential advisors, and lower echelons of the military construed the military operations as a rescue mission and made decisions accordingly.[12] Deputy Secretary of Defense Clements's confusion on this point expressed in the third NSC meeting is a case in point. He interrupts to say the group should not "lose sight of our objectives," which "are to get the Americans and the ship." The president quickly got the conversation back to punitive options by asserting it had to be assumed some Americans had already been killed. "This is tragic," he said, "but I think that we have to assume that it happened." Ford asked whether anyone disagreed. When no one dissented, the conversation swung back to reprisals. Similarly, Kissinger responded to Philip Buchen's interventions on behalf of crew safety with explanations for why the US response had to be punitive. If the United States only responded in kind to the provocation, "nobody can lose by challenging us," he said. He also insisted repeatedly that a disproportionate response was necessary: "We have to use the opportunity to prove that others will be worse off if they tackle us, and not that they can return to the status quo." He wanted to give the impression that the United States was "not to be trifled with" and "potentially trigger-happy."[13]

Schlesinger and senior military leadership are sometimes depicted as disagreeing with the need for a punitive use of force in the *Mayaguez* crisis,[14] but this is not the case. The secretary of defense also advocated punitive action. What Schlesinger insisted upon was a punitive use of force that was not so grossly disproportionate that it would be politically counterproductive. He believed a botched operation or overkill in the use of force would inflame public and congressional opinion and thus further undermine the credibility of US threats to use force. When Schlesinger tailored Pentagon orders to forces in the field to ensure US aircraft were on the lookout for the crew members, it was primarily to avoid killing them, which would have undermined the image of effective military power that Schlesinger wanted to burnish. The punitive actions he favored were those that were commensurate with the nature of the offense, which was a naval action, and discriminate, in order to minimize collateral damage—particularly with respect to the *Mayaguez* crew.

Schlesinger repeatedly voiced support for sinking Cambodian naval assets,[15] including using *Coral Sea* aircraft for this purpose. He said he wanted "to paste Cambodia to the point that they realized it was not worth it to them to keep the crew."[16] He argued for a sequence of military actions that would minimize chances of Cambodian reprisals. In the second NSC meeting he summarized US objectives as the need to prevent the ship from being taken to a mainland port, the need to recover the crew, and the need "to attack and sink the Cambodian Navy," but "later, after we have our ship and our people out, in order to maximize the punishment." Schlesinger worried that sinking Cambodian vessels might provoke them to retaliate against the crew, so he wanted to recover the ship and crew members on the island before punishing the Cambodians. Once the military operations began, however, Schlesinger wanted to inflict punishment.[17] When news of the Cambodian broadcast mentioning the release of the *Mayaguez* arrived, he argued with Kissinger that the airstrikes should continue and won him over on that point. As for General Jones—the acting chairman of the Joint Chiefs and the senior military officer advising the president and the NSC—he clearly understood the distinction between the recovery of ship and crew and punitive strikes, and he sided with Schlesinger on a more discriminate and proportional response. Despite this, Jones did not hinder the key leaders from pursuing their punitive purpose.[18]

It also is important to note that Ford, Kissinger, and Scowcroft were in agreement with Schlesinger that excessive, counterproductive military force should be avoided. Ford and Scowcroft were determined to prevent the military from using too much force against the ship, arguing it would be a disaster if they accidently sank it. Also, Kissinger came around to Schlesinger's view that the B-52s would probably elicit an unhelpful political backlash. Prior to this, Kissinger had leaked the possibility of using B-52s to reporters on his plane ride back from Kansas City. The angry response from the columnists may have convinced Kissinger that Schlesinger was right about a negative public response to the bombers.[19] He told Ford privately the B-52s might be too much, even though a few days later during a flight to Europe he again leaked to newsmen the fact that their use was contemplated, presumably to underscore how intent US leaders were on using punitive force.[20] Thus, the differences among these leaders over the purpose, level, and type of force used were matters of degrees and not principle.

Certainly this is true with respect to the tension between demonstrating American resolve and protecting the lives of the crew. At no point during the crisis were the lives of the crew accorded paramount importance by any of the key leaders. The assault on Tang put the lives of the crew at risk, as has long been recognized.[21] However, the iconic moment illustrating the latent incompatibility of punitive military operations and protecting the crew members occurred when US pilots reported "Caucasians" on the bow of the *Sinvari*, the wooden, 40-foot Thai fishing boat headed toward the mainland. Schlesinger's exacting rules of engagement made the report possible and ensured the decision making would take place in Washington. When the decision was put to the key leaders in the White House, they were disturbed and even angry that the Pentagon was procrastinating on implementation of the blanket order to sink all boat traffic. The third NSC meeting was called to force the issue with the Pentagon, and the conversation in that meeting made it crystal clear the lives of the crew were a secondary concern.

Kissinger was again candid about his reasoning, saying it would have been better if they had just said "we will simply hit anything that leaves the island." "Now," he said, "we are debating with the pilot." Kissinger's comment animated Ford, who insisted he had given just such an order but that his orders were being flouted by the Pentagon. Ford called the situation "inexcusable" and promised an accounting would be made. After acknowledging they were confronted by "a different situation" because of the pilot's report, Ford "reluctantly" agreed that destroying the boat after a positive sighting of Americans would be counterproductive. He then quickly drove the group to agreement on the need to destroy all the remaining Cambodian boats that could be found. When Counselor to the President John O. Marsh Jr. obtusely observed that some of those boats might "have Americans on it," Kissinger spelled it out clearly: "I think the pilot should sink them. He should destroy the boats and not send situation reports." Less information was better.

In all of this discourse it is clear that the lives of the crew were not the paramount concern. Schlesinger, by controlling the rules of engagement, had engineered circumstances so that the crew was discovered and would not be killed by accident. In that regard, he effectively imposed his position that a punitive demonstration of force had to be conducted without overkill or manifestly indiscriminate force. He succeeded in moderating the degree of force used, but the unanimous priority remained demonstrating US resolve and, as a corollary, avoiding humiliating hostage negotiations.

Execution Issues

Military operations were a foregone conclusion given the key decision makers' overriding priority. However, there were a number of other important decisions to be made about the means employed to achieve the decision makers' objectives. The diplomatic, military, and informational elements of national power had to be coordinated, and by and large the key leaders coordinated their activities well (figure 1). Yet individual decision makers sometimes misrepresented their true purposes, and in a few instances where they disagreed about the best way to achieve common goals, they acted in favor of their own preferences in ways that had a dramatic impact on the outcome of the crisis.

Diplomacy and Ultimatums

From the beginning Kissinger managed diplomatic communications to further the primary objective. While decision makers waited for US military forces to arrive on the scene, diplomatic communications and public statements were cast as threats so that,

FIGURE 1. KEY EVENTS AND DECISIONS

Cambodia Time — 12TH | MAY 13TH | MAY 14TH | MAY 15TH | 16TH

CAMBODIA:
- 2:10–2:18 p.m. Mayaguez stopped
- 11:10 a.m. US message delivered in China
- 1:18 p.m. Ship stopped at Tang
- 7:45–10:15 a.m. Crew on fishing boat moving toward mainland
- 8:55 a.m. Fishing boat with crew hit with riot control agents
- 3:56 p.m. US embassy in Middle East reports crew to be released
- 6:07–6:26 a.m. Cambodian radio says ship to be released
- 6:09–7:15 a.m. Marines assault Tang
- 7:05 a.m. 1st TACAIR leaves Coral Sea
- 7:25–8:22 a.m. Marines take ship
- 9:49–10:00 a.m. USS Wilson recovers crew
- 10:29 a.m. 2nd wave TACAIR strikes
- 10:50 a.m. 3rd wave TACAIR strikes
- 6:15–8:15 p.m. Marines leave Tang

DC Time — MAY 12TH | MAY 13TH | MAY 14TH | MAY 15TH

WASHINGTON:
- 5:30; 8:00 a.m Ford, then Kissinger notified
- 12:05–12:50 p.m. 1st NSC Meeting
- 1:50 p.m. White House calls it act of piracy
- 6:05 a.m. US forces ordered to isolate ship and island
- 10:22–11:17 a.m. 2nd NSC Meeting
- 10:40 p.m.–12:25 a.m. 3rd NSC Meeting
- 1:00–2:00 p.m. US message delivered to UN
- 12:27 a.m. Ford announces recovery of ship and crew
- 3:52–5:42 p.m. 4th NSC Meeting
- 6:40–7:47 p.m. Ford briefs congressmen
- 7:00 p.m. UN says talking to Cambodians
- 9:15 p.m. US responds to Cambodian radio message

as Kissinger explained, "we can get some credit if the boat is released." He said that if the Cambodians buckled while US forces gathered, the United States could say "the release is in response to our statement." As one commentator notes, the threats made it more difficult for the Cambodians to release the ship quietly without losing face, assuming they were ever inclined to do so.[22] Later in the third NSC meeting, explaining why he favored making it known publicly that they had sunk Cambodian boats, Kissinger again noted that "it is not inconceivable that the Khmers will cave," and if they did, it "should come in response to something that we had done."[23] In the second NSC meeting, which Kissinger missed, Joseph Sisco represented State and did not say a word. No diplomatic initiatives were discussed.

Kissinger refused to release diplomatic communications to congressional investigators following the crisis, but years later they were declassified and made public. Their content was not an appeal for assistance but a warning of military retaliation—that is, a repetition of public announcements from the White House. In his memoirs Kissinger said he had an unsigned "oral note" attached to the formal message in Beijing that intensified the threat, saying, "The United States demands the immediate release of the vessel and of the full crew" and "if that release does not immediately take place, the authorities in Phnom Penh will be responsible for the consequences," which, as Kissinger notes, obviously meant the use of military force.[24] These communications were intended to reinforce the American threat so that no matter what happened, US willingness to use force would be manifest.

As the congressional investigation noted, Kissinger did not explore options for discussing how to resolve the crisis without using force. He did not contact the Cambodians directly in Phnom Penh, Paris, or Moscow. He did not respond to the NSA intercepts suggesting Cambodian interest in a resolution to the crisis, or to the report from Tehran twelve hours before the military assault on Tang Island—both of which we know were developments that INR passed on to the upper echelons of the Department of State and NSC staff. Given the fuss Kissinger made about not being notified in a timely manner about the seizure of the *Mayaguez*, it is highly unlikely—not to say inconceivable—that he was uninformed of such developments. After the fact he did not deny knowledge of the Tehran cable but rather claimed it was news of dubious reliability. Kissinger mentioned all other diplomatic news in the NSC meetings, but not this cable. There is no mention of the report in the now declassified NSC minutes, and no NSC participant ever mentioned the cable in their memoirs or, with one exception, in any interviews.[25] Several are on record as not knowing about the report, and it is now easy to see why. Kissinger did not have to discuss the report because its Washington distribution was limited to the Department of State and a few members of Kissinger's NSC staff.[26] The other NSC members were not aware of the report, and Kissinger and Deputy Secretary Robert Ingersoll did not mention it during the fourth NSC meeting. Doing so would have been inconvenient given Kissinger's candid assertion in the previous NSC meeting that he feared a diplomatic development that might sidetrack the use of force. In contrast to Sisco, who moved with alacrity on diplomatic initiatives he proposed, Kissinger dragged his feet on these matters, personally holding up diplomatic outreach to the UN for more than two days. He only approved the release of the communication early on the afternoon of May 14, a few hours before the final NSC meeting where the president gave orders for the island assault and mainland bombing to begin.

The other diplomatic issue discussed during the crisis was the value of an ultimatum with a deadline. The idea originated at the Department of Defense, which was struggling with how to assault a defended island while communicating the desire for the release of the crew unharmed. Military officers came up with the idea of using a bullhorn to communicate a simple ultimatum: "Produce all the Americans immediately, or we will harm you."[27] Schlesinger mentioned this option in the second NSC meeting that Kissinger did not attend. The idea of a broader ultimatum was attractive to some in the White House, but when Ford called Kissinger in Missouri he argued it would cede the initiative to the Cambodians, who could feign interest in a diplomatic solution but request more time or otherwise complicate military operations. Kissinger thought, "The risks were greater than the benefits, and the benefits were really domestic" (i.e., reassuring domestic critics that the Ford administration had given peace a chance).[28]

Hours before the third NSC meeting, Schlesinger and Jones were discussing the operations, and Schlesinger asked about preparations for communicating with the Cambodians through pamphlets and broadcasts into their radio network. He wanted to know about the scripts for the messages.[29] It had occurred to the Pentagon that the ultimatum could be broadcast over Cambodian frequencies and international distress frequencies being monitored by the Khmer Rouge. DIA drafted the text for this version of the ultimatum, which was longer and had a deadline, saying the Cambodians had to "announce by 10:00 this morning their intention to release all crew members unconditionally and immediately" or "be fully responsible for the further consequences." It closed by noting, "We are monitoring international distress frequencies to receive response." General Jones mentioned the ultimatum during the fourth NSC meeting, which sparked an extended discussion.

Kissinger was again cool to the idea. Schlesinger, apparently understanding Kissinger's qualms about embracing an initiative that would put the ball in the Cambodians court, simply asked if it was okay to issue a local ultimatum (presumably on Tang during the assault). Kissinger had no objections so long as those using the bullhorns did not negotiate but simply stated US demands. Donald Rumsfeld was in favor of the ultimatum if communicated privately, and Buchen favored the ultimatum, believing it was the best means to prevent harming crew members and neutral ships during the fast-approaching US military operations. Kissinger and Buchen exchanged some barbs over the issue. Kissinger countered Buchen by arguing military operations should come first and if they failed to secure the ship and crew, then a "credible" ultimatum could be issued, promising even more punishment until the ship and crew were released.

Kissinger tightly controlled his staff at the Department of State.[30] He was furious that the *Mayaguez* had been seized without his being immediately notified. He demanded and received by close of business that same day an explanation for the tardy notification. He largely operated from his office in the White House, with Under Secretary Sisco keeping him apprised of developments at the State Department. A State Department official's remark—"We know what we have to do, we just have to wait for the means to do it to arrive on the scene"—perfectly reflected Kissinger's preferences but not the institutional proclivities of the diplomatic bureaucracy.[31]

However, with all the information now available, it is evident that career officials at State did try to get Kissinger to exercise more diplomacy.[32]

For example, Sisco tried to convince Kissinger to approve routine diplomatic communications, assuring him they were cosmetic only and would not interfere with the use of force. He wanted to notify US missions overseas and other nations, provide guidance to the ambassador in Thailand (who was furious about being kept in the dark and had complained bitterly to the State Department about it),[33] and, most important, notify the UN Security Council. Sisco understood the substance of diplomacy was being bypassed, but he nonetheless pushed Kissinger to communicate with the UN and other countries at least enough to provide some political cover for the pending military operations. Kissinger finally approved notification of other countries by phone when it was too late for any interference. In doing so he stipulated that he did not want the "usual pansy briefings" or "to give the impression of super reasonableness." The whole point was to signal a ready willingness to use force. In that same conversation Sisco sought quick approval for his other three diplomatic communications, offering to read them over the phone or have them hand-carried in the next five minutes for Kissinger's approval. Kissinger said he wanted to see them but left them unattended on his desk.

Later, after the Cambodian broadcast prompted a response from the White House that was released to the press, Kissinger passed this news to Sisco, who thought the attempt to communicate with the Cambodians made good political sense. In that conversation Kissinger told Sisco he could notify the UN Security Council if he wanted, but added "I just don't see why it can't wait until first thing in the morning." Sisco convinced a reluctant Kissinger to do it right away to avoid criticism and had the message sent to Ambassador Scali within ten minutes. Later, after the crew was recovered, Kissinger again spoke with Sisco, admitting the three messages hand-carried to him earlier were still on his desk. Concerning the notification of overseas posts, Sisco said he considered it a "dead" issue at that point. However, Kissinger told him to do it anyway because he wanted other countries informed on the successful US operations.[34]

Initially Kissinger was concerned about staging military operations from Thailand, which he knew would not grant permission. In the first NSC meeting he argued that aerial reconnaissance, but not combat missions, were permissible. Otherwise the Thais would demand that US forces depart, which would further weaken the US position in Southeast Asia. However, as the crisis progressed the injunction against using Thai-based forces relaxed. Thai-based fighters were ordered aloft by Scowcroft to interdict the *Mayaguez* when it was thought to be moving toward the mainland. In the third NSC meeting there was debate over conducting operations out of Thailand a day earlier or waiting a day until the Marines arrived from Subic Bay in the Philippines on board the carrier USS *Hancock* and the amphibious assault ship USS *Okinawa*. Kissinger said the Thai government would be upset, "but they will also be reassured" and "the Thai military will love it." He, along with others, eventually supported the earlier operations even at the expense of irritating the Thais. Later, after the recovery of ship and crew, Kissinger and Sisco discussed notifying the embassy in Thailand so that the ambassador could reassure the Thais. Sisco thought the Thais were most interested in getting the Marines off their territory, but Kissinger corrected him, saying that "the major thing the Thais want to know is that it worked."

Kissinger knew from the CIA that Thai military leadership was privately "extremely pleased" the United States was acting decisively. So when the Thai premier complained about US operations, he was ignored, as was the US charge d'affaires's cable admonishing Washington to "play by the rules" and respect Thai sovereignty. In the fourth NSC meeting, Deputy Secretary of State Ingersoll's only intervention was to ask about removing the Marines from Thailand quickly to avoid further irritating the Thais. Kissinger did not say anything then, but when Ingersoll raised the issue again on the morning of the sixteenth in the State Department staff meeting, Kissinger cut him off, saying, "First of all, I want that panic to stop about Thailand." After joking about sending tranquilizers to the US ambassador in Thailand, who had complained of "an unbelievable lack of coordination and foresight in failing to keep me informed,"[35] they discussed Thai reactions, and Kissinger's view was that it would blow over. When Philip Habib, assistant secretary of state for East Asian and Pacific affairs, pushed back and suggested an apology to Thailand, Kissinger repeatedly dismissed the idea as "absurd." He finally cut off the persistent Habib with the definitive comment: "We will not apologize."[36]

In sum, and contrary to other accounts,[37] Kissinger was not interested in using diplomacy to resolve the crisis.[38] Like Schlesinger, he used his control of his department to promote his preferred outcome. With good reason[39] he was "worried that in the next 48 hours some diplomatic pressure will occur" that might interfere with military action, and he used his control of diplomatic communications to prevent that development. Apparently unbeknownst to Ford,[40] he ignored direct communications with the Cambodians and signals that the Cambodians were looking for a peaceful resolution, delayed contacting the UN secretary-general for two days, and kept news of the cable from Tehran from the NSC.[41] If he had handled any of these issues differently, the diplomatic surprise he feared could have taken place, strengthening arguments in favor of waiting longer for more forces to arrive on the scene. Kissinger also used his influence with Ford to ensure the use of military force was as demonstrative as possible. He prevailed upon Ford to keep airstrikes going after the Cambodian broadcast announced an intent to release the ship, and he did the same after the news of the crew's safe recovery.

Lethal Quarantine

The first of three key execution issues for military operations was how to manage the quarantine of the *Mayaguez* and its crew from the mainland. Ford's initial orders on the ship were highly discriminate compared to later orders for the quarantine of Tang Island. When Scowcroft woke Ford at 2:23 a.m. on the morning of the May 13 to tell him the *Mayaguez* apparently was just fifteen minutes from Kompong Som, Ford wanted US aircraft to interdict the ship as Scowcroft recommended but not sink it:

> **Scowcroft:** With your approval, Mr. President, if we can get some planes in the air . . .
> **Ford:** I think you ought to try that. It doesn't seem to me there is any other alternative, Brent. But dammit, they hadn't better sink it now!!!
> **Scowcroft:** No sir; that would be disastrous.
> **Ford:** That would be the ultimate in stupidity . . .[42]

During the second NSC meeting when Kissinger was absent, there was a discussion on the use of force to interdict naval traffic between the island and the mainland. In response to Ford's question about whether they were keeping the gunboats at bay, General Jones told him, "We have not opened fire on them. We have scared some of them away by making passes at them." Rockefeller suggested they should just sink gunboats until the Cambodians gave in. In response, Schlesinger made his argument in favor of conducting punitive action after recovering the ship and any crew members found on Tang Island to reduce the likelihood of Cambodian retribution. Acknowledging this, Ford agreed, saying, "You do not sink them, necessarily, but can you take some preventive action?" Continuing, Ford said that in addition to preventing boats from leaving the island, the Pentagon should also "stop all boats coming to the island." When he summarizes the agreed-upon actions at the end of the meeting, Ford reiterated that these two steps should be taken.

Returning to the Pentagon, Schlesinger and Jones discussed the guidance from the president in the second NSC meeting and how the quarantine of Tang would be managed. Schlesinger emphasized to Jones the modulated use of force he wanted, saying boats headed for the mainland should only be sunk if they could not be turned around any other way. "I don't want indiscriminate shooting," he said.[43] Jones passed

these orders along, specifying that Tang Island would be isolated by intercepting all boats with carefully modulated force. The guidance was so restrictive it greatly reduced the possibility of accidental sinkings. It highlighted the importance of careful reconnaissance and emphasized "the decision to fire on or sink any boats resides in Washington." In effect, the Pentagon extended Ford's specific guidance on carefully modulated escalation of force for dissuading movement of the *Mayaguez* and applied it to all naval traffic between Tang and the mainland. Schlesinger elaborated on Ford's guidance, but his instructions were not inconsistent with Ford's guidance on some sort of "preventive action" short of sinking boats leaving Tang Island.

Between the second and third NSC meetings Ford decided to provide more specificity about the interdiction effort. He could see that sinking the ship they were rescuing would be disastrous. He called Schlesinger to emphasize the need to prevent the movement of the *Mayaguez* with very carefully calibrated escalation of force. Scowcroft followed up with similar instructions to Wickham, emphasizing that if the ship moved it should be interdicted with as little force as possible and that the president would make the decisions on each escalation of force. The guidance from Ford and Scowcroft happened to be fully consistent with the orders the Pentagon had already given the on-scene commander, with one exception. The White House wanted highly discriminate escalating force options for the ship but automatic interdiction of all other Cambodian naval traffic, even though it was not known whether the Cambodian gunboats carried *Mayaguez* crew members. This point was not so subtly underscored when Scowcroft revealed Ford's lack of trust by telling General Wickham the White House would need a copy of the execute orders on interdicting Cambodian boats.

Subsequently, Scowcroft monitored the interactions between US planes and boats as best he could by having his aide, Major McFarlane, monitor Pentagon communications. Scowcroft kept Kissinger and Ford informed on how aggressively the quarantine was being enforced.[44] The White House impression was that the Pentagon was stonewalling when it came to sinking Cambodian gunboats in accordance with Ford's blanket interdiction orders for Cambodian gunboats. Ford said as much during the third NSC meeting. After a discussion on why the boats had not been sunk, Schlesinger, and then Kissinger, argued it would be too problematic to explain attacking a boat after Caucasians were sighted on it. The president then relented but was still upset about what he believed was lack of compliance with his standing orders.

Ford clearly understood the risks he was running and was willing to take responsibility for his decision. When the NSC members discussed how to explain publicly the one boat sunk, Ford embraced his decision: "My answer would be, that we have ordered that no enemy boats should leave the island or go out to it, but that if they did, they would be sunk." And when Kissinger and Schlesinger discussed how and whether this could be kept "low-key," Ford again emphasized his personal decision: "The order was issued that no boats should leave."

The Pentagon at that point complied. Following the third NSC meeting, the Pentagon sent out top secret orders to field commanders with the requirement to "sink all Cambodian small craft in the target areas of Koh Tang, Paulo Wai, Kompong Som, and Ream" without knowing whether they held *Mayaguez* crew members or not. Ford was not mollified, however. He later expressed his anger at the Pentagon in a private conversation with Kissinger and Scowcroft: "I am disturbed at the lack of carrying out orders. I can give all the orders, but if they don't carry them out. . . . I was mad yesterday."[45] He was also quite angry in the fourth NSC meeting after Kissinger asked why boats were not being sunk and why US destroyers were not placed between Tang Island and the mainland for that purpose. From the president's point of view, his directions were clear but not being followed.

Years later Kissinger bluntly characterized the Pentagon's delaying tactics from the White House's point of view. He said that despite presidential orders in the second NSC meeting to quarantine the *Mayaguez*, Schlesinger "balked at military action" and basically stalled:

> Wickham (later army chief of staff), requested instructions as to what to do about that vessel. In light of the President's explicit orders to sink every ship approaching or leaving the island, the query was inexplicable except as a maneuver to avoid being blamed should anything go wrong [i.e., killing crew members]. Scowcroft, meticulous as always, checked with the President, who confirmed his original directive. . . . An hour and a half later, at 9:48 P.M. Washington time, Wickham was back with a new query [when a pilot observed the Caucasians on the bow of the fishing vessel].[46]

Based on all the discussions about carefully modulated force for interdicting the ship, the Pentagon could have argued it was complying with the spirit of presidential direction and logically applying it to all vessels capable of carrying the *Mayaguez* crew. Moreover, in the second NSC meeting Ford had insisted on "the quickest possible communication to me" and, as noted above, summarized his approved actions by saying "we would use the aircraft to stop any boats leaving the island," not to "sink them necessarily" but to take "some preventive action." Ford reinforced this guidance by calling Schlesinger, who reassured Ford the military would use carefully escalated force, beginning with riot control agents. It was further reinforced by Scowcroft's passing the same guidance to Wickham.

For all these reasons, it might seem that the Pentagon's extreme care in vetting the use of force against vessels, including Wickham's request for additional presidential guidance (which Schlesinger approved),[47] was consistent with Ford's guidance on wanting to be kept informed and call the shots. Also, the request for presidential reconsideration could be, and was, justified by noting the new information available: the sighting of possible *Mayaguez* crew members on deck. Finally, presented with the very choices and control the White House demanded, the president ultimately chose not to sink the boat with Caucasians.

However, the Pentagon made no such excuses. Rather than trying to explain away perceived Defense Department recalcitrance, both Schlesinger and Wickham have gone on record confirming it.[48] Wickham acknowledges that he and General Pauly gave the "do not shoot" order "in defiance of the instructions from the NSC." Wickham said it would seem a "serious offense" but that it was "real-time interceding," which he argues "saved the lives of that crew."[49] Schlesinger also acknowledged stonewalling the White House. "I refused to sink the boat," he said, because "to say the least, it seemed to me it would destroy our own purposes to sink a ship which would have killed the Americans we were trying to save."

> **Interviewer:** Did you apprise the White House of this ship with the Caucasians aboard?
>
> **Schlesinger:** Yes, indeed.
>
> **Interviewer:** And it was then that the White House said to sink it?
>
> **Schlesinger:** Yes, the White House said, "We told you to sink all ships, so sink it!" Obviously this would have been self-defeating. So I spent the next three hours [the time needed for the ship to sail to the Cambodian mainland] fending off calls asking why I had yet to sink the ship.
>
> **Interviewer:** What reasons were you giving for not doing it?
>
> **Schlesinger:** I started by saying the ship had Caucasians on it and [I] didn't want to risk killing the crew. I got orders back saying I'd been instructed to sink all traffic and therefore to sink it. I'd say, "Go back and talk to the President about this."
>
> **Interviewer:** This is clearly a critical point, because had you followed the order the entire outcome would have been much different.
>
> **Schlesinger:** It would have been tragic. We would have combined the humiliation of the United States with another example of alleged Defense Department fumbling. It would have been tragic and ludicrous at the same time.

Interviewer: Your strategy was essentially to keep the White House at bay?

Schlesinger: I stalled for three hours.[50]

The three hours Schlesinger referred to ran from approximately 8:15 p.m., when Wickham responded to the order to sink the boat by saying "we may lose the thing here in the next few minutes," until approximately 11:00 p.m. when President Ford, in the midst of the third NSC meeting, gave the orders to use riot control agents on the vessel with the Caucasians but sink all other boats.

Timing

The second key military issue was the timing of the operations. Here the Pentagon was compliant with senior civilian preferences, arguably more so than necessary or advisable. There was much discussion in NSC meetings about the arrival times of US forces, how long they needed to prepare for their missions, and the risks attendant to assaulting the island and retaking the ship, all of which were interrelated. In the first NSC meeting it was agreed little could be done until US forces assembled, but the urgency of the situation was clearly agreed upon and communicated down the chain of command. In the second NSC meeting there was more detailed discussion of timing, mostly with respect to the anticipated arrival of various US force elements. However, participants also noted the tradeoffs between waiting for more force and moving more quickly. For example, with respect to retaking the *Mayaguez*, there was discussion about using Marines and helicopters from Utapao or waiting until the USS *Holt* arrived. Schlesinger said:

> The Navy people are trained in boarding. It might be preferable to wait for the Holt because it will be manned and able to do it. We will then have the dominant force in the area. But, of course, this may give the Cambodians time to change the situation or to try to prepare themselves. Therefore, it may be better to go by first light tomorrow.[51]

After returning to the Pentagon following the second NSC meeting, Schlesinger told Wickham that he considered a twenty-four-hour delay reasonable, and a few hours later, he told Scowcroft the same thing, saying his "inclination is to go first light Thursday" but also noting they "could wait until Friday for the USS *Hancock* to arrive," which would have added its large compliment of Marines and ten helicopters, including four AH-1J Super Cobra attack helicopters.[52]

Rockefeller argued in favor of quick action, saying, "The longer we wait the more time they have to get ready." But he also understood the risks of quick action. In an eerily prescient moment, he worried that in an island assault we "may lose more Marines trying to land [on the island] than the Americans who were on the boat originally." He was not comfortable with the island assault, reminding Ford again toward the end of the meeting that "I think we have some questions about operating on land against the Cambodians." Scowcroft thought the urgent need was to prevent the crew or ship from being taken to the mainland and that once the *Holt* was between the island and mainland the situation would be more stable. The decision makers also discussed using lethal force against the Cambodian boats, acknowledging that doing so might convince the Cambodians to relent but also might precipitate reprisals.

In the third NSC meeting the relative risks of delaying or accelerating military operations were again discussed at length. With the risk of humiliating hostage negotiations negated by the decision to isolate Tang Island by sinking boat traffic, Kissinger emphasized the risks of using insufficient force: "Later you can do more. It might work with the 270 [Marines]. But it is a risk. It should be decisive and it should look powerful." And again, "If anything goes wrong, as often does, I think against 100 [Khmer soldiers] you would lose more Americans because you do not have overwhelming power." "On balance," he said, "I would like to get a more reliable force." When dominant force was available, Kissinger said it would be possible to "seize the island, seize the ship, and hit the mainland." A few moments later General Jones emphatically agreed:

> I would urge against going this daylight. The Marines would just be landing at Utapao. The helicopter pilots would be tired. Nobody would be mated up yet. It would be a difficult operation to be launching at that time, especially since we could not follow up the same day.[53]

With Schlesinger, Kissinger, and Jones all in agreement on the need to delay, Ford backed away from authorizing early operations on the fourteenth.

The debate then revolved around whether to go on the fifteenth or sixteenth. The Pentagon's option paper that Jones had distributed[54] explained why a forty-eight-hour delay was advantageous. The primary risk of military operations on the fifteenth was the "serious disadvantage of slow insertion (270 men per wave at 4+ hour intervals)." Alternatively, a "coordinated assault at first light on May 16 would "carry lower military risks" and "enhance the prospects of quick success and minimize the loss of life." However, the paper noted that the disadvantage of going on the sixteenth was less chance of surprise and more time for the Cambodians to "put forward preconditions for the return of the ship and/or crew."

The discussion of military risk seesawed back and forth over this issue of whether a one- or two-day delay was necessary. Schlesinger thought 270 Marines probably could take Tang but said the Pentagon preferred "to land with 1000." He argued for the two-day delay, saying, "We need the morning of the 16th for a coordinated assault." He considered it a "close call," and acknowledged that delaying gave the Cambodians more time, during which they might "decide to execute our men." Schlesinger also said delaying gave the forces on the island more "time to prepare" and to "scuttle the ship."

Jones then weighed in: "The suggestion is to go with the first light on the 15th," which Kissinger agreed with, remarking "I would go for the island at daybreak of the 15th." Schlesinger objected to this, declaring "the problem with that is that the *Coral Sea* will not be there" and that "if you want an overwhelming force on the island, you should wait until the 16th." That seemed to sway Kissinger, who then said, "The ideal time for what I have in mind is the 16th. That would not just include the island but Kompong Som, the airport and boats." Ford agreed: "If you wait until the 16th, you have maximum capability." But then he mused, "We do not know what will happen in 24 hours. They have options also. We can make a decision tomorrow if we want to. But we should have orders ready to go so that they can move within 24 hours." Kissinger agreed, summing up why he preferred a one- to a two-day delay: "Forty-eight hours are better militarily. But so much can happen, domestically and internationally," the implication being that political or diplomatic developments might complicate or remove the opportunity to use force. With that hanging in the air, Ford stated, "We should be ready to go in 24 hours," but he added, "We may, however, want to wait." Schlesinger then acknowledged that the Department of Defense would "be prepared to go on the morning of the 15th."

A few moments later, Ford discussed military preparations and concluded that "unless there is some unusual development, the actual action will take place 24 hours later." It was not clear whether he meant the twenty-four-hour delay already agreed upon or another day's delay. Schlesinger encouraged him to mean the latter, clarifying, "On the 16th." Kissinger encouraged Ford to make that decision later, but Ford responded, "The preferable time is 24 hours later," seemingly indicating his inclination to wait until the sixteenth. Kissinger demurred, citing not the *Pueblo* crisis but the April 1969 EC-121 crisis when the North Koreans shot down an unarmed American reconnaissance aircraft. He agreed the sixteenth was "when the best forces will be available," but argued "that has to be weighed against other considerations for the extra 24 hours that you lose." He believed long delays while forces were assembled could eventually lead to inaction and acceptance of the new status quo, which happened in the EC-121 crisis.[55]

As the discussion continued Kissinger told the NSC members he thought that "we should do something that will impress the Koreans and the Chinese." Rumsfeld worried about further delay, and Kissinger agreed, saying that "if we are going to do an integrated attack, I think we have to go in 22 hours [i.e., the fifteenth]. We should not wait for a later cycle." But he quickly added, "I cannot judge if there would be a problem in taking the island. We're saying that it will be one annihilating blow. I cannot judge if 270 Marines can do it." Rumsfeld said there would be 500 Marines, and Kissinger showed he understood the limited rotary lift available to transport the Marines, stating "but there will be 270 for four hours." Ford wondered if there were Marines on the *Coral Sea* who could help, and Kissinger noted the *Coral Sea* could support the attack on the island but insisted on the importance of the initial landing:

> **Kissinger:** . . . We have to be sure that the landing has a chance of success.
> **Jones:** The probability that the Americans are gone causes the problem. I think we have a high probability.
> **Kissinger:** Then my instinct is with Rummy [Donald Rumsfeld]. We should go tomorrow night or earlier.
> **Ford:** Everything will be ready. But, if you do it in the next cycle, you have the problem of Thailand.
> **Kissinger:** The ideal time would be Thursday night [i.e., the sixteenth]. But I am worried that in the next 48 hours some diplomatic pressure will occur, or something else. So we have to weigh the optimum military time against the optimum political time. For foreign policy and domestic reasons, tomorrow is better.
> **Ford:** The Thai [*sic*] will be upset.
> **Kissinger:** That is correct, but they will also be reassured.
> **Rumsfeld:** Can we be sure there is anybody on the island? We might just take a walk.
> **Kissinger:** If the Americans are on the mainland, then we have to rethink.[56]

In short, the question of whether to wait another twenty-four hours hung delicately in the balance and easily could have been influenced by advice from General Jones. All the decision makers agreed the military risk would be lower if they waited another twenty-four hours, but they also believed it quite possible they would lose the entire crew, and thus their reason to use force, or that some political or diplomatic development would arise that precluded the use of force. (Less than five hours later the cable from Tehran arrived at the Department of State, which was just the sort of potential diplomatic development Kissinger worried about.) At the beginning of the fourth NSC meeting, William Colby's intelligence update verified at least some of the crew was already on the mainland. As Kissinger had observed in the previous NSC meeting, if it was discovered (from such sources as imagery, signals intelligence, or Cambodian broadcasts) that the entire crew was on the mainland, they would "have to rethink." There would be no point in attacking the island if it was known there were no crew members there. Similarly, there would be no excuse for the mainland airstrikes, which were justified as support for the island assault.[57]

There were numerous opportunities for General Jones to argue the assault on Tang was too risky. He urged a twenty-four-hour delay in the third NSC meeting because he believed going sooner would be too risky, but he otherwise indicated US forces could and would be ready to go on the fifteenth with acceptable risk. Between the third and fourth NSC meetings the need to delay another day was discussed at both the White House and the Pentagon. Rumsfeld weighed in with Ford privately, arguing that "the longer the delay the weaker the United States looks, the greater the danger to the lives of the people, and the greater the likelihood that the critics will get into the act." The Pentagon felt differently. Schlesinger in particular had been outspoken about the advantages of delay in the third NSC meeting, more so than General Jones. There was a reason for this.

Before the fourth NSC meeting, Jones had met with the other Joint Chiefs to review the question again. Presumably they knew that subordinates such as Vice Admiral George P. Steele, the Seventh Fleet commander, were asking for more time.[58] However, the Chiefs decided another delay was not necessary. In an interview not long after the crisis, Jones said the Joint Chiefs were concerned about the need to move before the crew was imprisoned on the mainland. Thus, "on balance the Chiefs decided that the degree of risk in going as planned on the fourteenth [i.e., the fifteenth in Cambodia] was acceptable and that the urgency of the recovery should govern."[59]

This explanation for the Joint Chiefs risk assessment is hard to understand. The decision had been made in the previous NSC meeting to allow the boat with Caucasians to reach the mainland and to sink all other patrol boats. Hence, any further risk of the crew being taken to the mainland was virtually eliminated. The only remaining reasons to accept higher than necessary military risk were the hopes that moving quickly would encourage the Cambodians to capitulate rather than conduct reprisals[60]—a debatable proposition—and Kissinger's expressed fear that delaying another day might result in some kind of diplomatic breakthrough or gambit that would sidetrack military operations. It seems most likely that the Joint Chiefs wanted to accommodate White House preferences. Jones essentially acknowledged this years later in an oral history interview, saying, "There was great pressure to act very quickly and to act before all the forces were in place, to take that risk," which the Chiefs decided to do.[61]

When the president asked for the Pentagon's recommendation in the fourth NSC meeting, Schlesinger deferred to General Jones, and Jones did not ask for twenty-four more hours. Instead he said, "We recommend that we land tonight on the island and on the ship." He told the NSC members the island could be taken with "high assurance of success." He thought, "The 175 Marines can secure themselves, *with gunships and tactical air* [emphasis added]," indicating his understanding that the assault would have close air support. Jones continued: "When the second group arrives, we can cut off the neck of the island and move out." He then showed the NSC members a picture of the island and noted that

> the Marine in charge has reconnoitered it. A close check indicates an open
> area with trails leading into the woods. This is the preferred landing zone.
> Also, they might land on the beach. It is wide enough. It is the only opening on
> the island. Later, we would want to cut the island in two. With somewhat over
> 600 Marines by nightfall, we should have a good feel for what is there. We can
> perhaps withdraw the next day.[62]

Jones concluded his presentation by saying "that is the operation as we recommend it, as a joint recommendation from all the Joint Chiefs."

With Jones's presentation concluded, the NSC discussed timing and synchronization of the island assault with the retaking of the ship. In doing so it became apparent that the schedule was slipping and that attacking at "first light" might be a "moot question." When Ford observed the Marines already appeared to be "40 minutes behind your schedule," Jones did not ask for a delay but replied, "They should still make it." With that reassurance, the orders were given to launch, and the NSC turned its attention to whether B-52 or *Coral Sea* strikes would be authorized.

Thus, after all the discussion, civilian decision makers were left with the impression that taking the island was not a high-risk endeavor. Accordingly, and consistent with their overarching goal, they gave priority to conducting the military operations sooner rather than later, recognizing that unnecessary delay ran the risk of having all military operations suspended by some unexpected development. Having been advised by senior military leadership that the military operations were not high risk, the NSC members discussed how long to hold the island and what to do with prisoners taken, but they did not delve deeper into Kissinger's inquiry as to whether 270 Marines [actually 175, given the rest were sent to take the *Mayaguez*] in the first wave were sufficient.

Punitive Mainland Strikes

Ford, Kissinger, and Scowcroft were correct in thinking the Pentagon was reluctant to implement the blanket order to sink all boats. They also believed the Pentagon was chary of attacking the mainland. Indeed, Ford came to believe Schlesinger was "far less eager to use *Mayaguez* as an example for Asia and the world" than Kissinger or himself. Worse, he thought Schlesinger had "contravened" his authority on mainland airstrikes.[63] In reality, Schlesinger and the Pentagon were less obdurate on the issue of mainland strikes than the president believed.[64] Indeed, in retrospect it is clear Schlesinger worked to ensure the punitive strikes took place even after it was known that the crew had been safely returned and that the Marines needed the *Coral Sea* for recovery operations.

The issue of whether and how to strike the mainland had three major components. The first issue was whether striking the mainland could be justified in terms of the Cambodian provocation. The Pentagon options paper noted that bombing mainland targets might "convince the Cambodian government of our resolve" and "serve as a potent warning" to others. But it also noted the "paucity of useful military targets," the minimum effectiveness of bombing an agrarian society, the possibility the crew would be executed in retaliation, and that the act was of "questionable legality."[65]

The question of international law was discussed in the third NSC meeting, and the group settled on Kissinger's argument that "our aircraft are suppressing hostile action against our operation." The problem was identifying any real Cambodian military threats to US operations. Pentagon leaders did not think there were any on the mainland, but Colby helpfully observed "there are about three T-28's at Kompong Som airfield" that were "a potential threat . . . against our forces." Ford focused on this, asking twice that Colby verify the information and thereafter accepting the argument that mainland strikes could be justified as necessary to protect the Marines.

The next issue was whether to use B-52s or carrier aircraft. This matter emerged in the press as a key difference between Kissinger and Schlesinger during the crisis, which it was. However, neither man was as adamant as sometimes depicted.[66] Kissinger came to see Schlesinger's point that the use of B-52s would exact too heavy a political penalty and made that point privately to Ford. Schlesinger was always against using B-52s, but the Pentagon made them ready to strike in accordance with the president's orders. Also, Schlesinger did acknowledge in an NSC discussion that "B-52s may represent the best image for what Henry [Kissinger] is trying to accomplish." An advantage of the B-52s was that they could launch from Guam without any other country's permission and could reach their targets within six hours. Ford privately told Kissinger before the fourth NSC meeting that he only kept the B-52 issue alive to encourage the Pentagon to deliver the full set of carrier strikes he wanted. If so, he made a convincing show during the fourth NSC meeting, sparking substantial discussion about how the B-52s could damage the port (for example, destroying the breakwater) in ways that carrier aircraft could not.

That left the question of how many carrier airstrikes there would be. Ford specified continuous airstrikes, but because the *Mayaguez*'s crew was returned shortly after US military operations began, only four waves of aircraft launched from the *Coral Sea*. Ford learned that two of the four strikes never hit targets, and he was furious about it. Already suspicious that the Pentagon was reluctant to implement his decisions to use military force, Ford became convinced that Schlesinger had contravened his orders for the first and fourth airstrikes. For decades it looked like Ford was correct, but with all the information currently available, it is evident that poor communication played a much larger role than previously assumed.

Ford, Kissinger, and Scowcroft have all expressed surprise that the first strike was cancelled.[67] They all insist they ordered the strike "put on hold" pending a quick presidential decision about the import of the Cambodian broadcast suggesting the crew would be released. Somehow that order to hold was translated at the Pentagon into an order to cancel all strikes. Ford later claimed that when he spoke to Schlesinger a short while later, the Defense Secretary reported "first strike completed," which Ford took to mean targets had been hit. To make matters worse, the White House came to understand the first wave of aircraft had been assigned a mission of "armed reconnaissance," and according to one source, told not to expend ordnance unless attacked.[68] Ford called the Pentagon mishandling of the first mission "high-level bumbling."[69] Kissinger indicates the White House did not understand what armed reconnaissance meant:

> At our daily morning meeting the next day, Ford was still irate that the first wave had not used its ordnance. He recognized that there could have been some confusion due to the pause ordered to discuss the Khmer Rouge statement; what rankled him was that he had never been told of the "armed reconnaissance"—whatever that meant—and that, in fact, Schlesinger had left him with the opposite impression when he had reported "first strike completed" after the first wave.[70]

The Pentagon assigned the armed reconnaissance mission to suit its preferences for more discriminate and proportional military operations. When Schlesinger and Jones discussed military operations prior to the fourth NSC meeting, Schlesinger emphasized that any mainland attacks were to be "surgical" and avoid hitting the two ships of unknown nationality in Kompong Som harbor. The two men agreed on the initial "armed recce mission" to identify water and shore targets of opportunity more closely related to the military operations for recovering the *Mayaguez* and assaulting Tang Island—such as Cambodian gunboats in Kompong Som harbor that had been sighted—and to reduce chances of collateral damage. This decision was consistent with the Pentagon's draft concept of operations, which envisioned the *Coral Sea* strikes as supporting the operations to recover the ship and crew. *Coral Sea* planes were "to engage Cambodian shipping in designated area," "maintain continuous armed reconnaissance during daylight," and "prepare to strike mainland targets, if directed."[71]

Contrary to what Kissinger claimed in his memoirs, the Pentagon told the White House its intent. In the fourth NSC meeting, General Jones described the *Coral Sea* strikes, saying they would "be used with great precision. We would first send armed reconnaissance and then go for heavy targets like construction, POL [petroleum, oil, and lubricant facilities], the warehouses, etc." No one asked for a definition of "armed reconnaissance," which meant "a mission with the primary purpose of locating and attacking targets of opportunity," but Jones and Holloway later clarified the mission. Jones said the first wave "would go after mobile targets" and Holloway said it "will hit targets connected with the operation" (i.e., naval vessels and aircraft that could theoretically reach US forces).

When Ford said the Pentagon should expect the cyclic *Coral Sea* operations to be continuous and Kissinger added they should be done "ferociously" and "not just hit mobile targets, but others as well," Schlesinger promised, "We will hit whatever targets there are." Buchen jumped in, worrying about the possibility of hitting neutral shipping. Acknowledging this, the president said he wanted to "hit the planes, the boats and the ships *if they are Cambodian* [emphasis added]." Schlesinger promised Ford that "we will make a positive identification that they are Cambodian," and Admiral Holloway quickly added that the first wave of aircraft would report back, implying their eyes-on-target experience would make later waves of aircraft more effective. Ford, Kissinger, and Scowcroft presumably thought this mean more destructive, whereas Schlesinger, Jones, and Holloway no doubt were thinking more discriminate.

When Holloway left the NSC meeting to communicate the president's orders to the Pentagon and on down to forces in the field, he specified that the "first event" was to be "armed reconnaissance with principal targets aircraft and military watercraft and avoidance of merchant ships in Kompong Som until their identity has been clearly established as Cambodian."[72] Holloway also noted the armed reconnaissance was to support the operation to capture the *Mayaguez* and assault Tang Island, which the NSC had agreed would be the justification for the mainland attacks. Thus, those receiving the orders without the benefit of hearing NSC deliberations had the impression the mainland strikes were supporting actions of secondary importance.

When news reached the White House about the Cambodian broadcast, Kissinger decided to put the first strike on hold while he explained the situation to Ford and then Schlesinger.[73] He told Scowcroft to call the Pentagon to have the first wave "proceed on course *but drop no ordnance* until the President had made his decision [emphasis added]." Scowcroft is similarly explicit about the message he gave the Pentagon at 8:30 p.m.: "I called the Pentagon and said *don't call them off, but don't release them yet* [emphasis added]." Wickham's notes on the call from Scowcroft simply read: "*Coral Sea* not to release any ordnance on mainland. HAK [Kissinger] in w/Pres at this time. Will call back in 2 minutes."[74]

Minutes earlier, however, using the White House direct channel to the NMCC, another member of Kissinger's staff, William Stearman, also intervened for the same purpose. At about 8:25 p.m., Air Force Brigadier General Charles E. Word, the deputy director of operations at the command center, was providing an update to White House Situation Room personnel[75] when Stearman interrupted to ask about the first wave's time-on-target. Word said the planes would reach their target area at 8:45. Stearman then told Word: "Do not execute the Navy TACAIR [tactical air operations] against Kompong Som," adding "this is from the President." Word immediately picked up his red phone and broke into a conversation going on between the national command center's conference room and Admiral Gayler's Pacific Command headquarters. Identifying himself, Word said he had "just got a call from White House SITROOM [situation room] to hit area but do not release ordnance on harbor. In other words, Navy TACAIR is not to release any ordnance, period!" In the rush to stop the bombs the message that went to General Burns's headquarters (code-named Blue Chip) and the Airborne Command Post (code-named Cricket) emphasized that *Coral Sea* aircraft were not to release any ordnance. With multiple communications from the White House, Kissinger's intent that the strike be put on hold pending a presidential decision was lost. Stearman's message, delivered directly to the military command center, confused the more specific guidance Scowcroft gave Wickham.[76] In this instance, the White House insistence on direct access to the NMCC backfired and undermined its control of operations.

Pacific Command followed up a few minutes later, requesting clarification about the White House instructions. Since General Word had emphasized not hitting the "harbor," Gayler wondered if other mainland targets could and should be hit. Word checked and confirmed that the prohibition on dropping ordnance "extended to all mainland targets as well as targets in the immediate vicinity." However, the island landing and boarding of the ship could continue. Gayler also asked the command center if they had seen the report of the Cambodian broadcast. At 8:44, Word said he had further orders. General George Brown, the chairman of the JCS who did not attend NSC meetings but who was monitoring the military operations in the Pentagon's command center, said he had

> just talked to the White House and that he was "going to stop all launches off the Coral Sea." Admiral Holloway, from the Conference Room, rogered and said, "understand, cease cyclic strike operations form the Coral Sea immediately." This order, which was heard on the red phone teleconference circuit, was confirmed by PACOM [Pacific Command], Blue Chip and PACFLT [US Pacific Fleet]. Authority to use Coral Sea assets for support of the island operations was reconfirmed by Admiral Holloway at [8:46 p.m.] to Admiral Gayler.[77]

It is not clear who Brown spoke to at the White House, but he believed he had approval to stop the mainland strikes and concentrate on supporting the Marines who were under duress. For Brown, who did not sit in on the NSC meetings, it must have seemed logical and consistent with presidential guidance to turn the strikes off and use the *Coral Sea* to support the Marines with close air support and as a recovery platform. After all, the official line captured in military orders relayed by Holloway was that the mainland strikes were, in fact, for the purpose of supporting the Marine assault.

Meanwhile, at the White House, Kissinger discussed the issue with Ford from 8:29 until 8:37. According to Kissinger, Ford was against calling off the strikes until the fate of the crew was known. In his memoirs, Ford confirms he wanted "to hold up the first strike until we had a better idea of what was happening."[78] With the dinner for the Dutch prime minister just getting started in the State Dining Room, Major McFarlane was asked to pass Ford's decision to General Wickham at the Pentagon, which he did at 8:47. McFarlane told General Word to turn the first strike back on, adding the requirement for a bomb damage assessment prior to additional strikes (thus demonstrating the White House assumption that the first wave would hit something, but also delaying the next strike). General Word passed these instructions along one minute later, at 8:48, causing Admirals Gayler and Holloway to "compare notes over the teleconference as to their mutual understanding of the series of instruction from the White House." While Gayler and Holloway conversed, the *Coral Sea* aircraft were checking in with the Airborne Command Post for their final instructions.

Schlesinger had no role in canceling the first strike because he was en route to the White House and, as it turned out, in favor of continuing the strikes. As he later said:

> When I arrived at the White House, there was a call waiting for me from the Pentagon informing me with some chagrin that the first airstrike had been called off by the White House. I immediately sought out Henry [Kissinger], and he handed me something from the FBIS [an information arm of the CIA], saying that Radio Phnom Penh had announced that [the Cambodian government was] ready to negotiate. I said this was a stall, and we could not give up the airstrikes. After a brief-but-intense discussion, he agreed we should restore the airstrikes. We both then went to the President and said this. The second airstrike went off as had been planned.[79]

With Schlesinger and Kissinger in agreement, Ford did not hesitate. He said, "Tell them to go ahead, right now." Scowcroft, finally having his answer (not two, but twenty-two minutes later) passed the order to the Pentagon to resume strikes. In the process of confirming all strikes were back on, Scowcroft corrected McFarlane's earlier orders and specified there would be "no pausing" for bomb damage assessments.

General Word in turn notified Gayler at 8:52 that "General Scowcroft directed operations proceed with all *Coral Sea* assets as planned." Gayler verbally passed these orders to General Burns at 8:58 and "all stations rogered." At that moment "the aircraft from the *Coral Sea were on station offshore of the target area under the control of the Airborne Command Post* [emphasis added]."[80] When Gayler gave his verbal order to Burns at 8:58 to proceed with the strikes, he reminded Burns that the aircraft still needed to identify the ships as Cambodian before hitting them. Repeating Brown's earlier caveat, he also added that Burns had the authority to use the aircraft to support the Marines if he thought it necessary. Once again, a senior military officer not present in the NSC meetings assumed the mainland strikes were envisioned as support for the Marines and that they could therefore be turned off if doing so benefited the Marines. Burns responded that the armed reconnaissance mission might not produce much bomb damage, which proved correct. The aircraft jettisoned their bombs and returned to the *Coral Sea*. Jones later explained to the NSC that they did so because the pilots "found the shipping of other countries and did not want to take the risk."

Thus, within a twenty-minute period of confusion stimulated by the Cambodian broadcast and multiple White House sources providing guidance, Stearman's intervention turned the "hold" order for the first wave into a cancellation, and Brown's guidance cancelled all the *Coral Sea* strikes one minute before the first wave was due over its target area. However, contrary to some accounts of the crisis,[81] the assorted and confusing interventions were sorted out in time to allow the first wave to complete its mission. It also is noteworthy that Schlesinger actually recommended the strikes continue despite the broadcast, that he was at the White House for the formal state dinner when the issue was being managed, and that the White House was issuing orders directly to the NMCC. All these points would later be forgotten or ignored as Ford and Kissinger came to believe Schlesinger was personally responsible for the failure of the first wave to hit targets.

After Schlesinger left the White House dinner for the Dutch prime minister, he returned to the Pentagon and was updated on developments. Admiral Gayler was pre-occupied with assisting the Marines, who were under heavy pressure. Between 10 and 11:30 p.m., Gayler was working on getting Marines who had seized the *Mayaguez* trans-ferred to Tang Island to assist their beleaguered colleagues, obtaining fire support from the *Wilson* for the Marines, investigating whether *Coral Sea* antisubmarine helicopters could ferry Marines to Tang, and getting *Coral Sea* air support for the Marines. Shortly after 11:00, news of the crew's recovery was received. This development led to two quick conversations between Ford and Schlesinger: one at 11:15 and the other at 11:45 p.m. In the first call Schlesinger updated Ford on the airstrikes according to Wickham's notes:

> **Schlesinger:** 1st wave Coral Sea Recce armed. 2nd wave on way.
>
> **Ford:** Second wave if on way, let them go ahead.
>
> **Schlesinger:** We should keep it up until [we] get the Marines out.
>
> **Ford:** Keep it up.[82]

Wickham's notes indicate Schlesinger was forthright about the first wave being armed reconnaissance, but he did not go out of his way to say no targets had been hit. What Ford remembered from this conversation was Schlesinger reporting "first strike com-pleted."[83] What Schlesinger took away from the conversation was that the mainland strikes should continue, a position he also apparently favored at that point. When Gayler called just before 11:30 to ask whether the third wave should strike in light of the crew's promise that airstrikes would cease, Schlesinger and Brown discussed it. Despite the return of the crew, Schlesinger complied with Ford's expectations and ordered the third wave to proceed.

At 11:45 Ford checked in with Schlesinger again to confirm the entire crew was safe before he made his nationally televised address on the *Mayaguez* recovery operations. This was the call where other White House participants recall Kissinger encouraging Ford to "look ferocious" and keep bombing the mainland. Schlesinger reassured Ford that the entire crew was safe and passed along Gayler's information that the *Maya-guez* captain, on his own initiative, bargained with the Cambodians, saying he would arrange an end to the bombing. The president repeated what Schlesinger had just said, presumably for the benefit of the others in the Oval Office. Schlesinger then told Ford the Pentagon was continuing with the third wave of *Coral Sea* aircraft (they actually hit their targets at 11:50 while this conversation took place). According to Wickham's notes, Ford responded by asking about the Marines:

> **Ford:** What's status of Marines?
>
> **Schlesinger:** Heavily engaged on island. We can divert Coral Sea attack to help out.
>
> **Ford:** 3rd wave diverted?
>
> **Schlesinger:** We are prepared to do this.
>
> **Ford:** Think this is right decision. HAK [Kissinger]?
>
> **Schlesinger:** 4th wave would go to the island.
>
> **Kissinger:** I would keep some attack on the mainland until we get Marines disengaged on island.
>
> **Ford:** Moderated—some. We divert rest to help Marines on island. We ought to have perception of continuing pressure.[84]

Wickham's notes record a confused conversation with the status of the third and fourth waves of aircraft in play. Schlesinger suggested giving priority to supporting the Marines, and Kissinger asked for continuing attacks on the mainland. Ford appeared to rule in favor of both positions, acting upon Kissinger's advice by indicating some aircraft should hit mainland targets while approving Schlesinger's suggestion by noting others could help the Marines on Tang.[85] In any case, White House interest in continuing pressure on the mainland was evident, despite Schlesinger communicating the value in diverting the fourth wave to help the Marines on Tang Island. After speaking with the president at 11:45, and then with two members of Congress[86] around midnight, Schlesinger went to the Pentagon's NMCC to better monitor ongoing military operations. In the center's conference room, he and General Brown received a phone update from Admiral Gayler.

After hearing Gayler's update, Brown recommended that all further efforts be devoted to extracting the Marines without further casualties. Schlesinger agreed. That order went out at 12:12. At 12:19 Scowcroft called Schlesinger and read him the statement that the president was about to deliver to the nation. Apparently during this conversation Scowcroft agreed there was no reason for the Marines to persist in taking the island. Brown related this point to the admiral but also mentioned that "there is some interest in continuing the pressure of the mainland." Brown asked Gayler for his views on additional mainland targets. Gayler's quick reaction was that there were "probably naval and air force targets in Cambodia as a whole," but Brown specified the target area of interest was Kompong Som, not all of Cambodia. Gayler thought "some shipping might be scarfed up." Brown's reaction was that going after shipping was "probably not too useful and entails some risk to third country vessels," which Navy aircraft reported seeing. Gayler, however, was told to "look at it and let us know what you think."

While Gayler did so, Brown and Schlesinger discussed the fourth strike. Schlesinger then decided to execute Ford's order, telling Brown that "we should mount a fourth wave against targets on the Cambodian mainland." This decision elicited pushback from Brown, Holloway, and Gayler, all of whom strongly weighed in against the fourth wave of airstrikes. They offered multiple reasons, the most important of which was the need to support the Marines:

> General Brown stated that the strikes had been turned off and recommended that we should not turn them on again. The major point, however, made by General Brown was that we had gained our objectives with the recovery of the ship and the crew and therefore there was no need for further strikes. Second, there were no appropriate targets worthy of strike in the Kompong Som area; and third, that the sorties from the Coral Sea were needed to help the Marines on Koah [Koh] Tang Island, who were not having an easy time. General Brown's final point was that it was necessary to stop cyclic operations off the Coral Sea so she could position herself to serve as a close-in helicopter platform during the extraction of the Marines from Koah Tang Island. As long as the cyclic TACAIR operations were going on, the ship had to continually turn into the southwest wind when she launched and recovered her fighters, thus taking her away from the Island to the north.

> Admiral Holloway was quick to join the conversation and agreed with General Brown, pointing out that we had what we wanted, that the operation had been "clean"—we had no aircraft shot down; we had no POWs [prisoners of war]; there was no need to mount an SAR [search and rescue] effort for a shoot down; and there were no appropriate targets worthy of strike. General Brown asked Admiral Gayler what his views and recommendations were on the feasibility of sending in another wave. Admiral Gayler wholeheartedly concurred with the above positions of General Brown and Admiral Holloway for the same reason. Admiral Holloway called Admiral Weisner [commander of US Pacific Fleet] and got the same response.[87]

Schlesinger listened while Brown queried the admirals on the subject of a fourth strike. It was apparent that all his military subordinates believed the fourth wave should not be sent in. Given that resistance, the fact that the Marines were hard pressed on Tang Island, and the lack of useful targets on the mainland, Schlesinger accepted Chairman Brown's recommendation and redirected the fourth wave from the mainland to assist the Marines on Tang. The decision would cost him his job, but it also hastened the recovery of wounded Marines and facilitated the hazardous nighttime Marine evacuation from Tang Island, which was accomplished with minimal further casualties. The *Coral Sea* aircraft could not conduct close air support because their planes could not communicate with the Marines, but positioning the *Coral Sea* closer to Tang Island did prove critically important for rescuing damaged helicopters and wounded Marines.[88]

At 12:35 a.m. on May 15, Schlesinger called Ford, who had finished his televised address to the nation and was preparing to retire for the night. Wickham's notes indicate Schlesinger told Ford the B-52s were being stood down and that the *Coral Sea* aircraft were being used against Tang and "not the mainland." There is no indication that he mentioned the fourth wave per se. Ford agreed that the main thing at that point was the safety of the Marines and that there was no reason to take the island, so they should disengage. Ford concluded the call by congratulating Schlesinger and the Defense Department for "a damn fine job." Although Ford agreed that assisting the Marines was the priority, it does not appear that Schlesinger explained this meant a cancellation of the fourth airstrike. Orders then went out to stand down the B-52s, use *Coral Sea* aircraft to support the Marines, and devote the total effort to extracting the Marines without further casualties. The message to Gayler at 12:49 was specific about no further consideration being given to additional strikes on the mainland.

In sum, the Pentagon configured the first strike on the mainland consistent with Schlesinger's preferences for a discriminate and proportional military response. The confusion surrounding the Cambodian broadcast was sorted out in time for the planes to attack, but given their assigned mission and rules of engagement, the first wave was not likely to hit targets. Once the crew was released, Schlesinger was fine with punitive strikes, recommending to Ford the continuation of the second strike as long as the Marines were engaged. When Schlesinger understood the pressure the Marines were under, he noted the third wave could be diverted to assist the Marines, and if not the third wave, then the fourth. Kissinger's advice won out, and Schlesinger dutifully ordered the third strike and then also the fourth strike before cancelling the latter in the face of united opposition from his military commanders, who strongly felt that it made no sense and that it was far more important to support the Marines.[89]

Thus, the primary difference between the White House and the Pentagon over mainland strikes was the scale and timing of the attacks, not the targets. Kissinger wanted asymmetric punitive strikes that made it clear Cambodia had paid a large penalty for seizing the ship, and he wanted them as early and for as long as possible. The Pentagon did not want so much force used that the strikes elicited political outrage, which would undermine the credibility of the US reputation for punishing provocations. In addition, Schlesinger wanted to delay punitive strikes until after the crew was released. Kissinger came to agree that B-52s would be too much if the carrier planes were available, but he still wanted as much force used as possible. The Pentagon never thought there were many good targets for that purpose, and Schlesinger preferred attacking the Cambodian navy rather than infrastructure on the mainland, but he was ready to oblige until it became clear the Marines were in trouble, at which point he gave priority to supporting the Marines.

However, the Pentagon was not as duplicitous about all this as the White House came to believe. Poor communications—some inadvertent and others less so—exacerbated White House perceptions of Pentagon noncompliance. Schlesinger, Jones, and Holloway technically reported the armed reconnaissance mission to the NSC and to Ford. Nevertheless, a suspicious White House, already upset over lack of Pentagon compliance, had the impression that all four strikes would and had hit targets. The multiple and direct lines of communication from the White House Situation Room to the NMCC contributed to the confusion surrounding the first strike and its cancellation, but the first wave was designed to avoid collateral damage and improve accuracy for subsequent strikes rather than destroy useful targets, which the Pentagon thought were in short supply. Ford's apparent willingness to listen to Schlesinger on the diversion of the third and fourth waves to assist the Marines was overtaken by interventions from Kissinger who advised in favor of the strikes. Perhaps Ford's own somewhat ambiguous instructions about helping the Marine extraction inclined Schlesinger to believe his decision to cancel the fourth strike would be understood by Ford when all was said and done.[90] If so, he was wrong. Unbeknownst to Schlesinger, the president's confidence in him was at low ebb.

Adjustments to the Description of Crisis Behaviors

There was a great deal of information about decision making in the *Mayaguez* crisis soon after the event. Pleased with the outcome, Ford immediately granted in-depth interviews to two journalists and made his president's daily schedule available to them.[91] Because Ford was displeased with the performance of the intelligence community and the Pentagon, he ordered an immediate search for all verbal and written military communications and intelligence activities during the crisis. Individual members of the NSC leaked accounts of the council's decision making, some flattering and some not. Congress, displeased with the way the crisis was managed, held hearings and launched an investigation that uncovered a great deal of primary information, including a detailed chronology of incoming information and resultant decisions. Also, a few years after the crisis an NSC staff member with insider knowledge coauthored a book providing additional details on the crisis decision making. Shortly thereafter memoirs from the administration appeared providing more insider insights, including Ford's 1979 memoirs that made it clear he believed the Pentagon had been insubordinate[92] in executing his orders about airstrikes. Since then, numerous memoirs, interviews, and declassified documents have trickled out, enabling an even sharper depiction of crisis decision making—the milestone event being the declassification of the NSC minutes in 1996.[93]

It is worthwhile summarizing the most important enhancements to the detailed description of crisis behaviors enabled by new sources and scholarship over the past several decades. Doing so sets the stage for evaluating their impact on explanations of crisis behavior. The most important insight from the new sources, and particularly the NSC meeting minutes, is that US leaders attached even greater importance to a demonstrative use of force than previously believed. Two revelations make this particularly apparent: their decision to sink boats that might have been carrying crew members,[94] and their decision not to delay military operations another day for fear of losing the opportunity to use force.

This desire for a demonstrative use of force and the willingness to risk the lives of the crew have long been noted, but the more recent declassified materials demonstrate just how explicit the decision making was on these points. Another substantial revelation, based on interviews and then circumstantially corroborated by NSC minutes, is that the White House was convinced that Schlesinger and the Pentagon were ignoring the presidential order to sink any boats coming and going from Tang Island, something Schlesinger later admitted was the case.[95]

This research also makes the following new contributions to a better description of the crisis:

- Schlesinger's support for punitive measures and his preference for their sequencing so as to minimize the possibility of retribution from the Cambodians.

- The extent to which Kissinger used his control of diplomatic communications to prevent interference with the military operations, including more evidence that he withheld the news of the Tehran cable from the NSC.[96]

- The actual manner in which the Pentagon stonewalled the White House for three hours, beginning with Schlesinger's restrictive rules of engagement, Wickham and Pauly's decision not to sink the boats, and Schlesinger's ex post facto support for their decision and for slow rolling the White House with requests for additional presidential guidance.

- The way in which the debate about delaying military operations was detailed, sustained, and provided ample opportunity for senior military leaders to request another twenty-four hours before launching the assault on Tang Island. Schlesinger later said he was inclined to keep pressure on the Cambodians, but it also appears that he and Jones acquiesced to accommodate White House preferences and because the rest of the Joint Chiefs were in favor of quick action.

- The Pentagon being less obstructionist and duplicitous about the airstrikes than the White House supposed, and White House behaviors, including the insistence on direct access to the NMCC, actually contributing to the misunderstandings about the airstrikes.

- The significance of the NSC risk assessment on assaulting Tang Island being based on a smaller estimate of Cambodian strength issued by the Pacific Command rather than the higher estimate from DIA.[97]

Other minor descriptive details offered here also help illuminate crisis behaviors. Perhaps the most noteworthy are the Joint Chiefs' hard-to-explain conclusion that the assault on Tang had a high assurance of success and the way Kissinger managed to isolate and deepen Ford's suspicions about Schlesinger, both of which are discussed in the next chapter.

CHAPTER 6

Explaining Decisions, Behaviors, and Outcomes

G iven the safe recovery of the ship and crew and the fact that casualty figures were unknown for days, the military operations were initially considered a great success. It did not take long for concerns to arise, however. The full extent of the casualties suffered, the bombing of the Cambodian mainland an hour after the return of the crew, and the invasion of an island to rescue people who were not there raised numerous questions about the way the crisis had been managed. Among the most pressing issues raised by reporters and members of Congress was why US forces sank gunboats leaving Tang Island. If the gunboats were carrying the crew to the mainland, sinking them would harm the people the United States was trying to rescue. If they were not carrying *Mayaguez* crew members, their exodus from the island only weakened the defensive forces there.

Once it became clear that Tang Island had been much more heavily defended than the Marines were led to believe, critics also expressed concerns about the planning and execution of the military operations. It became clear that the assault on Tang narrowly avoided a complete fiasco. As one general noted, "We were lucky all of the Marines did not get killed." The pilot of Jolly-11 agreed: "We were very lucky or someone was watching out for us, because the casualties we suffered don't reflect the level of opposition we encountered."[1] Twelve of the fifteen men killed in action[2] died in one downed helicopter, and worse could easily have happened to any of the helicopters, almost all of which were knocked out of action by enemy fire. The Marines also suffered around fifty wounded in ground fighting, a surprisingly low figure considering they were outnumbered by better armed and entrenched Cambodian forces familiar with the terrain.

The risks run by US forces were not only consequential for the lives of the crew and the forces themselves; they also carried major strategic implications. As John Guilmartin has argued, if the Marines had been defeated, it would have "entailed immense damage to American credibility and prestige," with "the only real historical precedent being the 1961 Bay of Pigs debacle," where "the units overrun were not American and the men captured were not members of the United States military."[3] Thus, above and beyond the lives lost during the military operations, it is worth pondering why the United States came so close to suffering a major debacle and how it avoided that fate.

Operational and Tactical Issues

It is widely agreed that only the skill and valor displayed by US forces prevented much higher casualties and a complete disaster. Many servicemen took extraordinary risks to execute the mission and, particularly, to save the wounded or otherwise evacuate the Marines and downed airmen. The bold tactics of the Marines to join their groups divided on the western side of the island also helped salvage the situation. As Guilmartin notes, many small decisions made by the forces before and during the event had a critical impact on outcomes:

> The decision by the Aerospace Rescue and Recovery Service to install explosion-retardant foam in the 450-gallon auxiliary tanks of HH-53s probably saved the United States a humiliating defeat. The marines' insistence on going into what was advertised as a walkover fully armed and ready for battle probably had the same effect. The PACAF [Pacific Air Forces] decision not to install explosion-retardant foam in the 650-gallon auxiliary tanks of CH-53s in the interests of cost containment very nearly reversed the outcome.[4]

It is also worth noting that there were no US casualties as a result of inaccurate supporting fire, which is rather amazing considering the poor communications, proximity of US and Cambodian forces, and amount of ordnance expended. The creative measures employed by the Marines and airmen on Tang, the OV-10 forward air control aircraft and their pilots, and the AC-130s are largely responsible for that.

Why US forces came so close to defeat is also widely agreed upon. One critical concern raised by critics in this regard is why a numerically inferior assault force assaulted Tang Island when Marine Corps doctrine calls for a 3-to-1 numerical superiority during this type of operation. For many years the most common answer to this question was the failure to disseminate the best intelligence to the local Marine commanders. They ostensibly operated on the basis of intelligence estimates of approximately twenty Cambodian defenders on Tang. What made this seem particularly odd in retrospect was that Deputy Secretary of Defense Morton I. Abramowitz testified to Congress on the day of the assault that at least one hundred Khmer Communist troops were on the island. The failure to share the best available intelligence with the Marines was perhaps the most egregious military error made, but there were others.

Over the years, trenchant analysis by Guilmartin and others has raised a number of other salient questions about the planning and execution of military operations during the crisis:

- Why were the Marines denied permission to use the 1st Battalion, 9th Marines, which was fully trained and on alert?[5]

- Why were Navy SEALs or Marine Force Reconnaissance units not used to reconnoiter enemy positions on the island prior to assault?[6]

- Why did "no one in the operational chain of command above . . . a captain and a gunnery sergeant [do] a worst-case tactical assessment" of enemy capabilities?[7]

- Why were available reconnaissance aircraft not used to reconnoiter Tang Island defenses?[8]

- Why were the Cambodian antiaircraft gun emplacements identified prior to the Marine landing not neutralized?[9]

- Why was the assault planned for sunrise as opposed to just prior to first light, which ensured the helicopters would be easily visible to the defenders?[10]

- Why was an AC-130 gunship not on station when the Marines began their assault?[11]

- Why were Marine requests for the slow-flying OV-10 forward air control aircraft ignored until late in the afternoon, many hours after operations commenced?[12]

- Why was there "no workable plan to coordinate air and naval gunfire support with the assault?"[13]

- Why was there a gap in AC-130 coverage of the assault force from late morning until late afternoon, when up to that point these aircraft had provided the only effective close air support?[14]

Most but not all of these issues have been resolved by careful scholarship. In general, the answers fall into three categories: command failure, insufficient jointness (defined as lack of familiarity with, or a disinclination to collaborate with, other service elements), and insufficient interoperability (e.g., inability to communicate between ground and air forces). These problems were exacerbated by the rushed operations and ad hoc, geographically dispersed command and control arrangements.[15] Depending on the commentator, these factors are sometimes understood as extenuating circumstances. More often, the charge of micromanagement is levied against senior leaders to explain the planning and execution errors.

As we shall see, the evidence for the micromanagement charge is mixed. However, the persistent concern expressed about micromanagement raises profound issues about the requirements for the "mission command" concept codified in joint doctrine. The micromanagement charge against senior leaders in the *Mayaguez* crisis also has contributed to the fraying of civil-military relations. Most of the commentators who attribute micromanagement to senior uniformed leaders are civilians, and most of those attributing it to civilian leaders are military or former military officers. This trend erodes the trust necessary for civil-military teams of leaders to manage national security challenges well.

A more important issue than the extent to which senior leaders micromanaged military operations is the question of what they were trying to achieve and why. US leaders' risk calculations were critically affected by what they thought was at stake during the crisis, and their inclination to use force sooner rather than later must be evaluated in light of those concerns. Put differently, if we are confused about why leaders made the decisions they did—and many commentators are—it will not be possible to evaluate those decisions well. Thus, a compelling explanation for the US response to the seizure of the *Mayaguez* is a prerequisite for evaluating the senior leader decision making, and for drawing lessons from the experience about such higher order issues as mission command and civil-military relations.

Popular Competing Explanations

From the beginning, several alternative hypotheses for US behavior have been offered and embraced to varying degrees by commentators and analysts over the years.[16] The diverse explanations are not necessary, however. One explanatory variable accounts for all US behavior with great consistency: US leaders' determination to reinforce deteriorating American credibility and, in particular, to signal North Korea that they would defend South Korea despite developments in Indochina. The vast amount of new sources in the form of declassified documents and memoirs, carefully analyzed, makes this singular explanation more evident, not less.

Knowing senior leaders' overriding priority and how they managed the execution of diplomatic and military efforts to secure their objectives makes it possible to quickly assess the validity of alternative hypotheses for US behavior. Four popular explanations for US behavior circulated immediately following the crisis. *Newsweek, Time, US News and World Report*, and other news media depicted the US military response to the seizure of the *Mayaguez* as a rescue, an effort by Ford to shore up his sagging domestic political fortunes, a knee-jerk emotional reaction to the humiliation of losing Indochina, and a punitive use of force to chasten the North Koreans and other countries who suspected they could take advantage of a United States in strategic retreat.

Newsweek's reporting is illustrative of the multiple explanations long considered relevant for understanding why the United States reacted to the seizure of the *Mayaguez* with force. The magazine's cover carried the headline "The Rescue," reflecting official US explanations for the quick military action. *Newsweek* also suggested Ford was motivated by domestic political concerns, citing a Republican congressman's tagline for the affair—"Marines Rescue Ship, Crew and Ford"—to suggest Ford used force to resurrect his failing presidency, crippled by the fall of Vietnam and the unpopular decision to pardon President Nixon. The magazine also called US military operations a "two-day punitive expedition" and said Ford was "putting adversaries . . . on notice that the United States is not after all a paper tiger."[17] Finally, it suggested the US response was an emotional reaction to the humiliation of losing Vietnam, something to compensate for the "image of America's despairing retreat from Indochina." It quoted politicians expressing ardent satisfaction, such as Vice President Rockefeller, who "exulted," "I'm very proud to be an American today." It said Ford's supporters "celebrated the recovery of the *Mayaguez* as though it were the battle of Thermopylae." It ran a cartoon depicting Uncle Sam calmly evaluating responses to the seizure of the *Mayaguez* before succumbing to a first-class hissy-fit and lashing out militarily.[18]

All these competing explanations appeared plausible and were embraced to varying degrees by commentators and analysts.[19] Now, however, it is more evident than ever that the perceived need for a demonstrative and punitive use of force was the central motivation of US decision makers. The new sources and materials documenting the decision making during the crisis and the analysis of key decisions reinforce this core explanation for US behavior. The inadequacy of the most popular alternative explanations can be demonstrated with a quick review of their merits.

A Rescue

There is no doubt decision makers hoped the crew would be released unharmed, but they did not have the means to rescue the crew and could not even ascertain their whereabouts with certainty. Moreover, they had higher priorities, which became clear to close observers of their behavior.[20] The lack of military justification for mainland bombing, the willingness to run risks to the crew and to the Marines, and the admissions of key decision makers about their motives have long made a compelling case that the primary goal of decision makers was a punitive use of force that would reinforce US credibility, deter a belligerent North Korea, and perhaps encourage the Cambodians to release the crew.

New evidence reinforces this conclusion. During the first NSC meeting, when deci-sion makers thought the crew was already on the mainland, the only options discussed were punitive measures. When decision makers learned the crew could be isolated from the mainland, they embraced a quarantine even at the significant risk of killing the crew and carried on with the plan for punitive strikes. It was hoped the Cambodians would release the crew, but the manifest willingness to sink boats possibly carrying the crew makes it perfectly clear decision makers had higher priorities than the lives of the crew.

Domestic Politics

Those who believe "Ford used the crisis for political advantage"[21] make the mistake of reasoning from effect to intent. There is no doubt that the initial public response to the use of force was highly favorable. A day after the crisis the White House had received 3,254 telephone calls, 3,062 of which were in favor of the president's actions, and 5,404 telegrams, 5,068 of which also favored the president.[22] However, those effects were short lived and, most important, were not likely and could not have been anticipated.

At the time the nation was torn and deeply ambivalent about the use of force in Vietnam. Respect for the presidency was at an all-time low. Public, news media, and con-gressional reactions during and after the crisis indicate "another example of ineptitude and failure was not likely to elicit much sympathy" and that the "only hope for public plaudits required the successful rescue of the ship and crew, the president's publicly stated objective."[23] This is not to say the White House ignored political reactions and consequences. Ford and his advisors considered and monitored congressional reactions throughout the crisis.[24] They discussed how to portray their decisions to Congress and the public, especially but not only with respect to the use of B-52s. They did observe that there were signs of support for a firm response.[25] There were, for example, some colorful remarks from congressmen and senators favoring the use of force, which are often cited as evidence of the country's mood or to imply the president knew or could have expected the use of force to be popular. For example, when initially contacted by the White House, Senator James O. Eastland (D-MS) said, "Blow the Hell out of them," and Congressman Tip O'Neil responded, "Those bastards, we can't let them get away with this. They'll harass us forever."[26]

However, other members of Congress were mildly supportive or noncommittal, just thanking the White House callers for the information. Still others objected to the use of force as a matter of principle. The White House knew from questions posed by reporters, interest groups,[27] and members of Congress that many preferred a diplomatic solution and would question Ford's decisions if any harm came to the crew. They had a foretaste of the likely reaction from the heavily Democratic Congress (which held fourteen- and fifty-seat majorities in the Senate and House, respectively) when Ford and his advisors met with "the most important" members of Congress during the crisis.[28] The elected representatives applauded Ford when he entered the Cabinet Room but immediately offered up tough questions, taking their oversight role and the War Powers consultation provisions seriously. They asked whether there were Americans "on the boats that will be destroyed"; "why are we going into the mainland of Asia again [with ground forces]"; "can't we wait"; why "are we just going into Koh Tang shooting"; and "did we give Cambodia a deadline"? Democratic leader Michael J. Mansfield (D-MT) said, "I want to express my deep concern, apprehension and uneasiness at this near-invasion of the Indochina mainland."[29] Similarly, in congressional hearings held on May 14, congressmen asked administration officials to explain how sinking Cambodian boats that might hold crew members was consistent with rescuing the crew.[30] Congressional concerns were so manifest at the time that Kissinger told Ford he thought Schlesinger had changed Ford's orders on bombing the mainland to assuage congressional ire.[31]

Even after the fortunate release of the crew and the *New York Times* ruling that Ford had pulled off a "domestic and foreign triumph," many pundits and members of Congress were critical and wanted an investigation of the president. Gaylord A. Nelson (D-WI) said he did not question the popularity of Ford's decision but nevertheless thought it was wrong, noting that "these incidents are matters for negotiation, not force." Senator George S. McGovern (D-SD) said, "I continue to be alarmed and puzzled as to why military action of this kind was taken before an opportunity was given to the diplomatic process." Congresswoman Elizabeth Holtzman (D-NY) went further, saying the president's resort to force "appears to have been illegal and unconstitutional" and an "overreaction."[32] As Ford noted in his memoirs,

> Predictably, liberals in both the press and Congress were harshly critical of my decisions. In a column entitled "Barbarous Piracy," Anthony Lewis of the *New York Times* intoned: "Once again an American government shows that the only way it knows how to deal with frustration is by force. And the world is presumably meant to be impressed." In Congress, Senator Mansfield and Representative Holtzman assailed me for my alleged failure to observe the War Powers Act. . . . Missouri Senator Thomas [F.] Eagleton went several steps further. He introduced three separate amendments to the War Powers Act designed to plug its "loopholes" and prevent me—or any President who followed me—from taking the steps I had taken to save American lives. Then he asked the General Accounting Office, the auditing arm of Congress, to deter-

mine whether I had ordered the bombing of Cambodia "for punitive rather than defensive purposes." Such reactions, I thought, were hopelessly naive.[33]

It was not just partisan politics that induced Eagleton and others in Congress to launch the investigation into Ford's management of the incident. The nation was deeply divided over the lessons of Vietnam. As Ford suggests, those who had concluded the use of American military power in Vietnam was misguided, if not actually counterproductive, were predictably bothered by the quick resort to force in the case of the *Mayaguez*,[34] and they were a whole lot more skeptical of executive branch use of force than Congress had been when it passed the Tonkin Gulf Resolution giving President Lyndon B. Johnson authority to expand the Vietnam War.

Similarly, the news media were alert to any missteps by the administration and could be counted upon to ask hard questions and advertise any perceived deficiencies in Ford's decision making. Indeed, in the middle of the crisis, when the press learned that US aircraft had attacked Cambodian vessels, reporters immediately wanted to know whether the *Mayaguez* crew members might have been killed during those attacks, asking questions such as "so, are we to destroy these men in order to save them?" Reporters also asked whether the sinkings meant diplomatic efforts had been exhausted, given that Kissinger had said the previous evening that no military action would take place otherwise.[35] It was so clear that reporters were in a hostile mood that one of their own, White House correspondent John F. Osborne, chastised them, saying he had "the impression that some of the reporters would have been happy if the *Mayaguez* affair had proved to be an unmitigated disaster rather than a flawed success." Osborne thought Watergate, foreign policy reversals, and other factors had "created a deep and seemingly insatiable media appetite for disaster and official victims."[36] His comment enraged his readers, leading Osborne to comment that they too seemed anxious to find another catastrophic failure by senior leaders. The hostile media and the great divide in public opinion wrought by the Vietnam trauma helps explain why Ford's great surge in popularity was so short lived. His public approval ratings fell off quickly and precipitously as details of the incident and casualty figures became better known. Within days the news that more men died than were saved set off a new round of commentary complaining the incident had been mishandled. Within a few short months, nothing was left of Ford's briefly enhanced popularity.[37]

More pertinent than the public and congressional response after the fact is what Ford and his advisors thought the likely reaction to the use of force would be before the outcome was known. They knew there would be support and opposition to using force, which they discussed. They knew a great deal would hinge upon what the Cambodians did, and they were not optimistic. The odds of recovering the ship were good, but they agreed the Cambodians might scuttle or sink it. The odds against success were great,[38] and decision makers admitted as much when they acknowledged after the event that they had been "lucky."[39] Ford knew he would be harshly criticized if the crew was harmed, which seemed a likely outcome. The decision makers repeatedly observed the Cambodians might kill crew members in retaliation at any time. They already assumed crew members taken to the mainland were effectively "lost" and likely dead. They also knew that twenty-three US Air Force personnel had been killed in the helicopter accident, and they guessed that as many or more Marines could be killed in taking Tang Island.[40]

What is most relevant to this discussion is whether Ford based any of his decisions on anticipated public and congressional reactions. With one exception, the opposite is the case. The president made it clear in the first NSC meeting that he would do what he thought was necessary, saying, "I can assure you that, irrespective of the Congress, we will move." He was equally resolute in the other NSC meetings and in private conversations about doing what was in the nation's best interest. In the fourth NSC meeting, when discussing the upcoming meeting with selected members of Congress to "consult" in accordance with the War Powers Act, Rockefeller asked what should be done if the group opposed the president's plans. Kissinger quickly said Ford "would have to go ahead anyway," and Ford did not disagree.[41]

Ford's decisions backed up his assertion that he would act regardless of political consequences. Early on he told multiple people, including his wife and a congressman, that he had a very hard decision to make. He made the decision, agreeing with Kissinger that the lives of the crew were "unfortunately a secondary consideration,"[42] and, as he later said several times, he was not inclined to revisit difficult decisions once he made up his mind. He was resolute in NSC meetings and private conversations about doing what was in the nation's best interest rather than what might be popular. He used force earlier than what the Pentagon recommended, consciously ran high risks of killing the crew members, and knew in advance that employing force would entail significant human and political costs. But he was undeterred by these considerations. NSC members spent considerable time discussing how to manage public perceptions of their actions.[43] Kissinger told Ford to ignore the idea of an ultimatum because its benefits were only "domestic," (that is, a sop to domestic critics) and warned him he would "take as much heat for a big strike as for a small strike." Ford took that advice, and in fact, by some accounts, he was more steadfast than Kissinger about the matter.[44]

Reading all the recorded deliberations, it seems evident decision makers were bracing for a storm of criticism[45] and yet never let that fact influence their decisions.

Kissinger even opined that acting in the face of political opposition could be helpful, convincing foreign observers that Congress and public opinion could not tie the hands of a willful president. The one exception was Ford's decision not to use the B-52s, which his advisors thought would elicit a political backlash.[46] Even then Ford only relented in the last NSC meeting after being reassured by the Pentagon that it could deliver the desired amount of aerial bombardment with carrier aircraft that would conduct cyclic strikes until he ordered them to stop.

Emotional Catharsis

It is difficult to parse out emotion and reasoning in the decision-making process, especially when they appear mutually reinforcing. This might seem to be the case in the *Mayaguez* crisis. The evidence against decision makers using force as an "emotional catharsis" is the purposeful strategic reasoning of those who favored asymmetric punitive force and the relative restraint of those who demonstrated a concern with avoiding indiscriminate and grossly disproportionate force. Again, the NSC meeting minutes, other deliberations, and telephone conversations reinforce the conclusion that the key decision makers were highly purposeful during the crisis and driven by strategic reasoning rather than emotion. They also knowingly took risks that increased the chances of failure—including rushed military operations and foregoing B-52 strikes, which would not have been the case if they were driven primarily by the desire to bludgeon Cambodia in pursuit of an emotional release.

Kissinger and Rockefeller reacted to the news of the seizure with the most emotion, but both had strategic reasons for doing so. Unlike the rest of his staff at the State Department, Kissinger immediately was alarmed by the news. He cursed and insisted, "We are not going to sit here and let an American merchant ship be captured at sea and let it go into the harbor without doing a bloody thing about it." He demanded immediate action, saying he wanted to see if the Navy could intercept the ship. "We haven't reached the point yet where American ships get captured by Cambodians," he said. When William Hyland asked him what could be done about it, he shot back that he was not the chief of naval operations, before musing "but if we cannot handle the Cambodians . . ." and leaving the thought unfinished. One thing he was certain about: "I know you damned well cannot let Cambodia capture a ship a hundred miles at sea and do nothing."[47] Yet, as Kissinger made clear in the first NSC meeting, he had a firm geostrategic rationale for his reaction, and as the crisis went on, he articulated that rationale time and again.

Vice President Rockefeller is the other senior leader who initially characterized the event in emotive terms. He favored a "violent response," he said, because the Communists "only understand force." He said it was imperative "to show that we will not tolerate this kind of thing," without being specific about the thing that was intolerable. Other NSC members discussed the ruthless nature of the Khmer regime but also speculated that Cambodia might be motivated by territorial sovereignty and oil reserves. In contrast, Rockefeller immediately ascribed hostile motives to the Cambodians in seizing the *Mayaguez*. He claimed that "if we do not respond violently we will get nibbled to death" and that "unless the Cambodians are hurt, this pattern will not be broken." At one point he argued for unconstrained action, telling Ford, "You should do everything you can as soon as possible." His rationale for this was again the blanket assertion that "if the communists do not think that you will react strong and fast, they will keep on doing this."

Like Kissinger, Rockefeller offered a strategic rationale for his recommendations from the beginning, arguing the American response would "be seen as a test case" in Korea and elsewhere and that it was imperative not to get caught in an extended hostage crisis. He did acknowledge political risks, saying, "Public opinion will be against it [the use of force] in order to save lives" but arguing the president had to act anyway. While always emphatic about the need for a forceful response, he did distinguish between alternative courses of action and their attendant risks. He favored airpower, including B-52s, over an assault on the island with ground forces, which he feared might lead to high casualties. Thus, his interventions were not devoid of strategic logic or unrefined by relative risk assessments.[48]

In sum, all the key decision makers carefully reviewed incoming information and its impact on courses of action. They considered the relative risks of different military operations and of launching them on three alternative days, the likelihood of successfully recovering the ship and crew and the risk to the forces involved, and the potential domestic and international reactions to their decisions. They also discussed likely Cambodian motives throughout the crisis and decided they were irrelevant given the Khmer Rouge had the hostage option so long as they held the crew. With respect to risking the lives of the crew, the declassified conversations underscore the ruthlessly cool purposefulness of the decision makers who, as one critic observed early on, "preferred the risk of killing our own men to the risk of 'humiliating' negotiation."[49] *Newsweek* reported that from the first NSC meeting onward "there wasn't a dove in the place," but neither were there any Dr. Strangeloves.[50]

Devaluing Explanation

Journalists in May 1975 were able to identify the primary contending explanations for US behavior during the *Mayaguez* crisis from senior leader pubic statements, inside sources, and expert opinions. But, as a columnist in the *Christian Science Monitor* noted, journalists did not have the wherewithal to assess the relative explanatory value of those explanations. He argued the real explanation for the US response to the seizure of the *Mayaguez* remained murky because news accounts were "shaped by conflicting and what appear to be self-serving reports of what happened in those behind-the-scenes presidential sessions." He hoped "at some point historians may be able to provide a clear chronicle of the President's decision making process" but said, until then, the public would not know "what really happened."[51]

This eventually came to pass. A copious amount of information about the Ford administration's decision-making process during the crisis became available. What is surprising is that scholars did not translate that abundant information into a compelling explanation for US behavior. Instead, the cumulative effect of scholarship has been to *undermine* understanding of US behavior in the crisis. Scholars have concentrated on description at the expense of explanatory analysis, embracing multiple explanatory variables rather than critically examining the evidence for its explanatory efficacy. As a result, multiple competing explanations for US behavior in the *Mayaguez* crisis have persisted for decades. A quick overview of scholarship on the crisis illustrates the point.

The two most notable studies done soon after the crisis, both of which stood out for their access to primary information, were the August 1975 General Accounting Office (GAO) report and 1978's *Crisis Resolution: Presidential Decision Making in the Mayaguez and Korean Confrontations*.[52] The authors of the GAO report did not claim to explain US behaviors, noting they were "restricted by the executive branch from analyzing the decision making process at the highest levels." Like the GAO, the authors of *Crisis Resolution* also took a pass on explaining US behaviors. Instead they sought insights from a descriptive model that did not specify relationships among its diverse variables.[53] In describing crisis decision making they note that the desire to rescue the crew, avoid another *Pueblo* humiliation, and demonstrate US resolve were all motives for US behavior. They do not establish the priority of these competing objectives, and by concentrating on Ford as the key decision maker, overlook the important roles played by Kissinger and Schlesinger.[54]

My research in the 1980s took a different approach. A 1985 article in *Political Science Quarterly* and a longer treatment in the 1989 book *Belief Systems and Decision Making in the* Mayaguez *Crisis*, published by the University of Florida Press, offered a belief system explanation for crisis behavior. With the information now available, it is clear that my original research missed or misstated important aspects of the crisis decision making.

It missed the Pentagon's insubordination in initially refusing to sink all boats coming and going to Tang Island. It overstated the extent to which the decision makers had conflicting priorities. We now know the concern with a demonstrative use of force was consistently the higher priority. It also overestimated the extent to which Schlesinger viewed the military operations as a rescue mission when in reality he consistently supported punitive measures as well, but with his preferred sequencing and timing. It noted but underestimated the willingness of Ford and his advisors to risk the lives of the crew, and it portrayed Ford as an arbiter among strong subordinate experts when in reality he was consistently guided by Kissinger's advice.[55]

For these reasons *Belief Systems and Decision Making in the* Mayaguez *Crisis* is no longer adequate, but its basic explanation for US behavior still holds true and is actually strengthened by the new data available:

> The broad decision that force was necessary resulted from the belief shared by four key US decision makers that deteriorating American prestige and credibility were threatening developments that had to be arrested. In particular, the decision makers were concerned about the probability of North Korean aggression based on perceptions of American weakness and lack of resolve. . . . From this . . . flowed two corollaries, one positive and the other negative, which explain US behavior with more specificity. First, the United States needed a show of force to substantiate the deterrent efficacy of US power. Second, the United States absolutely could not afford another blow to its prestige, especially not a gratuitous humiliation from a minor power which had just recently participated in the forced removal of US influence from Indochina. Subject to whatever constraints might arise at the scene of the event, these two propositions guided the specific US military actions.

First, the *Mayaguez* and Tang Island were quarantined to facilitate the recovery of the ship and forestall the internment of the crew on the mainland. It was hoped that these actions would prevent a display of Cambodian insolence, even though they risked the lives of the crew. Then, as soon as barely sufficient US forces were available, the assault on Tang Island began, with strikes conducted against mainland targets, ostensibly to rescue the crew but primarily to influence perceptions of American power and credibility. This explanation holds despite the belief of many in the military that their orders were motivated primarily by a desire to rescue the ship and crew since it was the motivations of the key decision makers that defined US objectives.[56]

In 1993 Oxford University Press published Lucien Vandenbroucke's *Perilous Options*, a well-researched book containing multiple in-depth cases studies, including a multichapter analysis of the *Mayaguez* crisis. It benefits from numerous interviews with both White House and Pentagon participants and was the first source to raise the allegation that the Pentagon was slow to implement the presidential order to sink all boats coming from and going to Tang Island. Vandenbroucke takes an eclectic approach to explaining US behavior, embracing all the explanatory factors originally identified by *Newsweek*.[57] He seems to place the most emphasis on the emotional catharsis explanation. "Anger at the new Communist regimes in Indochina . . . ran high," he says. "The administration ended up displaying an almost unthinking preference for the language of force." He concludes: "the administration's handling of the *Mayaguez* fell short of cool, careful deliberation. When the ship was seized, the administration reacted with deep anger. From the start, there was strong sentiment among the president's advisers to lash back."[58]

But Vandenbroucke also embraces other explanatory factors. He argues that "Ford's domestic fortunes also subtly influenced . . . White House perceptions" and that "from the onset Ford 'was not unconcerned with the effect of the crisis on his popularity.'" Furthermore, he asserts that "US policymakers were also gravely concerned about the country's image," "the real purpose of the mainland strikes [was] to provide a lesson for the Cambodians and the others," and "the Ford administration was determined to prevent another such humiliation [that is, a *Pueblo* incident]." Vandenbroucke also sees the military operations as a genuine rescue effort, arguing Ford "was seriously concerned about the welfare of the crew." Vandenbroucke contends all these concerns influenced US decision makers, but over time the concern for the crew diminished in comparison with other factors, especially for Ford:

> Ford's original reaction was more reserved; at the outset he also showed strong concern about the safety of the crew, and his first decision was to explore military as well as diplomatic responses. But as the crisis wore on, the urge to retaliate and restore US prestige gained sway. By the time the Marines took off for Koh Tang, the crew's welfare had become merely one consideration among many others. Ultimately, the fear of another national humiliation, the urge to punish Cambodia, and the wish to show US resolve seem to have generated almost blind enthusiasm for a forceful response.[59]

Thus, he argues that "notwithstanding Ford's concern about the crew, hostility toward Cambodia and the administration's bellicose mood influenced White House decisions and attitudes from the start."[60] He believes blind enthusiasm for force led to cognitive dissonance as US leaders "rapidly concluded that the Cambodians' failure to respond to the diplomatic messages delivered in Beijing meant that they were not interested in a peaceful solution." He also thinks US leaders were so "eager to retaliate against Cambodia" they "apparently wished away key shortcomings of the plan."[61]

As the foregoing analysis demonstrates, it is now clear that US leaders were not driven by anger, or domestic political calculations, or concern for the welfare of the crew; it is also evident that Ford did not change his mind on his priorities over the course of the crisis. On the contrary, the NSC minutes reveal decision makers who were calm, resolute, and calculating, men who from the beginning gave priority to geostrategic purposes and consistently ranked the lives of the crew a secondary consideration. Neither were decision makers blinded by cognitive dissonance and wishful thinking. They correctly identified likely Cambodian motives in their first meeting and dismissed them as irrelevant.[62] They carefully and repeatedly assessed risks as the crisis progressed. The risks of assaulting Tang Island were not correctly assessed, especially by subordinate military commanders, but the Joint Chiefs and the NSC did not ignore or wish the risks away. They discussed the risks at length and delayed operations a day as a result. Then the president accepted the unanimous recommendation of the JCS that the operation could be executed with acceptable risk and a high assurance of success, which in the end and in terms of anticipated casualties, proved an accurate assessment, largely because of good fortune and the incredible efforts of US servicemen.

The senior leaders also directly confronted, and debated, the risks of military operations harming the crew, which they considered a secondary concern. Schlesinger differed from the other key decision makers on how much the crew should be put at risk by US military operations, but Ford, with support from Kissinger and Scowcroft, consciously decided to risk the crew by sinking Cambodian boats until Schlesinger's imposed rules of engagement led to a pilot reporting the likelihood of crew members being sighted. At that point, they debated again and Schlesinger won over Kissinger to the view that the political blowback from killing the crew would be too detrimental to the image they wanted to project of a United States prepared to defend its geostrategic interests. Risks to the crew, like the risk of the island assault, were not overlooked or wished away.

In 1995 John Guilmartin's *A Very Short War* was published by Texas A&M University Press. Guilmartin was a participant in the military operations during the crisis. He makes good use of new primary source material from military sources, such as command and unit histories and interviews with military participants. He examines the "interactions among policy, strategy, operations, and tactics" but devotes most of the book to an examination of the military operations, especially command and control arrangements. Relying heavily on numerous primary sources involved in the *Mayaguez* military operations, Guilmartin demonstrates how unpredictable developments (i.e., Clausewitzian "friction") affected outcomes. He finds fault with on-scene commanders for failing to anticipate enemy opposition and identifies numerous other command failures, including the fact that there was "no workable plan to coordinate air and naval gunfire support with the assault."[63] Disaster was only averted by truly heroic efforts by the forces hastily assembled and sent into combat. He draws particular attention to the performance of the OV-10 pilots who intervened to coordinate fires and the helicopter pilots who repeatedly flew into withering Cambodian fires, but he argues the fighting forces themselves were most responsible for saving the situation:

> The problem was resolved and catastrophe averted not by superior high-level communications but in spite of them. It was done by subordinate commanders, junior officers, and NCOs [noncommissioned officers] acting on their own initiative in response to the demands of the tactical situation, employing a general awareness of strategic objective and policy goals.[64]

Guilmartin indicates he relied on *Belief Systems and Decision Making in the* Mayaguez *Crisis* for his brief depictions of Washington decision making,[65] but his conclusions about US leader priorities differ significantly. He believes decision makers "were prepared to give priority to the avoidance of hostage negotiations at the expense of the crew's welfare," and that in turn, those two objectives (avoiding negotiations and the welfare of the crew) "clearly took precedence over a demonstrative application of force." He offers no evidence for this ranking of priorities; he just argues it makes sense because the bombing "could be orchestrated at leisure," whereas the assault on Tang Island was where "the enemy ability to interfere was greatest." He thinks it stands to reason that US leaders would give priority attention to the assault on Tang Island.[66] This conjecture gets decision makers' priorities exactly wrong. US leaders consistently gave priority to the demonstrative use of force, with the avoidance of hostage negotiations a secondary priority. The assault on Tang Island was rushed to accommodate those priorities.

The final university press book on the crisis is Robert J. Mahoney's *The Mayaguez Incident: Testing America's Resolve in the Post-Vietnam Era*. Mahoney's 2011 work is the only scholarly analysis to date that benefited from the declassified NSC meeting minutes.[67] Like Guilmartin, Mahoney stresses the strategic import of the crisis, which he considers underappreciated, and generally sympathizes with the decision makers. He provides a comprehensive account of the crisis, moving back and forth between events in the field and decisions in Washington to depict senior leader decision-making and its impact. Using the NSC minutes, Mahoney clarifies the extent to which the White House was willing to risk harming the crew, the fact that Kissinger strongly dissented from other NSC members who advised against any delays in military operations, and other descriptive details not previously disclosed.[68] However, Mahoney gets some descriptive details wrong,[69] in part by uncritically accepting Ford's and Kissinger's memoirs.[70] More importantly, he too weakens his explanation by embracing multiple explanatory factors.[71]

On the all-important question of what the United States was trying to achieve, Mahoney asserts that "the NSC's first priority was to send a strong message to the Cambodian government, as well as the world writ large, that the United States, although stung by setback in Vietnam, was not a hollow power."[72] Actually, the intended audience was North Korea and its patrons, not Cambodia. In any case, a few paragraphs later he seems to hedge on this conclusion. He cites Kissinger's memoirs, which claims White House leaders "were primarily worried about the safety of the crew" but also concerned about international perceptions. Mahoney observes, "The two main priorities, advancing (or restoring) American prestige and the rescue of the *Mayaguez* and her crew, were so interrelated that it was possible one could not have been accomplished without the other." Nevertheless, after reviewing White House decisions on risks to the crew, Mahoney acknowledges "the prioritization of punitive action over the release of the crew."[73]

Elsewhere, however, he weakens and confuses this apparent explanation by giving credence to other explanatory variables. He believes the US response was "shaped by the assumptions and predispositions of the members of the NSC" that in turn were "shaped in part by the pressures at all levels—international, domestic, political, and personal."[74] In describing crisis behaviors, he sometimes implies beliefs drove behavior,[75] but he only explicitly assigns explanatory weight to a few factors. One such factor was fear of another *Pueblo* humiliation, which he believes was particularly influential for Ford. Mahoney argues Ford refused to delay military operations another twenty-four hours because he "was determined not to allow a repetition of [the *Pueblo*]."[76] Like Vandenbroucke, he also thinks Ford was influenced by domestic political considerations, saying "Ford needed to address his weak power position as an unelected president and head of a party in shame."[77] Unlike Vandenbroucke, he rejects the emotional catharsis explanation, stating "the NSC's direction was not simply a reckless, emotional reaction to an apparent challenge to US power." He argues decision makers accessed risks carefully and quickly, concluding "their actions were on the whole logical."[78]

In short, *The Mayaguez Incident* appears to ascribe the greatest significance to the decision makers' desire for a demonstrative use of force for geostrategic reasons but confuses this explanation by assigning explanatory efficacy to other variables without adequately assessing their import. Ford was *not* influenced by domestic political considerations. Instead he was determined to act forcefully regardless of domestic political consequences. Also, the *Pueblo* crisis was not a critical factor in Ford's decision on when to launch military operations. Mahoney asserts the contrary based on Kissinger's and Ford's memoirs, which contain a number of major inaccuracies. The *Pueblo* was not mentioned during the fourth NSC meeting when Ford decided against further delays. By then Ford had done what he could to prevent a humiliating hostage scenario by quarantining the ship and Tang Island. At that point the primary argument against delay was the threat of a sudden diplomatic or political development that might preclude the opportunity to use of force at all.[79]

Other Noteworthy Explanations

University press books are the focus of this inquiry because they carry the presumption of academic rigor. What is interesting about the record of scholarship from these sources is how, despite an ever-increasing amount of primary data, they confuse rather than clarify the explanation for US decision making. The three most recent university press books use new primary sources to make valuable contributions to a fuller description of the crisis decision making, but they do not do justice to explanatory analysis.[80] All three books largely jump from detailed description to findings and prescriptions, lightly passing over explanatory analysis, which readers must ascertain on their own. The deleterious consequences of this trend in scholarship have been explored elsewhere.[81] The basic point is that devaluing explanation diminishes an understanding of the *Mayaguez* crisis and retards the growth of cumulative knowledge in the field.

What is true for the field also holds for individual learning. Those wanting to understand the *Mayaguez* crisis and, by extension, what it can teach about crisis decision making need a careful examination of the best evidence for alternative hypotheses and a clear conclusion as to what explanation is best supported by the evidence. In that regard, we need to evaluate two additional explanations for decision making and outcomes in the *Mayaguez* crisis that have currency: faulty intelligence and misperception.

Faulty Intelligence

From the beginning, faulty intelligence has been cited as a key factor in explaining crisis decision making during the *Mayaguez* incident. Early on key leaders were upset by conflicting and frequently changing reports from the field. Kissinger makes this point in his memoirs, giving the faulty intelligence argument a big boost. His overall assessment was that "intelligence had been poor throughout. At too many stages, starting with the very first NSC meeting, decisions were made on the basis of information that had turned out to be almost totally wrong." Kissinger said Colby's first briefing to the NSC "turned out to be wrong in every detail" and argued that "in the absence of accurate intelligence, no meaningful course of action could be formulated." More recently, Donald Rumsfeld has made similar arguments.[82]

It is true that reporting on the ship's location assumed it was being taken to the mainland and that assumption was incorrect. The Cambodians did want to take the ship to the mainland, but the wily captain of the *Mayaguez* convinced them it was not possible for technical reasons (e.g., broken equipment, shallow waters).[83] Ford, Kissinger, and Scowcroft also were irritated by rapidly changing reports of the ship's location. Now, however, with access to the NSC minutes and other data, we know Kissinger was grossly exaggerating the impact of poor intelligence.

Colby's first briefing was not wrong in every detail (he was correct in his depiction of likely Cambodian motives, for instance), but more to the point, those details were not critically important to Kissinger, who knew what he wanted to do from the beginning and just had "to wait for the means to do it to arrive on the scene."[84] The discovery that the ship was anchored off an island instead of moored at a mainland port shifted the debate from general punitive operations to those that would quarantine the ship and crew and punish Cambodia until they were released or retaken, but it did not change the decision makers' priorities or critically impede the formulation of policy in the crisis. Indeed, we now know that Kissinger at one point argued for *less* information on the crew's whereabouts because it complicated the punitive military operations he favored.

In the immediate aftermath of the crisis, Kissinger acknowledged faulty intelligence was not a major factor. Columnist Joseph Kraft, who called Kissinger on May 16 for insider information about the crisis, opined the intelligence was "off," particularly with respect to the location of the crew members.[85] "You can't blame them for not knowing about the island," Kissinger said. "Why should the CIA have up-to-date intelligence on every island off Cambodia?" Kissinger went on to say intelligence believed some of the crew were moved off the island, but it turned out that all of them had been, and he again concluded, "You can't blame them, the intelligence, for not having known that they were moved."[86] Schlesinger made the same arguments when questioned about "faulty intelligence" in a May 18 interview on ABC's *Issues and Answers* program. He said intelligence was not wrong; he and the other decision makers just did not know if the entire crew had been removed from Tang or not. And General Jones in a later interview said the same thing with respect to the location of the crew.[87]

The actual performance of the intelligence community during the fast-moving crisis was much better than characterized by senior leaders in their memoirs. Colby pushed back against those who wanted to blame faulty intelligence in his community's postmortem report on intelligence performance.[88] Recent scholarship agrees, concluding the problem was not so much poor intelligence as Colby's (and others') failure to sufficiently emphasize the imperfect nature of the incoming information offered to the NSC, which has been characterized as "a failure of expectation management."[89] However, General Jones did on several occasions remind the NSC that estimates of enemy strength were guesses, and the general discussion in NSC meetings acknowledged points of uncertainty.

There were, however, two very real failures involving intelligence during the crisis, one of which has received much commentary and the other none at all. Congressional investigators quickly discovered that the Marines conducting the assault on Tang only received the initial intelligence estimate of 20 to 30 (or fewer) irregular soldiers defending the island with light weapons and not the later and more accurate assessments of 90 to 100 Khmer soldiers rereinforced by a heavy weapons squad of 10 to 15 persons (from IPAC), or the DIA estimate of 150 to 200 heavily armed troops that circulated in the Washington area. The Marines also did not receive the May 13 report from an AC-130 gunship that its sensors suggested a sizeable ground force on Tang Island with at least three gun emplacements positioned in a one-hundred-yard curve.[90] A 6,000-foot minimum altitude restriction also hampered the Marine assault commander, Lieutenant Colonel Randall Austin, when he conducted aerial reconnaissance of Tang Island in an Army U-21 aircraft. The minimum altitude restriction had been imposed by local commanders to protect Navy P-3 reconnaissance planes from 20- and 40-mm weapons thought to be on the Cambodian gunboats, but later permission was received to fly lower.[91]

A Pacific Command inspector general's report later indicated the proximate cause of the Marines not getting the latest intelligence was that the command locations hosting the Marine assault forces were inadvertently omitted as addressees on message distribution. Other missed opportunities to get the intelligence to the Marine commander seemed the result of time pressure; unwieldy command structures (including the fact that General Burns did not have a dedicated intelligence officer); insufficient jointness; and, according to some accounts, personality conflicts.[92] In light of all the factors involved, the egregious breakdown in intelligence dissemination is probably better understood as a command and control collapse than an "intelligence" failure.

The critical import of the failure to disseminate the updated intelligence to the Marines has been questioned for two reasons. Some argue the Marines had no choice but to fly into the teeth of Cambodian defenses given the mission they were assigned. Lieutenant Colonel Austin made his decisions on the assumption that he would be facing relatively few irregular forces but also in light of his assigned rescue mission:

> I learned of the Air Security Police Plan after arriving in Utapao. This, tied with the talk of leaflets and bullhorns [to inform the Cambodians of US demands for the release of the crew] led to the conclusion we would not be faced with a large force. Our major concern was devoted to how we would release the crew if the villagers were holding them as hostages. [I] just didn't think this kind of intelligence existed.[93]

Austin's views on whether he would have landed elsewhere if he had known the higher intelligence estimate changed in the aftermath of the crisis and years later. He initially said he would have conducted the mission "more covertly," but a little later said that, given the mission, he would not have changed the landing location in any case.

Senior officers up the chain of command were also of mixed minds.[94] Some argue the higher intelligence estimate would have required a reconsideration of the plan, and others emphasize that even those who had the higher estimate judged the risks acceptable given the pressure from Washington to act quickly.[95] Like Austin, Burns seemed disposed to think of the Cambodians as an inconsequential force given the assigned mission:

> I honestly believe—and people may deny it, but having seen the events that took place—the people in Washington were convinced that it was a very inconsequential force on the island. Otherwise they wouldn't have had me be prepared to go in with 75 or 100 air policemen.[96]

At the same time, Burns later said he understood the mission was high risk, but again, the nature of the mission affected the risk assessment:

> When the plan came forward on what we were going to do, it bothered me. We only had 175 Marines we could put in that first wave if all the choppers were mechanically sound and arrived. You normally like to have something in the neighborhood of 3-to-1 superiority plus preparatory fire. I told them, "We can't afford preparatory fire," but I did say, "We can use 20-millimeter or gas." [Later,

when] Hunt [Major General Ira A. "Jim" Hunt, his deputy commander] came and showed me where they were landing, I was really concerned. I thought that was an awfully risky operation because obviously they were going to be landing right within a couple of hundred feet of the inhabited area. He said he had been talking to the Marines, that the Marine commander had in fact flown over the island, and had selected the landing zone himself. I thought, for example, it might have made more sense to land in the south where there was no inhabitants that we knew of and work your way up. He said, "Well, I am told by the Marines who looked the island over that it would take them a full day to work from the south end of the [4-mile-long] island to the north. By that time the crew could all have their throats cut. If they could quickly envelop them, they had a better chance of securing the crew." I said, "Okay, I will accede to the guy's judgment that has to do the job."[97]

Burns had the better intelligence on enemy strength and yet decided to trust the judgment of his subordinate commander, characterizing his plan as "gutsy." He was unaware that the Marine commander made his decision on the false assumption that he would be facing a smaller force, but the general was quite aware that his superiors in Washington believed there were larger stakes involved and the risk of assaulting Tang quickly with the forces available was acceptable. Burns noted Admiral Gayler had raised the question of "why the hurry" a number of times and "the answer coming back from Washington didn't really address that question" but rather "indicated that we should proceed." So they did.

After the crisis, Burns's military and civilian superiors in Washington took responsibility and said they believed the assault on Tang was a reasonable risk,[98] which raises the question of how military and civilian leaders in Washington calculated risks. With the NSC minutes now declassified, we better understand how the NSC assessed the risk of assaulting Tang.

In his memoirs, Kissinger again blames the intelligence community for a faulty assessment of Cambodian strength: "We were told some of the crew were being held by only a very few Khmer Rouge guards" on Tang Island.[99] Since Kissinger quotes the NSC minutes elsewhere, it seems he is dissembling on this point. In reality, the NSC members were told and assumed there were at least one hundred Khmer soldiers on Tang. In the third NSC meeting Schlesinger used the one-hundred Cambodian-force figure, saying it was a "Marine estimate." It does not appear that he cited this estimate of enemy forces to downplay risk, however, because he used the figure to explain why the Pentagon "would prefer to land with 1,000 [Marines]." When Kissinger and Colby questioned why one hundred defenders should be such a concern, General Jones explained the limited lift capacity, long cycle time, the need to split the Marine force between those taking the ship and those assaulting the island, and the fact that precise enemy strength was not known. When President Ford questioned the reliability of the one-hundred-defender figure, Colby observed it was probably reliable given that the Khmer regime had just arrived in power and probably not had the time to man the island with more defenders.

What is still unknown is why Colby and other NSC members were using the IPAC estimate of 100 Khmer forces on Tang Island rather than the larger estimate of 150 to 200 Cambodians that DIA put out and that, in retrospect, appears to have been more accurate. Colby was one of the decision makers encouraging fast action; thus, his response to Ford's question about the reliability of the 100-defender figure might seem like wishful thinking, but it must be remembered that all the estimates of enemy strength were based on extrapolations and guesswork. Khmer forces on Tang Island were estimated based on gunboat activity and radio intercepts that suggested a Khmer battalion size force, which were known to be typically understrength (i.e., 200–220 rather than 540 men). Since the actual size of the Cambodian defending force was unknown, it may be that the intelligence analysts working the issue and preparing Colby for the NSC meeting just decided to go with the IPAC estimate as the middle ground between a grossly optimistic estimate of twenty or so irregular forces and the DIA assumption that a near battalion-sized force had been placed on the island.

At one point in the NSC discussions, Schlesinger asked, "Is there any change in our estimate regarding the forces on the island?" Colby responded, "No," indicating he was the final arbiter on intelligence estimates. However, it is not known how CIA analysts adjudicated the differing intelligence assessments. The intelligence community's postmortem assessment ignores this issue,[100] which really was an in-house difference of opinion between two Defense Department intelligence entities. Defense officials told congressional investigators "that the Defense Intelligence Agency and Intelligence Pacific did agree on the nature of the probable opposition" and ignored the investigators' assertion "that the two estimates, which differed widely, were not reconciled."[101] There is some support for the assertion that the estimates were reconciled insofar as Morton Abramowitz, the deputy assistant secretary of defense for international security affairs (East Asia and Pacific Affairs), testified to Congress on the afternoon of May 14 that "the estimated strength on the island was 100 Khmer Communists." Presumably he would have given Congress the prevailing "best estimate," and in fact he said he did, acknowledging "we may be very wrong about the size [of the Khmer force but] that is a best estimate."[102]

Whatever the explanation, the use of the 100- rather than the 200-defender estimate was consequential. With 100 defenders the NSC decided to delay a day until more forces were on the scene. Presumably with an estimate of 200 defenders, they would have been even more worried about a potential military failure. With only 175 Marines in the first wave, the attack was being made with about half the force normally recommended (a 1.75 to 1 rather than a 3 to 1 advantage). Assaulting 200 entrenched troops with a numerically inferior force likely would have forced a reconsideration of the operation, making it also more likely that decision makers would have considered waiting another day until more Marines and helicopters were on the scene.

Misperception

Another line of reasoning used to explain the US response is misperception. Some sources conclude that US leaders, known to have been concerned about a repeat of the *Pueblo* affair, misperceived the dangers of the Cambodians holding the ship. Blinded by the powerful historical analogy with the *Pueblo* crisis, the argument goes, decision makers failed to consider that the seizure of the *Mayaguez* might have been a local commander's decision rather than a centrally directed act of hostility toward the United States.[103] In this vein it is often argued that if the United States had waited a little longer, the Cambodians would have released the ship and crew as they did in other cases. The disparity in the relative power of the United States and Cambodia is often cited as prima facie evidence that Cambodian leaders could not have had hostile intentions and would have released the ship and crew.

Ford inadvertently gave this thesis a boost in his memoirs when he claimed his decision to not use B-52s stemmed from an intervention by the White House photographer David H. Kennerly. According to Ford, in the fourth NSC meeting Kennerly suddenly asked if anyone had considered that the seizure might be just the action of a local commander, implying there was no centrally directed or malign intent on the part of the Cambodian government.[104] Ford said he believed the point had merit, so he ordered tactical instead of strategic bombing. By this account, Kennerly's observation was a revelation that influenced Ford's decision in favor of comparative moderation. Commentators frequently cite this passage from Ford's memoirs as evidence that up until that point US leaders were operating under the misimpression that the Cambodian actions were centrally directed as a "deliberate provocation by the new [Cambodian] regime."[105]

We now know that in the first moments of the first NSC meeting it was quickly surmised that the *Mayaguez* was stopped by a local commander on general orders to assert Cambodian sovereignty over offshore islands with their potentially "rich oil deposits," which were claimed by Vietnam as well.[106] Colby explained this was the likely Cambodian motive for stopping the *Mayaguez* and other ships previously, and Clements later reminded the NSC members of the same, saying, "We should not forget that there is a real chance that this is an in-house spat," with oil rights being the point of contention. Ford's response was, "That is interesting, but it does not solve our problem," a point upon which there was general agreement. Ford had already agreed with Kissinger on the overriding need for a demonstrative exhibition of US power, which rendered Cambodian motives of secondary importance. What was critical was demonstrating US resolve, and the discussion in the first meeting was all about punitive responses. Also, in a later Oval Office conversation with Kissinger and Scowcroft, Ford acknowledged that he was just using the B-52 option to encourage the Pentagon to conduct potent tactical airstrikes.[107] For both of these reasons, Ford could not have considered Kennerly's intervention eye-opening unless he forgot everything that he had previously said. Ford was either inserting some drama into his memoirs or just giving Kennerly, whom he considered "like a son,"[108] a flattering mention.

Many commentators echo Kennerly, portraying the Cambodians as innocent bystanders surprised by American belligerence.[109] Cambodian intentions cannot be known with certainty, especially given their lack of formal communications to US authorities. However, the longer the crisis went on the more evidence there was that Cambodian behaviors were centrally directed and hostile to US interests.[110] As has long been argued, the Cambodians did not just stop, search, and release the ship, thereby asserting their sovereignty. They fired on US reconnaissance aircraft and made determined efforts to get both the crew and the ship to a mainland port, at great risk to themselves and the crew. These behaviors made an impression on US leaders. Colby's comment to the NSC was that Cambodians' determination to get the crew to the mainland suggested they understood the value of the crew as hostages. Ford agreed, saying after the crisis was over that the Khmer Communists "didn't search the ship and release it" but rather "took control and kept it," inclining him to believe a confrontation was inevitable.

Later, more specific Cambodian behaviors were made known from interviews with the *Mayaguez* crew. The Cambodians repeatedly characterized the crew as "spies." The Cambodians' English-speaking interpreter told the ship's captain that the crew could be held captive for "two months possibly," but that only higher authorities in Phnom Penh could decide for how long.[111] He added, "You must stop the bombing before they will let you go." At one point, there was a press report suggesting the Cambodians would release the *Mayaguez* after "US apologies and return of Khmer aircraft that were flown to Thailand." One hundred and one planes were flown to Thailand by pilots loyal to the previous US-backed Cambodian government. Whether this was the quid pro quo the Cambodians hoped to obtain is not known. What is clear from crew interviews and communication intercepts is that Cambodian authorities in Phnom Penh told Ta Mok, the regional commander in Kompong Som, to release the crew in order to bring US military operations to an end.[112] Considering the contents of the Tehran cable, the Chinese may have helped authorities in Phnom Penh understand that larger US retribution was on the way.[113]

After the crisis, in a fifth NSC meeting, US decision makers again discussed the latest information on possible Cambodian motives. They surmised the Cambodians had moved the ship from the smaller island of Poulo Wai to the larger Tang Island because it was better defended. This, along with the fact that the crew was taken to the mainland for interrogation, suggested to Kissinger "that the operation was really centrally controlled." Then, a few days after the crisis Kissinger sent Ford a memo updating him on what had been learned from debriefing the crew:

> The account given by the MAYAGUEZ Captain ... does not, however, offer any explanation of what motivated the Cambodian authorities. From the Captain's account, it appears that the decision to release the vessel and crew was not triggered by our military actions on Wednesday evening (EDT) [i.e., the assault on Tang and mainland airstrikes] but was probably tied to the threats of those actions and to growing American military presence and activity. That is, presumably, why the Cambodians responded to the Captain's offer to turn off the American military if they released him and the crew.[114]

As Schlesinger later pointed out, given US objectives and Cambodian behaviors, it really did not matter how centrally controlled Cambodian behaviors were: "The fact of the matter is that we had to be sure that the Cambodian government acquired the responsibility at some point, because only the Cambodian government could deliver both the ship and the crew."[115] US leaders were intent on pressuring central authorities in Cambodia until they asserted control over their forces. At the same time, it is clear from the Cambodians' own behavior that they understood the value of controlling the crew and were determined to put themselves in a position where they could hold the crew for an indefinite period.

In short, there was little misperception on either side about the behaviors or motives of the other side. The Cambodians understood US behaviors and motives. They just responded too slowly to US threats to prevent US military operations, although releasing the crew when they did no doubt prevented worse from happening. US leaders had little to go on in interpreting Cambodian motives, but Colby appears to have gotten it right in the first NSC meeting where it was also agreed Cambodian intentions were of secondary importance since they were positioning themselves to hold the crew hostage if they concluded there were benefits from doing so.

Correcting the Record

Recent scholarship has confused the basic explanation for US behavior in the *Mayaguez* crisis. Concern about declining US credibility was not a lesser, tangential concern or one among several or many influential concerns. It was the *overriding* concern of US decision makers and their controlling objective. All the new evidence from declassified documents makes this more evident, not less. Worse, however, scholarship has also forgotten or ignored the major intended target of the US military operations, which was not Cambodia or Southeast Asia but rather North Korea.[116] Although US leaders hoped the resort to force would signal US resolve to protect its interests more generally, their immediate concern was the Korean Peninsula.

All the key US decision makers believed North Korea was the most likely candidate to test American resolve, and the subject came up quickly and repeatedly in the NSC discussions during the *Mayaguez* crisis. Vice President Rockefeller insisted that "many are watching us, in Korea and elsewhere." Kissinger was particularly adamant about signaling China and North Korea that they should not underestimate US resolve (see sidebar). When Kissinger argued, "We should seize the island, seize the ship, and hit the mainland," he added, "I am thinking not of Cambodia, but of Korea and of the Soviet Union and of others." Later he emphasized again that "the Koreans and others would like to look us over and to see how we react" and yet again: "I think we should do something that will impress the Koreans and the Chinese."[117] The day after the crisis Ford confided to the shah of Iran that he had perhaps "overreacted" in order "to show the Koreans and others our resolve."[118] In a phone conversation with a reporter after the crisis, Kissinger said Ford acted "decisively; enough so it didn't look like we were blinking," and then added "even China and North Korea," thus identifying the countries he considered the primary participants in the stare down.[119]

Of the four tentative explanations for US behavior offered by *Newsweek* immediately following the crisis, the most accurate was the assertion that US military operations were a "two-day punitive expedition" designed to compensate for the "image of America's despairing retreat from Indochina." *Newsweek* also accurately identified the intended target of the demonstrative use of force; its reporters wrote that the Ford administration wanted to hearten allies and caution adversaries—"especially the trigger-happy

North Koreans"—by demonstrating the US could and would still aggressively defend its interests and honor its treaty commitments.[120]

What *Newsweek* reported was common knowledge at the time. In 1975 US leaders emphasized their apprehensions about North Korea, and the media parroted them before, during, and after the crisis. *Newsweek*'s coverage was hardly unique in singling out the "trigger-happy North Koreans" as the target US leaders hoped to impress with the punitive strikes on Cambodia.[121] The *New York Times* did the same, reporting that "leading Administration officials" said military operations during the *Mayaguez* crisis were "undertaken in part to alert North Korea and other Communist countries that the United States was ready to meet force with force to protect its interests." Under the subheading, "A Korean Crisis Feared," the *Times* noted that "there have been no overt signs that North Korea is preparing to attack South Korea," but "administration officials have said for some time that the next major trouble spot in Asia would probably be the Korean Peninsula."[122]

Kissinger was the likely source for the *New York Times* article. He had been particularly diligent and forthright about his concerns in this respect. For example, he had been lobbying senators outspoken in their opposition to the Vietnam War to enlist their support in signaling North Korea that the United States would defend South Korea. On the day the *Mayaguez* was seized, these senators released a statement intended to head off a Korean crisis.[123] Whoever the senior administration official was, he told the reporter that "he believed the North Koreans, at the least, would have to consider more seriously the American commitment to South Korea than they might have immediately after the fall of South Vietnam to the Communists in April." The article also noted North Korea's leader, Kim Il Sung, visited China in April "to seek support for an invasion of South Korea but apparently did not receive it."[124]

In Schlesinger's interview on *Issues and Answers*, his interlocutor specifically asked him whether the "salutary" message delivered during the *Mayaguez* crisis had gotten through to North Korea. The interviewer wanted to know how the United States would react "if the Koreans should start something." Schlesinger said the United States would apply the lessons of Vietnam, which the interviewer misconstrued to mean possible use of nuclear weapons. Schlesinger clarified that he was talking about "destroy[ing] the heart of enemy power," rather than

> simply spend[ing] our time parrying their offensive operations. Now, whether this is overwhelming power immediately, what the precise reaction of the United States would be, I cannot at this time state, but I would emphasize that it's necessary for us to recognize, and the North Koreans to recognize, that the United States is bound by a mutual defense treaty to South Korea.[125]

Other news media and pundits around the time of the event also underscored the extent to which North Korea figured in the US leadership's calculations.[126] When I interviewed Scowcroft in 1980, he volunteered that "to the extent that we were looking anywhere specifically, it was . . . Korea."[127] In addition to being worried about North Korea aggression, there was also the concern that South Korea, doubting US security guarantees, might be tempted to acquire nuclear weapons.[128] Since then, however, scholars have forgotten or ignored the North Korean factor. For instance, the 1978 *Crisis Resolution* study downplayed the decision makers' concern with North Korea. The authors emphasized other elements of the international context and relegated the specific concern with North Korea to a footnote.[129] The next two scholarly treatments of the *Mayaguez* noted the importance of North Korea. My 1989 book *Belief Systems and Decision Making in the* Mayaguez *Crisis* argued US leaders were primarily interested in a demonstrative use of force and that North Korea was the principal concern. It drew attention to South Korean anxiety about North Korean intentions:

> William Colby, the man responsible for providing the National Security Council with intelligence estimates, five years later remembered Kim Il Sung's trip well: "Kim Il Sung trotted over to Peking and he was obviously trying to drum up trade for an attack in Korea. . . . The fact is, he thought, the Americans are weak, I can take advantage, why don't I do it, all I need is support from my big sponsors." The Japanese and the South Koreans had reached a similar assessment of North Korean motives. On 29 April, South Korean President Park Chung Hee predicted a North Korean attack sometime in 1975. On 10 May, two days before the seizure of the *Mayaguez*, more than one million South Koreans rallied in Seoul to express support for renewed vigilance against the North Koreans. Even politicians opposing Park Chung Hee's government attended. The South Koreans adopted a resolution calling on the United States not to "forget the lessons of Vietnam" and urging America to strengthen its defense treaty with South Korea.[130]

Ironically, the concern about North Korea that was well understood decades ago has been obscured by scholarship since then. Vandenbroucke's *Perilous Options* in 1993 focused on the US "overreaction" to the seizure of the *Mayaguez*, but it noted that the US response "may have had a sobering effect on foes of the United States in Asia, helping, perhaps, restrain the North Koreans, who had been increasingly belligerent toward South Korea."[131] Both Guilmartin's *A Very Short War*, published in 1995, and Mahoney's 2011 *The Mayaguez Incident* ignored North Korea, not mentioning it as a key concern of US decision makers.[132]

The North Korean Factor

Recent declassified documents and other new materials reinforce the notion that US leaders were concerned about an aggressive North Korea. In the period leading up to the *Mayaguez* crisis, Kissinger was using David Rockefeller as a secret channel to the North Koreans with the mission of making sure they knew the United States would respond with alacrity to a North Korean attack.[133] Kissinger personally delivered the same message to China. Three days before the *Mayaguez* crisis, Kissinger met with Huang Chen, chief of the People's Republic of China (PRC) liaison office in Washington, and other Chinese diplomats. A briefing paper from Kissinger's staff encouraged the meeting, observing that although "we have no hard evidence that Kim came to China seeking support for military action against South Korea, it seems likely that he was reviewing his options in the wake of developments in Indochina."[134]

Kissinger opened discussions with Huang Chen by saying he had read an editorial in the *People's Daily* asserting "the United States is in a period of strategic passivity." Kissinger explained how wrong and dangerous this misperception was:

> My main point is that we are not in a period of strategic passivity, and we will not remain passive. We now need a brief period of reassessment, but in many respects we are in a psychologically stronger period as we don't have to debate Vietnam every week. So, my main point is that we have absolutely no intention of remaining passive. . . . With respect to Korea, I want to make clear that under no circumstances will we tolerate a military attack on Korea, and a military attack on Korea will involve the certainty of American involvement. We will support peaceful evolution on the Korean Peninsula. We are prepared to discuss measures which would bring about the dissolution of the United Nations Command. And we will work to create conditions for coexistence on the Peninsula. But we are not prepared to accept another attack on the American presence.[135]

Kissinger also made his case for the North Korean threat to a group of liberal senators who had been outspoken in their opposition to the Vietnam War. In the period leading up to the *Mayaguez* crisis he tried to convince them that the danger of North Korean aggression was real and imminent. Coincidentally, on the day of the *Mayaguez* seizure these senators released a statement intended to head off a crisis on the Korean Peninsula. The statement's opening line bore witness to Kissinger's influence: "Let no nation read the events in Indochina as the failure of American will."[136]

William Stearman, the NSC staff member who argued with Kissinger against more airstrikes after the return of the crew, noted in an oral interview that

> I realized later the reason he was doing this had nothing to do with Cambodia. It was aimed at North Korea. At that time, we had a lot of intelligence that North Korea was planning to launch a strike against South Korea because they thought we had been so demoralized by the fall of Indochina that now would be a good time to attack. So Henry [Kissinger] was sending a message to Kim Il Sung by continuing the bombing. In retrospect, I think he was right.

As a matter of fact, I was quite concerned myself about a possible North Korean attack at that time. Many of us were. There was a lot of intelligence that indicated they were seriously thinking about it."[137]

Two months after the crisis, Kissinger argued in a personal memo to Ford that his actions had reassured South Korea, but he also observed, "The Korean peninsula remains, however, the single most dangerous area in Asia."[138]

Over time scholars have overlooked the focus on deterring North Korea for two reasons. The tendency toward descriptive, multivariate accounts of the crisis weakens understanding of the basic explanation for US behavior, thus diminishing the focus on deterrence and increasing the chances that scholars will also overlook the focus on deterring North Korea. Also, with the passage of time and considering the fact that North Korea never initiated war, it is natural for decision makers as well as scholars to downplay the concern about such a threat. For example, Kissinger does not even mention this motivation in his memoirs, preferring to talk about international perceptions of US resolve more generally.

Yet those studying North Korea and its external relations per se have moved in the opposite direction over time. Scholarship on North Korea now stresses that it was clearly the case that Kim Il Sung in April 1975 wanted to reunite the Korean Peninsula by force and that he asked for Chinese support to do so.[139] Even after being rebuffed by China, Kim continued to pursue diplomatic and military efforts to reduce international support for South Korea in hopes of setting the conditions for a successful conflict. Throughout the first half of 1976, North Korea pursued an all-out diplomatic offensive to build international support for a UN resolution to dissolve the UN Command in Korea and force the withdrawal of foreign forces under the UN flag.[140] North Korea made considerable progress toward this goal before making a fatal misstep. After more than a year of escalating tensions with threats, destruction of UN Command property, and gang assaults on UN Command guards, the North Koreans brutally hacked to death two US Army officers with axes on August 18, 1976. The grotesque murders backfired, alienating many nonaligned states and severely undermining the North Korean diplomatic position. Observers at the time concluded the North Koreans wanted a lethal overreaction from the United States that would substantiate North Korean allegations that the US presence in Korea was aggressive and likely to trigger a war. However, under Scowcroft's leadership the US response (contrary to Kissinger's recommendations[141]) was a restrained show of force that produced no North Korean casualties. The restraint apparently worked to the United States' advantage: "The pro-North Korea draft resolution was withdrawn on September 20, just before the UNGA [UN General Assembly] was convened, apparently because of North Korean expectations that its resolution would be rejected while the pro-South Korea resolution would be adopted."[142]

The United States continued to monitor Kim Il Sung's diplomatic and military moves closely throughout the following year. In January 1976 a top secret military assessment of North Korea produced for the NSC noted two trends that were consistent with Pyongyang's long-standing priorities. There had been an "across-the-board strengthening of military capabilities so as to enable the North Korean armed forces to implement a variety of military options with maximum effectiveness," and an effort to "maximize the capability to move rapidly, undetected, and in strength from forward positions in close proximity to the DMZ [demilitarized zone]." Nevertheless, the assessment concluded, "We see no evidence either in these military developments or in North Korea's political posture to suggest the imminence of an invasion or a major military probe."[143]

US leaders never assumed a North Korean invasion of the South was imminent. They hoped and eventually believed China had turned Kim down when he requested support for war and that it was unlikely the North Koreans would risk an armed conflict without Chinese support. Yet they knew North Korean leaders were drumming up support for war and that they would initiate a conflict if they could secure the requisite support and take advantage of American fatigue and disarray. In order to deter China and other countries from siding with North Korea, Kissinger and other US leaders wanted to signal that the United States was ready and fully determined to protect South Korea—regardless of public opinion and congressional restrictions. For all these reasons, it is not possible to fully appreciate what US leaders were trying to do and what they thought was at stake during the *Mayaguez* crisis without understanding their deep concern about possible North Korean aggression.

CHAPTER 7

Refining the Explanation | Rationality, Bureaucracy, and Beliefs

F oreign policy analysis arose from dissatisfaction with the assumption that states behave as unitary rational actors. Graham T. Allison's classic study on the Cuban missile crisis, *Essence of Decision*, makes this point.[1] The book "focuses principally on explanation" because, Allison says, we naturally want to know why the Soviet Union and the United States acted as they did.[2] "The logic of explanation," he argues, "requires singling out the relevant, critical determinants of the occurrence, the junctures at which particular factors produced one state of the world rather than another." However, Allison does not actually explain the missile crisis. He is straightforward about this, stating he did "not settle the matter of what happened and why." Instead, he tried to "uncover many new or previously underemphasized features, and afford a rich source of hypotheses about the causes of various outcomes."[3]

Ultimately, however, knowledge can only advance if scholars settle on best explanations for discrete cases so that, over time, comparative analysis can yield discernable behavior patterns. Given the imposing data requirements of most decision-making models, anything less is difficult to justify. The point is to simplify and clarify alternative explanations for behavior so that they can be compared with the best available empirical evidence to determine the best possible explanation for the state behavior in question. Self-consciously examining alternative explanations helps reduce subjectivity and increases confidence in the findings. It also makes it easier for researchers with additional empirical evidence to update results in a compelling manner. One luminary of foreign policy analysis labels this a "disciplined-configurative" case study approach and contrasts it with a "configurative-ideographic" case study approach.[4] The configurative-ideographic approach allows "facts to speak for themselves or bring out their significance by largely intuitive interpretation, claiming validity on the ground that intensive study and empathetic feel for cases provide authoritative insights into them."[5]

The argument here is that the configurative-ideographic approach has not served us well with respect to the *Mayaguez* crisis. Ole Holsti notes the danger of theoretically uninformed case studies is that they will add "levels of analysis" that result in an undisciplined proliferation of categories and variables. It may then become increasingly difficult to determine which are more or less important, and ad hoc explanations for individual cases erode the possibilities for broader generalizations across cases.[6]

This is what happened with scholarship on the *Mayaguez*. Multivariate descriptive accounts of the crisis, combined with ex post facto assertions from prominent leaders that their primary objective was the safe return of the crew, have encouraged numerous mischaracterizations of the crisis as a "rescue operation."[7] Assessing the behaviors of decision makers while assuming they were primarily interested in rescuing captives rather than signaling North Korea and other countries has led to false conclusions about decision-maker behaviors, including the assertions that their decision making was plagued by cognitive dissonance and wishful thinking.

If scholars researching the *Mayaguez* crisis had used a "disciplined-configurative" case study approach, they at least would have been obliged to consciously make an argument for the weight of the diverse explanatory variables they cited. However, too many researchers doing case studies of crisis decision making follow Allison's example rather than his advice. That is, they propound multiple competing hypotheses about what motivated behavior without making a case for which hypothesis is best supported by the available evidence. Raising multiple explanatory variables without making a case for the most compelling one muddies the explanatory waters.

Such confusion is unfortunate, weakening our understanding of specific cases like the *Mayaguez* and retarding the growth of cumulative knowledge in the field. It also is unnecessary—at least for the *Mayaguez* crisis. It is possible to imagine cases where multiple variables carry explanatory weight, and yet impossible to determine when and where they mattered. That is not true of the *Mayaguez* crisis. The evidence has long favored a singular explanation for US behavior that also distinguishes when secondary but reinforcing concerns (such as preventing a *Pueblo*-like humiliation) mattered and why plausible but ultimately false hypotheses with little to no explanatory weight do not (such as a desire to further Ford's political fortunes). The abundant new data on decision making during the crisis reinforces the basic explanation for US behavior.

Although the primary concern of US leaders in the *Mayaguez* crisis is now clear, its origins are not. At issue is whether the pursuit of a demonstrative use of force was something any leader occupying the White House would have embraced at that time (i.e., because they were driven by environmental circumstances), whether it was the product of bureaucratic struggle in the White House between influential leaders with different viewpoints, or whether it was because of some other factor. I considered such questions in

Belief Systems and Decision Making in the Mayaguez *Crisis* by comparing the explanatory adequacy of alternative decision-making models, namely the rational actor, bureaucratic politics, and belief systems models. Here we will revisit these models briefly and consider their relative utility in light of the new primary sources now available.

Rational Actor

The distinguishing characteristics of the rational actor model are the simplifying assumptions that the national state is a unitary actor making decisions in a manner that maximizes the chances of obtaining priority objectives.[8] Thus, a rational actor explanation for US behavior in the *Mayaguez* would be inadequate if the behavior could not be explained on the nation-state level of analysis or if the behavior was insufficiently rational by the model's criteria. Initially the *Mayaguez* crisis seems like an ideal candidate for a rational actor analysis because "the basic decision to respond with force was reached with unanimity, based on geopolitical rationale, and not marred by any major misperception concerning the nature of the circumstances surrounding the event."[9] But in a 1985 *Political Science Quarterly* article, I argued that a rational actor analysis of the crisis was insufficient, in part because the decision-making process was insufficiently rational.[10]

Decades ago a strong case could be made that key decision makers "were unable to see that some of the decisions they supported ran the heavy risk of working against, instead of toward, their objectives." According to this view, Kissinger wanted a convincing demonstration of American power but pushed for the use of force so aggressively that "he almost produced the antithesis of his affective concepts: an unmitigated military disaster." Similarly, Schlesinger wanted a strong, proportionate use of force but resisted airstrikes that proved to be "the impetus for the release of the crew and the margin of victory in any assessment of which side took the worst beating."[11] We now know from new materials and particularly the declassified NSC meeting minutes that these arguments are flawed.

In reality, Kissinger was more moderate than depicted by postcrisis news reports. He backed away from supporting the B-52 strikes, which he agreed might entail too high a political cost, and he was careful not to rush the military response at the risk of failure. He preferred "overwhelming power" precisely because failed operations would be disastrous for the impression he wanted to make. He argued that, "on balance," it was preferable "to get a more reliable force" and helped persuade Ford to accept a twenty-four-hour delay. He even acknowledged that another twenty-four-hour delay had military benefits but questioned whether it was necessary and if it sufficiently offset the political risks of a sudden diplomatic overture. He claimed he was not competent to judge the military necessity of further delay and called upon

Pentagon leaders to do so. With the full benefit of all Kissinger's comments in the NSC meetings he attended, it is no longer possible to assert that he was not sensitive to the risk of military failure.

Likewise, we now know Schlesinger did not resist all airstrikes and that he wanted strikes sufficient to demonstrate to Cambodia that it made a grave mistake in challenging the United States. He insisted on controlling and sequencing air attacks to the extent possible, but he was not against airstrikes per se. In the third NSC meeting, he recommended to Ford that "we sink the speedboats" that were remaining, just not the fishing boat with suspected Caucasians. After the fishing boat was allowed to proceed to the mainland, Schlesinger again told Ford, "I think we should destroy the boats that still remain at the island [i.e., the patrol boats]." Later in the meeting he supported sinking twenty-five Cambodian patrol boats at Ream Naval Base.

In the fourth NSC meeting Schlesinger argued there was value in the news media knowing US forces were massing and in discovering the use of B-52s was being debated because it reinforced perceptions that the United States was willing to punish Cambodia. He believed the United States would benefit from the perception that it was willing to use force but was also for exercising some restraint in the means actually employed. In that regard, he said the news media should be told about "selective" rather than a "few" airstrikes to emphasize the targets were carefully chosen. Schlesinger favored continuing airstrikes even after the Cambodian broadcast mentioning the release of the *Mayaguez*. He ordered the third wave to strike even though the crew was safely in US hands and even though he asked Ford whether the third wave should be diverted to help the Marines on Tang. He only canceled the fourth strike because of the unanimous conviction of his military subordinates that doing so was necessary to assist the Marines, and perhaps remembering that the president had agreed some planes from that strike group could peel off to assist the Marines. He also argued for delaying another twenty-four hours so that Tang Island could be attacked with more force (1,000 Marines), which would have substantially reduced the risks associated with the island assault. With all this being known, it is clear that Schlesinger did not underestimate the importance of ensuring Cambodia paid a high price for seizing the *Mayaguez*.

Decades ago, it was possible to argue that, collectively, the decision makers were so anxious to demonstrate US resolve that they unnecessarily rushed operations and almost precipitated a military disaster that would have diminished rather than enhanced US prestige.[12] However, it is difficult to make that case today given the details of the decision makers' extended discussion of the advantages and disadvantages of another twenty-four-hour delay (see the discussion on timing in chapter 6). There was not a rush to judgment but rather an extended discussion that led decision makers to underestimate military risks compared with the political risks of further delaying operations.

The military risks seemed lower because decision makers were assuming Tang Island was defended by one hundred Cambodian defenders and not double that number. All the service chiefs estimated the military risks of assaulting Tang as "acceptable" and advised the president that the military operations could be conducted with a high assurance of success. It must be said that the Joint Chiefs were proved correct. The combat operations actually cost fewer casualties than the estimated twenty to thirty killed, although it now seems nearly miraculous given the level of resistance encountered and the number of helicopters shot down.

The risks of waiting seemed high to decision makers because they feared developments might preclude the opportunity for a demonstrative use of force. At any time it might have been discovered that the entire crew was already on the mainland or had already been killed by the Cambodians or that some new political development like a diplomatic overture precluded the use of force. These were realistic concerns, as brutal Khmer behaviors[13] and the cable from Tehran reporting the imminent release of the crew demonstrate.

In sum, we now know key decision makers fully understood they could fail from using too much and too little force and debated the right force levels at length. It is quite possible to disagree with their risk assessments and priorities but no longer possible to argue they were insufficiently rational. More generally, and contrary to postcrisis leaks to the press that mischaracterized the debate in the NSC meetings as a donnybrook between Kissinger and Schlesinger, the NSC meetings were notable for the extended and candid debate about options for using force and its attendant risks.[14]

For example, in the first NSC meeting, and before it was known that the ship and crew could still be quarantined from the mainland, the NSC debated means of coercion, considering the relative merits of mining the harbors, seizing a harbor, quarantining a harbor, and capturing an island with lucrative oil deposits. Schlesinger argued, "If we mine the harbor, they will simply sit. We have got to do something that embarrasses them." Kissinger saw "a lot of advantage in taking the island rather than mining the port," but said it was important to know "how big a battle it would be and other relevant factors." When the subject turned again to mining the harbor, Schlesinger mused that it might be possible to "accomplish the same thing by quarantine as by mining." But Kissinger thought that would lead to "a confrontation and a crisis regarding every ship," and Schlesinger agreed that "we would have to be tough in such confrontations."

Much of the NSC meetings are devoted to that kind of give-and-take, exploring options and their relative merits. Thus, with the major exception that the president was increasingly angry about perceived Pentagon efforts to thwart his will, the NSC minutes demonstrate that Ford ran a wide-ranging and reasoned discussion of alternative courses of action and associated pros and cons. After the crisis when some media accounts were playing up the feud between Kissinger and Schlesinger,[15] the president's political advisors insisted the NSC meetings were marked by calm deliberation and were not a "bare-knuckle backroom brawl."[16] The detailed meeting minutes indicate they were correct.

There is a more fundamental reason the rational actor model proves insufficient, however. The model's assumption of a unitary actor precludes any understanding of the impact of individuals on the outcome of the crisis, which in the case of the *Mayaguez* crisis was profound. With almost any secretary of state other than Kissinger, diplomacy would have played a larger role. A decision in favor of issuing an ultimatum or taking the Tehran cable seriously—or at least sharing it with the NSC—or giving the UN time to play a role could easily have delayed military operations and perhaps stopped the assault on Tang Island. Similarly, it now seems clear that if Schlesinger had not insisted on strict rules of engagement for sinking the boats or had strictly followed Ford's orders, the *Mayaguez* crew would have been killed when the fishing boat was sunk in compliance with Ford's standing instructions. It is also possible that more aggressive enforcement of the quarantine might have prompted the Cambodians to retaliate by killing the crew and blaming it on US warplanes, which some evidence suggests they considered doing.[17] In short, the rational actor model would have perhaps explained the general preference for a forceful response but not the actual decisions that determined the crisis outcomes.

Bureaucratic Politics

Bureaucratic politics is a subset of decision-making research that attempts to explain foreign policy decisions by examining what takes place inside the "black box" of state behavior assumed by the rational actor model. The central proposition in decision-making analysis is that "to reconstruct how nations deal with each other, it is necessary to view the situation through the eyes of those who act in the name of the state: decision makers."[18] The distinguishing features of the bureaucratic politics model are politicized decision making and decision makers with bureaucratic predilections and motives. Rationality is limited by leaders pursuing their department's or agency's interests in competition with other elements of the government. A bureaucratic politics explanation for US behavior in the *Mayaguez* crisis fails if the decision makers do not engage in bargaining, coalition building, and maneuvering for their own ends that affect outcomes, or if their objectives do not reflect their bureaucratic positions.

My 1985 article argued a bureaucratic politics explanation illuminates the differences between Kissinger and Schlesinger and the lengths to which they went to secure their preferred outcomes but not their respective policy preferences, which could not have been predicted from their department's institutional interests. Both points still hold, but the first point requires emphasis. With the new information available today it is especially apparent that the outcome of the crisis cannot be understood apart from the interventions of both men and their interaction.

Schlesinger and Kissinger fought an ongoing battle for influence inside the Ford White House that affected the outcome of the crisis. Kissinger withheld information from the NSC, slow rolled diplomatic efforts, and used his proximity and influence with Ford to engineer a demonstrative; disproportionate; and, with respect to the lives of the crew and mainland Cambodians, indiscriminate use of force that he thought would enhance the US reputation for use of power. Schlesinger used leaks to the press and control over military operations, even to the point of being insubordinate, to prevent what he thought would be a grossly disproportionate and indiscriminate use of force that would harm US prestige. Kissinger, backed by Ford, pushed back by demanding direct access to the NMCC for more timely information and to bypass Schlesinger with direct orders when necessary. Schlesinger and his Pentagon subordinates saved the *Mayaguez* crew by refusing to implement the blanket order to destroy boats leaving Tang and also likely saved some military personnel by reducing the number of airstrikes on the mainland. These actions also deflected more severe criticism of Ford's handling of the crisis.[19]

Although the conflict between Kissinger and Schlesinger was reported even while the crisis was underway, the precise extent of their differences and how they influenced the outcome of the crisis is now much better understood. For example, their differences over the blanket order to sink Cambodian boats had a greater impact on outcomes than their differences over bombing. Also, it is now more evident that the differences between Schlesinger and Kissinger actually became a broader struggle between Schlesinger and the Ford White House, including Ford, Kissinger, and to a lesser extent Scowcroft[20] and others.[21]

Kissinger was quite candid about his deteriorating relationship with Schlesinger in his memoirs. He discussed his policy differences with the defense secretary and noted they were substantive, not personal. "However justified Schlesinger's grievances were initially," Kissinger commented,

> he let them run out of proportion. He resented my close relationship with Ford and mistakenly saw me as the principal obstacle to comparable intimacy with the President. What had started out as a perhaps legitimate grievance turned

step by step into a systematic effort to reduce my influence. Whether the issue was Cyprus or arms control, supplies for Israel during the Middle East war, the Mayaguez crisis or East-West relations, Schlesinger behaved as if he were the leader of the opposition to me in a parliamentary system.[22]

Over time these substantive differences between Schlesinger and Kissinger morphed into a larger problem between Schlesinger and the White House that reduced Schlesinger's credibility and influence. By the time the *Mayaguez* crisis took place, there was already a track record of White House suspicion about the Pentagon's reliability under Schlesinger's leadership (see sidebar).

The Kissinger-Schlesinger Feud

Even before becoming president, Ford expressed his fondness for Kissinger[23] and his dislike of Schlesinger. His first act as president was to ask Kissinger to stay on, promising he would work to get along with him.[24] Ford respected Kissinger's acumen and experience and also appreciated his self-deprecating humor and respectful cooperation.[25] With Schlesinger, it was far different.[26]

While still vice president, Ford speculated he would keep Kissinger and cashier Schlesinger if he became president.[27] As Ford indicated in his memoirs, and many others have corroborated, Schlesinger's aloof and condescending manner irritated Ford.[28] Substantively, prior to assuming the presidency, Ford objected to Schlesinger's handling of congressional relations[29] and, over time, to other aspects of his performance:

> Within a week of inauguration, Ford heard that Schlesinger was taking credit for instructing the JCS to check with him on any orders from the White House during the presidential transition. The implication that Schlesinger wanted to preclude President Nixon from attempting some semblance of a military coup greatly upset Ford, who considered the move a slur against the uniformed military leaders and "an attack on the authority of the commander-in-chief."[30] Ford apparently never discovered that it was his own advisors (Philip Buchen and Clay T. Whitehead) who asked Schlesinger to be on guard against the possibility that Nixon might refuse to leave office and "call on the military to bail him out."[31]

Some of Schlesinger's communication problem with Ford was the president's own doing. Early on Kissinger obtained Ford's signature on a memo from Ford to Schlesinger specifying that the secretary of defense had to communicate to the president through Kissinger on anything of policy import and through military assistants on any other matters.[32] So, in addition to Kissinger's proximity to Ford in the White House, he also managed to insert himself between the president and his defense secretary. Kissinger also cultivated the sympathies of the number two person at the Defense Department, which did not work to Schlesinger's advantage. For example, the White House used Deputy Secretary of Defense Clements to investigate the flap about potential military loyalties during Nixon's transition and also to summon Admiral Holloway as White House doubts arose about General Jones's performance during the *Mayaguez* crisis.[33]

Schlesinger tried to counter Kissinger. He tried to get Clements fired, which did not enhance his reputation with Ford.[34] He also used White House restrictions on reporting channels to tighten his own control over the Department of Defense. When notifying all senior defense officials about White House instructions, Schlesinger instituted his own reporting rules—only he, Clements, or Wickham could communicate with the White House on national security or defense policy.[35] Schlesinger also used leaks to the press to get his point of view heard, mostly through his public affairs spokesman, Joseph Laitin, which often irritated the White House (including repeatedly during the *Mayaguez* crisis). Kissinger countered by keeping Ford informed about Schlesinger's leaks, describing them on one occasion as "very damaging" and making "it look like you—or usually I—are not doing our own jobs just right." The president was furious.[36]

Tensions between Kissinger and Schlesinger reached new heights during the excruciating withdrawal from Southeast Asia, an extended crisis that culminated the month prior to the *Mayaguez* crisis.[37] There was friction over the timing of the evacuation, over Scowcroft directly ordering military forces to move, and how the situation was represented to Congress, all of which frayed relations between the Pentagon and White House.[38] Kissinger explained the issues to Ford in a manner that was unflattering to Schlesinger.[39]

Kissinger ascribed underhanded political motives to Schlesinger and his department, saying, "C-141 transports were leaving Saigon each day with well documented empty seats to prove that, if there were any casualties, it would be someone else's fault—Ambassador [Graham A.] Martin's or mine."[40] With Kissinger controlling most communications to Ford on the matter, Ford not surprisingly came to believe Schlesinger was being insubordinate. In his memoirs Ford said he "later found out that many of those planes that I thought were being loaded were flown out empty" and "according to my sources, that order came from Schlesinger."[41]

Schlesinger believed the Department of State did not appreciate the urgency of evacuating refugees and Americans. On April 1 he told Ford that South Vietnam had sixty to ninety days at most before collapsing. The country fell before the month ended.[42] Schlesinger wanted Ford to order Martin "to remove Americans who may be in the line of advance."[43] Kissinger's own head of intelligence at State, William Hyland, said Martin's delays endangered both the American and Vietnamese lives Ford wanted to save. Hyland describes the Pentagon's airlift operations as a "triumph for the United States," but Ford thought otherwise and resented Schlesinger because of it.[44] Thus, going into the *Mayaguez* crisis, Ford's confidence in Schlesinger was already compromised.

White House suspicion of Schlesinger deepened as Scowcroft and Ford received what they considered untimely and inaccurate information from the Pentagon at the beginning of the *Mayaguez* crisis.[45] In the second NSC meeting Ford expressed irritation about late and inaccurate information from the Defense Department, asking do "you have people on the ball in the Pentagon?" "Quite a few," Jones responded. But Ford did not back off, demanding to know how information was flowing to "Brent [Scowcroft] and then to me." Scowcroft piled on, complaining about time lags and inaccuracy of the information provided. Ford then insisted on receiving information immediately, saying, "There must be the quickest possible communication to me."

Ford's frustration with Schlesinger grew along with his suspicion—correct as it turned out—that the Pentagon was not following his orders about sinking Cambodian boats. In the third NSC meeting, Ford raised the issue of insubordination. After Kissinger complained that the NSC was in the position of "debating with the pilot," Ford noted that should not be the case since "I gave the order at the meeting to stop all boats. I cannot understand what happened on that order, because I heard that it did not go out until 3:30." Schlesinger had to insist to the president that his sources were wrong:

> **Schlesinger:** It went out by telephone within half an hour after you gave it.
> **Jones:** We talked to Burns, the Commander out there, immediately. The confirming order went out later. But our communications are so good that we can get all the information back here immediately to Washington in order to make the decisions from here.
> **Ford:** Was the order given, and at what time, not to permit any boats to leave the island or come into it? I was told it was not given until 3:30. That is inexcusable.
> **Jones:** That was the written order, not the verbal order.
> **Ford:** Let's find out when it was given.
> **Clements:** To assist General Jones, I was with him in the Situation Room when he gave the order even before he left the White House.
> **Ford:** Let's find out what happened. It is inexcusable to have such a delay.[46]

This exchange reveals an extraordinary lack of trust on Ford's part. He was convinced his orders were being ignored and he was angry about it, as he later told Kissinger and Scowcroft during one of their Oval Office exchanges between the third and fourth NSC meetings. While encouraging Ford to be ferocious, Kissinger also encouraged his suspicions about Schlesinger and Pentagon foot-dragging:

> **Kissinger:** I think you will have to be clear you want a strong effort. I think you should take out the port. The airfields aren't so significant. You will take as much heat for a big strike as for a small strike.
> **President:** As I recall, I asked Jones to come up with targets, planes, and strike plans.
> **Kissinger:** But I have the sense the McNamara syndrome is so important that they will not be so ferocious. It may be the B-52 strike is too much. The *Coral Sea* may be better if they do it with vigor. It depends on the pilot's instructions. I think Gayler is disastrous—McCain wouldn't give us these problems. A pep talk by you to the Chairman in front of his DOD [Department of Defense] superiors will help get what we need. Using B-52's may be paying too much of a price.

President: We won't have carrier strikes unless they can convince me they are meaningful.

Ford went on to say he was "disturbed at the lack of carrying out orders. I can give all the orders, but if they don't carry them out. . . . I was mad yesterday." Continuing, he said again that he would make it known that he favored the B-52s "unless they can show they can do as much with tacair," which Kissinger thought was "a good way to get at the problem."[47]

In the fourth NSC meeting Ford again expresses his distrust of the Pentagon. He was surprised that the USS *Holt* was not immediately positioned between the island and the mainland to interdict boat traffic. He said he was "amazed at this" and that he could not understand why the *Holt* was rushed to the scene if it was not to be used for interdiction. Jones said the Pentagon "did not want to tip our hand to the operation" and added that he did not recall any specific instructions to use the *Holt* for interdiction. As the crisis progressed, Kissinger weighed in with Ford to keep the airstrikes going against the mainland, trumping Schlesinger's recommendation that the *Coral Sea* aircraft be used to help extricate the Marines.

Schlesinger fought back, leaking Kissinger's role to the press. In contrast to Kissinger, who clamped down on State's public affairs office to assist White House image makers who wanted to underscore Ford's management of the crisis, Schlesinger's spokesman fed the press information. One such leak quickly caught Kissinger's attention. Fred S. Hoffman of the Associated Press reported that while "Secretary of State Henry A. Kissinger favored tougher action," Defense Secretary "Schlesinger was concerned about a possible overreaction." Other news outlets reported the same theme with variations. The *Albuquerque Journal* said that "Kissinger wanted a quick and punishing strike even if the crew was put in danger" but "the defense chief advised caution for fear of over-reacting."[48] Kissinger saw the Associated Press report and called Schlesinger to complain just before 1 a.m. on the fifteenth. Schlesinger appeared ignorant of the news report, so Kissinger summarized the contents, telling Schlesinger "you and I differed throughout this" and that "you were for moderation and I was not." Schlesinger changed the topic to the Department of State panic over Thai reactions to the US use of force, but Kissinger quickly returned to the purpose of his call. He emphasized the management of the crisis "was the best cooperation," that he felt very good about it, and he encouraged Schlesinger to take the same line, trying to convince him that it was in the country's interest for them to present a united front to the press and the world.[49]

The next day, during a fifth NSC meeting where the results of the *Mayaguez* crisis were reviewed, Kissinger had an opportunity to stoke the president's suspicions about

Schlesinger. In describing military operations, and airstrikes in particular, Jones told Ford:

> There were four waves. The first was armed reconnaissance. They did not expend ordnance. They found the shipping of other countries and did not want to take the risk. The three subsequent waves went against the airport, against the POL facilities, and against support facilities.[50]

Apparently Jones was not aware the fourth wave was cancelled by Schlesinger based on the advice of Brown and others. Kissinger says he saw Ford's face reddening as Jones provided his explanation, but the conversation did not prompt Ford to articulate any concerns. The conversation carried on as Jones explained the operations against Tang Island. But then Kissinger returned to the airstrikes, asking "how many aircraft were used altogether." Jones mentioned thirty-two to forty. Schlesinger then stimulated the president's ire by adding "not the 81 that had been on the carrier."[51]

Either Schlesinger was so absorbed with his understanding of the value of limited force that he was unaware that he was on thin ice with Ford, or he was bluntly asserting his prerogative to manage the details of military operations to the president.[52] If so, Ford recognized the challenge. Kissinger recalls that "when it became clear that the *Coral Sea* had made far from the maximum effort he had ordered, Ford interrupted the meeting and invited me to step out of the Cabinet Room with him for a moment. He asked me to summarize my understanding of the orders he had given."[53] Kissinger did so in a brief conversation that lasted less than three minutes, failing to mention that he had asked the Pentagon to put the first attack on hold while Ford considered the Cambodian broadcast. Ford "returned to the NSC meeting without another word" and "coldly" told Schlesinger, "Jim, I would like a full factual report giving a summary and chronology of what happened. It should include orders, summary results, photographs, etc., and indications of what we did when."[54]

The next day, May 16, Ford was still fuming when he again discussed the issue with Kissinger and Scowcroft, both of whom pointed the finger of blame at Schlesinger:

> **Ford:** My recollection is I told Holloway to continue the strikes until I said to stop.
> **Scowcroft:** That is my recollection. And you told Schlesinger.
> **Ford:** I want a detailed summary of the orders which went out and any changes which were made. I want an assessment of the operation—including the time sequence of takeoffs and what happened.
> **Kissinger:** You should ask for all the orders that were issued from the beginning of the operation.
> **Ford:** That should include the orders from the Pentagon to CINCPAC [commander

in chief, Pacific Command] and from there to commanders on the scene. I want the DOD submission compared with the orders issued in the NSC.

Kissinger: I think Schlesinger, when he heard the Congressional attitudes, changed the orders.[55]

Ford responded to Kissinger's blunt charge of insubordination[56] by saying the orders might have been changed by CINCPAC (i.e., Admiral Gayler). Kissinger was not dissuaded, stating that "the whole operation was conducted not as a military operation but in order to demagogue before the Congress." Returning to the need to investigate Pentagon compliance, the president said, "It seems to me that what happens in the Situation Room is being bypassed by what goes on in the NMCC."[57]

The memorandum directing the investigation was prepared for Ford, and he signed it and provided it to Schlesinger on May 18, giving the defense secretary forty-eight hours to provide "a detailed and comprehensive chronological exposition of events and activities" and "a copy of each order, verbal or written, which was issued directing military plans and operations." He gave Schlesinger until the end of the week to make "any observations or suggestions which you consider would contribute to improvement in the ability of the National Security Council machinery to deal effectively with crisis situations." He also told Schlesinger to conduct the review on a "very close hold basis."[58]

Schlesinger's staff saw the investigation as an opportunity to raise the issue of the reporting chain and to complain about the multiple direct White House orders issued to the NMCC, including those from Major McFarlane.[59] Schlesinger decided against that, perhaps because, as he suggested to reporters the day after the crisis, he did "not believe there will be many inclined to persistently argue with what has been a laudable and successful operation."[60] He was wrong about that insofar as Ford was concerned. Ford remained furious over the insubordination he suspected in the case of the cancelled fourth airstrike and was determined to get to the bottom of it.

When the Department of Defense report arrived at the NSC, McFarlane analyzed it for the NSC staff. Then, reporting his findings, McFarlane said in a memo to Scowcroft that it appeared an honest effort had been made to comply with the president's request for an investigation but that the information raised many questions. What most impressed McFarlane, a Marine, were the "serious deficiencies in the planning and execution of the fire support plan" for the Marines. However, he also noted "breakdowns in command and control over mainland air strikes." He observed the "temporary suspension of the first wave" resulted in a halt to all strikes by General Brown. Orders to turn it back on were issued, but he says that, "mysteriously," "no ordnance was delivered by the first wave."[61] He made no mention of the fourth wave, which is the one that really upset the president, but questioned the small number of aircraft sent in each wave and the long separation between the launch of the first and second wave.[62]

Ford said the Pentagon response to his inquiry into the cancellation of the fourth strike was "not satisfactory" and that he never resolved the issue, deciding to "let the matter drop" because the operation had been successful. Yet Ford still held Schlesinger accountable, and a few months later he fired Schlesinger. Ford had multiple reasons for letting Schlesinger go, but a primary and perhaps decisive reason was Schlesinger's insubordination during the *Mayaguez* crisis.[63] Kissinger seems to agree, noting in his memoirs that "although no heads rolled then, Ford never recovered confidence in his Secretary of Defense."[64] Certainly Ford always associated Schlesinger with contravening his orders for the fourth airstrike. Years later the incident loomed large in his explanation as to why he dismissed Schlesinger. He said that he had ordered mainland strikes and "after one strike, [Schlesinger] terminated them without getting further orders from me. It was a deliberate case as I understand it, of not carrying out the order of the commander in chief. I don't know why."[65] For his part, Schlesinger was angry about his dismissal, no doubt believing he had served Ford better than Ford understood.[66]

The extent to which Kissinger and Schlesinger struggled to implement their preferred approach to their shared objectives is more evident now and certainly accords with behaviors predicted by the bureaucratic politics model.[67] However, it remains the case that their respective policy positions could not have been predicted from their department's institutional interests—which is a common complaint about the bureaucratic politics model that has been discussed at length previously.[68] But for a quick reprise, the behavior of the secretary of defense in the *Mayaguez* crisis and the Joint Chiefs contradicted the assumption of the leading advocate of the bureaucratic politics model that the military prefers a minimum of restraint if called upon to use force. A case can be made that Schlesinger's preferences were generally consistent with historic military ethos that emphasize proportional and discriminate use of force, but they were not identical.

Schlesinger favored a punitive response; he just did not want it on the scale that Kissinger and others recommended because he feared a counterproductive political backlash. He also wanted the punishment sequenced in a way he believed would be more likely to coerce the release of the crew, after which the punitive destruction of Cambodian naval assets could take place. Schlesinger refereed a difference of opinion between the Air Force and the Navy over the use of B-52s at the front end of the crisis, ensuring that debate ended consistent with his preferences. He also opposed turning off mainland strikes after learning of the Cambodian broadcast, whereas his subordinates canceled all strikes until the situation was clarified.

Schlesinger took advice from his subordinates, but he never acted inconsistently with his own beliefs and objectives. He crafted the original rules of engagement that ensured careful vetting of boats before lethal force was used, and when those rules led to a question about attacking the fishing boat with the crew members, he argued against indiscriminate use of force that would have collapsed any public support for the military operations. When Generals Wickham and Pauly took the initiative to stonewall the White House on sinking boats suspected of carrying *Mayaguez* crew, Schlesinger backed them up and later even assumed responsibility for the decision, claiming the behavior as his own. Schlesinger accepted the chairman of the Joint Chiefs' recommendation to focus on extracting the Marines without further casualties after the third wave bombed the mainland and to divert (in effect, cancel) the fourth wave for the same reason, but those decisions were consistent with his own preferences as his telephone conversations with Ford reveal.[69]

The nation's chief diplomat more assertively defied his department's institutional interests. Kissinger argued for and helped engineer a strong and quick military action and assisted this course of action by foregoing diplomatic opportunities. In sum, it still holds true that the belief systems of key decision makers had "more influence on their respective bureaucracies than vice versa," and that in the secretary of state's case, "the State Department operated as a virtual appendage of Kissinger's belief system."[70] Thus, the *Mayaguez* crisis substantiates previous research that concluded "the bureaucratic politics paradigm is useful in crisis studies mainly for its account of the bargaining process" rather than for an "explanation of why people's attitudes differ."[71]

Belief Systems

Belief systems analysis is also a subset of decision making research. Like bureaucratic politics, it acknowledges senior leaders compete to promote their own agendas. However, it ascribes the origins of senior leader preferences to their belief systems rather than the interests of the organizations they lead. Belief systems are "the set of lenses through which information concerning the physical and social environment is received," which "orients the individual to his environment, defining it for him and identifying for him its salient characteristics."[72] Belief system analysis tends to focus on the most senior leaders and often the titular leader in particular: presidents, prime ministers, and other heads of state.[73] A body of belief system research has focused on crisis decision making because crises accentuate the role of the most senior leaders "making cognitive theories potentially more relevant,"[74] as proved true during the *Mayaguez* crisis. A belief system explanation for US behavior would prove inadequate if the decision makers' behaviors did not reflect their established belief systems, or if their beliefs were the same that any decision maker in similar circumstances would have held—which would suggest the decisions were driven by environmental factors.

My 1985 article argued that "the general desire to use force was perfectly predictable from common knowledge of key decision makers' belief systems" and that senior leaders with different belief systems "would have reacted to the seizure of the *Mayaguez* differently."[75] The divisive Vietnam War reinforced a schism in the belief systems of senior American foreign policy experts. Those who supported the war believed the Vietnam experience validated the assumption that one country falling to Communism made it much more likely its neighbors would fall as well (the so-called domino theory) and underscored the necessity of honoring alliance commitments.[76] In contrast, critics of the war effort believed Vietnam illustrated the need to scale down the United States' international role and cooperate more with the UN. Thus, if the latter group had occupied the White House in May 1975, the *Mayaguez* crisis would have been managed differently. This assertion was further substantiated by comparing key leader beliefs in similar crises, particularly the *Pueblo* and Iranian hostage crises, where US leaders with different beliefs decided against the use of force.[77]

Declassified documents support these claims. On the day the *Mayaguez* was seized, Kissinger forwarded a memorandum on the "Lessons of Vietnam" to Ford that argued

> we need to shore up our positions elsewhere once our position in Vietnam is lost. We may be compelled to support other situations much more strongly in order to repair the damage and to take tougher stands in order to make others believe in us again.[78]

Similarly, after the crisis, Kissinger recommended that Ford exploit the results to reinforce perceptions of American resolve. When preparing Ford for his meeting with the shah of Iran the day after the crisis, Kissinger recommended that Ford "tell [the shah] you used more force than necessary." Ford did so, telling the shah that "we perhaps overreacted, to show the Koreans and others our resolve," adding the American response "showed the world we weren't hamstrung."[79]

These declassified documents and conversations demonstrate that the decision makers made the same points privately that they did publicly,[80] albeit with less reserve. As noted in the introductory chapter, Ford, Kissinger, and Schlesinger repeatedly went on public record explaining their concerns in the months leading up to the *Mayaguez* incident. They emphasized the deleterious consequences of the Communist victories in Cambodia and Vietnam, which ended thirty years of determined efforts by both

Republican and Democratic presidents to keep Indochina noncommunist. They appealed repeatedly to Congress for enough aid to forestall the demise of the two countries and argued their fall would precipitate a crisis in the credibility of US security guarantees. As a congressman, Ford habitually supported the use of American military force in Indochina, including bombing,[81] and said he believed the domino theory was essentially correct. After Southeast Asia fell and US forces were evacuated, Ford was "damned mad" about his countrymen's refusal to graciously accept the resultant flood of refugees. He said he was concerned about the further expansion of Communism and international perceptions of US weakness. Concerned about perceptions of US weakness, Ford was quoted prior to the *Mayaguez* crisis as saying "I have to show some strength in order to help us . . . with our credibility in the world."[82]

Kissinger was even more emphatic about the validity of the domino theory in terms of the impact on US credibility. He said, "I know it is fashionable to sneer at the word domino theory [yet] letting Vietnam and Cambodia go down the tube would have serious consequences in terms of our credibility." He believed the Southeast Asian debacle would inevitably lead other nations to test the will of the United States. When asked by a reporter if $150 billon and 55,000 American lives had not proved America's will and credibility, Kissinger's response was that past sacrifice notwithstanding, Indochina was dependent on US aid and if the aid was not forthcoming the United States would be held accountable. Kissinger so consistently reiterated warnings of an impending credibility crisis that he was asked during an interview on April 12 whether his harping on the topic made it a self-fulfilling prophecy. "No," he replied, arguing the problem would not go away by ignoring it. After the fall of Vietnam, Kissinger told reporters off the record that "the United States must carry out some act somewhere in the world which shows its determination to continue to be a world power."[83] During the crisis, he explained the stakes to his audience in Missouri: "Given our central role, a loss in our credibility invites chaos."[84]

Scowcroft, one of only three men privy to foreign policy formulation in the White House, was also judged a key leader during the crisis. Like Kissinger, he believed the domino theory was valid in terms of its effects on confidence and credibility, even if his subordinate role precluded making public statements to that effect at the time. Inside the White House he was regarded as Kissinger's alter ego by Ford and others because the two men worked so closely together and were the only two who briefed Ford daily on national security issues. Scowcroft later explained, "We worked so well together because we had similar outlooks and because we in fact knew what the other would have thought, would have done, in a particular circumstance. So while we had a few very sharp disagreements, there were rarely disagreements of philosophy." At the time of the *Mayaguez* crisis, he too believed it was essential to "project an air of strength and confidence and decisiveness to our friends; that they could still rely on the United States."[85] Scowcroft also shared Kissinger's preference for erring on the side of too much rather than too little force, supporting the B-52 strikes.

Like Ford and Kissinger, Secretary Schlesinger proclaimed the domino theory "overly discredited" and predicted the fall of Cambodia and Vietnam could be disastrous for US credibility. Schlesinger joined Ford and Kissinger in pushing a recalcitrant Congress to provide funds for Cambodia and South Vietnam, even evoking the onus of national disgrace: "Other great powers in history have earned the term perfidious because of their desertion of their allies, and I would hate to see the United States earn that particular reputation." He bluntly said it was important that the fall of Indochina "clearly be marked as the result of the ineptitude of the [Cambodian and South Vietnamese] governments rather than due to a cutoff of American aid," and he joined Ford and Kissinger in pressuring Congress to provide funds to forestall defeat.[86]

In sum, all four decision makers shared some similar, salient beliefs about their extant international environment. They believed a growing perception of US impotence was threatening and inimical to US interests. They expected a test of American security guarantees, most likely from North Korea, which served as a common focal point for the decision makers' acute angst about declining American credibility. Their concerns, expressed publicly and privately, were so evident that Lee Kuan Yew, Singapore's prime minister who was visiting the White House a week before the *Mayaguez* was seized, came away with a clear impression of the US leadership's frame of mind, saying that "they are looking for a crisis."[87]

Belief systems researchers sometime label such beliefs about behaviors in the international system as "cognitive concepts," which in the *Mayaguez* crisis drove the decision makers "affective concepts," that is, their perceived interests and objectives. Another category of beliefs are the actor's perceptions about the options available for a decision, which can be referred to as "procedural concepts."[88] In the *Mayaguez* crisis most of the key decision makers had some particular and less visible beliefs that were not evident from their public statements prior to the crisis. These concerns manifested themselves forcefully during the crisis but could only be reconstructed in retrospect after examining crisis behaviors.

Kissinger, for example, had specific views on the use of military force in crises. By 1975 he was already a veteran of several such crises and had reached some conclusions about the use of force. He believed it was better to use too much rather than too little force, and to use it quickly before the opportunity to do so was lost. He was particularly chagrined at the US performance during the EC-121 crisis. He mentioned the lessons he drew from this incident in his memoirs but also to Ford during the *Mayaguez* crisis. He thought it demonstrated that

> a leisurely process of decision-making creates a presumption in favor of eventual inaction. . . . In a crisis boldness is the safest course. Hesitation encourages the adversary to persevere, maybe even raise the ante. . . . Overall, I judge our conduct in the EC-121 crisis as weak, indecisive and disorganized. . . . I believe we paid for it in many intangible ways, in demoralized friends and emboldened adversaries.[89]

In addition to moving quickly, Kissinger believed Vietnam demonstrated the need to use more rather than less force:

> The bane of our military actions in Vietnam was their hesitancy; we were always trying to calculate with fine precision the absolute minimum of force. . . . Perhaps the most difficult lesson for a national leader to learn is that with respect to the use of military force, his basic choice is to act or to refrain from acting. He will not be able to take away the moral curse of using force by employing it halfheartedly or incompetently. There are no rewards for exhibiting one's doubts in vacillation; statesmen get no prizes for failing with restraint. Once committed they must prevail.[90]

With the benefit of declassified NSC meeting minutes and conversations between Kissinger and the president, it is now clear that the secretary's behavior perfectly reflected these beliefs. His concern that indecision and weakness led to demoralized friends and emboldened adversaries weighed heavily on Kissinger in the *Mayaguez* crisis, and his belief that power must be committed decisively or not at all reflected his advice to the president during the crisis. Believing American prestige was fast approaching a nadir, the last thing Kissinger wanted was an emboldened North Korea or another American military failure due to halfhearted use of force.

Schlesinger shared Kissinger's concern about American credibility but not his predilection for rapid and overpowering military force. The Vietnam experience inclined him to believe disproportionate and indiscriminate use of force would tarnish US prestige and elicit a political backlash. After the crisis was over he underscored his preference for a proportional and discriminate use of military force by saying US military operations were a "very prudent use of force" that constituted a "firm and measured response to the highhanded and crude use of force" and one that compared favorably with the period before he became secretary of defense "when we were running a thousand, approximately, B-52 sorties a month and several thousand tactical air sorties."[91]

The only belief that seemed to weigh particularly heavy with Scowcroft was the *Pueblo* analogy. Kissinger never mentioned the *Pueblo* incident and was more impressed by the parallels with the EC-121 crisis. In NSC deliberations Schlesinger emphasized the Cambodians already had the crew and could kill them at will, so preventing another *Pueblo*-type incident was a moot issue from his point of view. Later he said he hardly remembered any discussion of the *Pueblo* and that it had not influenced his own thinking. Scowcroft, however, was very aware of the *Pueblo* analogy and was anxious to prevent its repetition by blocking the movement of the ship and crew to the mainland. He thought the *Pueblo* very naturally came to mind and, although he did not know if it was a stronger preoccupation on his part than anyone else's, said, "I know I felt very strongly about it."[92] Following the crisis Scowcroft repeatedly explained the decision making by referring to the desire to prevent a recurrence of the *Pueblo* incident.[93]

Perhaps befitting a new president leaning on the advice of his national security experts, none of Ford's discernible beliefs differed substantially from his subordinates' views, or more specifically, from Kissinger's and Scowcroft's. His growing conviction before and especially during the crisis that he could not trust the Pentagon under Schlesinger to execute his orders fully and with alacrity inclined the White House to monitor operations more closely and open direct channels to the NMCC. However, this degree of intense oversight had no discernible impact on outcomes. Concern about Pentagon compliance led to the late-night third NSC meeting, during which Ford made the decision to let the fishing boat proceed to the mainland. This was Schlesinger's recommendation, which Kissinger eventually seconded, and which Ford finally accepted. If the meeting had not taken place, Schlesinger would have been free to pursue his preferences, and the outcome likely would have been the same. One might argue that intense White House supervision inclined the Pentagon to comply with White House preferences for hasty operations, but the NSC minutes belie this interpretation. There was obvious White House interest in moving before the opportunity for military operations was lost, but no one wanted a military failure. The reason operations were not postponed an additional twenty-four hours, as Schlesinger and Jones personally preferred, is that the USS *Hancock* was further delayed and because the Joint Chiefs favored taking action. So, Jones faithfully passed along their collective recommendation and assurance that the operations had a high chance of success.

It is possible that if Ford had trusted Schlesinger more than he trusted Kissinger, he might have accepted some of his recommendations on the ultimatum or operational delays, and doing so could have dramatically changed outcomes. But there was no chance of such a development going into the crisis, and his distrust of Schlesinger intensified during the crisis. The only outcome that might have been changed by a lessening of Ford's anger was Schlesinger being fired. If Schlesinger had better communicated the reason for the cancellation of the fourth strike, and perhaps reminded the president that he said the strike could be divided between attacking the mainland and assisting the Marines, it might have mollified the president. However, even that is doubtful since Ford was correct in his understanding that the Pentagon was choosing not to automatically sink boats as he ordered.[94] Thus, Ford's suspicions about Schlesinger and the Pentagon—which were correct to some extent, if not in all particulars— doomed Schlesinger as secretary of defense but otherwise had no impact on crisis outcomes.

The correlation between precrisis beliefs and crisis behavior was compelling, particularly for Secretary Kissinger. He predicted the United States was going to be tested in an international crisis, probably by the North Koreans. He feared America would lack the will to respond. When he heard the news of the *Mayaguez*'s seizure, he moved quickly to convince Ford of the situation's seriousness and argued forcefully in the first NSC meeting for a demonstrative military response. In Kansas City he publicly predicted a quick and firm American reaction, which is what happened. He stifled a plan to give the Cambodians a deadline that might have complicated military operations, and he argued repeatedly for using more rather than less force. His diplomatic communications were threats of retaliation, and his appeals to the UN were delayed until they could not affect military operations. Direct communications with the Cambodians were ignored in favor of using the slower and less-effective international news media, and he chose not to share with the NSC the news that the Chinese expected the crew to be released soon. He constantly briefed and guided the president, twice encouraging him to launch additional airstrikes even though the crew had been safely returned. Kissinger prevented a repeat of what he considered an inept handling of the EC-121 crisis, and he was ecstatic with the results. Not only had he signaled American determination to a doubting world and a belligerent North Korea, he also reaped the unexpected bonus of the safe recovery of the crew, which precipitated a significant but short-lived boost in Ford's popularity and the attendant perception that America could and would still use force to protect its interests.

Schlesinger's behavior also consistently reflected his belief system. He favored making an example out of Cambodia but wanted a proportionate and discriminate military response that was managed to minimize any military blunders, including unacceptable collateral damage—particularly to the *Mayaguez* crew. He wanted to concentrate on Tang Island, where he preferred delaying and using more force, and on Cambodian naval assets, which he wanted attacked with great care. He wanted to avoid disproportionate airstrikes on the mainland and particularly the use of B-52s, thinking they would constitute overkill and foster an image of a blundering America lashing out indiscriminately. Although he lacked Kissinger's access and influence with the president, he had the advantage of controlling the details of military operations. His behaviors—both his advice to the president and his orders to his subordinates—closely reflected his beliefs, even to the point of insubordination. He ensured decisions to sink each Cambodian naval asset were made in Washington, and he disregarded orders to the contrary from the White House. He argued repeatedly against B-52s, for delaying military operations, and against taking undue risk with the lives of the crew. He did his best to ensure mainland attacks were limited and discriminate, and he ignored Ford's order for a final strike against the mainland when it became clear it could only be conducted by accepting greater risk to the Marines.

Scowcroft shared Kissinger's reluctance to take chances on calculating "with fine precision the absolute minimum of force." He generally supported more rather than less force, including B-52 strikes. On other issues, such as the ultimatum or timing of military operations, he agreed with Kissinger or remained silent. Scowcroft rarely spoke in the NSC meetings, and when he did, it was only to provide factual information. However, during the second NSC meeting, with Kissinger absent in Kansas City, he made one of his rare remarks in response to a direct request by Ford for his views, and it revealed his preoccupation with preventing the crew from reaching the mainland. He told Ford two military operations were needed, the first against the ship to "stop it from going to Kompong Som," and the second against the island to "stop the Americans from going to the mainland."

It is evident from the third NSC meeting minutes that Kissinger and Scowcroft agreed on the need to isolate the crew from the mainland. However, Scowcroft personally considered it imperative to prevent a recurrence of the *Pueblo*, which would have exacerbated the post-Vietnam image of American impotency. He behaved accordingly, especially when Kissinger's absence in Kansas City afforded him more latitude for decision making. Scowcroft then took on a larger role, working to prevent the Cambodians from delivering the crew to the mainland. He monitored news about the ship's location and on efforts to quarantine Tang Island, keeping Ford well informed on both issues. At one point, pressured by time constraints, Scowcroft took direct action by ordering

American jets into the air to prevent the *Mayaguez* from reaching the mainland, before going to Ford for his authorization. He also recommended to Ford and received permission to destroy boats that might be moving the crew to the mainland. He was later crystal clear on why he did so: "What we were trying to do in the *Mayaguez* was prevent . . . the ship and especially the crew from being spirited away somewhere, where we'd certainly lose the possibility of rescuing them, and then be subject to the kind of humiliations that we were with the *Pueblo* and appear powerless."[95]

Ford relied heavily on his advisors, but he also realized the final decisions were his and, when made, they reflected his concern with deteriorating American credibility. It is clear from his positions in Congress and his comments before the crisis that he believed his advisors were right about the need to shore up perceptions of American credibility. After the significance of the situation was brought to Ford's attention, he displayed a consistent preference for a military response, and later said repeatedly that once he made a tough decision, he was not inclined to second-guess it. His behavior during the *Mayaguez* crisis was consistent on this score, demonstrating his determination to punish Cambodia as an example to others even at the risk of harming the crew.

Yet, in some important respects the picture of Ford's belief system and its impact on his behavior has changed thanks to more recent information. Earlier I argued Ford appeared to be the most flexible of the key leaders, often choosing compromise positions between his two formidable senior advisors, Kissinger and Schlesinger; two of his compromises included delaying military operations twenty-four hours but not forty-eight and ordering tactical airstrikes on the mainland but not B-52s.[96] We now know this depiction of Ford as the arbiter between two strong personalities was flawed, and that on both of those issues, Ford followed Kissinger's advice. Ford made a point of hearing everyone's views and was the commanding presence in the meetings, announcing his decisions with authority. However, from the beginning he accepted Kissinger's interpretation of the significance of the *Mayaguez* seizure and how to respond to it.

Ford first learned of the *Mayaguez* seizure from Scowcroft but made no decisions until he had a chance to talk with Kissinger a little later that morning.[97] After discussing the situation with the secretary of state, and accepting Kissinger's interpretation of the event and what needed to be done in response, Ford displayed a consistent preference for a military response. Per Kissinger's recommendation, he called the first NSC meeting and thereafter made a point of getting Kissinger's views on every major decision, following his advice in each such case. Indeed, it is evident from the details of conversations that Ford sided with Kissinger over Schlesinger because he trusted him more. When Schlesinger raised an issue that Ford was unsure about, he consistently sought Kissinger's advice.

For example, this was the case with operating out of Thailand, the ultimatum, firing on the fishing boat with Caucasians, delaying a second day, and continuing the airstrikes on the mainland rather than giving priority to helping the Marines.

When Schlesinger asked about operating from Thailand, Ford checked with Kissinger and got back to the defense secretary with instructions. The same thing happened with the Pentagon's suggestion of issuing an ultimatum. Ford only passed up opportunities for quicker and more decisive use of force when Kissinger advised doing so, that is, when Kissinger advised not to sink the boat suspected of transporting crew members, to delay military operations twenty-four hours, and to forego B-52s because of political fallout. Schlesinger supported all of these positions as well—before Kissinger did—but Ford only agreed after Kissinger came around to supporting Schlesinger's position. Schlesinger's views only prevailed if he first convinced Kissinger to agree with him. When Kissinger and Schlesinger did not agree, Ford sided with Kissinger every time, as was the case with aggressive enforcement of the quarantine, not issuing a time-based ultimatum, and insisting on a fourth set of airstrikes against the Cambodian mainland. Ford's reliance on Kissinger[98] was widely assumed at the time[99] but obscured by his political aides, who were anxious to portray the president as firmly in command during the crisis.[100]

Summing Up the Best Explanation

Not surprisingly, the relative efficacy of the decision-making models corresponds well with their information requirements. With a general awareness of the international context and recent events, the rational actor model could hypothesize state behavior, drawing the likely explanation that the United States was reasserting itself after significant setbacks. However, it could not demonstrate that was actually the case or explain why US leaders in similar situations acted differently. The bureaucratic politics model required more detailed information about leadership relations and behaviors in the crisis. It anticipated and illuminated the ongoing struggle between Kissinger and Schlesinger but not their true motives during the crisis. The belief system model requires detailed information on individual leader beliefs and behaviors, which is difficult to acquire and substantiate. Nevertheless, it provides the best and fullest explanation for all the major decisions made and behaviors manifest during the crisis.

A minimally satisfactory explanation of US behaviors during the *Mayaguez* crisis needs to sort out competing explanations for why US decision makers ordered risky military operations not commensurate with their publicly stated objective of rescuing the ship and crew. The belief system explanation does that, demonstrating the rescue of ship and crew was not the decision makers' top priority. Nor were Ford and his primary advisors driven by a desire to shore up Ford's lagging political fortunes, by the need for emotional catharsis following the tragic fall of Vietnam and Cambodia, or by faulty intelligence or misperceptions of Cambodian motives. Instead, the basic explanation offered decades earlier still holds. The decision to use force quickly was due to the belief shared by all key US decision makers that they needed to reinforce deteriorating American prestige and credibility, in particular to signal North and South Korea as well as other countries, that the United States would still honor its security commitments.

With the benefit of new information and analysis, this basic explanation has been refined. We now know that the decision-making process was more driven by the decision makers' geostrategic goals and more rational than previously thought. In other words, the agreement on the need to signal US resolve and willingness to use force was more controlling than previously appreciated, and although decision makers did not correctly assess the risk of rushed military operations, they did not overlook the issue. We also now know there was much more conflict between the White House and the Pentagon than previously understood and that it was fueled primarily by differences of opinion among key leaders as to which actions would best accomplish their collective goals. In that regard, the beliefs of the key decision makers were more powerful predictors of crisis behaviors than previously realized.

The belief system analysis also explains the important subsidiary decisions made during the crisis about how to execute diplomatic and military options, including the slow-rolling of diplomacy, the decision not to issue an ultimatum with a deadline, the timing of military operations, and the number and purpose of the punitive mainland strikes. The most important subsidiary decisions were the order to sink boats that might have been carrying crew members, which was made because the lives of the crew were secondary to the larger geostrategic objectives of the decision makers, and the timing of the ill-fated invasion of Tang Island, which was rushed in order to minimize the chance of a political or diplomatic development that would have robbed decision makers of the opportunity for a demonstrative use of force.

One indication of the adequacy of the belief system explanation is how easily it allows researchers to separate truth from fiction in decision makers' postcrisis comments. The official line from the White House, communicated by press secretary Ron Nessen to the media, was that the decision to use force "was based 100 per cent and entirely on a single consideration, and that was getting the crew back and the ship back."[101] All the senior leaders made this point publicly.[102] But they also indicated there were complementary objectives or serendipitous benefits from the rescue operations.

In other words, they reordered their actual motives for public consumption, and only a detailed account of crisis decision making makes the correct ordering manifest.

The greatest misrepresentation was the insistence that the lives of the crew were the primary objective throughout the crisis. The next most misleading assertion was that the mainland airstrikes were necessary to protect the Marines on Tang Island. In fact, continuing the strikes on the mainland put the Marines at greater risk by denying them support from the *Coral Sea*. There were other less significant deceptions, including Kissinger's insistence that "there was no chance during the crisis to resolve it diplomatically,"[103] his assertion that B-52s were only considered briefly before it was known that *Coral Sea* aircraft could be used,[104] and his claim that "we decided to end the air attacks as soon as we knew that the crew had, in fact, been released."[105]

Some of these senior leader statements and others identified in the foregoing analysis and at greater length elsewhere[106] are merely misleading; others are blatantly not true. However, the decision makers also promulgated their actual motives, about which they were quite candid. They were explicit about the benefits of demonstrating US resolve, or in Kissinger's words, that "the United States is prepared to defend [its] interests and that it can get public support and congressional support for those actions." More starkly, off-the-record, "high-ranking sources" told the *New York Times* that "the seizure of the vessel might provide the test of American determination in Southeast Asia . . . the United States has been seeking since the collapse of allied governments in South Vietnam and Cambodia."[107] Scowcroft candidly acknowledged the determination to prevent the crew from being held captive on the mainland, a prime concern of his, and Schlesinger underscored his preoccupation with a "measured response" that compared favorably with previous, less discriminate uses of force.[108] It is not difficult to sort out which of the decision makers' public explanations for US behaviors are true given the details now available about their beliefs and crisis behaviors.

Remaining Issues

Two consequential issues remain that would benefit from further illumination. The first is why the estimate of Cambodian strength on Tang Island used in NSC meetings and congressional testimony was the lower IPAC estimate of 100 Cambodian defenders instead of the higher and ultimately more accurate DIA estimate of 150 to 200 Khmer troops. The second is why the Joint Chiefs estimated the risk of attacking Tang Island as acceptable with a high assurance of success. The answer to the first question may be as simple as some senior intelligence official making a determination to go with the IPAC estimate because they were closer to the scene.[109] Lieutenant General Burns indicates that the 100-defender figure was a compromise between IPAC, which leaned more heavily on a human intelligence source, and DIA, which leaned more heavily on signals intelligence.[110] It may be that the CIA accepted this compromise and it became the figure used to brief the NSC.

The Joint Chiefs' risk assessment is more puzzling. It ignored Marine Corps doctrine in several key respects,[111] beginning with the rule of thumb that the attacking force should have at least a 3-to-1 superiority in numbers. For reasons explained above, it seems clear that senior leaders in the Pentagon were not familiar with the details of the plan; for example, they erroneously assumed the Marines would have the benefit of close air support while making their assault. If they had been assuming the larger number of defenders on Tang, it would have increased the chances of the Joint Chiefs reassessing their risk estimate. However, even assuming the lower estimate of 100 defenders, the judgment of military leaders favoring a helicopter assault with 175 Marines against 100 entrenched defenders is surprising. If either decision had been made differently, the chances of military operations being postponed another day—and thus indefinitely because of the crew's release—would have increased substantially. Barring some unexpected revelation about how these two issues were decided, the basic explanation for US behavior during the crisis is not likely to change.

CHAPTER 8

Findings, Issues, and Prescriptions

===========

A good description of the *Mayaguez* crisis has merit for both academic and policy purposes. For academics, a case study with an accurate depiction of crisis behaviors and a compelling explanation for them is useful for historical accuracy and for increasing the validity of studies generalizing from multiple cases. The *Mayaguez* incident figures prominently in a range of historical issues concerning the Ford presidency and the legacy of the Vietnam experience. For example, one historical account claims the crisis sidetracked the bureaucracy's attempt to extract lessons from the Vietnam experience.[1] The crisis also is considered a key case in a wide range of other social science topics, from presidential compliance with the War Powers Act to assessments of NSC performance during crises. All such studies benefit from an accurate depiction of decision making during the crisis.

Among other things, the depiction of crisis decision making offered here ought to prompt a reassessment of James Schlesinger's place in history. McFarlane testified to Congress that Schlesinger showed "poor judgment" in his decisions on how to use the military during the crisis and was "not really as knowledgeable as the crisis demanded."[2] Schlesinger receives even harsher treatment from Ford and Kissinger in their memoirs. The detailed account provided in this study offers a more balanced perspective on his performance.

Schlesinger's strong disapproval of using B-52s, and his tight rules of engagement for all air attacks on Cambodian shipping, saved the *Mayaguez* crew and, along with them, Ford's reputation. He owned up to resisting the president's direct orders to sink all boats traversing between Tang Island and the mainland, but it appears the stalling began with Generals Wickham and Pauly. In addition, we have shown that the president's instructions insisted upon carefully modulated force. Ford's two sets of instructions—carefully modulated force and automatic sinking of boats—were arguably confusing and inconsistent, which makes Schlesinger's acknowledged insubordination seem less egregious. Similarly, it is clear from the detailed record provided in the preceding chapters that Schlesinger made an effort to carry out all the mainland airstrikes. Confusing miscommunications complicated the first strike, and the last strike as well. Schlesinger told Ford in the last conversation before he went to bed that the *Coral Sea* aircraft were being used against Tang and "not the mainland." Ford's response was to agree the safety of the Marines at that point was paramount. Presumably Ford would have agreed with Schlesinger's decision to cancel the last strike if he had been reminded about the details of his conversation with Schlesinger and knew that Schlesinger initially complied with the order and only relented in the face of united opposition from his military subordinates in order to save the lives of wounded airmen and Marines.

With Kissinger standing between Schlesinger and the president, the defense secretary was often blamed unfairly for developments that irritated Ford. Examples have been provided above, but another case is the casualty figures in the *Mayaguez* operations. Nessen claims that the five-day delay in accurate figures undermined the credibility of the administration, and that "despite prodding from Ford, the Defense Department stalled" because it was "trying to avoid dampening the good news of the crew's safe return."[3] But according to Wickham's notes, there was genuine confusion in the Pentagon about the real figures. Wickham reported "one KIA [killed in action], 13 MIA [missing in action], 22 WIA [wounded in action]" on May 16. Later Wickham noted two calls from Scowcroft to Schlesinger about casualty figures. In the first, he told Schlesinger that "Rumsfeld and the President were angry at the casualty figures" and asked whether the wounded could be described as "injured as opposed to WIA?" Four hours later he called Schlesinger back to tell him that the "number of wounded was being cut back to 40 for the time being."[4] In other words, an effort to disguise the extent of casualties originated in the White House, not the Pentagon.

By all accounts, the normally affable Ford did not like Schlesinger, and Schlesinger's departure was even more unpleasant than his tenure as Ford's secretary of defense. Schlesinger was bitter about being fired by Ford. He argued with the president for almost an hour, trying to no avail to convince Ford that his performance was a benefit to the administration. The conversation between the two men "was one of the most disagreeable I ever had," Ford later said.[5] Schlesinger returned to the Pentagon steaming. When he submitted his personal letter of resignation, it might have carried a hidden barb: "I have the honor of tendering my resignation from this office, effective at a time in the near future as suits your desires. I wish you good *fortune* [emphasis added] in carrying the heavy and manifold burdens that you shoulder. Respectfully, James R. Schlesinger."[6]

Schlesinger's parting comment might be interpreted as "good luck, you're going to need it" if you cannot recognize a competent subordinate. Adding insult to injury, Schlesinger left the Pentagon without a proper farewell. Wickham liked Schlesinger and considered him a competent, dedicated leader. He heard from someone that Schlesinger was going to be asked to step down and would be offered a different job of some sort. When he called Schlesinger to apprise him of this rumor, Schlesinger responded, "How interesting," and acknowledged he had been told to report to the White House to see the president the following day. When the Pentagon heard that Schlesinger was leaving, the Joint Chiefs conferred on whether to hold a departure ceremony for Schlesinger. According to Wickham, they decided not to since they did not want to be perceived as unsupportive of the president. So, Wickham said, Schlesinger "just packed his bags and left."[7]

History takes note of Schlesinger's poor relationship with Ford, and some sources understand it came to a head during the *Mayaguez* crisis. But Schlesinger's actual performance during the crisis has not been depicted accurately. Ford accused Schlesinger of incompetence,[8] and Kissinger blamed him for the Pentagon's torpor and even for inaccurate intelligence:

> Most of the communication mix-ups and sloppy intelligence reporting that plagued the *Mayaguez* crisis happened because the doubts of the Secretary of Defense compounded the trauma of the military. Clements excepted, the Pentagon seemed above all determined never again to be cast in the role of villain. The absence of the Chairman of the JCS, who was away on a trip to Europe, magnified the problem because his stand-ins were reluctant to use the direct access to the President which is the Chairman's prerogative by law. In this case, the only channel of the White House to the Pentagon was via a Secretary of Defense who was extremely ambivalent about the President's strategy.[9]

Nothing in this indictment of Schlesinger is correct. Pentagon military leaders argued their views directly to the president, who reflexively checked with Kissinger each time before making a ruling. Schlesinger was concerned with being competent, not avoiding charges of villainy. He favored punitive strikes, just not counterproductive B-52 strikes, a point Kissinger eventually agreed had merit.

Ford probably had cause to fire Schlesinger for insubordination over the resistance to automatically sinking the Cambodian boats. However, if he had better understood the consequences of Schlesinger's interventions and accurately recalled the conversations he had with Schlesinger, which demonstrate the defense secretary was much less duplicitous than Ford thought, he might have concluded that Schlesinger deserved some leniency. But the president seemed unaware of the extent to which Kissinger had "gone out of his way to put it in [his] mind that Schlesinger had been willfully insubordinate."[10] So Schlesinger departed, and Kissinger had the opportunity to see if partnering with Rumsfeld would be easier.[11]

In addition to correcting inaccurate historical findings, this case study's compelling explanation of decision making is useful for improving research designed to substantiate generalizations based on multiple cases. An explanatory case study of US crisis decision making stipulates how or why something happened.[12] In the case of the *Mayaguez*, we want to know why the United States reacted with military force, and *how* decision making affected the crisis outcome.[13] It is not enough to examine multiple plausible explanatory factors and assert they all played a role. We must postulate and substantiate the factor that best explains behavior. If we cannot discriminate among competing explanatory factors, assessing which serves as the best independent explanatory variable, the ideal of the discipline—cumulative knowledge about political behaviors—is not possible.

Scholarship on the *Mayaguez* crisis has not followed this pattern, a deficiency this study hopes to correct. The explanation of the *Mayaguez* crisis offered here provides a firmer foundation for cumulative knowledge than previous studies. It corrects previous assertions made about the crisis, many of which have been identified above. For instance, it should be clear from the foregoing analysis that Ford's decision making was not primarily driven by analogous reasoning based on the *Pueblo* crisis, as some have asserted.[14] It should be equally clear that it was not based on domestic political considerations. On the contrary, and to use Kissinger's terminology, the president had steeled himself to be accused of villainy and went ahead and did what he thought was in the nation's best interest. Despite all the evidence to the contrary, scholars continue to mistakenly ascribe domestic political motives to Ford.[15]

On the other hand, this research also substantiates some generalizations made by previous scholarship. For example, David P. Houghton cites Robert Jervis on the tendency of powerful states to act belligerently in the aftermath of foreign policy reversals:

> Jervis contends that states are likely to resort to belligerent foreign policy acts when they have experienced recent losses abroad or at home. Powerful states, in other words, seek to restore their international reputation and prestige in the wake of defeats or losses of some sort, and he contends that one can at least partially explain Ford's *Mayaguez* operation or Reagan's Grenada invasion this way (the former being a reaction to the fall of Saigon, the latter to the Iran hostage situation).[16]

The research here certainly supports Jervis's supposition about the *Mayaguez* crisis and thus helps substantiate his broader generalization.

This examination of the *Mayaguez* crisis makes a contribution to the effort to build cumulative knowledge on the factors that drive foreign policy decision-making. Past research on crisis decision making and bureaucratic politics has been criticized for "overstating the impact of bureaucracy over human agency" and "not being sufficiently analytically accurate about how and under what circumstances the impact of the bureaucracy prevails over other elements in government."[17] It is generally agreed that the president is able to exercise more control during crises that demand the attention of the national security system's most senior advisors. Institutional forces are acknowledged to be more consequential in noncrisis decision making, but the precise way such forces influence the decision process is contested. Thus, "the extent to which bureaucracies either enhance or jeopardize prospects for rational decision making," remains "one of the key issues" in foreign policy analysis.[18] This study makes a contribution by demonstrating that even in crises individual leaders can undermine collective coherence and thus rationality, especially when they cannot resolve differences over group purpose or courses of action.

Beyond the contribution to scholarship, the *Mayaguez* crisis is also a valuable case study for policy analysis. The crisis has been dismissed as a mere "historical footnote,"[19] but this reflects a poor understanding of the significant issues raised by the crisis, including what decision makers thought was at stake, the organizational mechanism used to manage the crisis, and the insights that can be generated from a close examination of the roles played by key leaders during the crisis. Properly understood, the *Mayaguez* crisis can be used to illustrate a number of important policy issues and to impart important lessons for senior policy makers.[20] To further demonstrate the value of this case study and extract useful insights from it, we will now examine a number of such issues, beginning with whether US leaders accomplished their primary goal.

The Efficacy of Force

One scholar has argued it is ludicrous to claim that the *Mayaguez* was a successful display of resolve. He believes Cambodians and other observers in Asia drew different conclusions:

> The US military action was a spasmodic and ill-conceived response by the White House to the frustration of liquidating a failed two-decade commitment in Indochina, not a signal of American intentions to project force in Indochina.

> Only in the imagination of US national security managers could a botched rescue mission be considered a successful show of force. American allies were not impressed.[21]

We now know this assessment is completely wrong with respect to explaining US motives. US military operations in the *Mayaguez* crisis were not an emotional outlet or primarily a rescue mission. Moreover, as previously discussed, the intended beneficiary of the show of force was not Cambodia, or Indochina more generally, as commentators so often misunderstand. Even during the crisis US leaders dismissed the costs of alienating Thailand. A cable from the Department of State to the US ambassador in Bangkok explained this matter-of-factly: "We realize that there may be costs with the Thais but the balance of interests requires that we be willing to take whatever risks may be involved in our relations with Thais."[22] The decision makers cared even less about relations with the Khmer Rouge. Chinese officials at a meeting in New York the following September suggested to Kissinger that the United States take the initiative to improve relations with Cambodia. Kissinger said the Khmer Rouge would have to moderate their language first. The Chinese foreign minister responded by saying he did not "want to provoke a dispute," but then insisted that "the *Mayaguez* incident hurt their feelings. It will take them some time to forget." Kissinger's reply was blunt, "Well, it is up to them. They can't do much for us."[23]

Acknowledging the target of the show of force was North Korea, its patrons, and the rest of the world more generally, we still need to ask whether the *Mayaguez* response was a successful show of force—that is, did other countries interpret the event as a signal of American intentions to project force if challenged? Many commentators reviewing the *Mayaguez* crisis, like the one cited above, conclude the operations were a fiasco and could not possibly have had their intended effect. Almost all of these assessments do not bother to check the available evidence, perhaps assuming what other governments really thought is unknowable. However, public responses from other nations and declassified reporting from the Department of State on foreign government reactions do provide some indications of foreign reactions, and those indications suggest that most countries interpreted the event precisely the way US decision makers intended.

Publicly, there were diverse reactions in the foreign press, depending on whether the news outlet leaned left or right. Of those depicting the US response in negative terms, quite a few summed it up as an overreaction to the Communist victories in Indochina. However, many also depicted the US resort to force as an unhealthy exercise in realpolitik. Those depicting the US response in a positive light typically argued it was justified to rescue the crew and defend the principal of freedom of the seas. Yet, many commentators applauding the US operations also recognized their value for signaling US resolve. In other words, whether the pundits approved or disapproved of the actions taken by the United States, many interpreted them precisely as US decision makers hoped they would—as a signal of US intentions to defend US interests despite being forced to abandon Vietnam and Cambodia.

Like foreign media, the attitude of foreign governments depended upon their political orientation. For example, even during the crisis Ford received feedback from the left-leaning Dutch Labor Party prime minister, who counseled restraint. Ford did not appreciate the advice. He later said the inability of the Dutch to understand that "decisive action would reassure our allies and bluntly warn our adversaries that the United States was not a helpless giant," "annoyed the hell" out of him.[24] Other reactions were varied. A national intelligence bulletin for May 16, 1975, stated:

> Public reaction in Britain and West Germany has been generally favorable. French press commentary, however, has been mixed. A spokesman for the Japanese Foreign Ministry implied approval for the action by telling newsmen that ships and "open waters must not be subject to seizure," and said that Tokyo viewed American action as "limited." Official and unofficial commentary from South Korea and Taiwan has been predictably favorable as was the Australian press. Of the Arab nations, only Algeria has weighed in heavily with invective against Washington.[25]

Regardless of whether they liked the response or not, foreign governments were even more inclined than news outlets to interpret the quick US resort to force as a signal of resolve to protect US interests. Intelligence community and US diplomatic assessments of foreign government reactions, based in part on host government conversations with US diplomats, indicate there were a range of positive and negative reactions, but in most cases the US purpose was interpreted in geopolitical terms. Close allies who felt threatened by their neighbors were predictably quite positive. Great Britain, Israel, Iran, South Korea, and Taiwan were supportive. To a lesser extent, so were the Japanese, and to a much lesser extent, the Filipinos as well.

A cable from London reported strong support in Britain but noted that "important political figures and respected journalists in private conversation continue to show some unease" about the willingness of the American people and Congress to support their international obligations. It added, however, that "solid popular and congressional backing given to the president's handling of the *Mayaguez* incident has helped considerably to dispel this unease." Yitzhak Rabin, the prime minister of Israel, told

Ford, Kissinger, Sisco, and Scowcroft that "we appreciate very much the handling of the *Mayaguez* incident by the United States."[26] The shah of Iran also expressed appreciation to Ford the day after the crisis when they met.

Similarly, the South Koreans, disquieted by the fall of South Vietnam, were reassured by the use of force.[27] They viewed Kim Il Sung's visit to China with greater alarm than the United States but hoped and expected that he would receive a colder reception in the Soviet Union that would constrain his belligerence.[28] Both the South Korean press and South Korean government officials lauded the US response. The English language *Korea Herald* said, "The decisive counteraction will weigh heavily in returning trust and strength to the US alliance with Asian nations." Privately, the Korean ambassador to the nonproliferation treaty talks in Bern, Switzerland, told US officials that "the US handling of *Mayaguez* was exactly what Koreans and other Asians needed at this moment," who he argued, found "the deft, swift and effective action" to save the *Mayaguez* and its crew "reassuring." He added that the United States and its allies "could be thankful to Cambodians for setting up the *Mayaguez* affair at this time and making it possible for the United States to demonstrate its determination to use its power effectively in Asia even after Vietnam."[29] In Taiwan, editorials stressed the importance of the US show of strength, which was "the only language communists understand."

The Philippines and Japan were more circumspect, particularly given the US use of Thai bases without permission. Commentary in the Philippines stressed the Thai anger and suggested the experience was relevant for the Philippines, although the US embassy in Manila interpreted this as posturing for potential renegotiating of basing rights.

In Japan, US diplomats quickly moved to explain US behavior and reassure the Japanese that American resolve to honor treaty commitments was rock solid, that "the Secretary [Kissinger] had stressed the firmness of US resolve with regard to Korea" in particular, and that "Defense Secretary Schlesinger had gone a step further in warning the North Koreans against adventurism."[30] US diplomats in Tokyo noted little official reaction to the *Mayaguez* affair from the government. However, at least one Japanese official said he "understood the domestic psychological atmosphere" that impelled US action but wished the United States had waited a day or two for a diplomatic solution. The comment from the embassy was that despite this official's reaction and "the heavy criticism we are sure to get from Japan's left, we believe there will be substantial elements of the Japanese public" who would "at least 'understand' the decisive US action."[31]

A few weeks later the US embassy in Tokyo sent a long message apprising Washington of Japanese thinking on their security interests.

If the Japanese had been anticipating the fall of Saigon, they were not prepared for Kim Il Sung's apparent effort to capitalize on the trend of events in Southeast Asia. His mid-April visit to Peking, read by most Japanese as a bid for Chinese support for military pressure against the ROK [Republic of Korea], sent tremors throughout the political establishment in Tokyo. . . . Subsequent events have combined to calm Japanese apprehensions. Peking obviously had no enthusiasm for the use of military force to reunify Korea, and the tone of Kim Il Sung's statements on the subject (most recently in Romania on May 24) have moderated accordingly. Strong reaffirmations of the American security commitment to the ROK by President Ford, Secretary Kissinger and Secretary Schlesinger, and evidence of resurgent congressional support for this position were followed by proof during the Mayaguez rescue that the United States was willing and able to use force in defense of its principles when provoked.[32]

However, the embassy went on to note that "a residue of anxiety remains, hardened by a sense that Japan's leverage is limited and options are few." Countries in East Asia continued to mull the consequences of Indochina's demise for some time, particularly the Japanese. A few months after the crisis a Japanese source quoted a senior Japanese diplomat in Tokyo as saying "our whole defense policy must be designed to prevent a North Korean invasion of South Korea." The comment was explained as a reaction among Japanese defense thinkers due to "Communist victories in Indo-China and the withdrawal of American military power from the region." The article went on to note that the Japanese did not think war on the Korean Peninsula was imminent but that they did consider it "the most immediately unsettling factor in northeast Asia."[33]

Adversaries of the United States reacted negatively, of course, but in degrees, depending on their assessment of whether a strong United States was an impediment to their interests. North Korea's response to the incident suggests it understood the underlying US message. Kim Il Sung's regime called the US military response a "premeditated, villainous provocation against the Cambodian people."[34] Given that the United States followed up the *Mayaguez* operations with warnings that a new war in Korea might lead to the use of tactical nuclear weapons, it was hard to misinterpret the US message.

It does not appear Kim was intimidated. He continued his efforts to secure support from other Communist nations for an effort to reunify the Korean Peninsula. A now-declassified Bulgarian assessment of Kim's visit with Bulgarian leader Todor Zhivkov's in June 1975 is revealing. It noted that "Kissinger and the US Defense Secretary repeat over and again that they will not tolerate in South Korea what happened in Indochina and will continue their commitments." It went on to argue the correlation of forces were not in Kim Il Sung's favor for reuniting Korea by force. It noted that the United States had increased its forces in South Korea by 4,000 men and that they had better equipment than the North Koreans. The assessment did not mention the *Mayaguez*, but it clearly assumed American willingness to fight in the event the North commenced hostilities.[35]

China reacted with more anger than expected. Deng Xiaoping's response in Paris when asked about the *Mayaguez* inclined Kissinger to believe the Chinese had practically given the United States the green light for teaching their unruly pupils a lesson and, in the process, reminding the Cambodians that they needed the protection of a great power like China. China watchers in Hong Kong, for example, openly speculated that the top leadership in Communist China was pleased the United States took such a firm stand because it would serve to stabilize the area. However, such reasoning appears off the mark. There are many indications that the Chinese were genuinely angry about the US military operations. China watchers in the State Department noted what they considered three officially orchestrated Chinese reactions.

On May 15, Vice Premier Li Xiannian described the US response as an "act of piracy," which was reported in the Chinese press. The *People's Daily* on May 16 said that the United States responded on the pretext of a rescue when in fact the ship had been engaged in spying; therefore, the incident "shows that US imperialism has not yet learned the proper lesson from its defeats in Cambodia and Vietnam."[36] Later, more *People's Daily* commentary lampooned the US military operations as inept, claiming the "great hullabaloo" Washington was making about the incident was a "farce," "written and staged single-handedly by the very superpower which the small Indochinese countries completely defeated." The commentary insisted that "the Chinese government and people will, as in the past, resolutely support the Cambodian people in their just struggle in defense of state sovereignty and against U.S aggression."[37]

US diplomats ended up arguing the details of the *Mayaguez* incident with their Chinese counterparts. In one exchange Deputy Assistant Secretary William H. Gleysteen Jr. debated the issue in a luncheon conversation with China's deputy chief of its liaison office, Han Hsu. Han and colleagues argued the Cambodians had the right to stop and inspect vessels in their territorial waters, that the United States was at fault "because of all the bombs it had dropped on Cambodia," and that the United States was wrong to move militarily after the Cambodians had announced their intention to release the ship and crew. Gleysteen's rejoinder was that the seizure was in international waters and illegal and that the United States had not learned of the Cambodian broadcast until too late. The Chinese at least "seemed to agree tacitly with Gleysteen's point that bilateral relations would be better off without such incidents." Yet another indication of China's anger came from the shah of Iran's twin sister, Princess Ashraf Pahlavi. She shared impressions from her meetings with senior Chinese officials with Ambassador George H. W. Bush, who headed up the US liaison office in Beijing at the time. The May 22 cable reporting her comments said, "The princess mentioned twice that the Chinese were angry with us about the *Mayaguez*."[38]

The commentary from US diplomats accompanying the reports of Chinese reactions explained the uncharacteristically strong language used by China, saying China "undoubtedly felt compelled to criticize US action in order to maintain its credentials with Cambodians, to meet domestic requirements and to avoid any impression that it was willing to 'collude' with the United States in resolving the matter." The commentary also debated US responses to the Chinese rhetoric. Bush noted his advisors thought it better to let the issue fade away rather than prolonging the acrimonious exchanges. He said he understood this point of view, which had merit, but that on balance he thought it better to set the record straight about US attempts to communicate with Cambodia during the crisis through China, which had refused to assist. In addition, he thought it might be useful to remind the Chinese that such overblown rhetoric had a real impact on US-Chinese relations. A middle position of sorts was for Kissinger to again remind Huang Chen, chief of the PRC liaison office, in his next meeting with the Chinese in Washington that "the increasing references in PRC commentary to 'US defeat' in Indochina and our 'strategic passivity' and isolation" were misinformed and dangerous.[39]

Months later, in a large December 3 meeting with Ford, Chinese Vice Premier Deng Xiaoping, and others in Beijing, Chinese Foreign Minister Qiao Guanhua complained, "You are too emotional in your actions," adding "the *Mayaguez* was totally unnecessary." A little later he returned to the subject again, saying that

> you are always saying we are criticizing you, but I must say we think you have overdone it [in the *Mayaguez* affair] with regard to that small island. And according to our information, the Cambodian leaders did not know about the incident—it was the people on that small island themselves. And then the United States began the bombing after the Cambodian leaders agreed to return the boat.[40]

Kissinger replied, "We didn't know this until after our military operation had begun," which prompted laughter from the Chinese. President Ford thought it wise to remind China of its response to US diplomatic overtures, saying "it is accurate to say we made diplomatic efforts at the very outset, in order to find an answer without taking the military steps; and we were very disappointed those diplomatic efforts were not responded to." This too prompted laughter from Huang Chen and Foreign Minister Qiao, who pointed at Huang Chen in mock blame. Kissinger joked that the "Vietnamese have solved the problem anyway by taking over the island," which produced more laughter. Vice Premier Deng wrapped up for the Chinese, stating "anyway, you have slightly overdone it with that incident. Because you are such a big country and Cambodia is such a small country." The discussion then moved on to other topics.[41]

Both sides were making it clear to the other that they took their prestige seriously. The United States was suggesting that it would not tolerate provocation by small powers and that the Chinese were responsible for the behavior of their client. The Chinese seem to be saying that they understood the point, but that the United States should have acted with greater restraint. They argued the overreaction hurt US prestige, but perhaps their real concern was that the US bludgeoning of China's client embarrassed China, and they wanted US officials to know such measures would harm US-Chinese bilateral relations. In any case, there seems little doubt that the Chinese understood the United States was communicating its willingness to use force in the aftermath of the withdrawal from Vietnam.

The response by Russia to the *Mayaguez* incident was quite restrained compared to China. The US embassy in Moscow reported that Soviet media treated the issue in a reserved and "fairly straight" manner, reporting the facts for the most part. Later, the embassy speculated about the Soviet treatment of the issue. US officials commented that "the Soviet response to the *Mayaguez* incident was so conspicuously cautious that it suggests a conscious policy decision to avoid using the issue as a handle to criticize the United States in the aftermath of the fall of Indochina." The embassy explained that the Soviets

> presumably saw no reason to take the United States on in connection with an event which was marginal to their own interests and which they could not have affected anyway. Likewise, their apparent absence of ties to the new Cambodian regime suggests that they might see some virtue in "teaching" Phnom Penh that it needs more friends than Hanoi and Peking. The publicity for the US diplomatic efforts via the Chinese also suggests that either Peking was unable to affect the outcome (i.e., lacks clout with the Cambodians) or chose not to affect it (i.e., does not value sufficiently its relations with the United States). Both points serve Soviet interests in treating the Chinese invidiously. Finally, on the question of the ship's position at the time of its seizure, Moscow clearly wished to avoid taking a position which could backfire on its own [law of sea] position on innocent passage. Some Soviet media replayed the Cambodian

charge about the alleged "intelligence" functions of the Mayaguez, but even this was carefully couched as the opinion of others.[42]

The US embassy's explanation for the surprisingly subdued Soviet response to the *Mayaguez* makes sense and in no way suggests the Soviets were unaware of the point US leaders were making.

Taken as a whole, governments interpreting US behavior in the *Mayaguez* crisis seem to have arrived at the correct conclusion that the United States was signaling its willingness to use force despite recent reversals in Southeast Asia. In some cases, they also speculated that the degree of force employed was excessive because the United States was feeling insecure about its position in the world. However, there was more speculation about an emotional overreaction in the popular press than in private diplomatic channels, where the norm was to think in terms of realpolitik.

The final observation one might make about the US response and foreign reactions is counterfactual. We can speculate about what might have happened if the *Mayaguez* had never been seized, particularly with respect to efforts to deter North Korean belligerence. The next major crisis with North Korea came the following year when the North Koreans used axes to murder two US military officers who were in the demilitarized zone. The officers were supervising a work party that was cutting down a tree obscuring the view of UN observers. The region went on high alert as the United States and South Korea weighed options, including military retaliation. Ultimately the two allies opted for just a symbolic show of force. American and South Korean forces entered the demilitarized zone and cut down the disputed tree. It has been argued by those with inside knowledge of the Ford administration that "the overwhelming military retaliation during the *Mayaguez* incident probably reduced the perceived necessity to use violent force in Korea"[43] Although this observation is speculative, there is considerable evidence supporting the contention.

It is now clear that Kissinger favored the use of more force in response to the brutal axe murders. Habib remarked that "we took some very strong measures" but added "we didn't do some of the things some of the people wanted to do." He noted there were advocates for "great drastic actions that fortunately were not carried out." For example, Kissinger, who by this time had been relieved of national security advisor duties but was still serving as secretary of state, issued guidance requiring the JCS to examine the option of using artillery fire to destroy the North Korean barracks at the same time that US and South Korean forces surged forth to cut down the tree. The response from the Joint Chiefs was that they were "forced to recommend against the use of artillery fire in connection with H-hour in the strongest terms." They argued the forces cutting down the tree would be completely exposed to return fire from the North Koreans and that the barracks probably would be empty anyway. More to the point, they said, was the "gross superiority of North Korean army artillery." The Joint Chiefs said they were developing a range of alternative options which would use precision-guided air munitions, surface to surface missiles, and unconventional warfare (SEAL) teams to destroy North Korean installations of military or infrastructure significance. They also argued against other Kissinger-proposed options and concluded by noting South Korean President Park Chung Hee's "strong feelings against the use of firearms in the tree cutting effort."[44]

Kissinger was not happy with the muted US response to the incident. After the tree-cutting operation had taken place, he called Scowcroft to complain about the weak-kneed response. Scowcroft was then serving as Ford's national security advisor, and he was pleased with the way the provocation was handled with restraint. Kissinger, however, said he was "sorry we didn't decide to hit the barracks. I am not sure we still shouldn't do that." Scowcroft speculated on what the North Koreans "had in mind," observing "they were apparently quite docile when we cut the tree down." "Which," Kissinger responded, "means they were scared out of their minds."

> **Kissinger:** I am worried about how the other countries assess us. When you look at the Soviet and Chinese reaction it is very mild—you have to assume that they thought we would do something drastic. Now they see us just chopping down a tree—which looks ridiculous. Habib tells me it was illegal to fire across the zone.
>
> **Scowcroft:** God Henry. So it is not illegal to murder people.
>
> **Kissinger:** No, that was wrong but not illegal. They were doing it in the JSA [joint security area] where they had every right to be. They were illegally killed but two wrongs don't make a right. If you are not a Mormon you won't understand that. You can't build justice on two wrongs.
>
> **Scowcroft:** We are trying to keep them in their cage.
>
> **Kissinger:** Scowcroft you are getting too literal—I am being sarcastic.
>
> **Scowcroft:** I know, I know. . . .
>
> **Kissinger:** Let me get to another phone—I want to ask you questions and I don't want Habib to have another heart attack.
>
> **Scowcroft:** O.K.
>
> (Kissinger goes to another phone)
>
> **Kissinger:** Hello?
>
> **Scowcroft:** Yes.
>
> **Kissinger:** What do you think about shelling them after all?
>
> **Scowcroft:** I don't think it is a bad idea.

Kissinger: The negative is that [Senators Strom] Thurmond, [Charles H.] Percy, [Jacob K.] Javits and some others have called for going to the UN on it rather than doing anything.[45]

Kissinger went on, trying to enlist Scowcroft's support for more military action. He suggested that Scowcroft should tell Ford "we feel unfulfilled about this" and see if he would be open to additional options. When Kissinger closed the long conversation, he asked Scowcroft to "try to get to [Ford] as soon as you can and call me back." In the end, Ford and Scowcroft decided against any further military action. However, it seems clear that if the *Mayaguez* incident had not taken place, the Ford administration would have felt much greater pressure to respond to the North Korean provocation with military force, which would have entailed far greater risk of escalation and presumably greater loss of life.

A final point needs to be made about the *Mayaguez* crisis and the efficacy of force in international relations. In the years following the incident, the US response to the seizure of the *Mayaguez* became widely viewed in US policy circles as an unproductive overreaction. During the 1976 presidential campaign, candidate Jimmy Carter repeatedly castigated Ford for his handling of the crisis. When he became president and had to respond to the Iranian seizure of the US embassy in Tehran, Carter made it clear that he intended to avoid a repetition of the *Mayaguez* crisis. As late as April 1978, Carter was still referencing the *Mayaguez* when resisting efforts by his national security advisor, Zbigniew Brzezinski, to convince him that the threat of force was inherent in the conduct of foreign policy.[46] Thus, the *Mayaguez* crisis and perceptions of how it was managed became part of the ongoing national debate about the efficacy of force in a real and direct manner. Just as President Carter and his advisors made policy decisions based in part on their understanding of the *Mayaguez* crisis,[47] future leaders may do the same. In that regard it is important for policy makers to consider not only how they might have managed the crisis differently, but also to have an accurate appreciation for how other nations viewed the US response. To date, those researching the crisis have typically offered their own assessment of US performance while overlooking the evidence for how other nations reacted and whether US leaders accomplished their objective of signaling US resolve.

Mission Command and Micromanagement

It might be assumed that the *Mayaguez* crisis cannot yield insights on such contemporary command-and-control concepts as "mission command" because the incident took place so long ago, but that is not the case. The mission command concept predates the crisis, extending back at least to World War II. Also, despite the recent emphasis on the concept in joint doctrine, US military leaders have been struggling to apply and refine the concept for decades.[48] Moreover, many commentators on the *Mayaguez* believe the incident showcased the advent of global communications that present special challenges to executing the mission command approach. The overwhelming majority of those studying the crisis believe US decision making and operational performance were crippled by senior leaders using newly available communication technology to keep abreast of developments in the field and then micromanage their subordinates, which is precisely what the mission command approach seeks to avoid. By examining the charges of micromanagement during the crisis, we can gain insights on how and whether following the mission command approach currently advocated in joint doctrine would have improved performance during the crisis. If not, asking "why" may yield insights for the current approach to mission command.

The mission command concept requires conducting "military operations through decentralized execution based upon mission-type orders." To be successful, mission command "demands that subordinate leaders at all echelons exercise disciplined initiative and act aggressively and independently to accomplish the mission."[49] One issue is whether a commander taking aggressive, independent initiative at one level will issue direction to subordinates that impinges upon their ability to do the same. To avoid this, the concept requires commanders to be on guard against "micromanagement." Indeed, the concept's default position is for commanders to "demonstrate trust by exercising restraint in their close supervision of subordinates"[50] and to "delegate decisions to subordinates wherever possible."[51] Thus, "mission command begins with a bias to decentralized decisionmaking,"[52] which many consider appropriate for the increasingly complex decision-making environment.[53]

Micromanagement, considered the opposite of decentralized decision, is what many commentators on the *Mayaguez* crisis believe crippled US decision making. In fact, the most persistent and widespread lesson gleaned from the *Mayaguez* crisis, other than the general perception that the Ford administration overreacted, is the belief that the military operations were heavily micromanaged, particularly by civilian authorities, with nearly disastrous results. Many sources with military experience agree with the Marine brigadier general who summarized that the key lesson from the crisis was

> modern communications are wonderful but they also are deadly. The capability to talk over thousands of miles from the very highest levels to the frontline foxholes takes many of the important decisions out of the hands of the responsible commander, the man on the scene.[54]

It is hard to find a source on the *Mayaguez* crisis that does not attribute deleterious micromanagement to senior leaders,[55] and many argue the incident is noteworthy in part because it was a "harbinger of shifts in warfare and diplomacy enabled by new global communication technologies" that have encouraged deleterious micromanagement.[56]

However, this popular lesson from the *Mayaguez* incident is mistaken. The way command and control was exercised during the crisis does not demonstrate the dangers of micromanagement. Rather, command and control problems during the *Mayaguez* crisis illustrate the importance of distinguishing unhelpful micromanagement from helpful oversight. There actually were more egregious examples of insufficient oversight than there were of harmful micromanagement during the incident. And where there were cases of inappropriate micromanagement with potentially consequential results, they originated with military, not civilian, leaders.

To review the charges of micromanagement and determine which have merit, it helps to distinguish the roughly three levels of micromanagement asserted in the literature: those that are fictitious or offered without evidence or explanation, those that are accurate and substantive but not consequential, and those that are real and potentially significant. Many sources express the concern that modern communications facilitate micromanagement without making the case that it actually occurred:

> Despite the global distances, local commanders were now under the constant watch of their chain of command, from the President to their immediate headquarters. Commanders could now listen in, comment on, and override decisions by their field subordinates. The President could literally micromanage a tactical situation instead of focusing on a strategic or long-term view. A local commander's initiative and ability to make decisions was therefore at risk of disappearing.[57]

Similarly, Guilmartin claims global communications gave leaders in Washington a "false impression of positive control,"[58] but he does not provide evidence for this assertion. As previous analysis makes clear, the White House worked hard to exert control over the Pentagon precisely because Ford, Kissinger, and Scowcroft were increasingly concerned that the Pentagon was not complying with presidential orders. Rather than a false sense of control, the White House had an exaggerated concern about losing control over the operations. Ford in particular believed, and said, that he feared the Pentagon was acting independently in pursuit of its own priorities. Scowcroft demanded direct access to the NMCC, and he and his aide, Major McFarlane, tried to keep abreast of developments by listening directly to military communications. The Pentagon was irritated by this level of information gathering and White House decisions on the timing and extent of military operations, especially the number of mainland strikes. When Schlesinger was required to explain all orders given during the crisis and offer his views on how the national security system could be improved, he suggested that less management by the White House would be helpful:

> "Washington's role should be to define the larger goal . . . while attempting to avoid too many and too frequent interventions." The president and his White House advisers, Schlesinger asserted, "are concerned that nothing go awry—and are searching for apparent mistakes." By contrast, people in DoD "have far more information and are in the position of having to execute any decisions in a fast-moving situation."[59]

The Pentagon wanted latitude to conduct operations as it saw fit, but it did not make the case that White House oversight impaired operations or outcomes during the crisis.

Other sources insist micromanagement took place simply because Washington asked for information updates that were trivial and a nuisance. One such example was Washington asking the Marines, in the heat of battle, whether they had a Khmer interpreter with them.[60] Similarly, Mahoney argues that "Ford's questioning of Schlesinger, Jones, and the military went beyond micromanagement during the crisis. On several occasions he openly questioned the rapidity of movement of forces into the area."[61] Yet it is hard to see how asking questions about the ability to communicate with the adversary or how rapidly forces were moving to the area constitutes micromanagement. US leaders explaining their decisions to congressional leaders and the public needed to know whether it was possible for the Marines to communicate with Cambodians or only shoot them. The ability to speak to the Khmer Rouge might have enabled a helpful cease-fire after it was known that the crew members were safe. The arrival time of US forces also was highly relevant to Ford's decision on when operations would commence.

Still other sources falsely assert that Ford and Kissinger "gave long-distance orders to military commanders on the scene during the 1975 *Mayaguez* crisis" and that, ipso facto, doing so constituted micromanagement.[62] Edward N. Luttwak appears to have started this rumor. He argues "the advent of instant worldwide communications now permits all sorts of phenomenal interventions direct from the White House" and claims, without citing a source, that "during the 1975 *Mayaguez* incident, President Ford spoke directly with Navy pilots actually over the target, to make tactical decisions in minute detail."[63] Major General John K. Singlaub, USA, in his memoir goes a step further, claiming that at one point, Air Force fighter-bomber pilots orbiting the island where the *Mayaguez* crew was held by the Khmer Rouge were startled to hear the distinctive, Mittel-Europa murmur of Henry Kissinger in their earphones. The White House had used a command override channel to deal directly with the operation's air support. In so doing, Kissinger bypassed the entire local command structure and fouled up the operation. The operational commander, Lt. General John J. Burns, USAF, had been about to order the Marine helicopters not to land on an island held by the Khmer Rouge, but his radio channel to the operational aircraft was blocked by the Flash Override from Washington.[64]

As an Army War College study observes, this never happened, and in fact, could not have happened given the communications extant at the time.[65] Kissinger has also been personally blamed for the decision to drop the BLU-82 and for ordering the assault on Tang Island.[66] Luttwak's and Singlaub's theme, asserted but unsupported by evidence, is replicated in a number of war college papers.[67] There is no evidence Ford or Kissinger spoke to pilots or directed their tactical decisions in minute detail, unless this refers to Ford's decision on whether or not to sink the trawler with the undetermined number of Caucasians on board. As will be argued below, it was entirely appropriate for the president to make this decision.

Other sources making the case that micromanagement occurred offer concrete examples, but upon inspection, they are either appropriate acts of oversight or inconsequential. For example, one source argues that Admiral Gayler micromanaged when he bypassed both Lieutenant General Burns and Marine Colonel John M. Johnson to order Lieutenant Colonel Austin on Tang Island to neither "hazard his force" nor "take offensive action without waiting for reinforcements," and when he ordered the 15,000-pound BLU-82 dropped without consulting the Marines on Tang.[68]

Gayler informing the Marines not to hazard their force created confusion about their mission because they did not yet know the crew had been safely recovered. That should have prompted a conversation that updated and clarified the mission for the Marines, but the instructions from Gayler were not inappropriate. After the return of the crew, no one in the White House or the Pentagon wanted additional casualties or unnecessary risks taken by the Marines. The decision to employ the BLU-82 without consulting the Marines is more egregious, and it did complicate operations by dislocating aircraft and stunning the Marines. However, some believe it also at least temporarily suppressed Cambodian resistance and otherwise does not appear to have harmed the Marines. In any case, it should be noted that both decisions were made by a military, not civilian, leader.

Vandenbroucke also condemns micromanagement, implying it came from the White House: "both USSAG [Lieutenant General Burns] and the forces at Utapao received continuous guidance from higher commands. Recognizing the stake the White House had in a successful rescue, Burns anticipated that Washington would control the operation tightly."[69] He makes the case that Washington not only demanded information in inappropriate detail[70] but in such volume as to be debilitating:

> CinCPac's and the NMCC's thirst for information was unquenchable. They demanded that USSAG report almost continuously, and in extraordinary detail, on its planning as well as on the smallest developments in the Gulf of Thailand. USSAG chief of staff [Major] General [Earl J.] Archer [Jr., USAF] later described these demands as "crushing." "I sat there with my hand glued to the telephone," he recalled.[71]

It is true that the demand for information must be attributed in part to the White House. Ford and Scowcroft were insistent on the need for timely, detailed updates, and this pressure for information could only have increased the Pentagon's penchant for demanding information from the field. Although the continuous demand for updates must have been irritating, Vandenbroucke offers little to no evidence that it impaired operations or affected outcomes negatively. One might surmise that hastily assembled and untrained staff trying to coordinate joint operations would be distracted by such a barrage of questions, but no one has traced any major mishap back to supporting staff being overwhelmed with phone calls and issues from higher command.

Vandenbroucke makes a more serious case for micromanagement when he asserts senior military leaders interfered by directing the movements of individual units on the scene:

> During the *Mayaguez* operation, on-scene commanders were dismayed when the Commander in Chief of U.S. forces in the Pacific (CinCPac), located thousands of miles away in Hawaii, tried to direct the movements of individual units and planes on or above Koh Tang. Key on-scene commanders spoke acidly after the operation about the intrusive and excessive guidance they received from CinCPac and senior military commanders in Washington.[72]

It is true that field commanders resented the interventions by higher military authorities,[73] but it is not evident that they micromanaged operations. An example offered by Vandenbroucke is a telephone call from a general in the NMCC to the captain of the *Holt*. The general wanted to know how fast was the *Holt* was going, and when he was told it was proceeding at 80 percent power, ordered it to "make full power," terminating the call before it could be explained that "1052-class destroyers like the *Holt* were prone to engine trouble."[74] This exchange, as unhelpful as it was, had no impact on the crisis or its outcome. Again, it is also important to note that such examples of micromanagement involve higher military authorities, and not civilians, as is typically alleged. For all the strong language about micromanagement, there are only a few concrete and consequential examples, which brings us to the third and most important category of micromanagement described in the literature on the crisis.

One example of micromanagement with potentially great consequence was the selection of the Marine units for the assault:

> Often, senior officers in Washington and Hawaii decided on matters of the smallest operational detail, ignoring the traditional prerogatives of the commander in the field. Early in the crisis, III MAF [Marine Amphibious Force] commander [Major General Carl W.] Hoffman was amazed when he saw the orders from higher headquarters sending Marines from the Philippines and Okinawa to Utapao. The message designated a specific rifle company by name to execute the recovery of the *Mayaguez*. No one, however, had asked the commanders of the battalion the company belonged to which company they thought could do the job best.[75]

According to Wetterhahn, "the 1st Battalion, 9th Marines, were nearing the end of their one-year tour on Okinawa and could not be extended except in case of an emergency. The III MAF commander sought authorization to extend the unit, but it was denied." Wetterhahn believes administrative issues took precedence over performance at Marine headquarters, "so a fully trained unit stood down while an outfit just beginning its predeployment training cycle was chosen."[76] It cannot be known whether the Marines with the higher readiness would have planned and performed differently. It seems churlish to even raise the question, given how well the Marines performed in such harrowing circumstances. But it is possible that a different unit with higher readiness might have produced a better outcome, perhaps by interacting with Air Force personnel better and thus obtaining more realistic intelligence estimates of enemy strength. In any case, it does seem the decision on which Marines to use should have been left up to local commanders.

Another example of micromanagement comes from Vice Admiral George Steele, the Seventh Fleet commander, who asserted that

> we requested permission to fly reconnaissance flights in the area, and later, specifically over the island of Koh Tang. Despite repeated requests to do this,

it was denied until so late that the reconnaissance flight's photographic results could not be processed in advance of the actual assault on the island. I think that this is another example of a disastrous attempt to micromanage, from distant headquarters with inadequately trained staff, large operations in which communications play so great a part.[77]

It is unclear why the permission for reconnaissance flights was delayed or for how long and with what consequences. It seems possible better reconnaissance of enemy positions might have inclined the Marines to insist on better plans for fire support during the assault. General Burns ruled out preparatory fires in deference to the safety of the crew, which made fire support during the assault all the more critical. In this regard not having a plan for gunship fire support and forward air controllers on the scene from the beginning seems much more consequential than the delayed reconnaissance flights. Once again, none of these limitations were imposed by civilian decision makers.

Another example of Washington interference with potentially disastrous consequences concerns the timing of the assault on Tang Island. One source that concludes "Ford interfered in a major military operation" offers the following argument:

> One of the problems involved in having the president direct such an operation—as opposed to providing broad guidance and leaving the details to the military personnel on the spot—was that Washington was not always aware of all the issues involved in carrying out such an operation. And in the case of the operation to free the *Mayaguez*, a major problem arose from Washington's failure to understand what only those in the immediate area were aware of: the time of first light. The Marines' attack on Koh Tang was scheduled to begin at sunrise, but daylight at Koh Tang actually arrived twenty-six minutes before the official sunrise. As a result, when the Marines attacked, they did so without the advantage of surprise and in the full light of morning.[78]

We now know Ford asked Jones whether the Marines could make it to their destination at the prescribed time, and Jones replied that they could. If he had said otherwise, Ford might have considered another delay. In any case, it appears questionable as to whether the amount of light available was a decisive factor. The Marines ruled out a night insertion, and the Cambodians, exercising good fire control, waited until the helicopters were offloading before opening fire. Even if the assault had begun at the crack of first light, it is not clear the Cambodian defensive fires would have been any less devastating.

One of the most commonly cited examples of Washington interference with potentially critical consequences was the decision to turn off the second wave of Marines headed for Tang Island. Mahoney asserts that "after micromanaging many of the details of the rescue operation, Ford and Kissinger treated the extraction of the marines as an afterthought. Ford's order for the marines to 'disengage as soon as possible' resulted in the second assault wave on Koh Tang being turned off apparently by overzealous subordinates."[79] But the White House giving the Pentagon permission to terminate military operations is not a case of micromanagement. As Mahoney himself notes, it was a subordinate in the military chain of command—Admiral Gayler—who turned the general guidance from the White House into a specific order to cancel the second wave of Marines without consulting the Marine commander on Tang. Admiral Steele argued that "this complicated, jury-rigged command arrangement and detailed management from the JCS level endangered and nearly destroyed the forces on the island."[80] However, the order was quickly rescinded, so the impact of the delay was greatly reduced if not eliminated.[81]

Taken as a whole, the charges of micromanagement are overblown. The heavy reporting requirement was irritating rather than injurious. There are only a handful of cases where higher authority appears to have made decisions that would have been better left to subordinates (e.g., the choice of the Marine unit for the assault, the use of the BLU-82). None of these seem especially consequential given the other operational problems such as the failure to disseminate accurate intelligence and to arrange for good close air support. Moreover, and contrary to much of the literature, all the tangible examples of deleterious micromanagement came from military, not civilian, leaders.

One of the best-informed and most strident critics of US government performance in the *Mayaguez* crisis disputes this conclusion. Wetterhahn insists military operations were "micromanaged from no less than the office of the president of the United States" and that Ford even outdid President Lyndon Johnson in micromanaging military operations.[82] He reviews the White House decision on whether the pilot should try to disable the fishing trawler with the crew members and asks whether the president should be making that kind of decision. However, if the risks were explained by the pilot, why shouldn't the president be the one to decide whether to risk the lives of the crew? The outcome of the entire crisis turned on this issue. In any case, the president did not decide on whether to order the pilot to shoot off the boat's rudder. The pilot initially volunteered that he could do so, but later, perhaps after discussion with senior military leaders who apprised him of what was at stake, decided against it, concluding it was too risky.

Wetterhahn also raises the issue of the controversial mainland airstrikes, asking "whether a president should be deciding how many aircraft and strikes should be used to carry out a presidential order in the first place." His answer is that a president should "instead simply tell the navy to destroy mainland targets that might affect the Koh Tang operation and let the navy determine how and with what force to do the job." For Wetterhahn, the lesson from the Vietnam War, illustrated by the *Mayaguez* crisis, is that

> Washington and the Pentagon had over the years improved communication links and computer systems needed to automate battlefield actions. As a result, tactical decisions kept moving higher and higher up the chain of command, the domain where the larger, strategic decisions are customarily made.[83]

Ironically, Kissinger agreed with these points made by Wetterhahn. He argued during the NSC deliberations that managing the attacks on the boats was a tactical issue best left to the pilots, that they should have been allowed to act on the blanket orders to sink the boats and not have reported on their activities.

Schlesinger disagreed and did his best to impose strict rules of engagement that would allow Washington to calibrate the amount of risk taken. As a result, the crew survived and the United States avoided a worse outcome. Given all that was at stake, it was appropriate for Ford to make decisions about how far he was willing to go in risking the lives of the crew. It was also appropriate for Ford to decide how much of a risk he was willing to run with Congress by bombing the mainland after the recovery of the crew. Years later Scowcroft offered an explanation for why presidents will always insist on this level of control in a crisis, emphasizing the tension

> between the need for the president to manage these sorts of things, and the utility of the man on the scene being told what it is he is supposed to do and then letting him do it. As a military man, of course, I am attracted to the latter. As a practical matter, however, as I watch what is involved in these isolated kinds of military situations—I am not talking about a general conflict or anything—the president's political neck is on the line. As a matter of course, he is going to be very reluctant to leave in the hands of some unknown military commander decisions which could have a great impact on his political well-being. Therefore, the military has to expect that it is going to be subject to intense scrutiny in carrying out crisis interventions. Whether it is optimally the better way to do it is almost beside the point. . . . An incumbent president is simply not going to leave these things up to the vagaries of the local US military commander.[84]

Scowcroft is right but for the wrong reasons. It has less to do with the president's "political neck being on the line" and more to do with the fact that small military engagements for political purposes require intense scrutiny by senior leaders in order to ensure military operations do not risk the very objectives they are trying to achieve. During a major war, where everything hinges upon military victory and precedence is given to military success, the assumption that the president and his cabinet officials should limit themselves to broad strategy decisions and leave all other operational and tactical details to subordinates holds for the most part. But virtually all the great theoreticians and practitioners of operations "other than war" (also called small wars, irregular wars, and low-intensity conflict) conclude that in such matters even tactical operations can have strategic significance.[85] Thus, the details of tactical operations deserve scrutiny by senior leadership, and the president was right to concern himself with the details of how, when, and where Cambodian boats would be sunk and with when and how much mainland bombing would take place.

This is not to say expert views on risk or other antecedent elements of the decision-making process should be overlooked. On the contrary, senior leaders need to be well-informed on their subordinates' estimates of risk and likely outcomes. The key White House decision makers during the *Mayaguez* incident—specifically Ford and Kissinger—were quite solicitous of military judgment about the risks involved in various military options under consideration, including the assault on Tang Island. With those expert views known, however, they made the decisions about how much risk to their objectives they were willing to accept. They miscalculated the risk of the island assault not in spite of best military advice, but because of it.

In the *Mayaguez* crisis, insufficient oversight was a greater problem than harmful micromanagement. Higher authorities should have asked harder questions about the plans to assault Tang Island and the risks being run during the assault. Egregious omissions in the tactical plan should have caught the attention of higher military authorities who, if they had made determined inquiries, would have quickly discovered the Marine plan was based on the incorrect assumption of token resistance. As already noted, the assault plan violated Marine Corps doctrine on a large number of points, including the lack of pre-assault reconnaissance, pre-assault strikes, armed escort for the troop helicopters, dedicated airborne forward air controllers, and naval gunfire support. As a Center for Naval Analysis study concluded, "Except for the exclusion of pre-assault strikes, we have found no explanation of why the above tactics were not incorporated or, in the case of pre-assault reconnaissance, were not adequate."[86]

As previously noted, Lieutenant General Burns later explained his assessment of the Marine plan when he received it at his headquarters in Utapao. Unaware that the Marines did not have the better intelligence estimate that depicted a large Cambodian defensive force dug in on the island, Burns was alarmed at the apparent risk:

> When . . . Hunt [Major General Jim Hunt, Burns's deputy] came and showed me where they were landing, I was really concerned. I thought that was an awfully risky operation because obviously they were going to be landing right within a couple of hundred feet of the inhabited area. He said he had been talking to the Marines, that the Marine commander had in fact flown over the island, and had selected the landing zone himself. I thought, for example, it might have made more sense to land in the south where there was no inhabitants that we knew of and work your way up. He said, "Well, I am told by the Marines who looked the island over that it would take them a full day to work from the south end of the island to the north. By that time the crew could all have their throats cut. If they could quickly envelop them, they had a better chance of securing the crew." I said, "Okay, I will accede to the guy's judgment that has to do the job."[87]

Burns followed a mission command approach by exercising restraint in the supervision of his subordinates and delegating as much of the decision making to his subordinate as possible, given that the Marine commander was closer to the area of operations and responsible for executing his plan. However, under the pressure of limited time, fatigue, and dispersed command and control, both Burns and the assault commander, Lieutenant Colonel Austin, were operating under false assumptions. Burns thought the Marines had the higher estimate of enemy forces and knew there would not be pre-assault fires; the Marines assumed they had the latest intelligence and that there would be pre-assault fires.[88] More scrutiny from Burns and direct queries to the Marine commander might well have brought these erroneous assumptions to the fore. Simply asking Austin, "How do you expect to land your helicopters in the face of 100–200 well-armed and entrenched Cambodian defenders?" should have quickly revealed the differing estimates of enemy forces and the misunderstanding about preparatory fires.

Another example of insufficient oversight concerns the estimate of risk in assaulting Tang Island discussed in the NSC meetings. Ford acceded to one twenty-four-hour delay when his advisors agreed it was too risky to go on the fourteenth. He could have been convinced to delay another twenty-four hours. Scowcroft argued the urgency of military operations was driven by the need to prevent the crew and ship from being taken to the mainland, but that was a moot point given the decision to sink Cambodian boats. Kissinger, the most influential advisor to the president, was not interested in a fine calculation of force. He wanted to make an unmistakable international impression,[89] which meant avoiding any embarrassing military mishaps. He pushed back against Colby and Rumsfeld when they seemed to dismiss such risk too easily, explaining the danger of the small initial Marine assault force. He also invited the military's assessment of risk on several occasions by saying he was not competent to render judgment on the risks involved in the island assault. Schlesinger obliged, arguing for the sixteenth, but neither General Jones nor Admiral Holloway chimed in. Jones had qualms about going on the fifteenth, but the other Chiefs were in favor of doing so. He might have acquiesced to their views because he discovered the USS *Hancock* was moving toward the scene slower than first reported due a malfunctioning screw. Later Jones noted, "We were depending on that ship coming from Okinawa [he meant Subic] very badly," and at the time of the island assault it was still about thirty-five hours away.[90] So, when Schlesinger explicitly turned to Jones in the fourth NSC meeting to make the Pentagon's recommendations, Jones advised going on the fifteenth, saying, "We can do it with high assurance of success" and that doing so was "a joint recommendation from all the Joint Chiefs."

Although it is perhaps understandable that the Joint Chiefs assumed authorities further down the chain of command were ironing out the details of the plan, they were responsible for assessing and explaining risk to the White House. They knew that the greatest risk came from the limited transport available for the first wave of Marines and explained this well to civilian leaders. With only a handful of helicopters, the first wave of Marines could at best insert 270 men, after which they would have to wait another four hours for the next wave. But actually the Joint Chiefs, and their spokesman, General Jones, missed an important point. The first wave was at greater risk than acknowledged because a portion of the 270 Marines would be sent to the ship. This meant that only 175 Marines would be assaulting Tang Island in the first wave.[91] But neither the Joint Chiefs, nor the acting chairman of the JCS, nor any of the civilian advisors initially noticed the oversight. Instead of almost a 3-to-1 ratio of assault to assumed defending forces on Tang, it would be a 1.8-to-1 ratio—a significantly greater risk. Later, in the fourth NSC meeting, Jones noted it would be 175 Marines in the assault on the island, but he failed to mention that this meant higher risk for the assault. Arguably, compared to the absence of close air support, the difference between 175 and 270 Marines was of lesser import. But the point is that greater scrutiny of the plan by any of the Chiefs or by any of the civilian advisors who considered and debated this issue at length could very well have inclined Ford to delay the additional day that Schlesinger, and, to a lesser extent, Jones wanted.

The most serious charge of micromanagement leveled in the literature on the *Maya-*

guez crisis is that senior civilian leaders rushed military operations unnecessarily and at great cost to the servicemen they sent in harm's way. Mahoney, for example, argues that "the operation was being driven from the very top" and that "people at the strategic level not trained in military planning" were "making operational and tactical decisions," which "was a recipe for disaster."[92] This observation, common in scholarship on the *Mayaguez* crisis, has been widely accepted by policy makers and academics. For example, a study on the Iran rescue operations makes the following claim about the *Mayaguez* operation:

> Pressured by Ford and Kissinger to launch the rescue mission on 14 May instead
> of the following day, Jones argued that it would be difficult, if not impossible.
> The various forces involved in a rescue bid would have to be coordinated
> properly, and many of the necessary forces had not yet even arrived in the area.
> Nevertheless, Ford decided that the mission should be launched immediately.[93]

This is factually inaccurate, as is the broader charge of civilian micromanagement it suggests. Military operations were not forced over the objection of best military advice but in conformity with it. Military operations were driven from the top, but not inappropriately and not exclusively by people untrained in military planning. The acting chairman of the JCS, representing all of the Chiefs, weighed in heavily on the timing of military operations. He secured one day of delay, and there is reason to believe could have easily delayed them another day if he had made the case that the risks of failure were too high. Under pressure from the other Joint Chiefs, Jones did not make that case. We cannot know what he would have done if the issue of only 175 Marines assaulting Tang Island had come up, but it seems clear that more scrutiny to reveal the actual risks being run would have been helpful. For this reason we can argue more rather than less oversight was needed in the *Mayaguez* decision-making process.

With a clear picture of command and control during the crisis, it is possible to extract some pertinent insights for the mission command concept. What the *Mayaguez* crisis illustrates is that the mission command approach *can fail from lack of oversight* just as easily as it can fail due to micromanagement and *fail just as easily from "anticipatory compliance"* as from insubordination.[94] Subordinates like the Marines assaulting Tang and the Joint Chiefs advising the president must feel free to provide candid risk assessments and to question their superiors until they are confident they understand intent and operating parameters.

What this suggests is that the open, collaborative, no jeopardy, "just the truth from your viewpoint" kind of culture pioneered by the military for its after-action review processes is just as important prior to operations (when they are being planned) as it is during operations (when they are being executed) and afterwards (when they are being reviewed to determine why things went the way they did). That was not the case during the *Mayaguez* crisis. The Marine assault commanders realized they would encounter heavier resistance than a few irregular forces and yet did not question their mission assignment.[95] The Marines wanted close air support but did not successfully explain their concerns or the risks of their assault plan to Lieutenant General Burns. In turn, Burns did not probe the Marine plan seeking an explanation for the risks being run or discuss the types of fire support that could be made available.[96] If either side had shared more information and their concerns, the competing intelligence estimates of enemy forces would have been reconciled and the assault plan could have been improved with workable close air support. Similarly, General Jones did not question the assault plan closely enough to raise questions about the advisability of 175 Marines assaulting a large body of well-entrenched enemy forces with heavy weapons, or the adequacy of close air support. Ford's civilian advisors, and particularly the much-excoriated Kissinger, actually raised more concerns about the risks of the Marine assault in the NSC deliberations than military leadership in the Pentagon did when reviewing the plan. Thus Jones, as well as Schlesinger, was not able to successfully explain the actual risks of the assault to Ford and other members of the NSC.

The *Mayaguez* crisis suggests the need to be as concerned about the adequacy of oversight as with the danger of micromanagement. Yet the mission command concept disproportionately emphasizes the latter. It encourages commanders to "demonstrate trust by exercising restraint in supervision of subordinates."[97] However, trust should also allow appropriate questions to be raised to clarify intent and risk. When all concerned are trusting others to focus on mission success, it is easier to fully explore the reasoning behind decisions without raising concerns about competence, confidence, or credibility that tend to complicate communication.

In the *Mayaguez* crisis there was not enough trust between the Marine and Air Forces in the field to sustain tough questioning of the assault force plan or higher decisions on close air support. Nor was there enough trust between the White House and the Pentagon to support more penetrating analysis of the risks associated with assaulting Tang Island and less direction of mainland strikes. The Joint Chiefs relaxed their oversight of plans and their risk assessment in deference to perceived White House preferences for moving quickly, and Schlesinger offered cryptic responses to Ford instead of bluntly explaining why he canceled the last airstrike. In short, undue fear of micromanagement can encourage a lack of trust that complicates effective command and control. In some cases, subordinates may even refuse to share information with superiors in hopes of compromising their situational awareness and discouraging interference in their decision making.

For example, during the crisis on the Korean Peninsula precipitated by the North Korean axe murders of American officers, senior military officers chose to distance themselves from Washington. "Recalling the micromanagement by officials in Washington who had reacted to the seizure of *Mayaguez* the previous year," General Richard G. Stilwell, USA, commander in chief of UN Command, "took steps to head off the tendency to skip echelons in the command and control system with high-level queries." "To preclude Washington micromanagement," he and key members of the UN Command staff "cut potential communications links between the President and subordinate commands." General Stillwell did so even though he and his chief of staff, Major General John Singlaub, believed the operations they were overseeing could easily escalate to general war. Singlaub later noted, "It was my estimate, shared by many of the staff, that the operation stood a fifty-fifty chance of starting a war." Still, Stillwell and Singlaub felt safer being out of touch with the president and his senior advisors.[98]

Some students of mission command have questioned the concept's bias toward decentralized decision making, arguing that sometimes conditions favor more centralized decision making.[99] But the vast bulk of the literature on the subject, and recent senior leader statements, emphasize the dangers of micromanagement, not the lack of sufficient oversight.[100] The condemnation of micromanagement in the *Mayaguez* crisis over the past thirty years and up until the present day has contributed to this broader, ongoing concern with micromanagement, and thus encouraged widespread worry that information sharing will lead to micromanagement.[101] These trends suggests the possibility that in our current military culture, and even the culture operative in the national security system more broadly,[102] leaders have trouble distinguishing between and properly balancing oversight and micromanagement.

This is especially true for operations short of large-scale force-on-force warfare. The persistent tendency in military culture to ignore the distinctions between warfighting and politico-military operations, and their differing requirements for success, further complicates the exercise of mission command. Officers involved in leading politico-military operations need to appreciate the greater level of scrutiny they will receive from both military and civilian leadership, and senior leaders need to pay greater attention to subordinate behaviors to ensure they are consistent with senior leader priorities. For example, General Brown, who unlike General Jones did not sit in on the NSC meetings, apparently did not appreciate the punitive nature of the mainland strikes. He too readily turned White House guidance to hold off the strikes into a blanket order to call them all off, thus exacerbating White House–Pentagon tensions. Misconstruing information requests from higher authorities as micromanagement and evidence of insufficient trust is another problem. Senior leaders may rightly delve into the details of operational and tactical planning because their understanding of the political objectives allow them to identify and assess risks that may not be apparent to those conducting the operations. Even those who currently flag the danger of micromanagement acknowledge it is no virtue for superiors to be poorly informed of what lower echelons are doing. On the contrary, the imperative for shared awareness makes it critical that senior leaders be acutely aware of what is happening at lower echelons, which also implies they may need to intervene on occasion to ensure alignment with higher level priorities.[103]

Defense Reform

It is often remarked that the *Mayaguez* incident was one of a series of cases that propelled defense reform interest in Congress and concluded with the landmark Goldwater-Nichols legislation of 1986 that mandated greater jointness. It is less well known that Scowcroft's assistant during the crisis, Robert McFarlane, played a major role in the reform. His conviction that reform was required stemmed, in part, from his after action analysis of what went wrong during the crisis.[104] The *Mayaguez* crisis also inclined the Joint Chiefs to pay more attention to special operations[105] and stimulated direct input into the landmark legislation that created the US Special Operations Command. First Lieutenant Gary L. Weikel, an Air Force HH-53 pilot during the crisis, was deeply bothered by how special operations forces were not used or ill-used during the operations. The AC-130 gunships were underutilized, the SEALs were not used at all, and after the special operations helicopters proved their worth during Vietnam and the *Mayaguez* crisis, the Air Force "wasted no time in dismantling the C/HH-53 squadrons and capability."[106] Weikel wrote a National War College paper on the topic that impressed the faculty. More directly, he provided evidence of the Air Force's failure to support special operations aviation to the Senate Armed Services Committee that motivated Representatives Dan Daniel (D-VA) and Earl D. Hutto (D-FL) to support legislation to create the Special Operations Command.[107]

Flag officers who served during the *Mayaguez* crisis also became proponents of reform. Admiral Holloway led the investigation of Operation Eagle Claw, the failed attempt to rescue the Americans held hostage in Tehran, and drafted the conclusions of the resultant "Holloway report." As Holloway recalls, the report "was frankly critical of the planning process, specifically the Chairman's decision to conduct the planning with an ad hoc organization outside of the JCS structure."[108] Holloway's colleagues signed the report even though they thought it would "probably be the end of their military careers."[109] The Holloway report contributed momentum toward the Goldwater-Nichols and Special Operations Command reforms.

General Jones also emerged from the crisis convinced of the need for change. He would end up playing a key role in subsequent reforms. Authoritative sources consider Jones's testimony and public stance on the need for reform to be the "most important factor in the enactment of the Goldwater-Nichols Act."[110] Jones later explained the impact of the *Mayaguez* on his thinking about the need for reform in an interview:

> It convinced me also of some of the difficulty of the problems of the joint system. If you look at our record of joint activity, we have had great problems of execution. There have been exceptions: the landing at Normandy and Korea at Inchon. But we've had our Gulf of Leyte, and we had terrible problems in Vietnam in joint operations. We have had them since then—the Iranian Crisis and Grenada. We found out in the aftermath [of the *Mayaguez*] that the command arrangements were down through CINCPAC, but below that it tended to get divided. We somewhat lucked out. Although we lost some troops on the island, we were quite fortunate to get the crew members back.[111]

Weikel, Jones, Holloway, and McFarlane experienced the *Mayaguez* crisis in different ways, respectively as a participant in the operations, as acting chairman of the Joint Chiefs, as a service chief, and as a White House aide monitoring the crisis decision making and conducting the White House assessment of the Pentagon's after action report. However, they all saw the need for change and played major roles in bringing about defense reforms that have transformed the way the US military performs both in conventional and irregular wars. Because of what they and many others learned from the crisis, major defense reforms are an important part of the historical legacy of the *Mayaguez* crisis.

One lesson from this experience is that it is possible to learn from failure—although it is difficult—and that it requires "insider" and "outsider" perspectives to come up with solutions. Both the Goldwater-Nichols and Special Operations Command reforms were fiercely resisted by the Pentagon. This is to be expected, given that organizations naturally pursue autonomy and resist outside direction. Reform required some farsighted individuals within the system working with those outside the system who could clinically evaluate system performance as a whole.

The current chairman of the JCS, Marine General Joseph F. Dunford, has argued the Pentagon has another major performance challenge that requires organizational change. He noted the high likelihood of any future conflict being transregional, multidomain, and multifunctional:

> From my perspective, our current planning, our organizational construct, and our command and control is not really optimized for that fight. . . . In terms of true integration—in other words, decision-making authority that integrates a fight across a region, across a domain, or across a function . . . if you believe what I believe . . . and then look at the nature of what the fight might be against peer competitors in the future, I don't think we'll be able to be as responsive, I don't think we'll be able to generate the tempo, I don't think we'll be able to frame decisions and act in a timely manner as much as we should unless we make some fundamental changes, again, to our organizational construct—the way we plan, the way we develop strategy, and . . . our command and control.[112]

The kind of organizational change the chairman is talking about will not be easy, but neither were the reforms that improved joint and special operations capabilities. What the *Mayaguez* crisis teaches is that such reforms are possible, particularly if those involved in the military operations can learn from the shortcomings and are willing to act on what they have learned.

National Security Council Reform

An in-depth description and analysis of the *Mayaguez* crisis also can be used to impart lessons about NSC decision making. Two things immediately stand out. It was the only time a president ever used the NSC to directly manage a crisis. Ford used the council as his decision-making body rather than empowering a smaller group to manage the event as happened during the Cuban missile crisis and other similar events.[113] The other salient aspect of the decision making is the amount of conflict it generated. Despite all senior officials agreeing on overarching priorities from the outset, which should have boded well for a unified effort, they executed their decisions in a manner that contributed to competition, conflict, and ultimately Schlesinger's firing.

Kissinger believes the two issues are related. In his memoirs, he argues that managing the crisis directly through the NSC was a mistake, that it was too "unwieldy to supervise operations in that much detail," and that trying to do so allowed Schlesinger to thwart the president's will. He claims the two mainland strikes that did not hit targets "demonstrate the risk of planning military operations in the National Security Council without any preparatory work by a subordinate group and without some official short of the President being made responsible for the hour by hour coordination." Kissinger notes, "The NSC is better designed for overall decisions than for micromanagement" and explains why:

> The President had ordered all-out strikes at the NSC meeting and, in the absence of the Chairman of the Joint Chiefs of Staff, there was no military officer sufficiently close to him to transmit the orders unambiguously through the chain of command. This gave the Secretary of Defense—who is actually, in our system, not directly in the chain of command—what turned out to be a decisive voice. To those of us in hourly contact with the President, it was inconceivable that he could have meant that the first wave be confined to armed reconnaissance in which no ordnance would be expended. How various NSC members in less frequent contact with Ford perceived his directives should not have been left to their subjective interpretations. The NSC is too unwieldy to supervise operations in that much detail. This is why President Kennedy created the so-called Ex-Comm (Executive Committee of the NSC) in the Cuban Missile Crisis and why the Nixon and Ford Administrations generally backed up the NSC with the Washington Special Actions Group (WSAG) at the deputy secretary level. In this case, senior officials at the NSC meeting were dealing directly with the President on tactical questions or created the impression with their subordinates that they were doing so. That made it hard to trace the responsibility for individual acts.[114]

Boiled down, Kissinger is arguing that "those of us in hourly contact with the President" (i.e., those who knew Ford's intent) were fit to "supervise operations in that much detail," whereas "NSC members in less frequent contact with Ford" and who "perceived his directives" through "their subjective interpretations" wrongly "created the impression with their subordinates that" because they attended an "NSC meeting [they] were dealing directly with the President on tactical questions." In short, Kissinger believed his proximity to Ford gave him the right to supervise policy implementation on the president's behalf and that Schlesinger's attempt to manage Defense Department implementation of presidential orders was illegitimate and ineffective.

Kissinger is wrong about Schlesinger's role, both legally and bureaucratically. Legally, Schlesinger was in the chain of command (figure 2). As one history of the Joint Staff notes, Kissinger apparently was "unaware of the 1958 amendments to the National Security Act, which established the chain of command as running from the President through the Secretary of Defense to the combatant commanders."[115] Kissinger was primus inter pares in terms of his close relationship with Ford, but as a practical matter the secretary of defense and other cabinet officials had the authority to oversee the details of any presidential decisions involving their departments and agencies.

Bureaucratically, Kissinger's proximity to the president did not afford him the undisputed authority he thought it should. In saying "the NSC is better designed for overall decisions than for micromanagement," Kissinger was not saying he was against micromanagement.[116] Rather, he was saying the president did not have time to micro-

FIGURE 2. MILITARY CHAIN OF COMMAND IN 1975

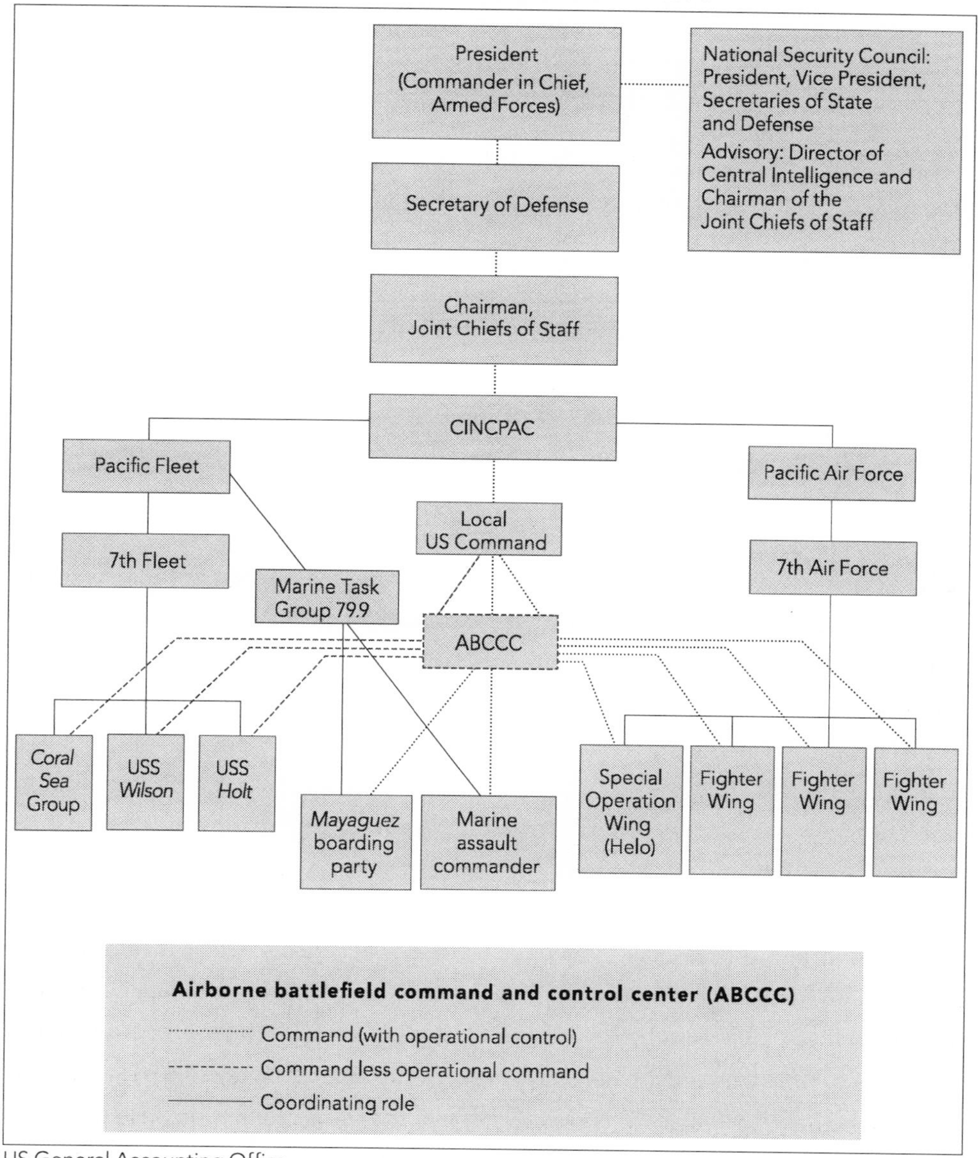

US General Accounting Office

manage and should have allowed Kissinger to do so through an interagency subgroup supporting the NSC. He is correct that presidents, and cabinet officials for that matter, typically are too busy to manage the details of complex national security problems. Presidents historically have relied upon smaller groups for both crisis support and routine policy formulation and implementation. Also, reading the NSC minutes, it is easy to see where Kissinger might have thought it difficult to keep discussion of fine points on track with so many people in the room. Minor players felt free to add their voices to the discussion and frequently sidetracked the debate.

However, it is not true that these interagency committees are better equipped to authoritatively oversee the implementation of policy. The *Mayaguez* crisis illustrates a president can have difficulty implementing his decisions through powerful departments and agencies. How much truer it is to say a presidential subordinate will face even more difficulties in this regard. Kissinger himself came to realize "that the more he was perceived as the controlling voice on policy the more likely the agencies and departments were to assert their prerogatives during implementation." He noted that it was easy making policy but not coordinating and implementing it. He found being dual-hatted as national security advisor and secretary of state increased his dominance in policy making but decreased his ability to implement the policies because the other departments, feeling they had not had a say in policy formulation, resisted policy implementation all the more.[117]

What Kissinger wanted was control so that he could impose coherence on both policy formulation and implementation. But he was not the president and did not have the formal or informal authority to control the Department of Defense.[118] Kissinger's relations with Melvin R. Laird and Rumsfeld, the secretaries of defense who preceded and followed Schlesinger, were just as fraught with tension. Also, as subsequent history illustrates, internecine battles between national security leaders are common (for example, between Zbigniew Brzezinski and Cyrus R. Vance, George P. Shultz and Caspar W. Weinberger, Colin L. Powell and Donald Rumsfeld). Typically these conflicts arise over inherently interagency issues that neither State nor Defense can manage alone but for which they refuse to follow the lead of the other or the national security advisor.

Moreover, Kissinger overestimates the value of one man's perspective dominating all the others. The decision making in the *Mayaguez* crisis was improved, not diminished, by having multiple perspectives advocated in the NSC. Ford's risk of catastrophic failure would have increased without the debate in the NSC about the wisdom of B-52 strikes and the need to delay operations a day. In retrospect, it is unfortunate the debate over delaying another day was not deeper and more protracted.

Despite his heavy reliance upon and confidence in Kissinger, Ford could see he benefited from multiple perspectives. When he fired Schlesinger, he also ended Kissinger's stint as both secretary of state and national security advisor. He later explained that doing so was "critical to restoring the proper functioning of the government's foreign policy apparatus," arguing that "from an institutional standpoint it was long overdue":

> The National Security Council was set up in 1947 so that a president would have an independent think tank in the White House that could make independent evaluations from the Pentagon and State Department and elsewhere so that the president wouldn't be captive of the bureaucracy. When Kissinger had both State and NSC, there was not an independent evaluation of proposals, and I never liked that arrangement that I inherited. And when the time came to make some [other] changes at the Pentagon and CIA, it was logical to tell Henry, "I'm gonna just leave you as secretary of state and upgrade Brent Scowcroft."[119]

Even if decision making is improved by multiple competing perspectives, as has long been argued,[120] we are left with the control issue that Kissinger raised. He charged Schlesinger with thwarting presidential intent. Kissinger overstated the case for insubordination on the airstrikes. Schlesinger and Jones did not hide the nature of the first strike package, and Schlesinger exercised what he (and probably most others) considered appropriate latitude in cancelling the fourth strike to aid the Marines on Tang Island. It has been argued that "Secretaries of Defense going back to Forrestal had routinely taken it upon themselves to cancel Presidential orders when they judged them to be . . . overtaken by events."[121] Arguably this was the case with the fourth airstrike.

However, by his own admission, Schlesinger was insubordinate on the orders to sink Cambodian vessels. He could have cited confusing presidential directives demanding a finely modulated use of force,[122] but his defense was that he did the right thing, both for the nation and for Ford's reputation. Regardless of how one adjudicates the propriety of what he, Wickham, and Pauly did in sidestepping the presidential order for sinking of all Cambodian vessels coming and going to Tang Island, their behavior underscores the control problem Kissinger raised. How can a president have high confidence that his policy will be implemented consistent with his will when he does not have time to personally supervise the issue and key actors on a sustained basis?

One option is for the president to designate an individual to lead the effort on his behalf. This is the solution Kissinger preferred, and as we have just examined, it does not work well. The other key presidential advisors resent the person designated as the lead and often refuse to take direction from that individual. They suspect the person assigned to lead the effort is pursuing their own interest and the interests of their organization, rather than the president's and/or nation's interests. This perceived conflict of interest is the same that General Jones identified in his testimony to Congress on the Joint Chiefs:

> Jones called the service chiefs' conflict of interest a "spokesman-statesman" dilemma. He said he did not see how the existing arrangement could work given the resource and mission issues that heightened this conflict. He called it "unreasonable to expect the service chiefs to take one position as service advocate . . . and a totally different position in the joint arena."[123]

Similarly, it is difficult to ask a cabinet official to both represent his or her department and also play the role of statesman, working for the national interest writ large. The Project on National Security Reform identified this problem in its lengthy report on national security system performance:

> In the national security system as currently constituted, Cabinet officials play dual roles. They are both advisors to the president on overall policy integration, and they are champions of their departments and agencies and those organizations' equities and agendas. Delegation of presidential authority does not work well because . . . "the needs of any President and those of his officialdom are incompatible." They are incompatible because Cabinet members must balance their roles as presidential advisors with their statutory obligations to build, manage, and safeguard strong departmental capabilities. Therefore, Cabinet officials bring their and their agencies' issues up to the president for settlement, while the president must try to impose a cross-cutting vision through his own "personal initiative, his mastery of detail, his search for information, his reach for control." The US government since World War II "has often tried . . . tinkering with structure" to reduce the tension between the president and his Cabinet officials, but to little effect.[124]

The Project on National Security Reform's remedy was to give the president the authority to appoint distinguished leaders without organizational leadership responsibilities to run empowered cross-functional teams dedicated to managing a high-priority issue full-time within a larger reform framework that assured departments and agencies that they would be able to weigh in with the president to define the scope of the team's purpose and strategy.[125] The way the teams should work has been explained elsewhere.[126] The point to be made here is that the *Mayaguez* is one of many cases that substantiate the need for reforming how the national security system currently integrates the efforts of diverse departments and agencies to pursue intrinsically interagency missions.

Civil-Military Relations

The *Mayaguez* crisis also has value as a case study in civil-military relations. The alleged micromanagement by the White House, the Joint Chiefs' desire to accommodate White House preferences that contributed to an underestimation of the risks of assaulting Tang Island, the insubordination by the Pentagon, and the firing of Schlesinger—in part because he accepted the unanimous recommendation of his senior uniformed officers to cancel the last airstrike—are all examples of friction in civil-military relations that deserve scrutiny. The loss of life, made particularly unbearable by the fate of the three Marines left behind,[127] still ignites indignation over these perceived shortcomings in the decision process.

The case of Pentagon insubordination in sidestepping presidential orders on the automatic sinking of Cambodian vessels is particularly poignant because it is so clear cut, yet so defensible in retrospect as having been responsible for securing "the margin of victory." If the boat with the *Mayaguez* crew had been sunk, many of the crew members would have been killed or badly injured. The United States would have suffered great damage to its reputation, and the public and Congress would have been furious, producing a backlash that would have further called into question whether the United States had the will and competence to protect its interests.

Yet the *Mayaguez* affair represents more than just a major case of frayed civil-military relations. The crisis and the way it was managed are often described as a fitting end to the nation's excruciating experience in Indochina, which broke the trust so necessary between the nation's leadership, military, and populace. As the novelist and Vietnam veteran Karl Marlantes put it,

> America didn't just lose the war, and the lives of 58,000 young men and women; Vietnam changed us as a country. In many ways, for the worse: It made us cynical and distrustful of our institutions, especially of government. For many people, it eroded the notion, once nearly universal, that part of being an American was serving your country.[128]

Many view the *Mayaguez* as the last act in an awful tragedy that began and ended with deception and poor leadership. In that sense the crisis was a harbinger of the direction civil-military relations would take over the next few decades as "no more Vietnams" became the silent rallying cry of many Americans. For many in the military, the *Mayaguez* showcased the civilian micromanagement they believed doomed military operations in Vietnam. Military officers widely believe civilian leaders second-guessed and tried to run military operations instead of making national strategy and ensuring the popular support and resources necessary to win the war were available. For many, the *Mayaguez*, with its near-catastrophic failure of the assault on Tang Island, tragic loss of life, and misleading explanations, seemed to epitomize the entire Vietnam experience.

For most civilian leaders, the *Mayaguez* incident did not reveal any such broader insights into the nation's military. To the extent Ford, Kissinger, and Scowcroft found Pentagon performance unsatisfactory, they attributed it to Schlesinger's poor leadership rather than the military more generally. However, well after the crisis Kissinger identified some institutional military characteristics that others have seized upon to help explain civil-military friction in more recent years.

When Kissinger explained the poor results and the "new crisis of confidence between the President and his Secretary of Defense" that, he said, "would culminate in Schlesinger's dismissal five months later," he also attributed some behaviors to the Pentagon more generally. In the same passage where he blames Schlesinger for "most of the communication mix-ups and sloppy intelligence reporting" during the crisis, Kissinger highlights the Pentagon's determination "never again to be cast in the role of villain." He attributes a more general Pentagon listlessness to the aftereffects of the Vietnam War:

> One of the most painful casualties of the Vietnam War was the morale of the Pentagon. The idea of reengaging in Indochina only two weeks after the evacuation of Saigon evoked revulsion. When the Pentagon is less than enthusiastic, it does not reinterpret orders—as the Foreign Service is wont to do—but fulfills them literally without any additional initiative on its part. Given the complexity of military deployments, the practical effect is the same as procrastination. Throughout the *Mayaguez* crisis, the Pentagon dutifully assembled the forces as it was ordered to do. But it was clearly reluctant, offered no ideas of its own, left it to the civilians to prod it into action, and—remembering the outcry after the B-52 bombing of the Hanoi area—reflexively opposed the use of the strategic bombers.[129]

Kissinger's charge of passivity is plainly false. The Pentagon had specific views on how military force should be used and acted on those views to the point of insubordination. Pentagon leaders also took the initiative on detailed rules of engagement and an ultimatum. Schlesinger and his top military leaders were not passive, but they did disagree with Kissinger on some specific issues like the rules of engagement, ultimatums, and B-52s.

It seems more likely Kissinger's real complaint was that the Pentagon was insufficiently pliant. It was too adamant about using proportionate and discriminate force, and given the documented insubordination present during the crisis, it seems like a fair complaint. The critical exception is the Joint Chiefs' willingness to accommodate the White House by supporting the hasty assault on Tang Island. But even that decision only serves to reinforce the popular view in the military that it is important for military leaders to help the White House make better strategic choices and calculate risks with greater precision. This willingness to challenge the White House perspective and work toward a Pentagon-preferred solution may be a long-standing military penchant, but it was greatly reinforced by the perceived failure in Vietnam.

Military leaders who believe Vietnam demonstrated that America's political elites are prone to poor and/or politicized strategic thinking and the micromanaging of military operations are more inclined to challenge, or even attempt to control, the way the military is used so that there will be "no more Vietnams." Over time, many senior civilians have come to believe the Pentagon will frame military advice in ways that encourage presidents to take Pentagon-preferred courses of action. In particular, the concern expressed by civilian leaders is that the Pentagon crafts an artificial set of military options to steer the president in the direction the Pentagon prefers.[130] In that sense, Kissinger's complaint that the Pentagon was insufficiently on board with President Ford during the *Mayaguez* crisis was a harbinger of future civil-military relations, as was the military's concern with civilian micromanagement.

By correcting the false narratives that have grown up around the *Mayaguez* crisis, this study can make a contribution to ameliorating strains in current civil-military relations. The analysis offered here disproves the heavy-handed micromanagement thesis that many military officers writing on the *Mayaguez* crisis emphasize. In reality, as a careful reading of the NSC minutes illuminates, civilian leaders were careful when it came to the issue of military risk. It is not hard to understand why. Political leaders need and want successful military operations as much as military leaders. They also, for political reasons, want to avoid allegations that they forced the military to act contrary to its recommendations.

The incident also amply demonstrates the limitations of the current NSC system. Even in a fast-moving crisis with a large degree of direct presidential management and senior leader agreement on priorities, it was not possible to achieve unified effort. In addition, the nation's senior military advisers were not able to calculate and explain well the risks of proposed military operations. The Goldwater-Nichols and Special

Operations Command reforms have remedied some of the joint planning and command and control issues revealed by the *Mayaguez* affair, but the larger NSC system remains essentially unchanged and inadequate.

In that sense it can be argued there is unfinished business from the *Mayaguez* crisis. Many leaders—military and civilian—have drawn attention to the need for national security reform over the past two decades, but reform has proven elusive. However, here too the example of the *Mayaguez* crisis is a balm to civil-military relations. After the crisis, military and civilian leaders were able to learn from experience and improve organizational performance for the benefit of all those who go in harm's way. Today no one believes the nation or its military would be better off if the joint reforms and creation of Special Operations Command had not happened. Similarly, if military and civilian leaders could partner again to improve the way the NSC and its staff manage critical national security issues, it would be a boon to better civil-military relations. The nation's military members, foreign service officers, intelligence professionals, and other civil servants who risk so much for the nation's welfare deserve nothing less than the best possible national security policy, strategy, planning, and decision-making system. It is not right, nor is it politically expedient, to ask them to serve in any other circumstances.[131]

The Morality of Force

This case study cannot resolve the moral issues surrounding the decision making during the *Mayaguez* crisis. It is not possible to study the crisis for long without becoming familiar with the names of the brave serviceman who lost their lives on or near Tang Island in mid-May 1975 and reflecting on their sacrifice and how their lives might have been saved. For many, their loss, juxtaposed with the apparent errors made during the crisis, is overwhelmingly tragic. Vice Admiral Steele is said to have remarked, "I just feel those men died in vain. . . . It was just a terrible rush to get it done."[132] This sentiment is understandable, especially because with the benefit of hindsight, it is clear that even a brief delay would have avoided much loss of life.

Others disagree, believing that despite the losses, the military operations were justified on several levels. Schlesinger took this view in a later interview:

> Much of the intellectual community had gotten to the point where they were opposed to any American military involvement in Southeast Asia. And I think that there were a number of people who were out to demonstrate that this incident was another failure of American decision-making. They were carried away

by issues that were secondary. For example, they often pointed out that we lost more lives [in the rescue effort] than there were members of the *Mayaguez* crew. That strikes me at least as secondary and possibly irrelevant. It was a matter of principle, and we were not going to allow acts of piracy against American vessels. There was a view that the United States was this "pitiful, helpless giant," to borrow a phrase from Mr. Nixon, and we could not let that view continue. And we had to get that crew back. We achieved everything we wanted, and in my mind, we did the right thing.[133]

Another White House participant, Robert Hartmann, the counselor to President Ford, reviewed the terrible losses, asking whether it was worth it and answering his own question in the affirmative:

Thirty-eight Americans lost their lives, including a whole helicopter load of twenty-three airmen who crashed in Thailand before the shooting started, and three Marines who were missing when the survivors pulled out of Koh Tang Island. Twenty to forty American lives to rescue thirty-nine other Americans. Was it worth it? Of course it was. Protecting unarmed US citizens in their peaceful pursuits is why we have police and military forces. It's what organized society, as opposed to anarchy, is all about.[134]

There are others who correctly understood the primary purpose of the military operations and still judged them worthwhile:

President Ford's swift action at the time . . . had a lasting effect for the good. It said to our enemies and to the world that while America might have withdrawn from Vietnam and been forced to acquiesce in the hostile takeover of that nation, our adversaries would make a mistake to think that we would ignore provocation, particularly when American lives were involved.[135]

While this research cannot resolve differences of opinion over the merits of the military operations balanced against their costs in lives lost, it can help sharpen that debate. Many commenting on the crisis attribute false motives to US leaders, or misunderstand what President Ford and his advisors thought was at stake. For example, Kissinger is frequently quoted for his explanation of the crisis in his memoirs where he concludes, "We had entered Indochina to save a country, and . . . ended by rescuing a ship."[136] But as Kissinger knows better than anyone, Ford did not order men into combat to rescue the ship. They were sent to underscore the resolve of the United States to protect its interests and more specifically to communicate to North Korea and its patrons that South

Korea was not theirs for the taking, even though the United States had withdrawn its military forces from Vietnam and Cambodia. It should at least be acknowledged that the president ordered military action during the crisis in pursuit of national geostrategic objectives and not for falsely ascribed and less worthy motives, such as burnishing his own political fortunes.

The debate also ought to be informed by a realistic assessment of the outcomes generated by military action. At this far remove it may seem that chances of conflict on the Korean Peninsula were too remote to risk lives in the Gulf of Thailand, but at the time the threat was widely perceived as real and significant in the press, the intelligence community, and among American leaders and US allies in Asia. It will never be known with certainty whether the use of military force during the crisis helped deter North Korea and other adversaries—thus helping to save lives by reducing the likelihood of war—or simply saved a lesser number of lives by helping mute the US response to the North Korean axe murders a year later. The results of any use of military force for purposes of posturing will be attended by such uncertainty. What can be said from a review of declassified intelligence and diplomatic assessments from the period is that the military operations successfully communicated to those countries in the region precisely the message US leaders wanted to send.

In addition, it should be recognized that although things went wrong during the execution of the military operations, no other nation could have projected military force in a similar manner. In that sense, the overall conduct of the operation showcased American military power. Schlesinger went further, saying "in my judgment this was a great triumph of American arms; that we could respond so quickly to an unexpected event, at such a distance, and respond so effectively, and with a high degree of discrimination against chosen targets."[137] Subsequent fine-grained analysis demonstrated how terribly wrong things had gone, how much better they should have gone, and how much the valor of US forces prevented a total fiasco, but the rapid projection of American military power to the scene was a stark reminder to other countries of inherent US capabilities.

Some who may not dispute the motives or the demonstrative impact of the military operations may nonetheless hold US leaders culpable for incompetence. To them, it may seem that the advantages of waiting another day clearly outweighed the disadvantages of not doing so, and that ordering the military to move too quickly was reprehensible. The analysis offered in this case study supports the conclusion that US leaders could have delayed another day without greatly diminishing what they were trying to achieve.[138] Yet there are mitigating factors that need to be considered before reaching that conclusion.

It should be acknowledged that the best military advice available to the president supported his decision to not wait another day. It also is important to remember that although the recovery of the crew members was a decidedly secondary objective that was considered an unlikely development, US leaders believed the only chance for such an outcome required maintaining pressure on the Cambodians. US leaders were conscious of the fact that the Cambodians could kill the crew any time they pleased, and thus there was an incentive to move as quickly as possible. Colby noted in the third NSC meeting that if the Cambodians started killing the crew members in reprisal, "it would be very difficult for us," meaning there would be great political pressure to cease and desist and appeal for a resolution by diplomacy. Schlesinger agreed, saying, "It is a close call." He also acknowledged "the pressures of time" and that it was "possible that the Cambodians will decide to execute our men." The reputation of the Khmer Rouge was such that the crew were considered "goners" if they got to the mainland.[139]

In such circumstances, and as Schlesinger later argued, the solution was to "paste Cambodia to the point that they realized it was not worth it to them to keep the crew."[140] In other words, he wanted the Cambodians to believe they were in the way of an oncoming train that would stop for nothing. To extend the metaphor, slowing the train or ushering it on to a side track temporarily ran the risk of releasing pressure and giving the Cambodians the impression they might be able to negotiate a better outcome. This is why Schlesinger was in favor of continuing the air attacks after receiving the news of the broadcast but in favor of discontinuing them after the crew was safely recovered in order to assist the Marines.

For some observers, none of these considerations lessen the moral opprobrium attached to the conscious decisions to risk lives for the purposes of "signaling" resolve to other nations. They will argue, as have US leaders in other crises such as the North Korean seizure of the *Pueblo* and its crew or the Iranian seizure of the US embassy and its personnel, that the top priority should be the lives of those captured and that military operations can only put those lives at risk. While this is a defensible position, making the lives of individual citizens a nation's top priority can have perverse effects, as other countries have discovered.[141]

It also should be noted that many of those who go in harm's way on the nation's behalf do not expect that their safety will be their countrymen's top priority if a merciless power captures them. The captain of the *Pueblo*, Lloyd Bucher, has said that as his ship and crew approached the North Korean mainland he "accepted the realization that if any help was still contemplated by our Seventh Fleet or Fifth Air Force, its objective could no longer be rescue, only retaliation."[142] Later, commenting on the military operations in the *Mayaguez* crisis, he again said, "I certainly expected this type of operation to be mounted for us . . . we all expected it."[143]

Elizabeth Ann Swift, a diplomat held hostage in Tehran during the Carter administration, has made the same point at length in an oral history interview about her experiences. Interestingly, she was one of the foreign service officers who served on the Department of State task force for the *Mayaguez* operations, which perhaps influenced her perspective:

> The fact that the US government didn't break relations with the Iranian government within the first couple of days of us being held, is just mind-boggling to me still. I assumed that some sort of Cambodian type rescue like the *Mayaguez* would be run rather quickly, and was nothing but astounded that it wasn't run. [I] assumed we'd all be killed if they ran it but assumed that the government would have to.[144]

Swift was asked about whether she felt abandoned after so much time passed, and she said no, that she "had assumed all the way along that everybody back in the States was desperate and worried about us." Neither did she feel abandoned by her organization: "There was no way the State Department was going to abandon us. I had too many friends, and I've never quite understood how people could feel that they were abandoned."[145] Swift did not believe the country could afford to make her safety the top priority, and she understood the president might have to make the difficult choice to resolve the issue through military force:

> There was no question in my mind that the president had the right to make a decision that might cost me my life . . . that he might take some sort of decision that would get the Iranians so mad that they would execute us, or something like that. . . . When I signed up for the Foreign Service, I signed up for whatever happened. I cannot say that I was particularly delighted with the thought that I might get shot or killed, and if you'd asked me did I want them to come to our rescue physically, I would've told you no, because I thought a good many of us would get killed. But I would never have said it is not the right of the President of the United States to make that decision. And I know he would make it realizing that indeed he might get a lot of us killed, but that is one of those awful decisions you have to make as the president. A lot of my colleagues didn't feel that way.[146]

Bucher, Swift, and many others who serve their country in dangerous circumstances overseas believed there are limits to the extent to which their country can protect them or should, as a matter of first priority. But not all citizens feel this way. After their *Mayaguez* ordeal some crew members sued the government for putting their lives at risk. More recently, the Obama administration was harshly criticized for not making the welfare of hostages its top priority.[147] The debate about what citizens owe their country and vice versa will continue, but hopefully the analysis of *Mayaguez* crisis offered here clarifies the issue and brings some balance to the discussion.

There is always a long chain of factors affecting the risk to lives during combat: the priorities adopted by White House leaders; the risk assessment of the most senior uniformed officers in the Pentagon; the command and control arrangements military authorities put in place; the training US forces have received; the willingness of their fellow servicemen to repeatedly risk themselves in attempting to recover those under duress; the competency of those maintaining vehicles and aircraft; and the sheer chance of being confused, unaware, and lost in the pitch dark. Yet despite all of these uncertainties, the servicemen ordered into combat during the *Mayaguez* military operations went willingly. In light of that, the one moral certainty we have is the debt of gratitude we owe our fellow citizens who risk their lives for the collective security and prosperity the rest of us enjoy.

Conclusion

T he purpose of this study was to fill in or otherwise improve some key descriptive details about the *Mayaguez* crisis, provide a compelling explanation for US behavior based on all available evidence, and extract lessons about command and control of US forces and civil-military relations more generally. The results correct a body of research that, to date and on the whole, has mischaracterized motives for US behavior. As a result, the wrong lessons from the crisis have been promoted, and the significance of the crisis has been underestimated. In addition, the literature on the *Mayaguez* has been a source of additional friction for US civil-military relations by promulgating the false—and persistent—narrative that civilian leaders micromanaged the crisis at high costs to US servicemen. Military leaders commenting on the crisis almost invariably repeat the false narrative of micromanagement,[1] a misapprehension that unnecessarily complicates civil-military relations.

This study offers a more accurate description of the crisis and a more compelling explanation for US motives and behaviors, thus offering useful insights for scholars, defense leaders, and students of the national security system. For example, numerous sources mischaracterize the Cambodians as innocent bystanders abused by a bullying United States driven by emotional fallout from defeats in Indochina and a president intent on furthering his political fortunes at the expense of American and foreign lives. The truth is far different, as this study has shown:

- Cambodia was anxious to assert sovereignty over potentially oil-rich islands, but its determination to hold the *Mayaguez* crew was centrally directed, as were its military actions during the crisis. Cambodian authorities only relented when it became clear the US military response would be too costly for them.

- US leaders accurately assessed Cambodian motives in the first NSC meeting, but considered them irrelevant given circumstances and broader US objectives.

- President Ford was not motivated by domestic political considerations, nor even by the intent to rescue the *Mayaguez* crew, which he was in a poor position to achieve. In fact, he was willing to run substantial risks the crew would be harmed.

- US leaders' collective preference for the use of force was not an emotional reaction to the humiliation of withdrawal from Vietnam either.

Instead, US leaders were singularly motivated by geostrategic concerns. The decision to use force quickly was due to the belief, shared by all key US leaders, that they needed to reinforce deteriorating American credibility and, in particular, signal North Korea (and to a lesser extent, South Korea) that the United States would honor its security commitments. In order to deter China and other countries from siding with North Korea, US leaders wanted to signal the United States was ready and fully determined to protect South Korea—regardless of public opinion and any congressional reservations. They also wanted to convince South Korea there was no reason to contemplate acquiring its own nuclear weapons. Only to a far lesser extent did they hope—while considering it unlikely—that their willingness to use force would incline the Cambodians to desist and release the crew.

Thus, it is impossible to fully appreciate what US leaders were trying to do and what they thought was at stake during the *Mayaguez* crisis without understanding their concern about possible war on the Korean Peninsula. Their desire to use force, and the ultimate value of the sacrifices made by US servicemen, must be understood in that light. This explanation differs from the bulk of the *Mayaguez* literature and especially the university press books on the *Mayaguez* over the past several decades. A detailed explanation for how scholarship went awry has been offered elsewhere,[2] but it should be noted here that the problem was not the one cited in recent commentary about the irrelevance of academia to public policy.

In recent years, prominent national security practitioners and theoreticians have raised the concern that the academy is too cloistered,[3] too focused on "models and methods,"[4] and insufficiently willing to comment on policy issues—to the point that academic work is unintelligible and irrelevant.[5] The conclusion here is that scholarship on the *Mayaguez* crisis does not suffer from these faults but rather the opposite. The scholarship erred by "jump[ing] from detailed description to 'findings' and strong commentary, passing lightly over explanatory analysis" and the attention to methodology it requires.[6] In paying too little attention to methodology, and rushing past explanatory analysis to commentary, these studies lost sight of basic factors in the decision-making process, such as the primary role North Korea played in decision-makers' geostrategic calculations.

For the defense community, the study challenges some deep-seated prejudices and encourages introspection. The dominant narrative among military authors and senior military leaders commenting on the *Mayaguez* crisis is wrong. The event was not an iconic example of gross civilian micromanagement. Instead, it is better understood as a caution against insufficient oversight:

- The only detailed military issue that civilian and military leaders disagreed about was the sinking of Cambodian boats. Given the stakes and import of the issue for US objectives, it was appropriate for President Ford to make this judgment call.

- What micromanagement there was came from military leaders, and arguably, it was not consequential in terms of outcomes.

- What was consequential, and might have reduced or eliminated the tragic loss of life during the crisis, was better joint military planning and risk assessments. In particular, better oversight should have revealed the inadequacy of plans for close air support and the actual risks of the assault plan for Tang Island.

Leaders involved in the crisis or responsible for evaluating it later came to appreciate the need for reforms that would provide improved joint planning and operations, and a more robust special operations capability. In this regard, major defense reforms are an enduring legacy of the *Mayaguez* crisis, and a positive development that hopefully will supplant the false micromanagement narrative currently so dominant in the literature.

In retrospect, it is surprising that the *Mayaguez* crisis facilitated defense reform but not national security reform. Congress was able to get beyond the widespread confusion about Ford's motives and the assumption that the crisis was simply an emotional overreaction to defeat in Indochina, and arrive at accurate conclusions about the need for defense reform. However, the *Mayaguez* crisis also perfectly depicts the need for NSC reform, and yet to date neither Congress nor the executive branch have been motivated to act on that need. The principal argument for NSC reform is the inability of the president to consistently generate unified effort from the executive branch. Despite the president's personal involvement, the lack of unified effort was a major problem during the *Mayaguez* crisis as it has been in so many other national security issues.[7]

News media quickly picked up on major differences between Kissinger and Schlesinger, and later the level of angst Ford had about his ability to control his own Department of Defense became evident. Research has revealed other major challenges to unified effort during the *Mayaguez* crisis as well, such as the following:

- Kissinger used his control of diplomatic communications to ensure military force was used, including withholding news of a diplomatic initiative from the NSC.

- Pentagon leaders consciously stonewalled the White House for three hours to avoid sinking boats that might be carrying *Mayaguez* crew members.

- The White House assessment of Pentagon obstruction and duplicity on airstrikes was exaggerated and uninformed as to how White House behaviors and the president's own guidance helped limit the number of strikes on the mainland.

The import of the *Mayaguez* crisis for NSC reform has been confused by scholarship and senior leader memoirs that cast blame elsewhere, such as Kissinger's assertion that the intelligence community's failure dramatically impaired the decision-making process. However, it also is true that NSC reforms are especially difficult because congressional committee structure is built around departments and agencies and no one committee has responsibility for considering the performance of the NSC system as a whole.

As numerous studies have shown,[8] the inability to consistently generate unified effort and other shortcomings indicate the current national security system, which has been in effect since 1948, is outdated and needs to be reformed. For decades, presidents and their key subordinates have had to work around the system to try to engineer the outcomes they desired, a task that has proven fraught with conflict and frequently led to poor outcomes. The *Mayaguez* crisis is just one case among many that demonstrates the need for managing high-priority national security issues with small empowered teams built for collaboration rather than competition.[9]

A final, editorial comment about the crisis and its relevance for civil-military relations may be in order. The research findings offered here underscore several additional observations:

- Only good fortune and the skill, initiative, and valor displayed by US forces prevented much higher casualties and a complete disaster.

- The merits of using military force in the *Mayaguez* crisis will always be debated, but it is clear US leaders pursued geostrategic goals and that they successfully conveyed their deterrent message.

- In that regard, the sacrifices made by US servicemen during the final battle of the Vietnam War might have been avoided, but they were not in vain.

The first point about the skill and valor of US servicemen is made better elsewhere and in greater detail,[10] but the latter two points are uncommon and deserve elaboration.

Thirty years ago the epigraph I chose for a book on the *Mayaguez* crisis was a quotation from Thucydides' history of the Peloponnesian War. Pericles believed a strength he and his fellow Athenians shared was that they were "capable at the same time of taking risks and of estimating them beforehand." My thought was that American citizens need the same ability to assess risks realistically, especially when it comes to foreign powers seizing hostages. Aware of the decision-makers' dilemma, the community "ought not to demand the most improbable outcomes: that military operations will be perfectly executed rescue missions or that tolerance and inaction will impress friends or influence enemies."[11] Decades later it is not clear from commentary on the *Mayaguez* crisis, or the quality of national debate over security issues in general,[12] that our collective understanding of such basic leadership dilemmas has increased. Perhaps a final contribution this study can make is to reinforce appreciation for the onerous decisions senior leaders have to make in such circumstances, thereby helping ameliorate our sometimes fractious civil-military relations while also honoring the sacrifices US servicemen and civil servants are often called upon to make.

Notes

Preface

1. Secretary of Defense Robert M. Gates, Address at the United States Military Academy (speech, West Point, NY, February 25, 2011), http://archive.defense.gov/Speeches/Speech.aspx?SpeechID=1539.

2. Jim Garamone, "Dunford Urges New AF Officers to Lead in Academy Graduation Address," DoD News, May 26, 2017, http://www.af.mil/News/Article-Display/Article/1195252/dunford-urges-new-af-officers-to-lead-in-academy-graduation-address/.

3. For example, in keeping with this sentiment, the Air Force named its Enlisted Heritage Research Institute at Maxwell Air Force Base in Montgomery, Alabama, after Chief Master Sergeant Wayne Fisk, "the last man off of Koh Tang Island during the rescue of the crew of the SS Mayaguez" and "truly a warrior's warrior." See http://www.airuniversityfoundation.org/enlisted-heritage-hall.html for more on Sergeant Fisk and the institute.

4. "The Mayaguez rescue could have served as a fitting metaphor for the whole of our war in Southeast Asia. Like the war, the Mayaguez incident is recalled, when it is recalled at all, more for its mistakes than for the lessons of duty and honor exemplified in the conduct of the men who fought it. That is unfortunate. For in that encounter, as in the war that preceded it, Americans fought for love and honor, and their service should be remembered in this country as an affirmation of human virtue and a priceless element of our national self-respect." John McCain, "Address to United States Air Force Academy" (speech, Colorado Springs, CO, October 18, 1996), https://www.mccain.senate.gov/public/index.cfm/1996/10/post-8a71f4b4-541f-4186-8f49-8a919d6f1a12.

5. This is as true for the popular press as it is for scholarship on the crisis. See "A Military Mission Gone Wrong," CBS News, January 24, 2001, https://www.cbsnews.com/news/a-military-mission-gone-wrong/; and Matthew M. Burke, "The Truth about the Lost Marines of the Vietnam War's Last Battle," *Newsweek*, January 24, 2017, http://www.newsweek.com/2017/02/03/us-marines-disappeared-mayaguez-last-battle-vietnam-war-547106.html.

6. Stephen Randolph, "Uncovering the Lessons of Vietnam," *Foreign Service Journal*, July–August 2015, 52–53.

7. Burke, "Truth about the Lost Marines." Burke's article notes "the brutal war that started with a lie may have ended with one as well."

8. Christopher J. Lamb, "The *Mayaguez* Crisis: Correcting 30 Years of Scholarship," *Political Science Quarterly* 133, no. 1 (Spring 2018).

9. Christopher Jon Lamb, *Belief Systems and Decision Making in the* Mayaguez *Crisis* (Gainesville: University of Florida Press, 1989), 279.

10. John McCain, "Dedication of the Mayaguez Memorial" (speech, US embassy, Bangkok, Thailand, November 11, 1996).

Introduction

1. There is disagreement over when the Vietnam War ended, but the Vietnam Veterans Memorial Fund maintains the participants in the *Mayaguez* rescue were part of the Vietnam conflict and the names of those lost during the *Mayaguez* operations are inscribed on the Vietnam Veterans Memorial. See William Triplett, "Out With a Whimper: The Tragedy of the *Mayaguez*," *Veteran*, July 1994.

2. Ford considered the crisis the "tensest moments" of his presidency. See Thomas M. DeFrank and Gerald R. Ford, *Write It When I'm Gone: Remarkable Off-the-Record Conversations with Gerald R. Ford* (New York: G. P. Putnam's Sons, 2007), 63.

3. The Ford and Kissinger quotes in this section are from Christopher J. Lamb, *Belief Systems and Decision Making in the* Mayaguez *Crisis* (Gainesville: University of Florida Press, 1989), 63–76.

4. US Congress, House Foreign Affairs Committee, Subcommittee on International Political and Military Affairs, *Seizure of the* Mayaguez, *Hearings on the* Mayaguez *Incident*, pt. 4 (Washington, DC: General Accounting Office, 1976) (hereafter GAO report), 80. This report details fifteen killed in action, three missing in action, fifty wounded in action, and twenty-three nonbattle deaths. The nonbattle deaths comprise eighteen Air Force Security Police and five crewmen who were killed on May 13 when their helicopter crashed in Thailand as they were assembling for possible use in retaking the *Mayaguez*.

5. The first university press book on the crisis was the author's *Belief Systems and Decision Making in the* Mayaguez *Crisis*. It was a distillation of my doctoral dissertation, which in turn drew upon research published a few years earlier: Christopher Jon Lamb, "Belief Systems and Decision Making in the *Mayaguez* Crisis," *Political Science Quarterly* 99, no. 4 (Winter 1984–85): 681–702.

6. Some key participants have gone on record multiple times about what they thought, said, and did during the crisis. Some recent studies on the crisis rely heavily on the memoirs of Ford and Kissinger, but these sources must be used with caution as they sometimes contradict what they actually said and did during the crisis. The general approach taken in this book is to assign greater credibility to a participant's remembrances offered during or shortly after the crisis rather than years later, unless corroborated by other sources.

7. Tapes of conversations among major participants in the Cuban missile crisis have been made public, but issues have been raised about their accuracy. See Ernest R. May and Philip Zelikow, *The Kennedy Tapes: Inside the White House during the Cuban Missile Crisis* (1997); and Sheldon Stern, "What JFK Really Said," *Atlantic*, May 2000, http://www.theatlantic.com/past/issues/2000/05/stern.htm.

8. For a discussion of why the event should be classified as a crisis, see Lamb, *Belief Systems and Decision Making*, 5–11.

9. Vandenbroucke says the US response was "an improvised, flawed operation that narrowly avoided defeat." Guilmartin argues it "nearly produced disaster," and Mahoney claims it "came perilously close to ending in disaster." Lamb, "Belief Systems and Decision Making," 682; Lucien S. Vandenbroucke, *Perilous Options: Special Operations as an Instrument of U.S. Foreign Policy* (New York: Oxford University Press, 1993), 72; John F. Guilmartin, *A Very Short War: The* Mayaguez *and the Battle of Koh Tang* (College Station: Texas A & M University Press, 2010), 155–56; and Robert J. Mahoney, *The Mayaguez Incident: Testing America's Resolve in the Post-Vietnam Era* (Lubbock: Texas Tech University Press, 2011), 261.

10. There are even conspiracy theorists who assert the *Mayaguez* was consciously led into Cambodian waters to precipitate an international incident and that it held classified cargo, which was the cause of the quick US military response. The sparse and circumstantial evidence for these claims is not reviewed here due to space constraints. The ship, owned by Sea-Land Corporation, was en route to Sattahip, Thailand, from Hong-Kong, and carrying a non-arms cargo for military bases in Thailand.

11. Marines and sailors from the USS *Pawnee* boarded the West Indies schooner *Susan Jane* on September 10, 1861, as part of the Union blockade of the Southern states. James E. Wise and Scott

Baron, *The 14-Hour War: Valor on Koh Tang and the Recapture of the SS* Mayaguez (Annapolis, MD: Naval Institute Press, 2011), 18.

12. Scowcroft cited in Robert L. Pfaltzgraff and Jacquelyn K. Davis, *National Security Decisions: The Participants Speak* (Lexington, MA: Lexington Books, 1990), 273–74.

13. National Security Council meeting minutes, May 12, 1975; May 13, 1975 (10:22–11:17); May 13–14, 1975 (22:40–0025); and May 14, 1975 (all declassified March 20, 1996), Gerald R. Ford Presidential Library, Ann Arbor, MI (hereafter NSC meeting minutes). Unless otherwise noted, all quotes from dialogue in NSC meetings come from these minutes.

Chapter 1

1. Scowcroft notes that when he first mentioned the *Mayaguez* to Ford, they were not sure if the news was "fact or fiction." Pfaltzgraff and Davis, *National Security Decisions*, 273; and Bartholomew H. Sparrow, *The Strategist: Brent Scowcroft and the Call of National Security* (New York: PublicAffairs, 2015), 156.

2. Henry Kissinger, *Years of Renewal* (New York: Simon & Schuster, 2011), 548.

3. Hyland would try hard to stay abreast of the fast-moving developments, telling INR he needed detailed chronologies and situation reports.

4. James Cannon, *Gerald R. Ford: An Honorable Life* (Ann Arbor: University of Michigan Press, 2013), 376.

5. Ron Nessen, *It Sure Looks Different from the Inside* (Chicago: Playboy Press, 1978), 118.

6. Just before noon on May 12, Defense Intelligence Agency (DIA) message traffic confidently assessed Cambodian motives for stopping the *Mayaguez* and the earlier Panamanian freighter. DIA noted there were "long-standing disputes between the Cambodians and Vietnamese over ownership of Poulo Wai and several other small islands in the Gulf of Thailand." Based on intercepted communications, DIA asserted the Cambodians were "eager to reassert their claims to this territory." Indeed, it appears Vietnamese threats prompted Cambodia to increase its garrison of 10 soldiers on the island to 300 on September 5, 1974. See *Defense Intelligence Agency (DIA) update on the Cambodian Khmer Rouge seizure of the US merchant ship MAYAGUEZ in the Gulf of Siam about 60 miles off the Cambodian coastline. The ship, owned by Sea-Land Corp., was en-route to Sattahip, Thailand, from Hong-Kong, carrying a non-arms cargo for military bases in Thailand.* Department Of Defense, May 12, 1975. *U.S. Declassified Documents Online*, tinyurl.galegroup.com/tinyurl/3nUUn6. Accessed April 3, 2017. For the 1974 augmentation of Cambodian forces on Poulo Wai, which is based on reporting in the *Far Eastern Economic Review*, see Luanne J. Smith, "An Analysis of Events Leading to the Chinese Invasion of Vietnam," (thesis, Naval Postgraduate School, 1980), 9–11.

7. Mahoney points out that this assumption was introduced in messages from the embassy in Jakarta and the defense attaché in Manila based on the captain of the *Mayaguez*'s distress message. Mahoney, *Mayaguez Incident*, 21–23.

8. Gerald R. Ford, *A Time to Heal: The Autobiography of Gerald R. Ford* (Norwalk, CT: Easton Press, 1987), 276; Richard G. Head, Frisco W. Short, and Robert C. McFarlane, *Crisis Resolution: Presidential Decision Making in the* Mayaguez *and Korean Confrontations* (Boulder: Westview Press, 1978), 110; and Walter Isaacson, *Kissinger: A Biography* (New York: Simon & Schuster, 2013), 649.

9. NSC meeting minutes.

10. Trevor Armbrister, *A Matter Accountability: The True Story of the Pueblo Affair* (London: Barrie & Jenkins, 1970), 259. A more recent account is Jack Cheevers, *Act of War: Lyndon Johnson, North Korea, and the Capture of the Spy Ship* Pueblo (New York: Penguin, 2014), 115, 167. Cheevers agrees

Clifford argued against a military response, saying he did not think it was worth risking a resumption of the Korean War.

11. For comparisons of the US responses in the *Pueblo* and *Mayaguez* crises, see Lamb, *Belief Systems and Decision Making*, 252–55; and David P. Houghton, "Spies and Boats and Planes: An Examination of US Decision-Making during the *Pueblo* Hostage Crisis of 1968," *Journal of Cold War Studies* 17, no. 4: (2015) 6, 32–35.

12. Major General John A. Wickham, USA, Military Assistant, Secretary of Defense, 92 pages of declassified personal notes from two spiral notebooks, one dated April 28 to May 14, 1975; the other May 14 to June 2, 1975, from the James R. Schlesinger Papers, Library of Congress; declassified January 5, 2017 as OSD MDR Case 15-M-2584 (hereafter Wickham notebooks).

13. Document 286, Telegram from the Department of State to the Liaison Office in China; Washington, May 13, 1975, 0013Z, in *Foreign Relations of the United States, 1969–1976*, vol. 10, *Vietnam, January 1973–July 1975* (hereafter *FRUS 1969–1976*, vol. 10).

14. Ibid., Document 299, Telegram from the Liaison Office in China to the Department of State; Beijing, May 15, 1975, 0253Z. By one account, US representatives in Beijing persisted, and shortly after midnight in Washington, DC (but late morning on the thirteenth in China), Ambassador George H. W. Bush, then chief of the US liaison office in Beijing, interrupted a picnic at the Ming Dynasty tombs to present a diplomatic note to Chinese foreign ministry officials. See John Prados, *Keepers of the Keys: A History of the National Security Council from Truman to Bush* (New York: Morrow, 1991), 364.

15. Some sources indicate Air Force General George S. Brown, the chairman of the Joint Chiefs of Staff, was in Europe for NATO meetings, but his director of operations, Lieutenant General Ray B. Sitton, indicated he had taken a fishing vacation in Canada. Sitton and Brown's assistant, General John W. Pauly, sent a helicopter to fetch him back to the Pentagon. Edgar F. Puryear, *George S. Brown, General, US Air Force: Destined for Stars* (Novato, CA: Presidio, 1983), 259.

16. Burns notes that Gayler returned to his headquarters in Honolulu after the initial planning and before the military operations were executed. Lieutenant General John L. Burns, USAF, oral history interview, June 5–8, 1984, transcript, Air Force Historical Research Agency, Maxwell Air Force Base, Montgomery, AL, 437 (hereafter Burns interview).

17. General David C. Jones, USAF, oral history interview, August 5 and October 15–17, 1985; March 13–14, 1986, Air Force Historical Research Agency, Maxwell Air Force Base, Montgomery, AL (hereafter Jones interview); Burns interview; and Wickham notebooks.

18. NSC meeting minutes. Kissinger was initially concerned about a competing geostrategic objective: shoring up defenses in Southeast Asia against further potential Communist aggression. He told the NSC, "Lee Kuan Yew [prime minister of Singapore who had visited the White House the previous week] has asked us to stay in Thailand as long as possible to give him time to work on getting the defenses of Malaysia ready. Bombing from Thailand will get us out quickly." Kissinger would later change his mind and give higher priority to a faster military response even at the expense of irritating Thailand.

19. This misunderstanding is emphasized by Herspring, who cites the *Crisis Resolution* book as his source. Dale R. Herspring, *The Pentagon and the Presidency: Civil-Military Relations from FDR to George W. Bush* (Lawrence: University Press of Kansas, 2006), 225; and Head, Short, and McFarlane, *Crisis Resolution*, 111–12.

20. Head, Short, and McFarlane, *Crisis Resolution*, 112.

Chapter 2

1. From the moment his ship was commandeered, Captain Miller had "proceeded at half speed" in a "delaying action," "figuring that our military should take some action." Miller at a press conference at Singapore following the incident, quoted in "The Captain's Log: A Tale of Terror," *Time*, May 26, 1975.

2. GAO report: 113, 117; Central Intelligence Agency, *Post-Mortem Report: An Examination of the Intelligence Community's Performance Before and During the* Mayaguez *Incident of May 1975*, August 1975 (declassified December 2010), 12 (hereafter CIA Post-Mortem Report).

3. Limited translation capability was available at Udorn, Thailand, and the resources were further drawn down by the Marines' request to borrow six Khmer-speaking linguists. Thus, much intercepted material had to be sent to Fort Meade in Maryland for translation, and some reports, after evaluation, had to be corrected. It was not until 4:37 a.m. that a "flash" message from the signals collection station at Udorn reported "that Commander of the KC 3rd Division was to move the 42 Americans and 9 VNese to Koh tang Isle." This information made it into DIA's briefing for the chairman of the Joint Chiefs at 0830 that morning. *Cryptolog*, no. 2 (1989), declassified (Fort Meade, MD: National Security Agency [NSA]): 23, https://www.nsa.gov/news-features/declassified-documents/cryptologs/assets/files/cryptolog_115.pdf.

4. Some of the confusion might have been the result of McFarlane trying to ascertain the location of the *Mayaguez* by monitoring radio reports from the pilots circling overhead and plotting the presumed location of the ship on his own map in his NSC cubbyhole office. Nessen, *It Sure Looks Different*: 121.

5. Ford, *A Time to Heal*, 276; Kissinger, *Years of Renewal*, 556; Head, Short, and McFarlane, *Crisis Resolution*: 112–13; and Memorandum of Conversation between General Scowcroft and the President, 2:23, May 13, 1975, box 1, folder "Cambodia-*Mayaguez* Seizure (1)" of NSA Kissinger-Scowcroft West Wing Office Files, Ford Library.

6. *Commander in Chief Pacific Command History*, vol. 1, 1975, appendix VI—The SS *Mayaguez* Incident (declassified December 31, 1985), 16 (hereafter CINCPAC Command History 1975).

7. The president's Daily Diary records an unusual hour-plus conversation, whereas Roy Rowan suggests there was a series of conversations. Perhaps the two men held a line open while the president's orders were implemented because records indicate the execution message from the JCS with the rules of engagement went out thirteen minutes into their conversation.

8. CINCPAC Command History 1975, 16.

9. In a widely overlooked interview, Schlesinger says, "We received the order to sink all ships coming off the island at the [initial] NSC meeting, I believe. And I believe it was the President who said it. When I got [back] to the Pentagon, I gave the order that all ships would probably be sunk if they came off Koh Tang. But I said that before any ships are sunk, our pilots should fly low over the ships and see what they could see, particularly if there were any [*Mayaguez*] crew members aboard. If they did see them, they were to report back immediately before doing anything." "James Schlesinger on The *Mayaguez* Rescue: Interview with Bill Triplett," *Veteran*, February–March 1999 (hereafter Schlesinger Veteran interview). For one source that did take note of Schlesinger's interview, see Christopher Hitchens, "The Kiss of Henry," Nation, April 30, 2001, 9.

10. Wickham notebooks.

11. Ibid. The Pentagon did this, but not surreptitiously enough. Scowcroft called back at 9:15 a.m. to tell Wickham the press was reporting the movement of the Marines and that the Pentagon should say this information was "incorrect" and refuse to discuss the issue.

12. Ibid.

13. Memorandum for the President from the Secretary of Defense, Subject: Seizure of the US *MAYAGUEZ*, Top Secret, Declassified by Executive Secretary, DoD [Department of Defense], Feb 16, 1999.

This is the first of two Pentagon products detailing military options. The second paper was prepared in advance of the third NSC meeting and is the one most frequently referred to. See "Possible Scenarios for Recovery of Ship and Crew," in box 28, Folder: Department of Defense—General, National Security Adviser, NSC East Asian and Pacific Affairs Staff: Files, (1969) 1973–1976, Ford Library.

14. William Colby, Director, Central Intelligence Agency, Memorandum for the President, Subject: The Rescue of the S.S. *Mayaguez* and Its Crew, 23 May 1975, with attached Interagency Intelligence Memorandum, Subject: Chronological Listing of Intelligence Community Activities During the *Mayaguez* Affair (declassified December 2, 2010; hereafter Chronological Listing of Intelligence Community Activities).

15. Wickham notebooks. After returning to the Pentagon, Jones, in discussion with Schlesinger, expressed consternation about the president's dissatisfaction with the timeliness of Pentagon information. He underscored the point that the president was demanding to be informed within ten minutes of activities taking place.

16. NSC meeting minutes. The ultimatum language was even drafted. "Your operation order should include words saying that the helicopter with bullhorn should appear overhead coincidentally with the force intended to take Kas Tang (Koh Tang). The message from the helicopter should say words to this effect: 'Produce all the Americans immediately or we will harm you.'" Memorandum for the Director, J-3, From G. E. Cooke, Brigadier General, USAF, Secretary, JCS, Subject: Words to be Included in Operation Order, 13 May 1975, top secret, declassified by Secretary, JCS on December 31, 1985.

17. The close relationship between Kissinger and Rockefeller is well known. In his memoirs Kissinger describes Rockefeller as "one of the seminal influences on my life." They vacationed together in the Caribbean shortly after Rockefeller was confirmed as vice president. Although Rockefeller and Kissinger were known to be close and cooperative, and Rockefeller's interventions in the NSC meetings supported Kissinger's preferences, there is no evidence that they collaborated or coordinated their positions outside the NSC meetings. Kissinger, *Years of Renewal*, 184.

18. NSC meeting minutes.

19. In his memoirs Ford wrote about his apprehensions concerning the Cambodian boats, saying, "Once I've made a decision, I seldom fret about it, but this one caused me some anxiety. If the pilot had been right, crew members were on their way to the mainland where we would have a far more difficult time effecting their recovery. My concern increased [upon learning Cambodian patrol boats had been sunk]. Suppose those vessels had carried crew members from *Mayaguez* below their decks? There was no way to tell, and that possibility was awful to contemplate." Cited in Lamb, *Belief Systems and Decision Making*, 178–79.

20. This tactical message was straightforward. See note 16 above.

21. Roy Rowan, *The Four Days of Mayaguez* (New York: W. W. Norton, 1975).

22. Colonel Clinton Granger, a member of Kissinger's NSC staff, prepared him for the third NSC meeting with a preview of Pentagon planning that he picked up from his contacts on the Joint Staff. He called the planning "limited and very conventional" but noted among the summary conclusions the recommendation to move a SEAL team into the area and to have psychological operations leaflets used on the island to state US demands. A handwritten notation at the top of the memorandum reads: "HAK has seen. Smyser concurred." Document 290, Memorandum from Clinton Granger of the National Security Council Staff to Secretary of State Kissinger, Washington, May 13, 1975, in *FRUS 1969–1976*, vol. 10.

23. Wickham notebooks.

24. Rockefeller had an opportunity to kibbutz on this issue on the margin of his meeting with Ford and the Domestic Council from 12:19 to 1:10 that day (May 13). In a brief article, White House photographer David Kennerly asserts, "Ford, who had been president for nine months, waved off one

of the Joint Chiefs' recommendations, which involved a B-52 strike on Phnom Penh." In reality, the recommendations to bomb Phnom Penh came from Rockefeller, Rumsfeld, and Kissinger, not the Joint Chiefs. In the fourth NSC meeting, Rumsfeld raises the question of bombing T-28 aircraft at Phnom Penh airport. A little later Kissinger said, "I could be talked into taking out the 100 aircraft at Phnom Penh." NSC meeting minutes; and David Hume Kennerly, "Gerald Ford Becoming President," *International Herald Tribune*, December 29, 2006, 4.

25. Flash Message #1708 1332101; 132052Z May 75, From CINCPAC Honolulu HI and USSAG/7A/CC/NKP APRT THAI, Subject: SS *Mayaguez* Surveillance Operation (declassified February 3, 2005), Ford Library.

26. Burns interview, 435.

27. Donald Rumsfeld says that during this call Ford and Schlesinger discussed destroying the gunboat and that "the order stood for our forces to look carefully to see if friendly personnel had been loaded onto any boats." Wickham's notes on the conversation do not mention looking for friendly personnel but do make it clear that Ford told Schlesinger to destroy any boats leaving the cove. Donald Rumsfeld, *When the Center Held: Gerald Ford and the Rescue of the American Presidency* (New York: Free Press, 2018), 173–74.

28. For background on the incident and the impact on USAF Security Police, see Senior Master Sergeant G. G. Browning, "Background Paper on The *Mayaguez* Incident: An Enlisted Perspective of a USAF Security Police Tragedy," student paper, Air Force Senior Noncommissioned Officer Academy, April 15, 1992, AFEHRI File 100.072, Air Force Enlisted Heritage Research Institute.

29. Schlesinger told Ford about this contingency option in his 7 a.m. phone conversation that same day. Wickham notebooks.

30. This decision has been attributed to General Burns, the on-scene commander, but in his interview he says, "I was told to consider using the air police if necessary to recover the crew on the island." Burns interview, 432.

31. *Washington Post*, May 14, 1975; cited in Lamb, *Belief Systems and Decision Making*, 88.

32. Secret cable without subject, date 132158Z, declassified via CIA letter April 13, 2011, photocopy obtained from the Ford Library.

33. Presumably Schlesinger left after ruling the boat should be sunk at 8:12 p.m. because no mention is made of a communication with Schlesinger in Wickham's notebook until just before 10 p.m., at which point Schlesinger would have been on the verge of traveling over to the White House for the scheduled 10:30 NSC meeting. It seems likely Schlesinger cleaned up for the meeting and then stopped in to see Wickham for the latest update before heading for the White House.

34. Phone conversation between President Ford and General Scowcroft, 8:10 p.m., May 13, 1975; box 1, folder "Cambodia-*Mayaguez* Seizure (1)" of NSA Kissinger-Scowcroft West Wing Office Files, Ford Library.

35. Phone conversation between General Wickham and General Scowcroft, 8:15 p.m., May 13, 1975; box 1, folder "Cambodia-*Mayaguez* Seizure (1)" of NSA Kissinger-Scowcroft West Wing Office Files, Ford Library.

36. General John A. Wickham, USA (Ret.), interview by the author by telephone from 12:46 to 1:16 p.m. on May 26, 2015, hereafter Wickham interview.

37. CINCPAC Command History 1975, 17.

38. Burns interview.

39. Wickham interview.

40. This information may have reached Scowcroft directly from the NMCC because he called Ford at 9:41, and the two men had a ten-minute conversation.

41. Phone conversation between General Wickham and General Scowcroft, 9:48 p.m., May 13, 1975; box 1, folder "Cambodia-*Mayaguez* Seizure (1)" of NSA Kissinger-Scowcroft West Wing Office Files, Ford Library.

42. Document 294, Transcript of Telephone Conversation between President Ford and the President's Deputy Assistant for National Security Affairs (Scowcroft), Washington, May 13, 9:50 p.m., in *FRUS 1969–1976*, vol. 10; Phone conversation between President Ford and General Scowcroft, 9:50 p.m., May 13, 1975; box 1, folder "Cambodia-*Mayaguez* Seizure (1)" of NSA Kissinger-Scowcroft West Wing Office Files, Ford Library.

43. Phone conversation between General Wickham and General Scowcroft, 9:54 p.m., May 13, 1975; box 1, folder "Cambodia-*Mayaguez* Seizure (1)" of NSA Kissinger-Scowcroft West Wing Office Files, Ford Library.

44. See note 33 on page 225.

45. Lamb, *Belief Systems and Decision Making*, 147.

46. Captain John B. Taylor, "Air Mission *Mayaguez*," *Airman Magazine*, February 1976, 39–47.

47. Kissinger, *Years of Renewal*, 560.

48. NSC meeting minutes.

Chapter 3

1. Chronological Listing of Intelligence Community Activities, p. INR-5.

2. Department of State, US Embassy Tehran Cable 14MAY750856GMT: Chinese Embassy Tehran believes *Mayaguez* to be freed soon (Washington, DC: Digital National Security Archive, 1975).

3. A possible explanation for why China chose to pass this information through a Pakistani diplomat in Tehran is that Kissinger had used the Pakistanis as a conduit for communications to China when he and Nixon had opened relations with the Chinese a few years earlier. Also, the US ambassador to Tehran at the time was Richard M. Helms, the former director of the CIA. The Chinese might have assumed that he would quickly recognize the import of the information and get it to the right people in the White House. As it turned out, Helms had left Tehran to accompany the shah on his visit to Washington, so the deputy chief of mission, Jack C. Miklos, was in charge.

4. Donald Rumsfeld, *Known and Unknown: A Memoir* (New York: Sentinel, 2013), 211.

5. Telephone conversation, Mr. Sisco/Secretary Kissinger, May 14, 1975, 9:55 AM, released in full, Ford Library.

6. Wickham notebooks.

7. Ibid. All quotes in this paragraph are from the Wickham notebooks.

8. Ibid.

9. Memorandum of Conversation, President Ford, Henry Kissinger and Brent Scowcroft, Wednesday, May 14, 1975, 11:45 a.m., Oval Office, declassified, Ford Library.

10. Telephone conversation, Secretary Kissinger/Joe Sisco, May 14, 1975, 12:12 p.m., released in full, Ford Library.

11. Ron Nessen News Conference at the White House, 11:50 a.m., May 14, 1975, Ron Nessen File at the Ford Library.

12. Headquarters, Pacific Air Force, "History of the Pacific Air Forces, 1 Jul 74–31 Dec 75," vol. 1 (Hickam Air Force Base, HI: Office of Pacific Air Forces History, 1976), 444n1.

13. It appears that the Pentagon was able to make copies of its options paper available before the NSC meeting. There is a short cover note in the Ford Library's digitized files for box 1, folder

"Cambodia-*Mayaguez* Seizure (1)" of NSA Kissinger-Scowcroft West Wing Office Files at the Ford Library that reads "Henry, The Defense Options paper" and is signed, "Brent."

14. NSC meeting minutes.

15. Vandenbroucke makes the noteworthy point that Pentagon leaks (presumably from Schlesinger via Laitin) ran operational risks by potentially alerting the enemy. Although how closely the Cambodians monitored ABC and NBC is questionable, Vandenbroucke notes journalists from these media outlets were well informed on the general timing of the operations. Perhaps those sharing the information thought it was too general to benefit an enemy already on the alert and consistent with their desire to build pressure to convince the Cambodians to release the crew before US forces struck. Even so, it seems an egregious lapse of operational security and inconsistent with the Pentagon's explanation to President Ford that it kept the USS *Wilson* and USS *Holt* over the horizon to avoid tipping the Cambodians to the pending military operations. Vandenbroucke, *Perilous Options*, 101.

16. Holloway had been in Boston giving a speech when he was summoned back to Washington by Clements, who shared with him the general White House dissatisfaction with Jones's performance to that point. Holloway later claimed Ford told Clements to have him (Holloway) take over as acting chairman during the crisis and describes himself as representing the Joint Chiefs and accompanying Schlesinger for the rest of the NSC meetings. It appears Holloway was exaggerating. The NSC minutes record Jones as the acting chairman in all four NSC meetings, and he assumed that role in all four meetings. Clements references Holloway once in the first NSC meeting, indicating he was in touch with him, but there is no mention of Holloway in the NSC minutes for the second and third NSC meetings, either as an attendee or speaker. However, Holloway did attend the fourth NSC meeting and was used to convey the president's orders to the JCS, which might reflect Ford's suspicion that his orders were not being transmitted by Jones quickly and accurately. During the fourth meeting Schlesinger asked Jones to present the Chiefs' recommendations, and the general spoke throughout the deliberations (forty-three times). Holloway spoke twelve times during the first two-thirds of the meeting, particularly concerning details of naval activity. NSC meeting minutes; James L. Holloway, *Aircraft Carriers at War: A Personal Retrospective of Korea, Vietnam, and the Soviet Confrontation* (Annapolis, MD: Naval Institute Press, 2007), 397–402; and Puryear, *George S. Brown*, 259.

17. Schlesinger had given Jones verbal approval for the ultimatum at 4:54 p.m., and five minutes later that was communicated from the JCS down the chain of command with the caveat that the ultimatum should not be broadcast until the order was given. After the subsequent NSC conversation, the ultimatum broadcast was cancelled about two hours later. Department of Defense, *After Action Report: US Military Operations SS Mayaguez/Kaoh Tang Island*, 12–15 May 1975 (hereafter DoD After Action Report); and Chronological Listing of Intelligence Community Activities.

18. Targets of opportunity are often mobile. See Wetterhahn's depiction of an armed reconnaissance mission he conducted shortly before the *Mayaguez* crisis. Ralph Wetterhahn, *The Last Battle: The* Mayaguez *Incident and the End of the Vietnam War* (New York: Carroll and Graf, 2001), 274–75.

19. It has been noted that a civilian, Robert Hartmann, was the first to ask about estimated casualties and that he did so late in the decision process. Carol Van Voorst, "Looking Ferocious: The Ford Administration's Management of the *Mayaguez* Affair" (paper, National War College, Washington, DC, 1998), http://www.dtic.mil/dtic/tr/fulltext/u2/a441469.pdf.

20. Telephone conversation, Mr. Sisco/Secretary Kissinger, May 14, 1975, 6:16 p.m., released in full, Ford Library.

21. As Kissinger noted in his memoirs,

The congressional leaders were unenthusiastic, especially about attacks on the mainland. Senator Mike Mansfield wanted to know, "why are we again going into the mainland of Asia, especially at a time when we almost have the boat in our custody once again?" Even the usually stalwart Senator John McClellan expressed his uneasiness about the attack on the mainland. Speaker Thomas P. "Tip" O'Neill implied that the boat was a "Pentagon charter," as if this changed the reality of its having been hijacked in international waters; he continued low-key grumbling even after Schlesinger assured him that his suspicion was unfounded.

The day after the crisis in a conversation with Ford, Kissinger said, "I think Schlesinger, when he heard the Congressional attitudes, changed the orders [for ongoing airstrikes against the mainland]." See the discussion on page 149. Kissinger, *Years of Renewal*, 565; Memorandum of Conversation, President Ford, Henry Kissinger and Brent Scowcroft, Friday, May 16, 1975, 9:25 a.m., Oval Office, declassified, Ford Library.

22. Rowan, *Four Days*, 178.

23. Nessen, *It Sure Looks Different*, 124.

24. The depiction of military operations is an update of the account in *Belief Systems and Decision Making in the* Mayaguez *Crisis*, which was based on firsthand accounts available at the time. Since then many more participants in the operations have been interviewed or written about their experiences, and their insights were used to improve the overview of military operations provided here. In addition to Mahoney's *Mayaguez Incident* and Guilmartin's *Very Short War*, I also drew upon other recently published sources as indicated.

25. Mahoney, *Mayaguez Incident*, 131; and Wise and Baron, *14-Hour War*, 11. See Mahoney for a good explanation of helicopter availability, and Guilmartin for expert insights on the differences between the two types of helicopters and their missions. Guilmartin, *Very Short War*, 9, 40–43.

26. Mahoney, *Mayaguez Incident*, 144. See Mahoney for a good description of the planning and execution of the retaking of the ship.

27. R. W. Austin, 2nd Battalion, 9th Marines, *Koh Tang/Mayaguez Historical Report*, 9 December 1975; declassified.

28. Urey W. Patrick, "The *Mayaguez* Operation," (Arlington, VA: Center for Naval Analyses, 1977), 16.

29. Guilmartin, *Very Short War*, 150.

30. Wise and Baron, *14-Hour War*, 31.

31. Document 297, Telegram from the Mission to the United Nations to the Department of State; New York, May 14, 1975, 1817Z, in *FRUS 1969–1976*, vol. 10.

32. Cited in Mahoney, *Mayaguez Incident*, 125.

33. Kissinger, *Years of Renewal*, 568.

34. This may be what Richard B. "Dick" Cheney was alluding to years later when he said that during the *Mayaguez* crisis Kissinger "became very nervous and upset" and "wanted to back off and reconsider," but Ford said, "No, Henry, we've made the decision. It's the right thing to do and we're going to do it full speed ahead." Kenneth W. Thompson, *The Ford Presidency: Twenty-two Intimate Perspectives of Gerald R. Ford* (Lanham MD: University Press of America, 1988), 81. If so, this corrects the author's 1989 surmise that Kissinger encouraged Ford to persist with the punitive strikes after the news of the Cambodian broadcast. See Lamb, *Belief Systems and Decision Making*, 93.

35. Ford, *A Time to Heal*, 282.

36. Rowan, *Four Days*, 205.

37. Kissinger, *Years of Renewal*, 569; Schlesinger *Veteran* interview.

38. Kissinger, *Years of Renewal*, 569.

39. William Lloyd Stearman, *An American Adventure: From Early Aviation through Three Wars to the White House* (Annapolis, MD: Naval Institute Press, 2012); and Interview with William Lloyd Stearman,

Foreign Affairs Oral History Project, Association for Diplomatic Studies and Training, interviewed on April 15, 1992 (hereafter Stearman interview).

40. Stearman's assertion that Kissinger liked the idea but NSA did not is possible but not probable. In his memoirs Kissinger does not claim NSA interfered with the plan. He merely says, "After toying with the idea of breaking into Cambodian communications, we decided that the most expeditious way would be to release a statement to the news services." Also, at lower levels where concerns about protecting sources and methods also would have been acute, there was already a sustained pattern of cooperation between NSA and DoD personnel on broadcasting to the Cambodians through their own radio network. Wickham's notes record a situation report at 8:38 p.m. on May 14 indicating that US forces had retaken the *Mayaguez* and that they were planning to deliver the ultimatum to the Khmer forces through their radio network. These plans were worked on until nearly midnight on the fourteenth, with Stearman advising General Lincoln D. Faurer of the DIA not to cancel the plan to broadcast directly to the Cambodians until the situation could be clarified. When IPAC asked NSA which authority cancelled the broadcast to the Cambodians, NSA responded, "The White House." NSA had been leaning forward to execute the plan and actually had to query its local entity to see if the broadcast inadvertently had gone out to the Cambodians contrary to the White House's final decision on the matter. Five minutes before midnight they were told the ultimatum had not been broadcast directly through the Cambodian network. Then, at 1:30 a.m. on the fifteenth, NSA inquired as to whether it could cancel all actions pertaining to broadcast of a message to the Khmer Rouge, and Scowcroft responded in the affirmative. NSA then passed this news to the NMCC. At 6:11 in the morning the NSA representative at the command center learned that Nessen had said the United States transmitted a message directly to the Cambodians on frequencies we knew they would be monitoring. NSA asked the NSA rep at the command center to provide a copy of this communication. Similarly, as noted earlier, President Ford told the shah of Iran the following day that "we put a message through their frequencies and over the AP that we would stop when the crew was released." The president did not know the message was never broadcast over Cambodian frequencies, and Kissinger and Scowcroft apparently did not correct his misimpression. Nessen mentions the plan to broadcast the US reply over a radio frequency the Cambodians were known to be monitoring, but he did not know why the idea was rejected. Nessen, *It Sure Looks Different*, 126.

41. GAO report, 67.

42. Memorandum of Conversation, President Ford, Mohamed Reza Pahlavi, Shah of Iran, Dr. Henry A. Kissinger, Secretary of State, and Assistant to the President for National Security Affairs Lt. General Brent Scowcroft, Deputy Assistant to the President for National Security Affairs, Oval Office, Thursday, May 15, 1975, 11:00 a.m. National Security Adviser's Memoranda of Conversation Collection, Gerald R. Ford Digital Library, http://www.fordlibrarymuseum.gov/library/document/memcons/1553077.pdf.

43. Kissinger, *Years of Renewal*, 569.

44. Telephone conversation, Joe Sisco with Secretary Kissinger, 9:15 PM, May 14, 1975; declassified and released in full, February 10, 2003, Ford Library.

45. Robert C. McFarlane with Zofia Smardz, *Special Trust* (New York: Cadell and Davies, 1994), 163.

46. Nessen, *It Sure Looks Different*: 127–28. Rumsfeld also cites the leaks as an irritant in Pentagon relations with President Ford. Rumsfeld, *When the Center Held*, 172.

47. Stearman interview.

48. Nessen, *It Sure Looks Different*: 129. In making this comment, Kissinger echoed his advice to Ford in an Oval Office meeting between the third and fourth NSC meetings, during which he told Ford, "The [political] price will be the same. If you use force it should be ferociously." Memorandum of

Conversation, President Ford, Henry Kissinger and Brent Scowcroft, Wednesday, May 14, 1975, 11:45 a.m., Oval Office, declassified, Ford Library.

Chapter 4

1. Wise and Baron, *14-Hour War*, 37 and 47.

2. Ibid., 43.

3. Guilmartin, *Very Short War*, 102.

4. The AC-130s had been maintaining nighttime vigils, but on the morning of the assault, Spectre-61 left as the sun rose. Then, it was brought on station for support and was working feverishly to establish communications with the Marines and ascertain their positions so that it could safely direct its fires toward the enemy. Spectre-61 was returning to its base in Korat when it was redirected to Utapao Air Base to refuel. It relaunched at 0700 to Tang Island and was enlisted for close air support around 0830. Patrick, "*Mayaguez* Operation," 88; and Wetterhahn, *Last Battle*, 212.

5. Mahoney, *Mayaguez Incident*, 166.

6. Ibid., 166. Wise and Baron count 221 Marines on the western portion of the island at this time, *14-Hour War*, 47.

7. Nessen, *It Sure Looks Different*, 129.

8. All the Marine radio connectivity with *Coral Sea* aircraft had been lost when the first helicopter went down. Burns interview.

9. Generally speaking, once the second wave of Marines arrived and explained the crew had been recovered, the Marines on the ground stopped risking additional casualties in offensive actions. Wise and Baron, *14-Hour War*, 167–68.

10. Schlesinger *Veteran* interview and Wickham interview. "Yes!" said General Wickham. "They wanted to take the island and not pull back. Schlesinger thought that was unnecessary and would just cost more lives."

11. Mahoney, *Mayaguez Incident*, 173. Major Guilmartin, who later wrote a superb account of the military operations, flew Jolly-44. According to Guilmartin, the craft's fuel line was hit by a .50-caliber round: "The flight mechanic, Technical Sergeant Billy D. Willingham, assisted the Navy maintenance personnel" who cut out the "damaged line (one and one-quarter inch aluminum standpipe) with a hacksaw and put in its place a section of hose held together with radiator hose clamps. Certainly, not by the book, but despite concerns about fuel contamination by the pilots, it worked." Major George R. Dunham, USMC, and Colonel David A. Quinlan, Colonel, USMC, "Recovery of the SS *Mayaguez*," chapter 13 in *US Marines in Vietnam: The Bitter End, 1973–1975* (Washington, DC: History and Museums Division, Headquarters, U.S. Marine Corp), 258n.

12. Mahoney, *Mayaguez Incident*, 167.

13. Ibid., 171. All told, the *Wilson* fired 157 5-inch rounds. Malcolm J. Muir, *End of the Saga: The Maritime Evacuation of South Vietnam and Cambodia* (Washington, DC: Naval History and Heritage Command, 2017), 54–55.

14. Wise and Baron, *14-Hour War*, 48.

15. Ibid., 115, 199; and Wetterhahn, *Last Battle*, 231–32.

16. Commander J. A. Messegee, et al. "'Mayday' for the Mayaguez," *U.S. Naval Institute Proceedings*, November 1976, 258.

17. DoD After Action Report.

18. Gary Weikel, letter to the author, October 29, 1991.

19. Wise and Baron, *14-Hour War*, 52.

20. Mahoney, *Mayaguez Incident*, 174.

21. Greg Wilson, "Growth: Greg Wilson's Account of The *Mayaguez* Incident," Koh Tang/*Mayaguez* Veterans Organization, http://www.kohtang.com/kohtang-1975/growth-wilsons-account/growth-wilsons-account.html. The flare almost hit the *Wilson*'s gig, which surprised and worried the crew since the boat's deck was awash in ammunition. Wise and Baron, *14-Hour War*, 253.

22. Mahoney, *Mayaguez Incident*, 175.

23. Wilson, "Growth."

24. Davis had traded for the strobe light with a recon Marine back in Okinawa. Clayton K. S. Chun, *The Last Boarding Party: The USMC and the SS* Mayaguez *1975* (Oxford: Osprey, 2011), 70; and Wise and Baron, *14-Hour War*, 168.

25. Wise and Baron, *14-Hour War*, 244.

26. DoD After Action Report.

27. Lance Corporal Loney was killed early in the operation but lost when several Marines carrying his body to a helicopter were hit by enemy fire. Wise and Baron, *14-Hour War*, 231.

28. Ibid., 253.

29. Ibid., 57, 170–71.

30. The leaflets are available on the Koh Tang/*Mayaguez* Veterans Organization website. See Jim Butler, lithographer on board the USS *Coral Sea*, comments posted on Koh Tang/*Mayaguez* Veterans Organization website, http://www.kohtang.com/whats-new/whats-new.html.

31. Timothy L. Bosiljevac, "The Teams in 'Nam: U.S. Navy UDT/SEAL Operations of the Vietnam Conflict," (master's thesis, Emporia State University, 1987). Bosiljevac interviewed the SEAL commander.

32. Wetterhahn explains the differences of opinion well in *Last Battle*, 254–55.

33. Wise and Baron summarize the status of the debate over the fate of the lost Marines, including testimony and radio communications, indicating it should have been evident that not all Marines were able to get off the island on the last helicopter. Wise and Baron, *14-Hour War*, 55–56 and 66–84 (see page 71 in particular). Over the years, thirteen Marines and airmen killed in the *Mayaguez* operations have been identified, recovered, and buried in Arlington National Cemetery. But to date, forensic analysis of remains has been inconclusive about the fate of Hall, Hargrove, and Marshall. Ralph Wetterhahn made a sustained, meticulous effort to determine the fate of those three lost Marines. Based on his interviews of Cambodian sources, he believes they were captured and executed. The credibility of Wetterhahn's Cambodian sources—who seemingly have no reason to fabricate, other than perhaps to encourage more trips by Americans searching for their fallen comrades—needs to be balanced against the puzzling question of why the three Marines, if still alive, did not reveal themselves to the crew of the *Wilson*, which spent hours cruising the coast of Tang Island in hopes of seeing them. See also Wise and Baron, *14-Hour War*, 238–41; Matthew Burke, "Fate of Marines left Behind in Cambodia in 1975 Haunts Comrades," *Stars and Stripes*, April 4, 2013; and Matthew M. Burke, "The Truth About the Lost Marines of The Vietnam War's Last Battle," *Newsweek*, January 24, 2017, http://www.newsweek.com/2017/02/03/us-marines-disappeared-mayaguez-last-battle-vietnam-war-547106.html.

34. Mahoney, *Mayaguez Incident*, 180; 199–200. Mahoney notes forty-nine were wounded in combat, and thirty more received wounds that were not the result of hostile fire.

Chapter 5

1. Rockefeller echoed Kissinger's concerns and where he differed from Kissinger (for example, in being leery of attacking the island) he was ignored by Ford. A case could be made that Jones was a key decision maker, but more for what he did not do rather than what he did. If he had refused to pass the Joint Chiefs' recommendation for going ahead with military operations and insisted on another twenty-four-hour delay until a larger number of Marines could make the assault on Tang Island, he would have had a major impact on the crisis outcomes. Colby also might be considered a key player if it could be shown that he intervened to ensure the NSC was operating on the basis of the smaller estimate of Khmer defenders on Tang Island, but there is no evidence of this. Rumsfeld weighed in with Ford on the B-52 issue, encouraging him to use the *Coral Sea* planes instead, but again, this just reinforced the advice Ford had already received from Kissinger. As for Scowcroft, it is true his views overlapped with Kissinger's, and that Kissinger played an even larger role in influencing Ford than was assumed before the release of so much classified information on the decision-making process. Nevertheless, that same material makes it clear that Ford valued Scowcroft's views independent of Kissinger. Also, Scowcroft played an important role at several key junctures during the crisis, especially when Kissinger was away from Washington. For a discussion of why Ford, Kissinger, Schlesinger, and Scowcroft were considered key decision makers and Jones, Rockefeller, and others were not, see Lamb, *Belief Systems and Decision Making*, 55–61.

2. Brent Scowcroft, interview with author, Washington, DC, 1 February 1980, cited in Lamb, *Belief Systems and Decision Making* (hereafter Scowcroft interview).

3. Schlesinger *Veteran* interview.

4. Scowcroft interview.

5. This information is new and based on the declassified NSC meeting minutes. See the discussion of Kissinger and the EC-121 and on historical analogies during the crisis in Lamb, *Belief Systems and Decision Making*, 72–73 and 198–203, respectively.

6. The NSA recently declassified its top secret account of the incident: "The National Security Agency and the EC-121 Shootdown," National Security Agency, September 20, 2016, https://www.nsa.gov/news-features/declassified-documents/cryptologic-histories/assets/files/EC-121.pdf.

7. Bernd Schaefer, "North Korean 'Adventurism' and China's Long Shadow, 1966–1972" (working paper 44, Cold War International History Project, Woodrow Wilson International Center for Scholars, Washington, DC, 2004), 24–25.

8. Van Jackson, "The EC-121 Shoot Down and North Korea's Coercive Theory of Victory," *Sources and Methods* (blog), Wilson Center, April 13, 2017, https://www.wilsoncenter.org/blog-post/the-ec-121-shoot-down-and-north-koreas-coercive-theory-victory.

9. Kissinger, *White House Years*, 316, 318, and 321, cited in Lamb, *Belief System and Decision Making*, 72.

10. Peter Goldman with Thomas M. De Frank, Henry W. Hubbard and Bruce Van Voorst, "Ford's Rescue Operation," *Newsweek*, May 26, 1975, 16.

11. Right after the first meeting, Ford surprised Nessen by asking him, among other things, whether he would "go in there and bomb the Cambodian boat and take a chance of the Americans being killed?" This implies it had been made clear to him that it might be difficult to use punitive force and still protect the crew. See pages 12 and 113–14 and note 19 on page 224.

12. For example, General Burns refused to authorize an AC-130 gunship to fire back at Cambodian forces because he feared the crew, at least some of whom were believed to be on the island, might be hurt. Burns interview, 436. See also page 39 for his instructions that "all forces must be aware of the fact that the primary purpose for conducting ground operations is to secure the safe release of US/third-country national prisoners."

13. NSC meeting minutes.

14. For example, in Ford's memoirs he says that "punishing" Cambodia by airstrikes is "where Kissinger and I disagreed with Schlesinger." Similarly, Kissinger says that "Schlesinger, so stern when it came to arms control issues, balked at military action." Kissinger asserts this even though elsewhere he notes that Schlesinger and he were in agreement on basic philosophy. Mahoney accepts the depiction of Schlesinger by Ford and Kissinger, even though it does not reflect the record of the discussions in the NSC, as discussed here. Often histories of the Ford presidency, such as Douglas Brinkley's *Gerald R. Ford*, repeat these assertions. In reality, Schlesinger was a staunch realist and believed in the efficacy of force. The day after the crisis in another NSC meeting on the Panama Canal treaties, Schlesinger declared himself an opponent of the treaty being negotiated. He explained the geostrategic need for sovereign bases around the world and concluded with a commentary on world opinion, saying, "Worldwide reactions are likely to be mixed. When the U. S. shows strength and determination, it receives respect. When it recedes from its position, it whets appetites." NSC meeting minutes, May 15, 1975. For an indication of how much this is true with regard to the significance of the fall of Southeast Asia to Communist forces, see the March 27 telephone conversation between Kissinger and Schlesinger in Henry Kissinger, *Crisis: The Anatomy of Two Major Policy Crises* (New York: Simon & Schuster, 2003), 428–29. Ford, *A Time to Heal*, 279; Kissinger, *Years of Renewal*, 177, 557; Mahoney, *Mayaguez Incident*, 110, 113; Douglas Brinkley, *Gerald R. Ford* (Waterville, ME: Thorndike Press, 2007), 105.

15. Enough so that observers like James Cannon, one of Ford's presidential assistants who did not sit in on the NSC meetings, later related that from what he understood "Schlesinger contended that any military action should be limited to punishment of the Cambodian forces involved." James Cannon, *Time and Chance: Gerald Ford's Appointment with History* (Ann Arbor: University of Michigan Press, 1998), 398.

16. Schlesinger *Veteran* interview.

17. John Osborne is one of the few commentators to get this point right. Presumably Schlesinger was his source. See *White House Watch: The Ford Years* (Washington, DC: New Republic Book Co., 1977), 140

18. Many years later in an oral history interview General Jones recalled "there was great debate in the government between rescue and punitive action. There were some in the government, not the military, who wanted to bomb the airport at Phnom Penh with B-52s as punitive action." See the discussion below on the timing of military operations, which was the one issue where General Jones's military expertise might have been used to assess risk in a manner that would have complicated the punitive purposes of the key leaders. Jones interview.

19. Prados, *Keepers of the Keys*, 371.

20. Osborne, *White House Watch*, 139; Roger Morris, *Uncertain Greatness: Henry Kissinger and American Foreign Policy* (New York: Harper & Row, 1997), 288.

21. As the GAO report concludes, "The goal of safely landing the assault force on the island was in direct conflict with the goal of ensuring the safety of possible American prisoners." The report goes on to explain why the assault and supporting fires invariably put the crew at risk. The report was finally declassified in its entirety on June 10, 2003. GAO report, 95.

22. Vandenbroucke, *Perilous Options*, 77.

23. Kissinger kept this kind of thinking and how he managed diplomacy secret as long as possible, insisting that the portions of the GAO report that related the contents of diplomatic communications remain classified even though the Department of State and Department of Defense had no issues with its declassification. GAO report, vi.

24. Kissinger, *Years of Renewal*, 555.

25. This includes the author's interviews with William Colby and Brent Scowcroft, who had no recollection of the cable ever being discussed, but also formal communications in response to congressional inquiries about diplomatic communications immediately following the crisis. For example, a May 30, chronology prepared in response to requests from Congress by George Springsteen, the NSC executive secretary, makes no mention of the Tehran cable. Similarly, a June 20, 1975, letter prepared by DoD in response to congressional inquiries about "the exact sequence of communications, meetings, consultations, diplomatic initiatives, and military actions" makes no mention of the Tehran cable under its section that reviews diplomatic events. See Memorandum from George Springsteen, NSC Executive Secretary to Brent Scowcroft, Subject: Chronology of the *Mayaguez* Incident, dated May 30; and Letter to Honorable Melvin Price, Chairman, Committee on Armed Services, from Richard Fryklund, Principal Deputy Assistant Secretary of Defense (Legislative Affairs), June 20, 1975.

26. The cable went to diplomats in Beijing, Islamabad, and Bangkok and to CINCPAC. In Washington, however, distribution was limited to State and the NSC staff. Vandenbroucke agrees that "the White House disregarded evidence suggesting that the incident could be solved peacefully," but he discounts the assertion that Kissinger kept the Tehran cable from the NSC. He assumes the cable would have been distributed widely in Washington, which is not correct. The "tags" added by the embassy in Tehran categorized the content of the cable as relevant to foreign policy and relations, China/Mainland, Iran, and Pakistan. These tags automatically generated an office list and minimum distribution within the State Department, and then State's operations center manually added additional offices to the distribution. From those distribution tags, it is clear that the Pentagon, CIA, and NSA did not receive either electronic or paper copies of the cable. All copies were distributed internal to the Department of State except for five paper copies that went to the NSC (i.e., Kissinger's staff in the White House). Vandenbroucke also asserts that an unidentified NSC participant spontaneously mentioned the cable in a 1984 interview with him and said the NSC discounted its credence. The unidentified interviewee's assessment is consistent with the Department of State response to GAO investigators after they revealed the existence of the cable. State representatives said the cable was "an unevaluated report of questionable validity." However, that does not mean the cable was made known to the NSC at the time. If Kissinger had distributed the cable to other NSC members, it seems unlikely he (and other Department of State personnel) would have been willing to tell reporters and the GAO investigators that there were "no known diplomatic responses or initiatives carried out by Cambodia, the Chinese, or anyone else with regard to the seizure of the *Mayaguez*." GAO report, 10–17; US Congress, Seizure of the *Mayaguez*, pt. 2, 246; Vandenbroucke, *Perilous Options*, 85 and 205n59. See also the discussion on Mahoney's treatment of the Tehran cable in note 96 on page 240.

27. Memorandum for the Director, J-3, From G. E. Cooke, Brigadier General, USAF, Secretary, JCS, Subject: Words to be Included in Operation Order, 13 May 1975, Top Secret, declassified by Secretary, JCS on December 31, 1985.

28. Rowan, *Four Days*; and "Text of Statement to be Read Over Cambodian Frequencies and via Loud Speaker to Inhabitants of the Island," box 1, folder "Cambodia-*Mayaguez* Seizure (1)" of NSA Kissinger-Scowcroft West Wing Office Files, Ford Library.

29. Wickham notebooks.

30. Much later Sisco commented that Kissinger routinely cut State out of the action and that he had to fight to keep the department involved. Certainly that proved true during the *Mayaguez* crisis. See Joseph J. Sisco, Foreign Affairs Oral History Project, Association for Diplomatic Studies and Training, interviewed on March 19, 1990 (hereafter Sisco interview). See Nessen for his take on Kissinger's treatment of his staff, Nessen, *It Sure Looks Different*, 137.

31. See the discussion in Lamb, *Belief Systems and Decision Making*, 213–15.

32. Career diplomats at the Department of Defense did the same. Ambassador Abramowitz, then serving as deputy assistant secretary of defense for East Asian and Pacific affairs, advised Schlesinger to give diplomatic initiatives a chance to work before military operations or there would be "severe criticism." Wickham notebooks.

33. The ambassador's "flash" cable begins, "As the department is aware, I had absolutely no advance word that military action was to be taken." He argued, "Had I known what was contemplated I could have taken steps to contain the damage." Sisco drafted a cable back to contain the ambassador's ire and bring him into line. It stated, "We understand fully sensitivity of issue, but it is our judgment that if we begin to supply the Thais with advance information they would have no alternative but to pose strong objection. . . . You should understand that we will be required to utilize U-Tapao as may be necessary in order to secure promptly the release of the vessel and Americans. . . . You should not rpt not give any advance indication to the Thais. We realize that there may be costs with the Thais but the balance of interests requires that we be willing to take whatever risks may be involved in our relations with Thais." Document 289, Telegram from the Embassy in Thailand to the Department of State; Bangkok, May 13, 1975, 1315, in *FRUS 1969–1976*, vol. 10. Sisco's response is Document 292, Telegram from the Department of State to the Embassy in Thailand, Washington, May 13, 1975, 1754Z, in ibid.; and Ford Library, National Security Adviser, NSC East Asian and Pacific Affairs Staff Files, box 29, Department of State, Telegrams and Cables. Secret; Nodis; Flash. Drafted by Sisco; approved by Sisco, Johnson, and Eagleburger.

34. After the recovery of the ship and crew, Kissinger asked Sisco to add this information to the message going out to all overseas diplomatic posts, acknowledging he "hadn't even looked at the three I've got here" (i.e., the drafts Sisco provided earlier). Sisco said, "As far as I'm concerned, that's dead." He did not see the point of informing posts about the operations after the fact, but a few moments later acceded to Kissinger's point that they should emphasize the positive outcome.

35. Document 289, *FRUS 1969–1976*, vol. 10.

36. Document 400, Minutes of the Secretary of State's Staff Meeting, Washington, May 16, 1975, 8:08 a.m., in *Foreign Relations of The United States, 1969–1976*, vol. E-12, *Documents on East and Southeast Asia* (hereafter *FRUS 1969–1976*, vol. E-12). Ford adopted the same attitude in his memoirs, saying he "didn't give a damn about offending [Thai] sensibilities." Nevertheless, on May 19, Ambassador Masters delivered a note that the Thai government took as an apology. It stated, "The United States regrets the misunderstandings that have arisen between Thailand and the United States in regard to the temporary placement of Marines at Utapao to assist in the recovery of the SS *Mayaguez*." Telegrams 115952 to Bangkok, May 18, and 4359 from Bangkok, May 19; ibid., Central Foreign Policy Files). Ford, *A Time to Heal*, 276.

37. Mahoney overlooks Kissinger's manipulation of diplomacy and asserts Kissinger gave it an honest effort. Somewhat strangely, he also asserts his account is "the first to show that, contrary to popular opinion, diplomatic efforts were taken in parallel to the military response." Presumably he means the diplomatic efforts trickled out over the course of the crisis. The GAO report identified all the major diplomatic initiatives and when they occurred. What the delay in going to the United Nations, despite Sisco's urging, actually demonstrates is Kissinger's desire to avoid any untoward political developments that might have prevented the use of force. See Mahoney, *Mayaguez Incident*, xxii, 107, and 216, and the discussion on the cable from Tehran in note 96 on page 240. In contrast, a Kissinger biographer and a Scowcroft biographer both conclude the quick resort to military force was matched by a lethargic diplomatic effort. Seymour M. Hersh, *The Price of Power: Kissinger in the Nixon White House* (New York: Summit Books, 1984), 639; and Sparrow, *Strategist*, 166.

38. Other members of the NSC were not necessarily interested in diplomacy either. In the first meeting when a public statement by the White House was being discussed, Colby said, "We may

wish to point out that they released other ships. This gives them a way out." Rumsfeld and Rockefeller objected, not wanting to identify an off-ramp for conflict or imply the United States was willing to discuss the issue.

39. Kissinger knew about the telegram from Tehran, but he also knew that Waldheim had promised to jump immediately into action. Kissinger approved Sisco's outreach to the UN in a 12:12 p.m. phone conversation. The US ambassador to the UN delivered the request to Waldheim within the hour and then sent a cable to State at 2:17 p.m. saying that Waldheim "promised to contact Cambodian authorities immediately," using China but also a channel to Phnom Penh, that "he used successfully to seek Cambodian help for first convoy of foreign evacuees." The cable said Waldheim broke off a meeting with UN representatives forced to leave Cambodia to give the matter his priority attention. Document 297, Telegram from the Mission to the United Nations to the Department of State, New York, May 14, 1975, 1817Z; Subj: Amb. Scali's Visit to Secretary General Kurt Waldheim Concerning US Vessel *Mayaguez*. Ref: State 112089, in *FRUS 1969–1976*, vol. 10.

40. Ford's lasting memory of the attempted diplomacy during the *Mayaguez* crisis was that it had been impossible to contact the Cambodians. He noted this months later when the subject of not being able to contact Cambodian authorities came up in another context. Document 85, Memorandum of Conversation, Washington, January 26, 1976, 4:43–5:30 p.m., in *FRUS 1969–1976*, vol. E-12.

41. The GAO report implies diplomacy was not aggressively pursued. Similarly, this author argued long ago "the popular perception that diplomacy had been tried and failed was not accurate," and that "a diplomatic settlement rated a very poor second on the list of American priorities." Some later accounts acknowledge this, while others continue to maintain diplomacy was tried and failed. Oddly, though, only I have made the case that Kissinger controlled the diplomatic bureaucracy as much as Schlesinger controlled the Pentagon in pursuit of his preferred approach to managing the crisis. This seems strange because of Kissinger's much commented upon penchant for recognizing the power of bureaucracy and insisting it had to be tamed or worked around. For example, see Lloyd Jensen, *Explaining Foreign Policy* (Englewood Cliffs, N.J.: Prentice-Hall, 1982), 126; and, for my original argument that Kissinger limited diplomatic initiatives, see Lamb, "Belief Systems and Decision Making," 692–93; and *Belief Systems and Decision Making*, 213–15, 246–47.

42. Memorandum of Conversation, General Scowcroft and the President, the Oval Office, 2:23 a.m., May 14, 1975 (declassified January 24, 2000), Ford Library.

43. Wickham notebooks.

44. For example, Colonel Graves passed information to Scowcroft that provided an exact accounting of Cambodian boat sightings, length of the boats, the number sunk, and the location of surviving vessels. Note from "Irene" to General Scowcroft, May 14, 1975.

45. Memorandum of Conversation, President Ford, Dr. Kissinger, and General Scowcroft, 11:45 a.m., May 14, 1975; box 1, folder "Cambodia-*Mayaguez* Seizure (1)" of NSA Kissinger-Scowcroft West Wing Office Files, Ford Library.

46. Kissinger, *Years of Renewal*, 559.

47. DoD After Action Report. Schlesinger approved making the request for presidential approval, which was consistent with his standing guidance and preferences. However, for two reasons it seems he may have done so without being aware that Wickham ignored the previous presidential order. First, Wickham says he explained later to the secretary what he'd done and that Schlesinger "realized the wisdom of what happened." Second, at the opening of the next NSC meeting, which was called to resolve the issue of what to do about the vessel with the Caucasians aboard, rather than justifying Pentagon lethargy by pointing to the possible presence of the crew, Schlesinger observed that the pilot "is not certain that there are Caucasians on board." In other

words, he undermined the best possible Pentagon defense for asking for presidential reconsideration of standing orders. Wickham interview; NSC meeting minutes.

48. All parties involved—Ford, Scowcroft, Kissinger, Schlesinger, and Wickham—agree it was crystal clear that Ford wanted all boats sunk as a matter of course. Kissinger, *Years of Renewal*, 559–60; Wickham interview; Schlesinger *Veteran* interview.

49. Wickham interview.

50. Schlesinger *Veteran* interview. Wickham's and Schlesinger's memory of the exact sequence of events is slightly at odds. See page 28 and note 33 on page 225.

51. NSC meeting minutes.

52. Wickham notebooks and on the ten helicopters, see Mahoney, *Mayaguez Incident*, 215.

53. NSC meeting minutes.

54. "Possible Scenario for Recovery of Ship and Crew," prepared by the Department of Defense, for the NSC meeting beginning at 10:40 p.m., May 13. Kissinger-Scowcroft West Wing Office Files, box 1, Cambodia, *Mayaguez* Seizure; cited by the Office of the Historian, Department of State: https://history.state.gov/historicaldocuments/frus1969-76v10/d290.

55. See pages 70–71 on EC-121.

56. NSC meeting minutes.

57. Clements baldly stated that he didn't think any Americans were on Tang Island, causing Kissinger to respond, "They could be. We do not know." That precipitated a discussion of how many Caucasians the pilots thought they saw, and it was agreed the pilots were not sure. Kissinger reasoned, "We do not know that they are not there [i.e., on Tang]" and "Taking the island if they are not there is easier to explain than failing to take it if they are." Schlesinger agreed, saying, "We have an obligation to get the Americans or to see if they are there."

58. According to Admiral Steele, "The sad part of the *Mayaguez* evolution is that we had sufficient force coming up with the Seventh Fleet, after it had been turned around from the evacuation of Vietnam stand down, to seize Southern Cambodia. I begged for another day or two, rather than commit forces piecemeal as we did." Dunham and Quinlan, *US Marines in Vietnam*, 239.

59. Head, Short, and McFarlane, *Crisis Resolution*, 121–22, based on an interview with General Jones. With respect to "going on the fourteenth," it should be noted that the issue was a twenty-four versus a forty-eight-hour delay, i.e., going on May 14 or 15 (Washington time) or May 15 or 16 (Cambodian time).

60. See Schlesinger *Veteran* interview.

61. Jones interview, 202. Vandenbroucke, who interviewed several senior officers involved in the crisis, claims Jones was out of step with the other members of the Joint Chiefs who were "eager to proceed without delay." This insight is consistent with a comment Scowcroft made to Wickham on the phone before the fourth and final NSC meeting before the military operations began. He told Wickham that there was considerable concern among the Joint Chiefs that General Jones was not being sufficiently inclusive of their views. Wickham notebooks.

62. NSC meeting minutes.

63. "What is harder for me to understand is why the fourth air strike—and I had specifically ordered four—was never carried out. I hadn't told anyone to cancel that attack. Apparently someone had, and I was anxious to find out who had contravened my authority." Ford, *A Time to Heal*, 284.

64. In that regard, the account provided here with the benefit of new sources helps correct the conclusions of this author's 1989 work, which for Schlesinger's views relied more heavily on leaked information to news media. See Lamb, B*elief Systems and Decision Making*, 104ff. and 208n67.

65. "Possible Scenarios for Recovery of Ship and Crew," in box 28, Folder: Department of

Defense—General, National Security Adviser, NSC East Asian and Pacific Affairs Staff: Files, (1969) 1973–1976, Ford Library.

66. Laitin was the source of most leaks according to Nessen. This greatly irritated Kissinger, who says in his memoirs that "Joseph Laitin, missed no opportunity to transform honest disagreements into aspects of a feud between the Secretaries of State and Defense. Newspaper columns kept describing our deliberations in terms of 'Dr. Strangelove' restrained by the humanistic Secretary of Defense. I was alleged to have advocated indiscriminate B-52 bombings in contrast to Schlesinger, who stood for a more precise 'tit-for-tat' retaliation." Nessen, *It Sure Looks Different*, 128; and Lamb, *Belief Systems and Decision Making*: 210–11.

67. See Lamb, *Belief Systems and Decision Making*, 104–14; and Kissinger, *Years of Renewal*, 572.

68. Head, Short, and McFarlane, *Crisis Resolution*, 303n30.

69. Ford, *A Time to Heal*, 284.

70. Kissinger, *Years of Renewal*, 571–72.

71. See the concept of operations as explained in the Pentagon's after action report on the military operations. DoD After Action Report.

72. Ibid.; see section on verbal orders relating to rescue of the SS *Mayaguez* and crew.

73. Kissinger in his memoirs indicates that he understood there was little time left before the first wave struck: "Since there was little time left, I suggested that the planes from the *Coral Sea* proceed on course but drop no ordnance until the President had made his decision." Kissinger, *Years of Renewal*, 568.

74. Wickham notebooks.

75. Direct communications between the White House situation room and the NMCC began once McFarlane called Wickham prior to the fourth NSC meeting to say the White House wanted direct reports not delayed by intervening echelons of command authority. Wickham notebooks.

76. Lieutenant General, USAR, Ray B. Sitton, Director for Operations, Joint Chiefs of Staff, Memorandum for the Secretary of Defense, Subject: Mainland Air Strikes During the *Mayaguez* Operation, Undated, Air Force (hereafter Sitton to SECDEF memo). Also, at 8:37 the CIA operations center heard from the White House situation room "that at 2027 (i.e. 8:27 p.m.) President Ford ordered a stop in the action planned against mainland Cambodia," which suggests that a general suspension of operations against the mainland was not just the Pentagon's selective perception. Chronological Listing of Intelligence Community Activities, CIA-5.

77. Sitton to SECDEF memo.

78. In his memoirs, Ford misremembers these conversations as being with Scowcroft rather than Kissinger, but Kissinger, Scowcroft, and Ford all agree on the timing and content of the communications. Ford, *A Time to Heal*, 282.

79. Kissinger in his memoirs notes Schlesinger wanted the controversial strikes to continue. It is notable, in light of Schlesinger's disagreements with Kissinger and his being fired, that he did not take the opportunity to blackguard Kissinger for the punitive mainland strikes when speaking on the record about them. An interviewer pressed him to do so, asking him to confirm that Kissinger wanted more airstrikes even after it was known that the crew had been safely recovered. Schlesinger declined. What stood out in his mind was Kissinger's reluctance to continue the strikes after the broadcast was received:

> **Interviewer:** Is it true, as has been alleged, that even after you received word about the crew's safe return, Kissinger still wanted to go ahead with the last air strike?
> **Schlesinger:** I don't think there's any justification for that. Our purposes had been achieved, and there was no point in inflicting additional punishment.
> **Interviewer:** You do not remember Kissinger saying anything like this?

Schlesinger: No, nothing of the sort. In fact, as I indicated earlier, after Radio Phnom Penh made that first broadcast, he was reluctant to inflict more damage.

Schlesinger *Veteran* interview.

80. Sitton to SECDEF memo. The first wave launched from the *Coral Sea* at 8:05 and were over their target area forty minutes later at 8:45. They made their shorter trip back to the *Coral Sea*, which continued to close the distance during their flight, by 9:30. If they were still on station above their targets at 8:58, that left only thirty-two minutes available for the flight back to the *Coral Sea*. Either they made their runs at the harbor targets very quickly or they had already observed the neutral shipping and decided not to risk expending ordnance. For reasons explained elsewhere, given the combat radius of the aircraft in question, the Pentagon's later explanation of fuel complications seems unlikely. See Lamb, *Belief Systems and Decision Making*, 105ff.

81. Mahoney notes that "no bombs had been dropped on the first wave per Kissinger's suggestion," implying Kissinger's intervention effectively ensured the first wave would not hit targets. Mahoney, *Mayaguez Incident*, 126.

82. Wickham notebooks.

83. This perceived failure to be straightforward was exacerbated by later Pentagon claims that the planes were low on fuel and had to turn back and is an explanation that some sources still cite despite being disproven long ago. See Lamb, *Belief Systems and Decision Making*, 110; and Herspring, *Pentagon and the Presidency*, 231.

84. Wickham notebooks.

85. In reviewing this decision for another mainland strike, Wetterhahn argues that no one considered the more important issue, which was whether another punitive strike made more sense than having "all available US forces . . . harnessed in getting the Marines safely off the island." But Schlesinger tried to do precisely that. Wetterhahn, *Last Battle*, 206.

86. Senator John Stennis (D-MS) and Congressman Melvin Price (D-IL). Wickham notebooks.

87. Sitton to SECDEF memo.

88. See MH-53 pilot Gary Weikel's account on landing on the *Coral Sea* in Orr Kelly, *From a Dark Sky: The Story of US Air Force Special Operations* (Novato, CA: Presidio, 1996), 229–31.

89. Sitton to SECDEF memo.

90. A few days after the crisis in an interview on ABC's *Issues and Answers* television program, Schlesinger responded to a question about whether the mainland airstrikes were really necessary by noting candidly, among other things, that "we did terminate the fourth wave." James Schlesinger interview, *Issues and Answers*, ABC, May 18, 1975.

91. Roy Rowan produced *The Four Days of Mayaguez*, a quick book on the event that contained much useful material. Hugh Sidey of *Time* magazine wrote an article titled "The Presidency: An Old-Fashioned Kind of Crisis," May 16, 1975. The Sidey interview can be found in box 26, folder: May 16, 1975 Time Magazine–Hugh Sidey, Ronald H. Nessen Files, Ford Library.

92. Mahoney notes Ford actually accused Schlesinger of being "downright insubordinate" in an interview he gave late in life. Mahoney, *Mayaguez Incident*, 12; and Thomas M. DeFrank and Gerald R. Ford. *Write It When I'm Gone: Remarkable Off-the-Record Conversations with Gerald R. Ford* (New York: G. P. Putnam's Sons, 2007), 92.

93. The minutes are not verbatim, having been "edited and transcribed" for administrative purposes, but they appear to be remarkably comprehensive. Participant accounts sometimes bring extra color or identify comments not recorded in the minutes. For example, see Robert T. Hartmann, *Palace Politics: An Inside Account of the Ford Years* (New York: McGraw-Hill, 1980), 326; and Sparrow, *Strategist*, 169.

94. Mahoney in particular notes this point. See *Mayaguez Incident*, 220.

95. Vandenbroucke is the first source to mention the Pentagon was resisting presidential orders, noting that one anonymous participant in a confidential interview said, "Officials reportedly withheld the order to shoot until it was too late for the planes to act." Guilmartin, who interviewed Schlesinger, is more specific, saying Schlesinger "'fluffed off' the White House for three hours." Vandenbroucke, *Perilous Options*, 81; Guilmartin, *Very Short War*, 55–56 and 148. Mahoney notes the White House's willingness to sink the boats and frustration with the Pentagon's reluctance to act, but not the Pentagon's conscious decision to stonewall the White House. All these sources missed Schlesinger's explicit explanation of Pentagon behavior in his interview with *Veteran* magazine. Schlesinger *Veteran* interview.

96. See the discussion of Vandenbroucke's treatment of the Tehran cable in note 26 on page 234. Mahoney asserts diplomacy was not neglected, citing the threats delivered via China, the outreach to the UN, and the US response to the Cambodian broadcast (which he says was delivered via the Voice of America, which is not accurate, as he notes himself on p. 127, saying the US response was delivered via news media). He also disputes that Kissinger kept the Tehran cable from the NSC, saying that "the NSC did not ignore the report." His source for this observation is Kissinger, who discusses the cable in his memoirs, saying the "information seemed to us too fragmentary to affect our decisions." Kissinger does not specify who the "us" was; it might have been Scowcroft and him or another NSC staff member, but Mahoney assumes it was the NSC. For the reasons provided here, it seems clear Kissinger's assertions during the crisis about fearing a diplomatic development should be given more weight than his vague explanation for discounting the Tehran cable in his memoirs. Mahoney, *Mayaguez Incident*, 103, 107, 212 and 216; Kissinger, *Years of Renewal*, 564.

97. Mahoney discusses intelligence at length but focuses on why the higher estimates of enemy strength on Tang Island never reached the Marines. See Mahoney, *Mayaguez Incident*, 96 and 251–55.

Chapter 6

1. Lamb, *Belief Systems and Decision Making in the* Mayaguez *Crisis*, 31.

2. With the twenty-three Americans who died in an accidental CH-53 helicopter crash in Thailand, forty-one lives were lost. Many observers noted this amounted to one more than the forty crewmen saved, which does not include the five Thai crewmen.

3. Guilmartin, *Very Short War*, 150.

4. Ibid., 155.

5. Wetterhahn, *Last Battle*, 63.

6. Patrick, "*Mayaguez* Operation." Many special operations forces have made this point as well. Gary Weikel, a HH-53 pilot, raised this issue in a National War College paper long ago, and other military students have done the same. According to Timothy Bosiljevac, "Delta platoon from SEAL Team One was available in Subic Bay for contingency operations. They were initially alerted and moved to Naval Air Station Cubi Point with ammunition and weaponry. Soon after, they were ordered to stand down." Gary Weikel, letter to the author, October 29, 1991; Bosiljevac, "Teams In 'Nam." See also T. L. Bosiljevac, *SEALs: UDT/SEAL Operations in Vietnam* (New York: IVY Books, 1990), 178–179. For a fuller treatment of what the SEALS might have contributed, see Edward G. Winters and Kent A. Paro, "The Misuse of Special Operations Forces" (thesis, Naval Postgraduate School, Monterey, CA, 1994).

7. Guilmartin, *Very Short War*, 156.

8. Vandenbroucke, *Perilous Options*, 100.

9. Ibid. General Burns decided against pre-assault fires for fear of endangering the *Mayaguez* crew. However, the Marines were not informed of this. The decision to forgo pre-assault fires made

escort suppressive fire all the more important, and yet this operational detail was also overlooked. More helicopters were not available for that purpose, but an effort to have the Marines better linked up with AC-130s and OV-10s as they approached the island could have been made. See Patrick, *"Mayaguez* Operation"; and Glenn T. Starnes, "The *Mayaguez* Incident: A Failure in Operational Leadership" (Naval War College, June 16, 1995).

10. Wetterhahn, *Last Battle*, 102, 112.

11. Guilmartin, *Very Short War*, 77. Head, an early student of the crisis, calls the underutilization of the AC-130s "puzzling." William P. Head, *"Mayaguez*: The Final Tragedy of The U.S. Involvement in The Vietnam War," *Journal of Third World Studies* 29, no.1 (Spring 2012): 63.

12. Vandenbroucke, *Perilous Options*, 101. Guilmartin asserts that Colonel Harry Goodall, the commander of the 56th Special Operations Wing, ordered the OV-10s launched on his own authority to help the Marines. Guilmartin, *Very Short War*, 112. See also OV-10 pilot Greg Wilson's explanation for why OV-10s were committed to the fight late instead of early on. Wilson, "Growth."

13. Guilmartin, *Very Short War*, 149.

14. According to Guilmartin, they were only dispatched in response to an order from the NMCC. Guilmartin, *Very Short War*, 153.

15. For example, Glen Starnes notes Marine Colonel John M. Johnson could not participate in the assault on Tang Island because of limited lift, so he and his staff remained at Utapao, thinking he would be able to communicate with the Marine assault force via the Airborne Command, Control, and Communication (ABCCC) aircraft. But, "for unknown reasons, the ABCCC never established the communications link to Utapao," and Colonel Johnson was largely excluded from on-scene decision making. Starnes, *"Mayaguez* Incident."

16. Lamb, "Belief Systems and Decision Making," 695–96. Perhaps the first scholar to make a case for the punitive nature of the US response was J. K. Baral, who argued, "The primary motive of Washington apparently was to punish Cambodia and thereby send the necessary signals to other adversaries." He weakened this conclusion a bit by identifying other possible motives, including Ford being "attuned to the requirements of the politics of the Presidential elections," the possibility of US espionage, and "the lurking suspicion that the *Mayaguez* incident was provoked by the United States by sending its spy ship deliberately" into the area. J. K. Baral, "The *Mayaguez* Incident: a Study of Crisis Management," *International Studies* 19, no. 1 (1980): 22, 39, 40.

17. Goldman et al., "Ford's Rescue Operation."

18. Ibid.

19. See a list in Lamb, "Belief Systems and Decision Making," 695–96.

20. The primary argument made by the author's 1985 article was that the US response to the *Mayaguez* "was essentially a punitive action and not a rescue attempt." See Lamb, "Belief Systems and Decision Making."

21. This explanation for Ford's behavior is widespread. See the discussion of Vandenbroucke below, but also Mattias Fibiger, "Redeeming the Ship of State: The *Mayaguez* Incident and the Legacies of the Nixon Administration" (Paper Prepared for the Student Research Conference, Richard M. Nixon Presidential Library, April 27, 2012), 20–22; and Greene, who asserts Ford launched "a punitive operation born of a political need." John R. Greene, *The Presidency of Gerald R. Ford* (Lawrence: University Press of Kansas, 1995), 150. Fibiger's research is otherwise excellent and well worth reading.

22. Martin Thornton, *Times of Heroism, Times of Terror: American Presidents and the Cold War* (Westport, CT: Praeger, 2005), 107.

23. The author originally made this case in Lamb, "Belief Systems and Decision Making," 696.

24. Although the senior members of Congress did not engage in any meaningful consultation in their short telephone conversations with the low-level aides who called them (sometimes only reaching them at home), their brief comments were taken down and passed along to the president. Cited in Fibiger, "Redeeming the Ship of State." Congressional Contacts of May 13, 1975, Box 122, Folder: *Mayaguez* Seizure – 5/14/75 (2), John Marsh Files, 1974–1977, Ford Library.

25. Proponents of asymmetric force such as the vice president cited congressmen and public feedback they had received to encourage the president to use force. For example, Rockefeller told Ford that in New York "people expect you to be doing things" and a business group "applauded when I said that you would be firm." He also noted that Congressman Clement Zablocki, a proponent of the War Powers Act (and a liberal Democrat), told the press that the United States "could bomb the hell out of them."

26. Eastland's behavior and comments were leaked to *Newsweek* (May 26, 1975 issue), which reported that he "sat slouched in his chair throughout the meeting, mumbling several times to himself, blow the hell out 'em." Mahoney provides a full description of the meeting with members of Congress and their mixed views, but titles the chapter on this topic "Congressional Leadership Approves," which seems an overstatement. Kissinger's review of the meeting, which notes "congressional leaders were unenthusiastic," is more accurate. Mahoney, *Mayaguez Incident*, 119–22; for Kissinger's comment, see note 21 on page 227.

27. Even as the crisis was ongoing the White House received input from interested parties, many applauding a strong stance and others notably hostile to the use of force and conditioned by opposition to the Vietnam War. Early on folk singer Joan Baez sent Ford a telegram asking, "Re Sinking of Cambodian Gunboats. What in [the Lord's] name do you think you're doing?" Hester G. Stoll, vice president of the Women's International League for Peace and Freedom, also sent a telegram to Ford to "strongly recommend that you keep our merchant marine out of questionable waters. A great country like ours should depend on patient diplomacy rather than military threat and actions." Even with the apparent success of the operations, many like the Steering Committee of the Joint Washington Office for Social Concern immediately contacted the White House to "strongly object to the hasty use of force in the *Mayaguez* incident, before all recourse to diplomacy was exhausted" and to "the violation of the sovereignty of Thailand" and "to the continued resort by the leadership of this nation to the diplomacy of violence." Joan Baez, Western Union Telegram to President Ford, May 14, 1975; 13:16 EST; Mrs. Hester G. Stoll, vice president of the Women's International League for Peace and Freedom, Western Union Telegram, to President Ford, May 14, 1975; 19:56 EST; Robert E. Jones, executive director, Joint Washington Office for Social Concern, letter to the president, May 16, 1975.

28. "Most important" is Nessen's depiction. Nessen, *It Sure Looks Different*, 124.

29. Ibid., 124.

30. Mahoney, *Mayaguez Incident*, 103.

31. The day after the crisis in a conversation with Ford, Kissinger said, "I think Schlesinger, when he heard the Congressional attitudes, changed the orders [for ongoing airstrikes against the mainland]." See the discussion on page 149. Kissinger, *Years of Renewal*, 565; Memorandum of Conversation, President Ford, Henry Kissinger and Brent Scowcroft, Friday, May 16, 1975, 9:25 a.m., Oval Office, declassified, Ford Library.

32. Robert Gates, in his first set of memoirs, claimed that "the first instinct of the Congress through the years was to be critical of any presidential use of force," and he cites the *Mayaguez* as one example. Only when it became clear force was popular with the public did the congressional attitude change. Robert M. Gates, *From the Shadows: The Ultimate Insider's Story of Five Presidents and How They Won the Cold War* (London: Pocket, 2008), 558.

33. Ford, *A Time to Heal*, 283.

34. The congressional hearings on May 15 focused in particular on whether any airstrikes had been "punitive" or not, which the administration witnesses testified was not the case. US Congress, House Subcommittee on International Political and Military Affairs, Seizure of the *Mayaguez*, 94th Cong., 1st sess. (Washington, DC: US Government Printing Office, 1975).

35. Ron Nessen News Conference at the White House, 11:50 a.m., May 14, 1975, Ron Nessen File, Ford Library.

36. Osborne describes how his positive assessment of Ford's performance at the time elicited a ferocious backlash, including from readers. Osborne, *White House Watch*, 152, 155.

37. According to Nessen, as the 1976 election year began, Ford's pollster, Robert Teeter, showed Ford and his political advisors the depressing results of a comprehensive survey of public attitudes toward Ford. In response to the question, "What has Ford done that particularly impresses you?" sixty-one percent replied, "Nothing." The next-largest group was 4 percent, which liked the tax cut; 3 percent praised Ford's honesty and integrity; and 2 percent mentioned the rescue of the *Mayaguez*. As William Hyland recalls, "At home the administration earned no public or political credit for using force to rescue the ship and free the crew. There was bitterness; the mood was sour and turning worse." William G. Hyland, *Mortal Rivals: Understanding the Pattern of Soviet-American Conflict* (New York: Simon & Schuster, 1988), 114.

38. Lamb, "Belief Systems and Decision Making," 157ff.

39. Decision makers acknowledged this after the fact. Ford told the journalist Rowan he thought they would be lucky to get the crew back alive. Three days after the crisis, Schlesinger admitted on ABC's *Issues and Answers* that there had been "an element of good fortune" in the outcome. Schlesinger also admitted, "The outcome was fortunate" in an interview with *Time* correspondent Joseph J Kane. Scowcroft's biographer notes he thought the same: "In regard to the safety of the *Mayaguez*'s crew, the Ford administration got lucky. It's easy to imagine one or more of the crewmembers being accidentally killed, whether by their captors or by US ordnance." General Jones also concluded we "lucked out" and "were quite fortunate to get the crew members back." The observation that Ron Nessen voiced the feeling of the administration when he told the press, "All's well that ends well," was not meant to communicate a callous disregard of the lives lost, but the great sense of relief that the return of the crew had been so fortunate. Ford in Rowan, *Four Days*, 140; Schlesinger interview, *Issues and Answers*; Scowcroft in Robert L. Pfaltzgraff and Jacquelyn K. Davis. *National Security Decisions: The Participants Speak* (Lexington: Lexington Books, 1990), 276; and Sparrow, *Strategist*: 165. Jones interview, 202; Nessen in Greene, *Presidency of Gerald R. Ford*, 24.

40. Deputy Secretary of Defense Clements made the observation in the fourth NSC meeting that the Air Force police fatalities would be linked with the crisis response "sooner or later."

41. NSC meeting minutes. In his recent book, Rumsfeld agrees, citing his own notes from the period and asserting "the president decided to notify the appropriate members of Congress, on an 'advisory basis,' rather than on a 'consultation basis'" because he concluded the War Powers Act was not applicable "in this particular instance." Rumsfeld, *When the Center Held*, 172.

42. *Newsweek*, May 26, 1975, 16.

43. They repeatedly considered how their decisions would be interpreted by Congress, the media, and the public. For example, in debating the presence of Americans on Tang Island and noting the entire crew might have been on the fishing boat, Colby commented, "We need to be braced against that pilot" (that is, the pilot who observed what he thought were crew members on the boat). NSC meeting minutes.

44. Memorandum of Conversation, President Ford, Henry Kissinger and Brent Scowcroft, Wednesday, 14 May 1975, 11:45 a.m., Oval Office (declassified January 24, 2000), Ford Library. Kissinger

reconsidered the B-52s and the continuation of the airstrikes, but, as others have noted, including Kissinger in his memoirs, Ford remained resolute. See Richard "Dick" Cheney's remembrances in Thompson, *Ford Presidency*, 81; and Kissinger, *Years of Renewal*, 569.

45. They frequently discussed how to justify their decisions to the public. Ford also several times mentioned to passersby that he had a tough decision to make about the ship and crew. What made the decision tough for Ford was that using force risked the lives of the crew.

46. For example, in the fourth NSC meeting when discussing a meeting with selected members of Congress to "consult" in accordance with the War Powers Act, Rockefeller asked what should be done if the group opposed the president's plans. Kissinger quickly said "he would have to go ahead anyway," which is what Ford had already said he would do in the first NSC meeting regardless of congressional preferences. Kissinger, *Years of Renewal*, 565.

47. Document 284, Minutes of the Secretary of State's Regionals Staff Meeting; Washington, May 12, 8-8:40 a.m., in *FRUS 1969-1976*, vol. 10.

48. It also is not clear that Rockefeller was particularly influential. Ford listened to everyone but acted upon what Kissinger and Scowcroft told him with great consistency, much more so than was the case with Schlesinger and Rockefeller.

49. I. F. Stone quoted in Lamb, *Belief Systems and Decision Making*, 276.

50. Over time, and with the release of the NSC minutes, researchers have moved away from the characterization of the decision-making process as highly emotional. For example, Scowcroft's biographer says the "transcripts of the NSC meetings show that the . . . discussions were serious, intense, and candid," and that decision makers were "trying to come up with sound decisions under conditions of immense pressure." Sparrow, *Strategist*, 169.

51. The commentary came out the day following the *Newsweek* article that provided the well-rounded description of possible US motives. A 1991 history of the NSC makes the same point, saying, "Someday the documentary record may reveal whether the attacks during this incident were instrumental or punitive in nature." See Godfrey Sperling Jr., "Manipulating *Mayaguez* News Coverage," *Christian Science Monitor*, May 27, 1975; and Prados, *Keepers of the Keys*, 372.

52. One of the coauthors of *Crisis Resolution*, Robert McFarlane, who was on the NSC staff at the time, spent a year and a half at the National War College writing the book. McFarlane and Smardz, *Special Trust*, 166.

53. The authors did not apply their stated approach consistently, however. At times they just described crisis behavior; sometimes they "suggested" relations between variables; and sometimes they asserted an intention to explain US behavior. For a longer critique of the study see Lamb, *Belief Systems and Decision Making*, 232–35.

54. More recent studies also miss this element of the crisis. Scowcroft's biographer misses all the tensions expressed in the NSC minutes, concluding they

> reveal no obvious rivalries or opposing coalitions. Although Schlesinger, Kissinger and Rumsfeld were known to oppose each other on various policy issues—SALT II for example—during the *Mayaguez* crisis they worked together effectively. . . . Only after the crisis had ended did the rivalry between State and Defense reemerge.

Sparrow argues the remarkable harmony was "largely because of Scowcroft" who was "at the center of it all" and "doing the little things that held the US government together." While it is true that key decision makers agreed on their overall objectives, they struggled mightily over how to implement decisions made in NSC meetings. Sparrow, *Strategist*, 169–70.

55. In one case the evidence even suggests that Ford bucked up Kissinger, who went wobbly after the news of the Cambodian broadcast. See note 44 on page 243.

56. Lamb, *Belief Systems and Decision Making*, 241–42.

57. Vandenbroucke, *Perilous Options*, 74–75

58. Ibid., 74, 86, and 92.

59. Ibid., 92–93.

60. Ibid., 75.

61. Ibid., 86–87.

62. See also Lamb, *Belief Systems and Decision Making*, 194.

63. Guilmartin, *Very Short War*, 149.

64. Ibid., 156.

65. He does not find other explanations for US behavior plausible, such as the assertion that Ford was trying to improve his domestic political standing.

66. Guilmartin, *Very Short War*, 38 and 148.

67. The first book on the *Mayaguez* to use the NSC minutes is Wetterhahn's *The Last Battle*. The book includes excellent research and great sympathy for the forces committed to combat but does not offer a balanced depiction of the NSC members and their decision making, which are presented in a uniformly and scathingly negative manner. The only other source more disparaging is a historical novel on the *Mayaguez* by Ejner Fulsang, *A Knavish Piece of Work: A Novel of the Mayaguez Incident* (Belmont, CA: Aarhus Publishing), 2006.

68. On the lives of the crew being a lesser priority, see Mahoney, *Mayaguez Incident*, 68–69 and 218–20; on Kissinger's dissent, see p. 71. Mahoney's work is packed with other useful descriptive details, including how Navy SEALs and others were not allowed to attempt a rescue of the three missing Marines, the impact of a malfunctioning propulsion screw on the USS *Hancock*, and more on Ford's ire with Schlesinger for canceling the last airstrike. Mahoney, *Mayaguez Incident*, 179, 37, and 185ff, respectively. Other notes highlight more new observations from Mahoney's research.

69. Mahoney overlooks Kissinger's manipulation of diplomacy (see note 96 on page 240) and gets some other descriptive details wrong. For instance, his account does not relate that Kissinger encouraged Ford to call the first NSC meeting, that it was Schlesinger's strict rules of engagement and intervention by Pentagon generals that saved the fishing boat and not the pilot's initiative, and that Schlesinger was not against punitive strikes. Mahoney, *Mayaguez Incident*, 24; 62 and 103; 49 and 113, respectively. It is important to review and compare Mahoney's multiple references to a subject because some of his conclusions run contrary to the descriptive evidence he provides. For example, he identifies Jones early in the book as someone who favored giving priority to rescuing the crew (p. 38, based on a much later interview with Jones), but he also relates Jones's intervention in an NSC meeting when he said the solution for preventing the movement of the crew to the mainland was to sink all boats (p. 50)—a step that obviously risked the lives of the crew and subordinated them to other priorities.

70. For example, he cites Kissinger in his memoirs attributing great significance to the *Pueblo* crisis as a key factor in Ford's thinking. As we have shown, however, Scowcroft was more influenced by the *Pueblo* crisis, and Kissinger actually drew Ford's attention to the EC-121 crisis to encourage him to act quickly. More generally, Mahoney cites the memoirs of Ford and Kissinger forty-five and fifty-eight times, respectively, for more than a tenth of his notes. Mahoney also uncritically takes Jones's later interview as the definitive account of his views at the time. On Kissinger and the *Pueblo*, see Mahoney, *Mayaguez Incident*, 29; and Lamb, *Belief Systems and Decision Making*, 198–200; on Jones's thinking, see Mahoney, *Mayaguez Incident*, 37–38 (and the previous note).

71. Mahoney comes closest to offering an explanation for US behavior in his analysis of strategic leadership where he makes seven observations, the sixth of which addresses US priorities in the crisis.

72. Mahoney, *Mayaguez Incident*, xiv–xv; 217–18.

73. Ibid., 218–22.

74. Ibid., 13.

75. For example, at one point early in the crisis he asserts (correctly) that "Kissinger had undoubtedly already decided that prompt military action was called for; his task now was to ensure it occurred."

76. Mahoney, *Mayaguez Incident,* 215, 221.

77. On the *Pueblo* and emotional catharsis, ibid., 215; on Ford and domestic politics, ibid., 259.

78. Ibid., 215. Even this conclusion is a bit confused, however, by Mahoney also asserting "the NSC's overall decision-making process to a large degree acknowledged the emotional aspect of the situation," and yet "set it aside."

79. This point was evident long ago. See Lamb, *Belief Systems and Decision Making*, 282. Mahoney does not describe the impact of the *Pueblo* analogy well and appears to take Kissinger's memoirs at face value on the issue. Kissinger asserts Ford was powerfully impressed by the *Pueblo* analogy, and Mahoney repeats this, claiming that "the NSC pointed to this possibility on several occasions, including lengthy tangential discussions regarding the similarities between the Pueblo incident and the *Mayaguez*." In reality, the *Pueblo* was only mentioned in the first of the four NSC meetings, and then only twice: once by the vice president and once by Schlesinger. The *Pueblo* analogy had the greatest impact on Scowcroft's beliefs and behaviors, driving his determination to prevent the crew from reaching the mainland. Kissinger, *Years of Renewal*, 551; and Mahoney, *Mayaguez Incident*, 29, 215, 221; see also discussion on pages 70, 121–22, 156 and note 103 on page 248.

80. It also might be noted that these books do not adequately address previous scholarship. Vandenbroucke does not mention previous scholarly works in his index and has few citations of the same. Guilmartin has three index entries on the present author's work but does not address why his findings differ. He also ignores Vandenbroucke's work (perhaps because he had already submitted his manuscript to editors before it became available). Mahoney makes brief mention of previous scholarship in his introduction but does not address previous findings in the rest of his book.

81. Christopher Lamb, "The *Mayaguez* Crisis: 30 Years of Scholarship," *Political Science Quarterly* (Spring 2018): 35–76.

82. Kissinger, *Years of Renewal*, 551–52; 556. Many years later Scowcroft also said, "We had very inadequate intelligence." Pfaltzgraff and Davis, *National Security Decisions*, 274. For a more recent source, see Rumsfeld, *When the Center Held*, 169, 170–71, 176. Rumsfeld complains about the tardy notification of senior leaders, not realizing Ford had been notified early on by Scowcroft and only interpreted the incident as a major provocation after speaking with Kissinger. Rumsfeld also argues that "there was no substantive analysis" of why "the Khmer Rouge [would] risk such a provocation" when in fact Colby laid out likely Cambodian motives right off the bat. Rumsfeld also claims the intelligence community's "two dozen ragtag Cambodians turned out to be between 200 and 300 reasonably well-armed, battle-hardened Khmer Rouge troops in embedded positions." He is apparently unaware that the NSC meeting minutes demonstrate the decision makers knew they were dealing with at least 100 well-entrenched Khmer defenders.

83. Captain Miller lied and told the Cambodians his chart was in meters, not fathoms, and thus he could not risk moving beyond Tang Island to the mainland. Gerald Reminick, *An Act of Piracy: The Seizure of the American-Flag Merchant Ship Mayaguez in 1975* (Palo Alto, CA: Glencannon Press, 2009), 25.

84. See page 77.

85. Mahoney explains well the thinking on the crew's location. See his explanation for AC-130 reports inclining decision makers to think the crew had been taken to Tang Island, and why they

thought the crew had been split up. Mahoney, *Mayaguez Incident*, 53, 66, 250. See also Captain Miller's explanation for confusion on the crew's whereabouts in Reminick, *Act of Piracy*, 73.

86. Telephone conversation, Mr. Joseph Kraft with Secretary Kissinger, 6:56 PM, May 15, 1975 (declassified January 18, 2005).

87. Schlesinger interview, *Issues and Answers*; Jones interview.

88. In his memoirs Colby cited the fast-evolving nature of the crisis but admitted there was room for improvement in keeping his analysts abreast of developments. CIA Post-Mortem Report; William Colby and Peter Forbath, *Honorable Men: My Life in the CIA* (New York: Simon & Schuster, 1978), 429. For an example of the extraordinary efforts made by the intelligence community on the spur of the moment, see David Mark, "The *Mayaguez* Rescue Operation Revisited," *Studies in Intelligence* 23, no. 2 (Summer 1979). Declassified from Secret/NOFORN and approved for release March 5, 2008 by the CIA.

89. Some sources, like Herspring, uncritically accept Kissinger's assertion that intelligence was uniformly poor and deleterious to decision making. It is manifest that the intelligence could have been better, and some students of the crisis make the need for better intelligence a major finding from their research (Vandenbroucke being a case in point). This author concurs with Mahoney, who reviews the intelligence issues at length and offers a more balanced assessment. He believes the intelligence was good considering the circumstances, but there was a tendency to oversell the certainty of information provided. Interestingly, Ford agreed, saying years later it would have been better if Colby simply said, "We don't know." Of the five key insights Mahoney says flow from his analysis (p. xxiii), his assessment of intelligence is the most original and helpful, although he does overestimate the extent to which the Marines were ignorant of enemy strength. See Herspring, *Pentagon and the Presidency*, 224; and Mahoney, *Mayaguez Incident*, 39, for his assertion that the Marines had "no idea what they were in for," and 47–48, 51, and 57 where he cites Jones for passing intelligence with more assurance than warranted, and also pages 345ff. For Ford's comment on Colby, see Cannon, *Honorable Life*, 379.

90. Chun, *Last Boarding Party*, 22–23. "The AC-130 returned from its 13 May night reconnaissance with IR and TV film (available today) 'showing in excess of fifty campfires on the island.' As the AC-130 crew later remarked, 'either the 13 bad guys were awfully afraid of the dark or there was a damn sight more than 13 bad guys.'" Gary Weikel, letter to the author, October 29, 1991. However, the AC-130 intelligence was factored in to the IPAC estimate of enemy strength on the island. See Pacific Air Force, "History," 438.

91. CINCPAC Command History 1975, 18.

92. It boils down to speculation about why communications between people did not take place. I concluded that "numerous interviews with Air Force and Marine officers after the incident paint a general picture of how the IPAC intelligence estimate failed to reach the Marine commander in charge of the Tang invasion: the members of each service were absorbed in their own responsibilities; they had not worked with each other before; the chain of command was geographically dispersed and unclear, and thus the responsibility for disseminating Intelligence was not clear either; and, finally, time for detailed planning was severely limited." Lamb, Belief Systems and Decision Making, 129–37. See also Mahoney's review of these factors, *Mayaguez Incident*, 251–55; and the CINCPAC IG report: Memorandum from BGEN Johnson to Admiral Gayler, Subject: SS *Mayaguez* Seizure, 17 November 1975; declassified 16 December, 1991 (hereafter CINCPAC IG report).

93. Lamb, *Belief Systems and Decision Making*, 131–32. More recently, Austin has said that he did not "put much credence" in the intelligence estimate of a small number of irregular forces, which "just didn't jive with what we knew at the time." As for the point of insertion, he said he chose "the north end of the island on both sides because these were the only already cleared areas," and it was

in "this general area that we suspected the crew might be." In addition, "a landing away from there could allow whoever was on the island to escape by boat from either of the coves." Wise and Baron, *14-Hour War*, 93–96.

94. It has also been suggested that, in addition to the mission objective, Austin's decision to land on the beach may have been influenced by Air Force preferences. See my discussion in *Belief Systems and Decision Making* (pp. 134–135), which focuses on Austin's decision and explanations, and Vandenbroucke's in *Perilous Options* (pp. 88–89), which takes into account more senior officer opinions up the chain of command.

95. This author concluded "the decision makers' haste was a more important factor than any intelligence [dissemination] failure in complicating military operations." Vandenbroucke seems to agree, emphasizing the "senior decision makers . . . unbridled enthusiasm for a military response," a category he construes to include the Joint Chiefs. However, he also cites Marines who insist they would have demanded preparatory fires if they had had the higher intelligence estimate of Cambodian forces. Burns precluded preparatory fires because of the potential danger to the crew members. See Lamb, *Belief Systems and Decision Making*, 134; Vandenbroucke, *Perilous Options*, 89–90 and 99–100.

96. Burns interview, 440.

97. Ibid., 442–43.

98. GAO report, 92. Also, as noted above, Wickham's notebooks indicate that the Marine Corps Commandant Cushman "had no concern about securing the assault area." Wickham notebooks.

99. Kissinger, *Years of Renewal*, 570. Kissinger selectively cites NSC minutes in his memoirs, so presumably he knew that the actual estimate of Tang defenders used in the NSC deliberations was one-hundred personnel.

100. CIA Post-Mortem Report. See also Burns interview, 439–44; Mahoney, *Mayaguez Incident*, 252–53; and CINCPAC IG report.

101. The Defense Department told the GAO that DIA and IPAC spoke often and coordinated their respective intelligence estimates, but noted the conflicting estimates were never reconciled. GAO report, 91. Burns asserts the same in his interview, where he notes his command argued with IPAC over their lesser estimate but never really understood why they insisted on the one-hundred-defender figure or why the DIA figure did not prevail. Burns interview, 444–45.

102. US Congress, House Committee on Foreign Affairs, Subcommittee on International Political and Military Affairs and Committee on International Relations and Military Affairs, Seizure of the *Mayaguez*, pt. 1, 7.

103. *Thinking in Time* is a case in point. The authors are careful to raise issues and not be definitive about the decision makers' motives, but their argument is that an historical analogy, in this case with the USS *Pueblo*, can obscure as much as it illuminates. They assert the *Pueblo* analogy "had a grip on the President's mind, and this probably influenced both his definition of the primary objective and his preferences for action." They seem to believe Ford and his advisors failed to consider differences between the *Mayaguez* and *Pueblo*, beginning with the fact that the *Pueblo* was a Navy ship with a crew that knew US secrets, whereas the *Mayaguez* was a merchant vessel. Ultimately, they ask, "Did the solution (i.e. use of force) precede, indeed, define, the problem?" Richard E. Neustadt and Ernest R. May, *Thinking in Time: The Uses of History for Decision-Makers* (New York: Free Press, 1988), 61.

104. Ford made no mention of Kennerly's insight when he was interviewed by Rowan immediately following the crisis. However, his recounting of the moment in his memoirs is dramatic:

There was a lull in the discussion. Then, from the back of the room, a new voice spoke up. It was Kennerly, who had been taking pictures of us for the past hour or so. Never before during a meeting of this kind had he entered the conversation; I knew he wouldn't have done so now unless what he had to say was important. "Has anyone considered," he asked, "that this might be the act of a local Cambodian commander who has just taken it into his own hands to halt any ship that comes by? Has anyone stopped to think that he might not have gotten his orders from Phnom Penh? If that's what has happened, you know, you can blow the whole place away and it's not gonna make any difference. Everyone here has been talking about Cambodia as if it were a traditional government. Like France. We have trouble with France, we just pick up the telephone, and call. We know who to talk to. But I was in Cambodia just two weeks ago, and it's not that kind of government at all. We don't even know who the leadership is. Has anyone considered that?" For several seconds there was silence in the Cabinet Room. Everyone seemed stunned that this brash photographer who was not yet thirty years old would have the guts to offer an unsolicited opinion to the President, the Vice President, the Secretaries of State and Defense, the Director of the CIA and the Chairman of the Joint Chiefs of Staff. Yet I wasn't surprised, and I was glad to hear his point of view.

Ford, *A Time to Heal*, 279–80.

105. Vandenbroucke, *Perilous Options*, 75–76.

106. The Cambodians were right to be concerned because Vietnam later took the islands. Indeed, just a month after the *Mayaguez* crisis, US communication intercepts revealed that the Vietnamese stormed Poulo Wai island and wiped out its Cambodian garrison. Ironically, it seems Kissinger may have helped convince the Vietnamese to later return the island to Cambodia. See National Security Agency, "American Cryptology during the Cold War, 1945–1989," top secret (declassified July 26, 2013; hereafter "American Cryptology during the Cold War"). For Kissinger's role in the return of the island, see Luanne J. Smith, "An Analysis of Events Leading to the Chinese Invasion of Vietnam" (thesis, Naval Postgraduate School, September 1980), 11ff.

107. Memorandum of Conversation, President Ford, Henry Kissinger and Brent Scowcroft, Wednesday, May 14, 1975, 11:45 a.m., Oval Office, declassified, Ford Library.

108. DeFrank notes Kennerly was Ford's "de facto fourth son." And Kennerly himself notes he was often the last person to see the president each day—often over drinks—which made other White House officials nervous. DeFrank and Ford, *Write It When I'm Gone*; and David Kennerly, interview by Richard Norton Smith for the Gerald R. Ford Oral History Project, December 14, 2009.

109. Vandenbroucke is a case in point, arguing it made no sense for the weak Cambodians to challenge the United States. Vandenbroucke, *Perilous Options*, 76–77

110. Cambodia's deputy premier, Ieng Sary, acknowledged the central direction in an interview a few months later, saying the Cambodian government in Phnom Penh decided to release the crew after three hours of deliberation. But, he said, "We did not broadcast our decision until the following morning," by which time US military operations had begun. Ieng Sary, interview by James Pringle, Lima, Peru, *Newsweek*, September 22, 1975, 39.

111. Henry A. Kissinger, Memorandum for the President, Subject: Debrief of the *Mayaguez* Captain and Crew, May 19, 1975 (declassified 1999).

112. Before going to sleep on the night of the fourteenth, Captain Miller was informed that an answer from Phnom Penh on the outcome of his negotiations would be received at 6 o'clock the following morning. See "The *Mayaguez* Story, Sea-Land Service, Inc. Special Issue for Sea-Land Employees." On the intercepts, see cable from DIRNSA to NSA/UNIFORM ECHO, 15 2131Z May 1975, approved for release by NSA on 01-28-2004, FOIA Case #18289; cited in "American Cryptology during the Cold War."

113. The US liaison office in China also suspected the Chinese and Cambodians had discussed the US threats and coordinated their nonresponse. The liaison office noted both the Chinese foreign ministry and Cambodian embassy had returned the US messages and commented: "Timing of the Cambodian Embassy's return of US message, i.e. morning after PRC [People's Republic of China] refusal to be of assistance, raises possibility that two actions were coordinated. Both rejections were predictable, but Chinese may in fact have discussed the matter with Cambodians here prior to the decisions being taken." Telegram from the Liaison Office in China to the Department of State, Beijing, May 15, 1975, 0253Z; Subject: Cambodian Embassy Returns US Message; source: Ford Library, National Security Adviser, NSC East Asian and Pacific Affairs Staff Files, 1973–1976, box 29, Department of State, Telegrams and Cables (2). Secret; Niact; Immediate; Nodis.

114. Henry A. Kissinger, Memorandum for the President, Subject: Debrief of the *Mayaguez* Captain and Crew, May 19, 1975; Ford Library. Oddly, Mahoney suggests it is a new finding to discover the Cambodians released the crew because of the US military buildup in the area and attacks on the gunboats and not because of the mainland strikes or assault on Tang Island. However, as Kissinger's comments to Ford suggest, this conclusion about what prompted the Cambodians to release the crew has long been evident from the testimony of the captain of the *Mayaguez* and long noted by multiple observers. For example, see Hartmann, *Palace Politics*, 327; and Lamb, "Belief Systems and Decision Making," 985, and *Belief Systems and Decision Making*, 189, 193, and 246.

115. Schlesinger *Veteran* interview.

116. This is true of much scholarship that examines the *Mayaguez* crisis, but there are exceptions. See Andrew Gawthorpe, "The Ford Administration and Security Policy in the Asia-Pacific After the Fall of Saigon," *Historical Journal* 52, no. 3 (2009): 709–10.

117. NSC meeting minutes.

118. Document 125, Memorandum of Conversation, Washington, May 15, 1975, 11 a.m., in *Foreign Relations of the United States, 1969–1976*, vol. 27, *Iran; Iraq, 1973–1976*.

119. Telephone conversation, Secretary Kissinger with Hugh Sidey, 11:15, May 15, 1975 (declassified 18 January 2005). General John Wickham noted there was always a concern with North Korea, "but yes, particularly at that time." He also thought there was concern with restraining South Korea from going nuclear. He noted one of Schlesinger's first trips as secretary of defense was to South Korea to convince them *not* to build a nuclear weapon and to assure them that our nuclear umbrella would suffice. Wickham said the South Koreans stuck to that agreement religiously. He mentioned that when he became the US commander in chief of UN Command and Combined Forces Command in July 1979 and first met with South Korean president Park Chung-hee, the president ordered everyone out of the room and in halting English, thanked Wickham for the United States allowing South Korea to find its own path to democracy. Wickham interview.

120. Goldman et al., "Ford's Rescue Operation," 16ff.

121. Ibid.

122. Bernard Gwertzman, "US Sees Foray for Ship as Signal to Communists," *New York Times*, May 16, 1975. See also Richard Halloran, "High South Korean Discounts Impact of Vietnam's Collapse," *New York Times*, May 1, 1975. The article describes South Korean officials expressing confidence in US security guarantees despite "fears expressed in Washington that the impact of the fall of Cambodia and Vietnam would be felt more in South Korea than anywhere else in Asia."

123. Lamb, *Belief Systems and Decision Making*, 72.

124. Gwertzman, "US Sees Foray," 14. The article elaborated on the administration's geostrategic reasoning in terms that emphasized Kissinger's known perspective. It explained the salutary effects of the *Mayaguez* for great power politics: "Mr. Kissinger and his aides have believed for some time that

Peking was interested in ties with the United States only so long as China though Washington would stand up militarily to Moscow if necessary." Thus, according to the article, the senior US official was confident that China would respect the response to the *Mayaguez* even though it might feel compelled to publicly criticize it.

125. Schlesinger interview, *Issues and Answers*.

126. *Time* magazine at the time reported that a "White House aide" bluntly explained "the aim was for our action to be read by North Korean President Kim Il Sung as well as by the Cambodians." "A Strong but Risky Show of Force," *Time*, May 26, 1975, 9. Mets cites three sources from 1975 and 1977 that noted the emphasis on deterring North Korea, including the Roy Rowan book. David R. Mets, "Last Flight from Koh Tang: the *Mayaguez* Incident a Generation Later," *Joint Force Quarterly* (2007): 115n4. Even severe critics of the Ford administration were aware of the focus on North Korea and grudgingly admitted it might have achieved its objectives. Shawcross says "the exhilaration which Ford derived (and the public support he received) from his handling of the *Mayaguez* incident . . . suggests that he would have full support for bombing North Korea if Kim ignored Chinese advice and crossed the demilitarized zone." See William Shawcross, "Making the Most of *Mayaguez*," *Far Eastern Economic Review*, May 30, 1975.

127. See page 70.

128. Wickham interview.

129. Head, Short, and McFarlane, *Crisis Resolution*: 301n25.

130. Lamb, *Belief Systems and Decision Making*, 186; and on North Korea, 99, 184–87.

131. Vandenbroucke, *Perilous Options*, 74–75, 113.

132. Guilmartin makes no mention of North Korea aside from the connection to the *Pueblo* incident. Similarly, Mahoney ignores North Korea, which is not found in the index or called out for special attention in the text. Mahoney instead emphasizes Cambodia, saying, "The NSC's first priority was to send a strong message to the Cambodian government, as well as the world writ large." Later Mahoney offers a passing reference to North Korean when describing US leaders' geostrategic concerns: "the United States was involved in the Cold War and had to maintain or improve its power relationships with China and the Soviet Union. American leaders were also concerned with North Korea and the Middle East, and a continued poor showing in Southeast Asia would further weaken the perception of American power in those areas." Mahoney, *Mayaguez Incident*, 218 and 259.

133. Telephone Conversation, David Rockefeller/Secretary Kissinger, May 16, 1975; 2:35 p.m. (declassified February 10, 2003). Their exchange is cryptic, but Rockefeller told Kissinger: "I thought it was important for them to know . . . in the event that they took from what happened in Vietnam. . . . That there would be an immediate response along the lines you suggested." A few months later Kissinger also sought a line of communication to Kim Il Sung through Nicolae Ceausescu, the Communist leader of Romania. See Memorandum of Conversation, Subject: US-North Korean Relations, August 3, 1975, lunch, Peles Castle, Sinaia (declassified December 2, 2003).

134. Habib prepared the May 8, 1975, briefing paper for Kissinger's discussion with Huang Chen, chief of the PRC liaison office in Washington. Briefing Paper for Secretary Kissinger; re your meeting with Huang Chen, May 8, 1975 (declassified July 3, 2008); box 5, Folder "China, unnumbered items – (12), 5/8/75 – 5/9/75" of the Kissinger-Scowcroft West Wing Office Files, Ford Library.

135. Memorandum of Conversation, Subject: Tour d 'Horizon with Huang Chen, May 9, 1975, 5:35–6:40 p.m., Department of State (declassified July 3, 2008).

136. Ibid., 72.

137. Stearman interview. This passage in Stearman's interview is also noted by Fibiger, "Redeeming the Ship of State," 11.

138. Document 60, Draft Memorandum from Secretary of State Kissinger to President Ford; Washington, July 18, 1975, in *Foreign Relations of the United States, 1969–1976*, vol. 38, pt. 1, *Foundations of Foreign Policy, 1973–1976*.

139. Yafeng Xia and Zhihua Shen, "China's Last Ally: Beijing's Policy toward North Korea during the US–China Rapprochement, 1970–1975," *Diplomatic History* 38, no. 5: 1083–1113. Xia and Shen explain "why the PRC declined to support Kim Il-Sung's proposal to attack the South in April 1975." They note that "George H. W. Bush, who was then head of US Liaison Office in Beijing, recorded in his diary of April 24, 'Kim Il-sung's talking militantly about Korea, China apparently downplaying this.'" Charles Armstrong agrees, saying, "Kim Il Sung's proposal to move aggressively toward the South in 1975 was rebuffed by China." Armstrong's source on this is East German documents reporting on Kim's April 1975 trip to Beijing, which detail "Kim's ambitions for a North Vietnam-style conquest of the South." Interestingly, European Communist governments suspected China of helping the United States by restraining North Korea. Charles K. Armstrong, *Tyranny of the Weak: North Korea and the World, 1950–1992* (Ithaca, NY: Cornell University Press, 2015), 139. See also James Hoare on China's refusal to support Kim's proposal for war in, "China's Korean Dilemma: Influence and Power on the Korean Peninsula," China Policy Institute, https://cpianalysis.org/2016/03/30/90512/.

140. Narushige Michishita, *North Korea's Military-Diplomatic Campaigns, 1966–2008* (London: Routledge, 2011), 83. Yafeng Xia and Zhihua Shen agree on this point, noting Kim promoted North Korea's cause internationally by active involvement in the non-aligned movement," which initially seemed like it might produce the UN General Assembly resolution Kim desired until the axe murders derailed North Korean diplomacy. Xia and Shen, "China's Last Ally," 1083–1113.

141. In a private conversation on September 15, 1976, National Security Advisor Brent Scowcroft and Ambassador Sneider (the US ambassador to South Korea) shared the view that the August 18 incident had "come out better than expected—and apparently to our net advantage." Kissinger disagreed. He thought chopping down the tree made the United States "look ridiculous," and he regretted the decision had not been made to destroy North Korean barracks. Kissinger was also consistent in relegating domestic political concerns to lower priority during this tree cutting crisis. When Kissinger first discussed the event in an interagency meeting, he was in favor of an aggressive response. The national intelligence officer at the time, Evelyn Colbert, asked, "How the media and the US people [would] react to that in this campaign year." Kissinger responded, "That has nothing to do with it. The important thing is that they beat two Americans to death and must pay the price." Interestingly, Colbert responded to that with a point similar to Schlesinger's position during the *Mayaguez* crisis. She said the North Koreans were hoping to see signs of a "Vietnam type mentality" in the United States so it was "important to have the right kinds of expressions of support from the media and opinion makers." Kissinger ignored the remark and asked about the possibility of "a B-52 exercise." On Scowcroft and Sneider, see Michishita, *North Korea's Military-Diplomatic Campaigns*, 85–90. For Kissinger's views, see the record of his telephone call to National Security Advisor Scowcroft: Telephone conversation, General Scowcroft/Secretary Kissinger, August 20, 1976, 8:04 p.m. (declassified July 24, 2015); and Document 282, Minutes of Washington Special Actions Group Meeting, Washington, August 18, 1976, 3:47–4:43 p.m., in *FRUS 1969–1976*, vol. E-12

142. Michishita, *North Korea's Military-Diplomatic Campaigns*, 85–90. Michishita cites information from a senior North Korean defector who described the axe murders as a mistake, but acknowledged North Korea thought about going to war if the South made a strong response. The defector thought China was ultimately the deciding factor, as "Kim Il Sung knew very well that such an attempt would wind up in failure unless North Korea could get both material and moral support from China."

143. Memo RE North Korea, Subject: Recent North Korean Military Developments, NSC File, 6/5/2007 30 January 1976; declassified.

Chapter 7

1. Graham T. Allison, *Essence of Decision: Explaining the Cuban Missile Crisis* (Boston: Little, Brown), 1971.

2. In the case of the Soviet Union, Allison points out the difficulty of understanding why Soviet leaders took the risk they did in 1962 and notes that to obtain an answer, "it is necessary to open the black box and look within the state actor to its disaggregated moving parts." Using competing models, Allison argues, can help "identify more fine-grained hypotheses, and ways to combine them in explanations and predictions." Ibid., 404.

3. Ibid., 99. Allison makes the same points in his coauthored second edition of the book. See Graham T. Allison and Philip Zelikow, *Essence of Decision: Explaining the Cuban Missile Crisis* (New York: Longman, 2010), 2–3, 4, 9, and 379.

4. Alexander L. George and Andrew Bennett, *Case Studies and Theory Development in the Social Sciences* (Cambridge, MA: MIT Press, 2007), 75. George and Bennett are borrowing from Harry Eckstein's long-standing distinctions in "Case Studies and Theory in Political Science," in *Handbook of Political Science*, vol. 7, ed. Fred Greenstein and Nelson Polsby (Reading, MA: Addison-Wesley, 1975), 118–20. George notes three prerequisites for disciplined-configurative case studies: the use of general variables for description and explanation, an adequate definition of the class of event being explained, and a selective investigation that focuses on one particular dependent variable.

5. Harry Eckstein, *Regarding Politics: Essays on Political Theory, Stability, and Change* (Berkeley: University of California Press, 1992), 136–37.

6. Ole Holsti, *Making American Foreign Policy* (New York: Routledge, 2006), 31.

7. Vandenbroucke's *Perilous Options* is a case in point. His penchant for characterizing the response as a rescue may have been influenced by the fact that the purpose of his multicase analysis was to examine strategic special operations and included other historic rescue attempts like the Son Tay and Iranian hostage operations. Neustadt and May also characterize the US response in the *Mayaguez* crisis as a "rescue mission," which may have been influenced by their focus on historical analogies. They argue the *Pueblo* analogy drove the US response during the crisis and incorrectly assert even Kissinger "seems to refer frequently to the *Pueblo* precedent." See Neustadt and May, *Thinking in Time*.

8. Lamb, *Belief Systems and Decision Making*, 38–39.

9. Lamb, "Belief Systems and Decision Making," 699.

10. Ibid.

11. Ibid.

12. "In retrospect, and using his own goals as a basis for analysis, it seems clear that Ford should have agreed to another delay since it would have reduced the risk of an embarrassing military failure without substantially reducing chances of accomplishing the decision makers' goals." It was further argued that "the import of this error, in terms of casualties, was reduced by having escaped from a near catastrophe with relatively low casualty figures (lower than originally estimated, in fact). The safe recovery of the crew also helped preserve the image of a successful military operation which US decision makers felt they needed." Lamb, *Belief Systems and Decision Making*, 265.

13. In the third meeting, Ford said, "I think we have to assume that the Americans were taken from the island and that some were killed," and the other NSC members agreed. In the fourth meeting

when Buchen worried mainland airstrikes might hit members of the crew, Schlesinger countered with the observation that he thought "they would have moved the Americans 20 miles inland as soon as possible." If considering crew members lost once they were on the mainland seems overly pessimistic since they were later released unharmed, it must be remembered there was reason to be concerned. US leaders knew what the Khmer Rouge was doing to its own people, and already suspected the scale of the atrocities. They also knew the Khmer Rouge had executed seven members of a Vietnamese fishing boat they captured. Vietnamese sources claimed that in May 1975 the Khmer Rouge kidnapped 513 Vietnamese civilians to do hard labor building fortifications and tunnels on Tang Island before killing them in a mass execution. Allegedly, the Khmer Rouge also executed the Marines left behind on Tang Island. Later it would become evident that being a Westerner or even a fervent supporter of Pol Pot's regime were no guarantees of better treatment. In August 1978, Pol Pot's regime killed a Canadian, Englishman, and New Zealander who were stranded on Tang Island by a storm; one was killed outright and the two others died after being tortured (one was burned alive) and forced to write confessions. A few months after that the regime killed British academic and avowed Marxist Malcolm Caldwell after a visit with Pol Pot. Caldwell was a consistent critic of American foreign policy and resolute defender of Pol Pot's regime. For US suspicions about the scale of Khmer Rouge atrocities, see "American Cryptology during the Cold War"; for the massacre of the Vietnamese, see Tuoi Tre, "Evidence of Koh Tang Massacre by Khmer Rouge," tuoitrenews: News Gateway of Vietnam, http://tuoitrenews.vn/features/16933/evidence-of-koh-tang-massacre-by-khmer-rouge; for the murder of the others, see Susan Pepperell, "Brotherly Love: Rob Hamill Wants Justice for Brother Killed by Khmer Rouge," *Sunday Star Times*, April 5, 2009; and Andrew Anthony, "Lost in Cambodia," *Guardian*, January 10, 2010.

14. Some research indicates that "contrary to the notion that normative (rational) decision-making is more likely in less dramatic settings . . . elevated threat encourages rational decision processing, whereas heuristic processing was more prevalent in less threatening situations." This finding is supported by behaviors during the *Mayaguez* crisis. See Allison Astorino-Courtois, "The Effects of Stakes and Threat on Foreign Policy Decision-Making," *Political Psychology* 21, no. 3 (2000): 489–510.

15. Kissinger was erroneously depicted by Pentagon sources as a Dr. Strangelove character, whereas Ford and Kissinger in their memoirs mischaracterize Schlesinger as preferring not to use any force at all. See sources and discussion in Lamb, *Belief Systems and Decision Making*, 209–10, and for Ford and Kissinger, see discussion on page 124.

16. Greene offers the typical take on Ford's demeanor: "Ford's behavior was calm and rational throughout the crisis and his demeanor spread to the team." *Presidency of Gerald R. Ford*, 145. Hartmann asserts the same, saying "the debates within the National Security Council in the Cabinet Room were never all that polarized." *Palace Politics*, 326.

17. The Cambodian broadcast said the Cambodian government had "no precise idea of the extent of the damage, or the number killed among our patrolmen and the American crew," which was not true and thus suggests the Cambodians might have been considering killing the crew and blaming it on US planes. The point was not lost on US decision makers according to Hartmann, who notes that in the broadcast "nothing about the *Mayaguez* crew was revealed except that some of them might have been killed by American bombs." *Palace Politics*, 328. See Lamb, *Belief Systems and Decision Making*, 191–92.

18. Using belief systems (also called cognitive maps, operational codes, evoked sets, and decisional premises) to explain decision making dates from the mid-1960s when Ole Holsti and other researchers began investigating the way senior leaders' perceptions of the world varied from reality and the consequent impact on their decisions and foreign policy behaviors. I follow Holsti's lead in using the term "belief system." Holsti explains the evolution of thinking and research on belief systems in the introduction to his 2006 book on foreign policy: Ole R. Holsti, *Making American Foreign Policy* (New York: Routledge, 2006), 4–7. The citations are from the same source, pp. 327–28.

19. See the discussion of the irony of Ford's opprobrium in light of Schlesinger's impact on the outcome of the crisis in Lamb, *Belief Systems and Decision Making*, 211–12.

20. Scowcroft was upset with the Pentagon during the *Mayaguez* crisis, but in general he was more collaborative than Kissinger. As he once remarked when asked to compare himself with Kissinger, "In general I was more solicitous of the need to try to co-opt people within the government in support of particular policies than Henry . . . who was more inclined to move and let the chips fall where they may, and rely on the president to back him up." Lamb, *Belief Systems and Decision Making*, 145n82.

21. See the commentary on page 54 and the sidebar in Chapter 7.

22. Kissinger, *Years of Renewal*, 178–79. The conflict was long-standing from Schlesinger's point of view as well. After Ford fired him, Schlesinger discovered Kissinger had interfered with his receiving formal invitations to visit China while he was the secretary of defense. He wrote a memo for the record documenting the fact, which is included in the papers he donated to the Library of Congress. James R. Schlesinger, memorandum for the record, Subject: Visit of AMB Han Hsu, Chinese Liaison Office, March 15, 1976, Schlesinger Papers, box 57, folder 8, Library of Congress.

23. Most histories of the Ford presidency document Ford's first act as asking Kissinger to stay on, promising he would work hard to get along with Kissinger, which prompted Kissinger to respond that it was his duty to get along with Ford, which he did.

24. Numerous sources make this point. Kennerly, for example, recalls Ford standing on his front lawn in Alexandria, Virginia, just before Nixon's departure from the presidency, reassuring the world and the foreign leaders at some length that everything would be fine because Henry Kissinger would still be working in the White House. David Kennerly, interview by Richard Norton Smith, December 14, 2009, Gerald R. Ford Oral History Project.

25. Coincidentally, on the first meeting of the first day of the *Mayaguez* crisis, May 12, Ford asked Kissinger to be part of his informal White House team conducting election strategy, and Kissinger promised support, noting Reagan and any Democratic candidate would be disastrous. Memorandum of Conversation: Monday, May 12, 1975. 9:15 a.m.

26. Mahoney notes the tension between Ford and Schlesinger was long-standing. Mahoney, *Mayaguez Incident*, 12–13.

27. A William Safire column in the *New York Times* headlined "Et Tu, Gerry?," cited in DeFrank and Ford, *Write It When I'm Gone*.

28. Cannon notes Ford's comment that "there are few people I can't get along with. Schlesinger was one of them." DeFrank quotes Ford as saying Schlesinger "was the one that I was not comfortable with." Ford considered Schlesinger "a talented guy, but we just didn't fit." Kissinger said the same, noting Schlesinger addressed the presidents he served with a "professorial tone, verging on condescension." According to Sisco, Kissinger thought that Ford "was a decent man, but he didn't give him very high grades intellectually. That was very clear." Cannon, *Honorable Life*, 380; Sisco is cited in Greene, *Presidency of Gerald R. Ford*, 119; DeFrank and Ford, *Write It When I'm Gone*, 179; Kissinger, *Years of Renewal*, 179–82.

29. Kissinger, *Years of Renewal*, 181–82.

30. Ibid., 181; and Barry Werth, *31 Days: The Crisis That Gave Us the Government We Have Today* (New York: Nan A. Talese/Doubleday, 2006), 182–85.

31. Mark Perry, *Four Stars: The Inside Story of the Forty-Year Battle between the Joint Chiefs of Staff and America's Civilian Leaders* (Boston: Houghton Mifflin, 1989), 258. Instead, with Clement's help, the story spread that Schlesinger had fabricated the entire thing. See Robert Shrum, "The Most Hated Man in Washington," *New York Times*, May 28, 1979.

32. The president's directive to Schlesinger said, "Communications on issues involving national security or defense policy will be channeled to Schlesinger through my Assistant for National Security

Affairs." Less important matters would be "channeled to Schlesinger through my Military Assistant, who will maintain liaison with your Special Assistant." Major General Richard L. Lawson, USAF, was military assistant to the president at the time, and Wickham was Schlesinger's military assistant. President Gerald Ford, Memorandum for the Secretary of Defense, Subject: Liaison Procedures, October 31, 1974, Schlesinger Papers, box 49, folder 4, Library of Congress.

33. In his memoirs, Ford describes how Deputy Secretary of Defense Clements was used to track down the truth about the incident. Clements discovered the armed forces were never put on "alert," but that Schlesinger discussed the issue with the press. Ford said he thought what Schlesinger did "was to stab our armed forces in the back. And that, in my opinion, was inexcusable." For an example of how Kissinger interacted with Clements, see their phone conversations recorded in Kissinger's account of the evacuation crisis and their conversation on February 10, 1976. Ford, *A Time to Heal*, 322–23; Kissinger, *Years of Renewal*, 529–46; Kissinger, *Crisis*, 488–89; Werth, *31 Days*, 182–85; and Secretary Kissinger to Bill Clements, TELCON, 3:20 p.m. 2/10/76, declassified by US Department of State Case No. F-2001-02979 Doc No. C18091241 Date: 07/24/2015.

34. Werth, *31 Days*, 185.

35. Schlesinger's directive said, "On issues directly involving national security or defense policy, the only channels of communications with the White House will be through me, the Deputy Secretary of Defense, or my Military Assistant." Secretary of Defense James Schlesinger, Memorandum, Subject: Liaison between the Department of Defense and the White House, November 29, 1974, Schlesinger Papers, box 49, folder 4, Library of Congress.

36. Ford responded, "I was so ——damned mad when I read the Star article last night about the 'unnamed Defense sources.' I want Schlesinger to put it [i.e., his objections] down in writing." Memorandum of Conversation, July 8, 1975, 10:15–10:55 a.m., Oval Office (declassified August 4, 2006), Ford Library.

37. Kissinger provides an overview of State-DoD differences over how best to manage the evacuation and implies Ford sided with him and told Schlesinger he would personally accept the greater risk to Americans, implying the president lacked confidence in DoD compliance with his orders. Kissinger, *Years of Renewal*, 529–37. See also Kissinger's account of the evacuation crisis in Kissinger, *Crisis*.

38. For example, Schlesinger and his legislative affairs assistant took to writing memorandums for the record to document State Department (particularly Ambassador Graham A. Martin in South Vietnam) and White House (particularly Brent Scowcroft, who was overseeing the evacuation) lethargy in evacuating Americans who were increasingly at risk. They also documented what they considered to be White House misrepresentations to Congress, including false numbers of Americans still in South Vietnam. Memorandum of Conversation, Subject: Telephone Conversation during call from the President, 11:45 AM, April 1, 1975, Schlesinger Papers, box 57, folder 8, Library of Congress; and Memorandum for the Record from John Maury, Assistant Secretary of Defense, Legislative Affairs, Subject: Conversation with Jack Marsh re Vietnam Evacuation, May 1, 1975, Schlesinger Papers, box 60, folder 10, Library of Congress.

39. According to Kissinger, the Pentagon wanted to evacuate as fast as possible and Ambassador Graham Martin in Saigon wanted to space the American withdrawal over the longest period of time possible in order to leave enough of an American presence to justify rescuing the Vietnamese. Martin "flooded us with cables, the gist of which was that I would be the one held responsible if any potential refugees were needlessly left behind." Kissinger, who noted his position on evacuation was "much closer to Martin's than to the Pentagon's," nonetheless admits the Pentagon was willing to evacuate Vietnamese "so long as this did not slow down getting all Americans out at the fastest pace possible." Kissinger, *Years of Renewal*, 529, 537.

40. Ibid.

41. DeFrank and Ford, *Write It When I'm Gone*, 92.

42. The quick fall was anticipated by many. Colonel Clifton Granger wrote to Scowcroft on April 5 saying he did not think South Vietnam would survive to the end of the month. David Kennerly, Ford's photographer, told him the same thing on April 4, saying "Mr. President, Vietnam has no more than a month left, and anyone who tells you different is bullshitting." For the Kennerly quote, see Greene, *Presidency of Gerald R. Ford*: 137; for Granger, see Memorandum From Clinton Granger of the National Security Council Staff to the President's Deputy Assistant for National Security Affairs (Scowcroft), Washington, April 5, 1975, http://www.mekong.net/cambodia/download/foreign_relations_vietnam_73-75.pdf

43. Memorandum of Conversation, 1 April 1975, box 57, folder 8 SUBJECT: Telephone Conversation during call from the President 11:45 AM, 1 April 1975.

44. Hyland, *Mortal Rivals*, 112.

45. As Mahoney notes, it was Rockefeller who called out Schlesinger and the Pentagon in the second NSC meeting for faulty information, stoking distrust between the White House and Pentagon. Mahoney, *Mayaguez Incident*, 46–47.

46. NSC meeting minutes.

47. Memorandum of Conversation, President Ford, Henry Kissinger and Brent Scowcroft, Wednesday, May 14, 1975, 11:45 a.m., Oval Office, declassified, Ford Library.

48. Fred S. Hoffman, "Military Options: Two Takes," *Albuquerque Journal*, Thursday, May 15, 1975, 2.

49. Telephone conversation, Secretary Kissinger to Secretary Schlesinger, 12:58 – 5/15/75; declassified by Department of State, Review Authority: Robert H. Miller, Date/Case ID: 10 Feb 2003 200102979. Later Schlesinger took a pass on portraying Kissinger as the zealot for force (see note 79 on pages 238–39). When Kissinger wrote his memoirs he also refrained from blaming Schlesinger, and instead attributed the press leaks to Schlesinger's spokesman, Joseph Laitin, who he says "missed no opportunity to transform honest disagreements into aspects of a feud between the Secretaries of State and Defense. Newspaper columns kept describing our deliberations in terms of 'Dr. Strangelove' restrained by the humanistic Secretary of Defense. I was alleged to have advocated indiscriminate B-52 bombings in contrast to Schlesinger, who stood for a more precise 'tit-for-tat' retaliation." Kissinger, *Years of Renewal*, 561.

50. NSC meeting minutes.

51. Kissinger, *Years of Renewal*, 571.

52. A Rumsfeld observation suggests it might have been the former. He says Schlesinger called him on May 16 to complain "that the State Department was circulating stories that they had been leaning forward while the Defense Department had opposed the use of force." That Schlesinger thought it wise to emphasize State's exaggeration of the Pentagon's opposition to force suggests he thought Ford might appreciate the truth—that he was in favor of discriminate, limited, punitive force. Rumsfeld, *When the Center Held*, 177.

53. Ibid.

54. The resultant investigation and products provide a bonanza of rich detail about the crisis for researchers. Pentagon staff put together a comprehensive chronology of the verbal and written orders issued in the fast-evolving crisis. Sitton to SECDEF memo.

55. Memorandum of Conversation, President Ford, Henry Kissinger and Brent Scowcroft, Friday, May 16, 1975, 9:25 a.m., Oval Office, declassified, Ford Library (hereafter Memorandum of Conversation, May 16, 1975).

56. In his memoirs, Kissinger said "the friction was not between Schlesinger and me. It was President Ford, the commander-in-chief, who felt that he had not been kept adequately informed. He learned of some key decisions only at the final wrap-up NSC meetings and then only by accident." Kissinger goes on, saying, "Only extreme frustration accounts for the usually so equable Ford lashing out at the military establishment, an institution he truly revered and in which he was so proud to have served as a naval officer." Kissinger, *Years of Renewal*, 571.

57. Memorandum of Conversation, May 16, 1975.

58. Memorandum for the Secretary of Defense, from the President, Subject: the Rescue of the SS *Mayaguez* and its Crew, May 18, 1975; box 29, folder "Department of Defense – Joint Chiefs of Staff-Report to the President, May 20, 1975 (1)" of the National Security Adviser, NSC East Asian and Pacific Affairs Staff: Files, Ford Library.

59. Schlesinger's Office of the Secretary of Defense staff complained that reporting through Kissinger generated allegations of DoD foot-dragging and being uncooperative or bureaucratic, and they advised Schlesinger to revisit the issue with the president. His staff cited examples such as McFarlane issuing orders to the NMCC during the *Mayaguez* crisis and incidents from the evacuation of South Vietnam where Scowcroft issued orders directly to the Pentagon.

60. From Tom Wicker, "Raising Some *Mayaguez* Questions," *New York Times*, May 16, 1975; cited in Lamb, *Belief Systems and Decision Making*, 152.

61. Apparently McFarlane pursued the issue. In his coauthored book *Crisis Resolution*, there is a footnote that describes the armed reconnaissance mission as the result of an inadvertent misunderstanding between the White House and Pentagon. The note also indicates the armed reconnaissance mission included the instruction to "not to expend ordnance unless attacked." The inadvertent misunderstanding appears correct insofar as the Pentagon explained the first wave would be armed reconnaissance and the White House failed to understand this point. However, the assertion that aircraft were not to expend ordnance (never documented) raises questions about the purpose of the mission. Reconnaissance aircraft (RF-4s) already had photographed mainland targets. See Head, Short, and McFarlane, *Crisis Resolution*, 303n30; and Lamb, *Belief Systems and Decision Making*, 105ff and 112.

62. R. C. McFarlane, Memorandum for General Scowcroft; Subject: Defense Report on *Mayaguez* Operations, May 20, 1975 (declassified August 9, 2002).

63. This author asserted it was the primary reason Schesinger was fired, based on insights from a major source in the crisis. See Lamb, *Belief Systems and Decision Making*, 211.

64. Kissinger, *Years of Renewal*, 573.

65. DeFrank and Ford. *Write It When I'm Gone*, 92.

66. After the crisis both Scowcroft and Rumsfeld called to warn Schlesinger that the president was angry, but as several months passed he may have felt he was on safer ground. Wickham warned him otherwise just before his dismissal. He heard from someone that Schlesinger would be called in and offered a different job the next day, so he called Schlesinger and alerted him to the rumor. Schlesinger told Wickham that was interesting because he had just been told by the White House that the president wanted to see him the next day. Wickham interview; see also discussion on page 166.

67. This finding is important. One criticism of foreign policy analysis is that "foreign policy implementation . . . remains barely examined." Although the general assumption that the "impact of the executive is . . . experienced most strongly in a crisis situation" probably holds true, the *Mayaguez* crisis supports the contention that it is nonetheless a challenge for chief executives to implement their decisions as they see fit. Chris Alden and Amnon Aran, *Foreign Policy Analysis: New Approaches* (New York: Routledge, 2012), 111.

68. Lamb, "Belief Systems and Decision Making," 698–99; and Lamb, *Belief Systems and Decision Making*, 211–26.

69. It might be argued that the Pentagon has an institutional preference for proportional and discriminate force rather than asymmetric and indiscriminate force, and thus Schlesinger was "captured" by his institution. But the key point is that these predilections were not inconsistent with Schlesinger's beliefs, and he made sure those beliefs guided Pentagon orders.

70. Here the author must diverge from Baral's conclusion that "Kissinger and Schlesinger reflected by and large the views of their respective agencies." That is particularly not true in the case of Kissinger. J. K. Baral, "The *Mayaguez* Incident: a Study of Crisis Management," *International Studies* 19 no. 1 (1980): 34.

71. Lamb, "Belief Systems and Decision Making," 699.

72. Cited in Lamb, *Belief Systems and Decision Making*, 43.

73. See for example, J. Philipp Rosenberg, "The Belief System of Harry S. Truman and Its Effect on Foreign Policy Decision-Making during His Administration," *Presidential Studies Quarterly* 12, no. 2 (Spring 1982).

74. Derek Beach, *Analyzing Foreign Policy* (Basingstoke, Hampshire [U.K.]: Palgrave Macmillan, 2012), 115.

75. Lamb, *Belief Systems and Decision Making*, 47–50; 52–61.

76. The schism was apparent among congressional leaders as well. During their meeting with Ford some members of Congress worried about the undue haste to use military force while others fully supported it. For example, when Senator McClellan asked, "Can't we wait," Senator Eastland jumped in and answered for the administration, saying, "No, we can't." For the general argument on the schism, see Ole R. Holsti and James N. Rosenau, "Vietnam, Consensus, and the Belief Systems of American Leaders," *World Politics* 32 (October 1979).

77. Lamb, *Belief Systems and Decision Making*, 247–55. David Houghton makes the same point:

Different occupants of the White House have viewed such situations differently and have been motivated by noticeably different policy considerations in dealing with them. To take one particularly striking example, President Gerald Ford reacted in a manner radically different to Carter when faced with the seizure of American hostages during the 1975 *Mayaguez* episode. While one president viewed the situation primarily as a threat to US credibility and "face" in the world, the other saw it primarily as a threat to human life; while one resorted almost immediately to the use of military force, the other tried negotiation for several months before selecting a military option that was probably the least forcible of the available alternatives. Ford's actions and reasoning were also markedly different from Lyndon Johnson's during the *Pueblo* crisis.

David P. Houghton, *US Foreign Policy and the Iran Hostage Crisis* (Cambridge: Cambridge University Press, 2001), 167.

78. Document 280, Memorandum from the President's Assistant for National Security Affairs (Kissinger) to President Ford, May 12, 1975, in *FRUS 1969–1976*, vol. 10, 956, cited in Fibiger, "Redeeming," 8.

79. Memorandum of Conversation, President Ford, Mohamed Reza Pahlavi, Shah of Iran, Dr. Henry A. Kissinger, Secretary of State, and Assistant to the President for National Security Affairs Lt. General Brent Scowcroft, Deputy Assistant to the President for National Security Affairs, Oval Office, Thursday, May 15, 1975, 11:00 a.m. National Security Adviser's Memoranda of Conversation Collection, Gerald R. Ford Digital Library, http://www.fordlibrarymuseum.gov/library/document/memcons/1553077.pdf.

80. For example, on May 12, the first day of the crisis, Kissinger was asked in a news conference whether US "prestige has suffered" as a result of the loss of Indochina and the Cambodian seizure

of the *Mayaguez*. He responded in the affirmative, saying that "our credibility has declined" and that "one of the most important challenges to our foreign policy is to restore it." Cited in Lieutenant Colonel Donald E. Carlile, "The *Mayaguez* Incident: Crisis Management," *Military Review* (October 1976), 6.

81. Ford believed the United States did not prevail in Vietnam because it did not use its full military powers, including strategic bombing. Cannon, *Honorable Life*, 374. See also Fibiger, "Redeeming," 5.

82. See the extended discussion of key leader belief systems in chapter 5, "Pre-Crisis Beliefs," in Lamb, *Belief Systems and Decision Making*: 62–78.

83. Lamb, *Belief Systems and Decision Making*, 62–78.

84. Baral, "*Mayaguez* Incident," 21.

85. Scowcroft interview, cited in Lamb, *Belief Systems and Decision Making*, 76–77.

86. Lamb, *Belief Systems and Decision Making*, 74–75.

87. Baral, "*Mayaguez* Incident," 21. Also cited in Vandenbroucke, *Perilous Options*, 74.

88. Lamb, *Belief Systems and Decision Making*, 49.

89. Cited in ibid., 72.

90. Cited in ibid., 72–73.

91. Ibid., 150.

92. Ibid., 176.

93. For a longer discussion of Scowcroft's focus on the *Pueblo* analogy see ibid., 176–77, as well as Pfaltzgraff and Davis, *National Security Decisions*, 274–75.

94. In his memoirs Kissinger says Schlesinger underestimated Ford's pique at his behaviors and overestimated Kissinger's interference in the relationship. In retrospect, it is not hard to see why on either account. In virtually all the meetings and phone calls during the *Mayaguez* crisis, Ford treated Schlesinger respectfully, and in the end, he congratulations him on a fine job. By all accounts, this was Ford's general demeanor with all his subordinates: calm, polite, and respectful. Apparently, this lulled Schlesinger into the false belief that he was on acceptable terms with Ford, and not even warnings from Scowcroft and Rumsfeld that the president was angry seemed to register with him. It is equally evident why Schlesinger thought Kissinger was using his inside position with President Ford to complicate Schlesinger's relations with the president—because he was.

95. Lamb, *Belief Systems and Decision Making*, 176.

96. Ibid., 180–83.

97. Immediately following the crisis Ford told a journalist that initially he was "hoping that the best would take place, and not the worst . . . that the Cambodian government would, after they got the ship, release it." But by the time he wrote his memoirs there is no mention of this, and he says he was from the beginning determined to protect US interests and so called an NSC meeting. Rowan, *Four Days*, 66–67. See also the discussion in Lamb, *Belief Systems and Decision Making*, 79–80.

98. At times Ford seemed deferential to Kissinger. For example, in one NSC meeting after Kissinger expresses his strong objection to a recommendation just made by Philip Buchen, Ford almost apologies, saying, "Phil and I have argued for years." NSC meeting minutes.

99. Hartmann observed: "The demonstration that we witnessed every day, of Kissinger disappearing into the oval office, [with] everybody else waiting patiently while their appointment times came and went—stacking everybody else in the government four or five deep—till he finished his long monologue instructing his new pupil in the Byzantine intricacies of the world, was not a happy example." Ford's advisers worried about the president's personal credibility in light of his reliance on Kissinger and resented Kissinger's habit of "putting the President of the United States in a pupil's role."

Rumsfeld and other presidential advisors were recommending to Ford that he seek a wider range of advice on foreign policy matters than just Kissinger. Ford's reliance on Kissinger was also substantiated later by inside sources. Sisco, for example, notes, "Ford was not inclined toward perceiving a lot of the complexities of foreign policy issues," so he "relied heavily on Henry" "when dealing with global affairs." Hartmann quoted in Michael Turner, *The Vice President as Policy Maker: Rockefeller in the Ford White House* (Westport, CT: Greenwood Press, 1982), 160; Sisco interview; see also Hartmann, *Palace Politics*, 329; and Nessen, *It Sure Looks Different*, 132.

100. Lamb, *Belief Systems and Decision Making*, 144–45.

101. Informal Briefing by Ron Nessen, 11:33 a.m., May 16, 1975; box 14, folder "*Mayaguez* - Press Releases and Press Briefings," Ron Nessen Papers, Ford Library.

102. This includes Scowcroft, who did not typically speak to the press. In a June 18, 1975 memorandum from Scowcroft to George Springsteen, executive secretary for the Department of State, Scowcroft told Springsteen to answer an inquiry from a senator by saying, "I am sure you are aware that the Administration's principal concern was to react swiftly and responsibly in order to save the lives of the crew and to recover the vessel." Then, as all the decision makers did, he elaborated on the basic explanation, saying, "The Administration acted to prevent that crew from being interned and their lives jeopardized, as the crew of the USS *Pueblo* was, and to make clear to the Cambodian Government and to all other governments that the safety of its sailors and the freedom of the seas for its vessels were matters of great concern to the American Government and people." Lamb, *Belief Systems and Decision Making*, 1; 17n7.

103. Secretary Kissinger's Press Conference, May 16. Kissinger added, "That is to say, we never received a communication, proposition that would have enabled us to explore a diplomatic solution." The Department of State response to the GAO report that suggested some diplomatic possibilities were overlooked was quite hostile. Lawrence Eagleburger responded on behalf of State on March 15, 1976, saying the GAO report was "by the most generous interpretation I can muster, an exercise in ex post facto diplomacy by amateurs." GAO report, 108.

104. Kissinger, *Years of Renewal*, 553; 561. In point of fact, Kissinger's closing comments in the first NSC meeting included the observation that "we can bomb from Guam with B-52s or from the carriers," and both options were debated until the end of the fourth NSC meeting.

105. Kissinger, *Years of Renewal*, 569. Kissinger was not averse to making it up on the fly, as John Prados has documented: "Shooting from the hip, Kissinger replied that a routine notification had gone to the insurance companies that insured ships like the *Mayaguez*. In the court case that flowed from the incident, however, the State Department was forced into an official admission that no records could be found anywhere which supported this contention." Joseph Sisco has also noted blatant inaccuracies in Kissinger's memoirs. Prados, *Keeper of the Keys*, 371; Sisco interview, 10.

106. See the discussion of "communication strategies" in Lamb, *Belief Systems and Decision Making*, 52–55, 66n12, and 144–52.

107. Baral, "*Mayaguez* Incident," 21.

108. See the discussion in Lamb, "Belief Systems and Decision Making" 694–95; and *Belief Systems and Decision Making*, 144–52.

109. It is also possible the issue was not explored in greater depth because Colby was not treated as an insider with important information. The CIA history notes, "On most issues Colby had to deal with Kissinger's deputy, Brent Scowcroft, and NSC staffers and was shut out from any meaningful, continuing access to the major policy players." Harold P. Ford, CIA History Staff, "William E. Colby as Director of Central Intelligence, 1973–76" (declassified and approved for release, August 10, 2011), 40.

110. Burns interview.

111. This point about violating Marine Corps doctrine was made by the GAO report and this author earlier, but Mahoney, drawing on Patrick, makes the case better and in much greater depth, demonstrating numerous conflicts with existing doctrine. Mahoney, *Mayaguez Incident*, 242–43; Patrick, "*Mayaguez* Operation"; GAO report, 95; Lamb, *Belief Systems and Decision Making*, 32.

Chapter 8

1. Stephen Randolph, "Uncovering the Lessons of Vietnam," *Foreign Service Journal*, July–August 2015, 52–60.

2. Sparrow, *Strategist*, 171.

3. Nessen, *It Sure Looks Different*, 130.

4. Wickham notebooks.

5. Cannon, *Honorable Life*, 384; Dick Cheney with Liz Cheney, *In My Time: A Personal and Political Memoir* (New York: Threshold Editions, 2011), 91.

6. Secretary of Defense James Schlesinger, Letter to the President, 3 November 1975, Schlesinger Papers, box 49, folder 4, Library of Congress.

7. Wickham interview.

8. Ford said his performance amounted to "high level bumbling." Ford, *A Time to Heal*, 284.

9. Kissinger, *Years of Renewal*, 558–59.

10. Steven L. Rearden, *Council of War: A History of the Joint Chiefs of Staff, 1942–1991* (Washington, DC: NDU Press, 2012), 384.

11. From Kissinger's memoirs, one wonders whether Kissinger came to rue his part in diminishing Ford's opinion of Schlesinger. It is interesting to note that during the first meeting of Ford, Kissinger, Rumsfeld, and Scowcroft, the president quickly revised the special reporting instructions that had disadvantaged Schlesinger, offering Rumsfeld more direct access to the president. Kissinger, *Years of Renewal*, 177–78, 559; and Memorandum of Conversation, Oval Office, Thursday, November 13, 1975, 9:40 a.m. (declassified June 4, 2004); and Memorandum of Conversation, Oval Office, Wednesday, November 26, 1975, 9:20 a.m. (declassified automatically, date not recorded).

12. Robert K. Yin, *Case Study Research: Design and Methods*, 4th ed. (Los Angeles: Sage, 2009), 141.

13. Objections that the case did not constitute a crisis because of the relative disparity between the protagonists and that it cannot contribute to generalized knowledge are addressed at length elsewhere. Lamb, *Belief Systems and Decision Making*, 1–4; and Yin, Case Study Research, 14–16.

14. Lamb, *Belief Systems and Decision Making*, 245–46.

15. For example, Richard Pious notes the argument that "the president did not act with regard to his personal political fortunes," but claims "the evidence points in the other direction." However, he offers no evidence to substantiate his assertion. Instead, he switches the topic to Kissinger's belief that the United States needed an opportunity to demonstrate its resolve, and then he lampoons the idea that the *Mayaguez* accomplished any such thing. Ford's motives and the outcomes his decisions generated are two different things. Pious is hardly the first to criticize Ford's decisions, but it is difficult to offer useful criticisms without understanding what actually happened and why. Absent evidence, a criticism is just a prejudice, perhaps useful for punditry but not for political science. Richard M. Pious, *Why Presidents Fail* (Lanham, MD: Rowman and Littlefield, 2008), 86.

16. Robert Jervis, *System Effects: Complexity in Political and Social Life* (Princeton: Princeton University Press, 1999), 266–69; cited in David P. Houghton, *US Foreign Policy and the Iran Hostage Crisis* (Cambridge: Cambridge University Press, 2001), 171.

17. Brian Ripley, "Cognition, Culture and Bureaucratic Politics," in Laura Neack, Jeanne A. K. Hey, and Patrick J. Haney, *Foreign Policy Analysis: Continuity and Change in Its Second Generation* (Englewood Cliffs, NJ: Prentice Hall, 1995), 88; and Chris Alden and Amnon Aran. *Foreign Policy Analysis: New Approaches* (New York: Routledge, 2012), 44, 119.

18. Neack, Hey, and Haney. *Foreign Policy Analysis*, 23.

19. This observation is ascribed to Dick Cheney in Thompson, *Ford Presidency*, 72. Cheney ascribes greater significance to the *Mayaguez* in his memoirs: Cheney, *In My Time*, 83.

20. Pious, *Why Presidents Fail*, 87.

21. Ibid. Not all sources quickly dismiss the efficacy of force. Wetterhahn, for example, judiciously and accurately assesses both Cambodian behaviors, which were centrally directed and hostile to US interests, and the impact of the US military operations. Wetterhahn, *Last Battle*, 258–59.

22. Telegram from the Department of State to the Embassy in Thailand; Washington, May 13, 1975, 1754Z; FRUS. Source: Ford Library, National Security Adviser, NSC East Asian and Pacific Affairs Staff Files, box 29, Department of State, Telegrams and Cables. Secret; Nodis; Flash. Drafted by Sisco; approved by Sisco, Johnson, and Eagleburger.

23. Document 119, Memorandum of Conversation, New York City, September 28, 1975, 8:10–11:55 p.m., in *Foreign Relations of the United States, 1969–1976*, vol. 18, *China, 1973–1976* (hereafter *FRUS 1969–1976*, vol. 18).

24. Ford, *A Time to Heal*, 281.

25. "National Intelligence Bulletin" news story concerning world reaction to US action to recover the *MAYAGUEZ* from the Cambodian Khmer Rouge. United States: Central Intelligence Agency, 16 May 1975. US Declassified Documents Online, October 5, 2016, http://tinyurl.galegroup.com /tinyurl/3nUcTX.

26. Document 183, Memorandum of Conversation, Washington, June 11, 1975, 10 a.m.–noon, in *Foreign Relations of the United States, 1969–1976*, vol. 26, *Arab-Israeli Dispute, 1974–1976*.

27. Scholars have argued that after the fall of South Vietnam it was apparent to many South Koreans that the threat of invasion from the North, even if it has in the past been used indiscriminately by Park as an excuse to consolidate his dictatorship, was nonetheless real. Donald S. Zagoria and Young Kun Kim, "North Korea and the Major Powers," *Asian Survey* 15, no. 12 (December 1975), 1017–35.

28. "South Korean Report on Kim Il Sung's Attempt to Visit the USSR in 1975," April 1975, History and Public Policy Program Digital Archive, South Korean Ministry of Foreign Affairs Archives, http:// digitalarchive.wilsoncenter.org/document/114588.

29. Cable from US Mission Geneva to SECSTATE, 15 May 1975 1835Z; Subject: NPT Revcon: *Mayaguez*: Korean Ambassador's Reaction; Margaret P. Grafeld Declassified/Released US Department of State EO Systematic Review, July 5, 2006.

30. Memorandum of Conversation, Subject: Japan's Security: Korea and Taiwan, May 23, 1975, declassified December 31, 1981. The participants were the US ambassador, deputy chief of mission, and two first secretaries and five senior Japanese political leaders. The US ambassador told his Japanese interlocutors he had duly reported Japanese concern over Korea and then tried to reassure them war was not imminent and that US resolve was firm.

31. Cable from American Embassy Tokyo, subject: Japanese reaction to *Mayaguez*, May 15, 1975, 0917Z, Declassified/Released US Department of State EO Systematic Review, July 5, 2006.

32. Cable from American Embassy Tokyo, subject: Japan's national interest in foreign policy in northeast Asia, June 4, 1975, 0857Z.

33. Takashi Oka, Tokyo, "Keeping A Wary Eye on Korean Affairs," *Daily Messenger*, Canandaigua, New York, July 3, 1975.

34. Cited in Fibiger, "Redeeming": Telegram from Secretary of State Kissinger to Delegate Secretaries, May 19, 1975, box 3, folder: Cambodia – Seizing of the *Mayaguez*, May 1975 (4), National Security Adviser Presidential Country Files for East Asia and the Pacific: Cambodia, Ford Library.

35. "Information on the Talks between Kim Il Sung and Todor Zhivkov," June 18, 1975, History and Public Policy Program Digital Archive, Political Archive of the Federal Foreign Office, Berlin (PolA AA), MfAA, C 294/78. Obtained and Translated by for NKIDP by Bernd Schaefer, http://digitalarchive .wilsoncenter.org/document/114282

36. Cable from SECSTATE WASHDC, subject: PRC comment on *Mayaguez* operation, 22 May 1975, 0032Z, Declassified/Released US Department of State EO Systematic Review, July 5, 2006.

37. Cable from SECSTATE WASHDC, subject: PRC comment on *Mayaguez* operation, 22 May 1975, 0155Z, Declassified/Released US Department of State EO Systematic Review, July 5, 2006. This cable followed the earlier one at 0032Z in order to provide the full text of the article by "NCNA Correspondent."

38. Cable from USLO Peking, subject: Call by AMB Bush on Princess Ashraf, 22 May 1975, 0300Z, Declassified/Released US Department of State EO Systematic Review, July 5, 2006.

39. Cable from SECSTATE WASHDC, subject: PRC comment on *Mayaguez* operation, 22 May 1975, 0032Z, Declassified/Released US Department of State EO Systematic Review, July 5, 2006.

40. Document 136, Memorandum of Conversation, Beijing, December 3, 1975, 9:25–11:55 a.m., in *FRUS 1969–1976*, vol. 18.

41. Ibid.

42. Cable from AMEMBASSY Moscow, subject: Soviet reaction to *Mayaguez*, 24 May 1975, 1103Z, Declassified/Released US Department of State EO Systematic Review, July 5, 2006.

43. Head, Short, and McFarlane, *Crisis Resolution*, 227. For more on this incident, see chapter 6, note 129.

44. "JCS Assessment," Box 10, folder "Korea - North Korean Tree Incident, 8/18/76 (1)" of the Presidential Country Files for East Asia and the Pacific, 1974–77 at the Ford Library.

45. TELCON, General Scowcroft/Secretary Kissinger, August 20, 1976, 8:04 p.m. UNCLASSIFIED US Department of State Case No. F-200V02979 Doc No. C 18093011 Date: 07/24/2015.

46. Brzezinski argued that Carter's foreign policy was too contractual (based on negotiated agreements) and that "in some cases, what is needed is a demonstration of force, to establish credibility and determination and even to infuse fear." Carter underlined "demonstration of force" and "to infuse fear" and then wrote in the margin "Like *Mayaguez*?" Document 76, Memorandum from the President's Assistant for National Security Affairs (Brzezinski) to President Carter; Washington, April 21, 1978, in *Foreign Relations of The United States, 1977–1980*, vol. 1, *Foundations of Foreign Policy*.

47. David Patrick Houghton, "The Role of Analogical Reasoning in Novel Foreign-Policy Situations," *British Journal of Political Science* 26, no. 4 (1996), 523–52; and Houghton, *US Foreign Policy*.

48. Anthony C. King, "Mission Command 2.0: From an Individualist to a Collectivist Model," *Parameters* 47, no. 1 (2017), 7.

49. Joint Chiefs of Staff, Joint Operations, Joint Publication 3-0 (Washington, DC: Joint Chiefs of Staff, 11 August 2011), cited in Mission Command White Paper, April 3, 2012, 1.

50. Mission Command White Paper, 7.

51. Joint Chiefs of Staff, *Joint Operations*, Joint Publication 3-0 (Washington, DC: Joint Chiefs of Staff, 17 January 2017), xi.

52. Andrew Hill and Heath Niemi, "The Trouble with Mission Command: Flexive Command and the Future of Command and Control, *Joint Force Quarterly* 86 (3rd Quarter/July 2017), 94.

53. A major spokesman for this point of view is retired General Stanley McChrystal. See General Stanley McChrystal with Tantum Collins, David Silverman, and Chris Fussell, *Team of Teams: New Rules of Engagement for a Complex World* (London: Portfolio/Penguin, 2015), 217–18; 221–23; and 232.

54. Dunham and Quinlan, *US Marines in Vietnam*, 265.

55. Of the major authors on the *Mayaguez* incident, Chun, Guilmartin, Mahoney, Vandenbroucke, and Wetterhahn all charge the Ford administration with micromanagement. Baron and Wise are an exception. They speak vaguely of "the perils of directing a war halfway around the world" but otherwise reserve comment. Baron and Wise, *14-Hour War*, x.

56. Mahoney, *Mayaguez Incident*, xiv–xv.

57. Chun, *Last Boarding Party*, 71. Similarly, another source emphasizes that "Washington frequently intervened directly in the ongoing operation" and, as an example, cites the calls to the USS *Holt* directly from the NMCC and even Chief of Naval Operations Admiral Holloway. Muir, *End of the Saga*, 54–55.

58. Guilmartin, *Very Short War*, 156.

59. Walter S. Poole, *The Decline of Détente: Elliot Richardson, James Schlesinger, and Donald Rumsfeld, 1973–1977* (Washington, DC: Historical Office, Office of the Secretary of Defense, 2015), 14.

60. "There was unfortunate micromanagement and interference from the upper echelons in Washington, District of Columbia. At one point in the heat of battle, Marines had to respond to an information request from Washington: did they have a Khmer interpreter with them?" Marius S. Vassiliou and David S. Alberts, *C2 Failures: A Taxonomy and Analysis* (Alexandria, VA: Institute for Defense Analyses, 2013). Vassiliou and Alberts cite Major Mark J. Toal, "The *Mayaguez* Incident: Near Disaster at Koh Tang" (thesis, Marine Corps War College, 1998).

61. Mahoney, *Mayaguez Incident*, 213–14.

62. Dan Caldwell, *The Cuban Missile Affair and the American Style of Crisis Management*, Rand Note (Santa Monica, CA: Rand Corporation, 1989), 5.

63. Edward N. Luttwak, *The Pentagon and the Art of War: The Question of Military Reform* (New York: Simon and Schuster, 1986), 86. Others have uncritically accepted Luttwak's assertion. See Houghton, *US Foreign Policy*.

64. John K. Singlaub with Malcolm McConnell, *Hazardous Duty: An American Soldier in the Twentieth Century* (New York: Summit Books, 1991), 376; cited in Lloyd J. Matthews, *The Political-Military Rivalry for Operational Control in U.S. Military Actions: A Soldier's Perspective* (Carlisle Barracks, PA: U.S. Army War College, 1998), 12.

65. Matthews, *Political-Military Rivalry*, 12. See also Matthews, 39n32. Nevertheless, the thought that Kissinger was running military operations has taken hold in some circles.

66. On responsibility for the BLU-82, see Christopher Hitchens, "The Kiss of Henry," *Nation*, April 30, 2001, 9; and for ordering the assault on Tang, see Wise and Baron, *14-Hour War*, 223.

67. See Edward J. Lengel, Charles R. Rambo, Shelley A. Rodriguez, and Michael D. Tyynismaa, "The *Mayaguez* Incident: An Organizational Theory Analysis" (thesis, Naval Postgraduate School, 2006). These authors assert that "through the radio connection established in the NMCC (National Military Command Center), he [Ford] spoke directly several times to fighter pilots and the Airborne Command and Control Center during the strafing of the Cambodian waters." The source for the assertion is *Seized at Sea: Situation Critical: The Story of the Mayaguez Crisis*, directed by Brian Kelly (Alexandria, VA: Henninger Productions, 2000), DVD.

68. Starnes, "*Mayaguez* Incident."

69. Vandenbroucke, *Perilous Options*, 95.

70. Ibid., 168.

71. Ibid., 96.

72. Ibid., 7.

73. Lieutenant General Burns later commented, "Gayler had now gotten back to Hawaii. I could tell the minute he walked in the command center. Admiral Gayler is a very courageous, very brilliant, take-charge sort of fellow who finds great difficulty in getting off the bridge. Sometimes that is not helpful." Burns interview.

74. Vandenbroucke, 97.

75. Ibid., 97.

76. Wetterhahn, *Last Battle*, 62–63.

77. Dunham and Quinlan, *US Marines in Vietnam*, 243.

78. Herspring, *Pentagon and the Presidency*, 230, 235. Herspring relies on Wetterhahn for this argument.

79. Mahoney, *Mayaguez Incident*, 224.

80. Ibid., 253.

81. Ibid., 214, 224. Vandenbroucke offers a detailed account of this incident. He notes the Marines were anxious for reinforcements, but somehow CinCPac had received information that the Marines were "in no imminent danger," with "the opposition forced back." Instructed by Washington to concentrate on withdrawing, Gayler ordered USSAG to recall the second helicopter wave. General Burns realized, however, how badly the Marines needed reinforcements and pressed Gayler to change his order. Colonel Johnson, who was monitoring communications, also protested, as did a Marine Corps general in Hawaii. Gayler reversed the order. Vandenbroucke, *Perilous Options*, 108.

82. Wetterhahn, *Last Battle*, 45–46. This charge is repeated by Herspring, *Pentagon and the Presidency*, 226.

83. Wetterhahn, *Last Battle*, 260, 262. Wetterhahn's biting conclusion is that Ford and Kissinger "improvised tactics, confusing political experience with military reality during a black-tie dinner" while "Americans lay bleeding and dying needlessly on a distant spit of sand" (314).

84. Pfaltzgraff and Davis, *National Security Decisions*, 276–77.

85. For a sustained argument on this point, see David Tucker and Christopher Lamb, "Peacetime Engagements," in *America's Armed Forces: A Handbook of Current and Future Capabilities*, ed. Sam Sarkesian (Greenwood: Westport, CT, 1996), 306–7.

86. Patrick, "*Mayaguez* Operation."

87. Burns interview.

88. According to one source, "Although CinCPac had authorized such fires and LtCol Austin had requested them, LtGen Burns decided against pre-assault fires, fearing endangerment of the *Mayaguez* crew. Neither he nor his staff informed the assault forces of his decision." Starnes, "*Mayaguez* Incident," 6.

89. In prepping Ford for a meeting with the shah of Iran the day after the crisis, Kissinger said, "Tell him you used more force than necessary." Memorandum of Conversation, President Ford, Henry Kissinger and Brent Scowcroft, Thursday, May 15, 1975, 9:45 a.m., Oval Office (declassified), Ford Library.

90. Jones interview, 204; Mahoney, *Mayaguez Incident*, 37; GAO report, 95.

91. Mahoney, *Mayaguez Incident*, 132; Guilmartin, *Very Short War*, 151. Also, within that 175-person first wave of Marines there were linguists, explosive ordnance disposal personnel, and a medic because, as Austin later wrote in his unit history, "it seemed logical that if the *Mayaguez* crew was found on the island, the assault force should be prepared to free/assist/treat them." R. W. Austin, 2nd Battalion, 9th Marines, *Koh Tang/Mayaguez Historical Report*, 9 December 1975, 2; declassified.

92. Mahoney, *Mayaguez Incident*, 229.

93. Houghton, *US Foreign Policy*, 88.

94. Vandenbroucke does a good job of examining anticipatory compliance as subordinates tried to meld with what they assumed were senior leader preferences. His account indicates the Marines would launch their assault irrespective of conditions because of their assumptions about senior leader preferences. Vandenbroucke, *Perilous Options*, 162.

95. Both Austin and his S-3 understood enemy strength was greater than twenty or so irregular forces. Lieutenant Colonel Austin "anticipated a tough time" (see note 93 on page 248), and according to Major John Hendricks, Austin's S-3, it was understood that enemy forces would be as high as 100 to 150:

> After our return [from the U-21 recon flight] to Utapao we met with members of the Air Force at Utapao, coordinators for fixed wing, a brigadier general from General Burns' staff at Nakhon Phenom, air intelligence, and the crew of a C-130 air rescue aircraft. The task force colonel and Lieutenant Colonel Austin took the lead in questions designed to elicit the most information about the circumstances of the seizure of the SS *Mayaguez* and the situation on the island. No maps and only a few localized photos taken by aircraft were available. Initial estimates were that about 60 to 70 former Royal Khmer Navy personnel from the sunken gunboats and a very few soldiers, believed to be Khmer Rouge, were on the island. All in all, less than 100 effectives were present on the island. This was based on information given by a Royal Khmer officer who had fled to Thailand. Aerial observation seem to confirm this.
>
> After we had almost finished with this coordination process, the major operations officer from the task force stopped me in a passageway and let me know that he had received more information about the Khmer on the island. He said that, rather than the "less than 100" originally briefed, there appeared to be at least 150. He had no further information about the makeup of the force. I relayed this information to Lieutenant Colonel Austin and our intelligence officer. After the exchange of information about the opposing forces and the assets available to rescue the crew, we returned to our hanger. Once there we set up a briefing board and got down to drafting options and began to develop an assault plan.

A platoon leader, Lieutenant Richard H. Zales, recalls a last second meeting with Captain Davis on the tarmac, who explained the revised intelligence estimate indicated the Marines would face "at least a reinforced company on the island equipped with heavy machine guns and mortars." In contrast, Gunny Sergeant Francis McGowin, Austin's S-2, only knew that "the last intelligence we received was that there were sixty to eighty militia troops occupying Koh Tang." Wise and Baron, *14-Hour War*, 95, 187, 234, 265.

96. Austin simply notes his requests for prep fires were not approved. Burns notes, "I told them, 'We can't afford preparatory fire' but I did say, 'We can use 20-millimeter or gas.'" Wise and Baron, *14-Hour War*, 95, 96; Burns interview, 440.

97. Mission Command White Paper, 7.

98. Richard A. Mobley, "Revisiting the Korean Tree-Trimming Incident," *Joint Force Quarterly* 35 (October 2004), 108, 112, 115.

99. Hill and Niemi, "Trouble with Mission Command," 94.

100. For example, the current Army chief of staff, General Mark A. Milley, sees micromanagement as a major concern despite official emphasis on the mission command approach:

> What we do, in practice, is we micromanage and overly specify everything the subordinate has to do, all the time. . . . It might be an effective way to do certain things. It is not an effective way to fight. . . . You will lose battles and wars if you approach warfare like that. . . . So we have to practice what we preach. We preach "mission command" but we don't necessarily practice it on a day to day basis in everything we do.

Sydney J. Freedberg Jr., "Let Leaders off The Electronic Leash: CSA Milley" *Breaking Defense*, May 5, 2017, https://breakingdefense.com/2017/05/let-leaders-off-the-electronic-leash-csa-milley/. The author is indebted to Colonel Robert M. Klein for this reference. See also note 53 above for retired General Stanley McChrystal's discussion of delegation of authority and his concept of "Eyes On, Hands Off," which emphasizes the dangers of micromanagement.

101. Commenting on information sharing in the Pentagon, two former officials observe:

> There is a fear among some at the Department of Defense that this type of data would facilitate micromanagement from leadership or—worse—from Congress. This is anathema to all in an organization that valorizes mission command. Yes, no one wants the secretary of defense to call up a battalion commander demanding better outcomes on measures only partly within that unit's control. But mission command—empowering lower echelons—does not mean that senior leaders should be kept in the dark. Mission command may be about "hands off," but it must be, as a corollary, "eyes on." Having better data (and the systems to use it) would allow the department to tailor interventions, share successes, and demonstrate what works and what doesn't.

Brad Carson and Morgan Plummer, "Defense Reform in the Next Administration," *War on the Rocks*, September 12, 2016, https://warontherocks.com/2016/09/defense-reform-in-the-next-administration/.

102. See the discussion of micromanagement and war planning in Christopher Lamb with Megan Franco, "National-Level Coordination and Implementation: How System Attributes Trumped Leadership," in *Lessons Encountered: Learning from the Long War*, ed. Richard D. Hooker Jr. and Joseph J. Collins (Washington, DC: National Defense University Press, 2015), 197–201; 214–16.

103. McChrystal is an interesting case in this regard. He emphasizes the importance of senior leaders being aware of subordinate activities:

> I told subordinates that if they provided me with sufficient, clear information about their operations, I would be content to watch from a distance. If they did not, I would describe in graphic terms the "exploratory surgery" necessary to gain the situational awareness I needed. They were free to make all the decisions they wanted—as long as they provided the visibility that, under shared consciousness, had become the standard.

This was the "Eyes On" part of McChrystal's dictum, but the "Hands Off" component of his injunction implies no interference with subordinate decisions. However, the importance of shared situational awareness suggests well-informed senior leaders occasionally will need to intervene and provide guidance to subordinates. McChrystal, *Team of Teams*, 217.

104. James R. Locher, *Victory on the Potomac: The Goldwater-Nichols Act Unifies the Pentagon* (College Station: Texas A & M University Press, 2004), 279. See all of chapter 14: "McFarlane Outflanks the Pentagon," 277–98.

105. Rearden, *Council of War*, 384.

106. Gary Weikel, letter to the author, October 29, 1991. At the time, military officers on the NSC staff noted how "conventional" the Pentagon military options were. See note 22 on page 224.

107. Richard Green, "Ted Lunger and the Creation of USSOCOM," *Tip of the Spear*, April 2014. Green works in US Special Operations Command's History and Research Office, and *Tip of the Spear* is the command's publication.

108. Holloway, *Aircraft Carriers at War*, 427.

109. Ibid., 402, 426.

110. James R. Locher, the lead SASC staffer for the legislation makes this point often in presentations. James R. Locher III, telephone conversation with the author, May 18, 2017; and James R. Locher III, email to the author, May 18, 2017.

111. Jones interview, 202.

112. General Joseph F. Dunford, USMC, Remarks in Q&A at the Center for a New American Security Next Defense Forum, Washington, DC, December 16, 2015.

113. Scowcroft has made this point. Pfaltzgraff and Davis, National Security Decisions, 273–74. It is often forgotten that Kennedy used the Executive Committee during the Cuban Missile Crisis rather than managing it directly through his NSC.

114. For Kissinger's negative take on Ford's use of the NSC as his decision making mechanism, see *Years of Renewal*, 572–73.

115. Rearden, *Council of War*, 389n66.

116. Mahoney cites and approves of Kissinger's observation that it was dangerous to have the NSC exercise oversight, thinking Kissinger was taking a stand against micromanagement. This is not the case, as Kissinger's subsequent argument for a subgroup exercising the requisite control indicates. Mahoney, *Mayaguez Incident*, 214.

117. See the discussion in Project on National Security Reform, *Forging a New Shield* (Washington, DC: Project on National Security Reform, 2008), which cites John P. Leacacos, "Kissinger's Apparat," in *Fateful Decisions: Inside the National Security Council*, Karl F. Inderfurth and Loch K. Johnson, eds., (New York: Oxford University Press, 2004), 86; Kissinger, *White House Years*, 28–29, 48, 805–806; Henry M. Kissinger, *Years of Upheaval* (Boston: Little, Brown, 1982), 435; and comments to Richard Holbrooke in *To End a War*, rev. ed. (New York: Modern Library, 1999), 117.

118. Kissinger once observed that "personality clashes are reduced; too much is usually at stake for normal jealousies to operate. In a crisis only the strongest strive for responsibility; many hide behind a line of consensus that they will be reluctant to shape; others concentrate on registering objections that will provide alibis after the event. The few prepared to grapple with circumstances are usually undisturbed in the eye of the hurricane." This was not true of the *Mayaguez* crisis, where Schlesinger had a strong influence on outcomes. Robert Shrum, "The Most Hated Man," *Time*, October 15, 1979, 44, cited in Major Ken Robinson, USA, "*Mayaguez* and National Security Decision Making in Crisis" (student paper, Command and Staff College, Marine Corps University, 1997).

119. DeFrank, *Write it When I'm Gone*, 91.

120. Alexander George, "The case for Multiple Advocacy in Making Foreign Policy," *American Political Science Review* 66, no. 3 (September 1972): 751–85.

121. Rearden, *Council of War*, 384.

122. For example, in his memoirs Kissinger describes the orders Ford issued in the first NSC meeting as "crisp" and quotes the first such order: "First, we use the aircraft to stop any boats leaving the island. You do not sink them, necessarily, but can you take some preventive action?" "Some preventative action" falls far short of automatically sinking the vessels and gave the Pentagon a significant degree of latitude. See also the discussion on pages 83–84. Kissinger, *Years of Renewal*, 558.

123. Locher, *Victory on the Potomac*, 38.

124. Project on National Security Reform, *Forging a New Shield*, 222.

125. Ibid., 587.

126. Ibid.; and Christopher Lamb, "National Security Reform," in *Charting a Course: Strategic Choices for a New Administration*, ed. Richard Hooker (Washington, DC: National Defense University Press, 2016).

127. Some sense of the remorse involved in the loss of the three missing Marines can be gathered from the interviews in Wise and Baron, *14-Hour War*. As for a "cover up," many recall being told not to discuss the fate of the Marines with the press, but Lieutenant Colonel Austin argues an extensive investigation was mounted and "nothing was covered up." See Wise and Baron, *14-Hour War*, 104, 111, 116, 144, 200, 254–56, 268.

128. Karl Marlantes, "Vietnam: The War That Killed Trust," *New York Times*, January 7, 2017.

129. Kissinger, *Years of Renewal*, 558.

130. Davidson does a good job of documenting this and other civil-military tensions that arise in civilian review of military plans. Janine Davidson, "Civil-Military Friction and Presidential Decision Making: Explaining the Broken Dialogue," *Presidential Studies Quarterly* 43, no.1 (2013): 129–45.

131. For an argument to this effect, see Christopher J. Lamb and Joseph C. Bond, "National Security Reform and the 2016 Election," *Strategic Forum* 293 (April 2016).

132. Cited in Vandenbroucke, *Perilous Options*, 113.

133. Schlesinger *Veteran* interview.

134. Hartmann, *Palace Politics*, 327.

135. Cheney, *In My Time*, 83.

136. Kissinger, *Years of Renewal*, 575.

137. Schlesinger *Veteran* interview.

138. That has always been this author's view. Lamb, *Belief Systems and Decision Making*, 262–65.

139. Ford made this point in an NSC meeting when he said if the boat got to the mainland, "and we have done the other things we are contemplating, there will not be much opportunity for them anyway." He also said it two days later when Hugh Sidey of *Time* magazine interviewed him, asking why he had not tried to negotiate for the crew after they were taken. Ford said that had not worked in the case of the *Pueblo* and that "we were dealing with a government that, by its recent actions, had shown a very abnormal attitude toward its own people and I could imagine how they might treat Americans." Thornton, *Times of Heroism*, 107.

140. Schlesinger *Veteran* interview.

141. See Ephron's reporting on how Israel now deals with citizens taken hostage. Dan Ephron, "Israel: Better Hostages Dead than Alive: Operation Hannibal," *Politico*, July–August 2015, http://www.politico.com/magazine/story/2015/06/operation-hannibal-119209_Page2.html#.WSR6FaqwefA.

142. Wetterhahn, *Last Battle*, 103.

143. *Stars and Stripes*, May 17, 1975, 2.

144. Swift also recalled the impact of Reagan's pronouncements, stating that "one of these Iranian guys came in and said, 'you all better hope you get out before Ronald Reagan comes in because he will take military measures, and all of us will die.' And I think that was quite possible too. They just figured that when Reagan came in that they believed his rhetoric, that indeed he would take action." Elizabeth Ann Swift, interviewed by Charles Stuart Kennedy, December 16, 1992, Association for Diplomatic Studies and Training, Foreign Affairs Oral History Project, 42.

145. Ibid., 44.

146. Ibid.

147. Barak Barfi, "How the White House Abandoned American Hostages," *Foreign Policy*, June 23, 2015, http://foreignpolicy.com/2015/06/23/how-the-white-house-abandoned-american-hostages-foley-sotloff-mueller/.

Conclusion

1. For example, Marine General James L. Jones, former Supreme Allied Commander, Europe, reiterated the micromanagement charge on the occasion of President Ford's funeral in 2007. Jones, who later would become national security advisor, commented on the *Mayaguez* crisis, saying: "One of the mistakes that was made in the senior echelons was that once the crew was released, the politicians wanted to stop the landing. So you had half the troops on the ground, another half waiting to go in; it was chaos." In 1975 Jones was a member of the Marines' 3rd Battalion, 9th Marines, but did not participate in the *Mayaguez* operations because he was on leave at the time. John J. Kruzel, "*Mayaguez* Incident Tested President Ford's Mettle," American Forces Press Service, January 3, 2007.

2. Lamb, "*Mayaguez* Crisis: Correcting 30 Years."

3. Patricia Cohen, "Field Study: Just How Relevant Is Political Science?" *New York Times*, October 19, 2009.

4. "Does the Academy Matter?," *Foreign Policy*, March 14, 2014, http://foreignpolicy.com/2014/03/15/does-the-academy-matter/.

5. Nicholas Kristof, "Professors, We Need You!," *New York Times*, February 15, 2014.

6. Lamb, "*Mayaguez* Crisis: Correcting 30 Years," 69.

7. See *Forging a New Shield*, 222, and particularly the 107 case studies that report draws upon.

8. For a quick survey of nine such studies, see the chart in Lamb and Joseph Bond, "National Security Reform and the 2016 Election," 4.

9. Lamb, "National Security Reform."

10. Wetterhahn's account, *The Last Battle*, is particularly good in this respect, as are the personal testimonies of participants in Wise and Baron's *The 14-Hour War*.

11. Lamb, *Belief Systems and Decision Making*, 279.

12. The vast majority of the literature on the *Mayaguez* is highly critical of the Ford administration. However, it should be noted that the most recent book on the crisis, Mahoney's The *Mayaguez Incident*, is on the whole sympathetic to the difficult decisions US leaders faced. More generally, many senior leaders have expressed concern about the quality of the national debate over security issues following the terror attacks on September 11, 2001. See Lamb with Franco, "National-Level Coordination and Implementation," 238–40.

Map Credits

Introduction

Mainland Southeast Asia
Marine Corps History Division

Chapter 1

Local Area Map
Adapted from *The Four Days of* Mayaguez by Roy Rowan (W. W. Norton, 1975)

Chapter 2

Locations of US Air Bases in Thailand
Map by the author

Chapter 3

Command and Control Communications, May 14–15, 1975
Adapted from *The Last Battle: The* Mayaguez *Incident and the End of the Vietnam War* by Ralph F. Wetterhahn

Planned Tang Island and Mayaguez *Actions: 0600 hrs, May 15, 1975*
Adapted from *The Last Boarding Party: The USMC and the SS* Mayaguez *1975* by Clayton K. S. Chun, © Osprey Publishing, part of Bloomsbury Publishing Plc.

Tang Island: Khmer Rouge Defensive Positions, 6:20 a.m., May 15, 1975
Adapted from *The Last Battle: The* Mayaguez *Incident and the End of the Vietnam War* by Ralph F. Wetterhahn

Tang Island: Situation 7:00 a.m., May 15, 1975
Adapted from *The Last Battle: The* Mayaguez *Incident and the End of the Vietnam War* by Ralph F. Wetterhahn

Chapter 4

Marine Forces on Tang Island after First Wave
Adapted from *The Last Boarding Party: The USMC and the SS* Mayaguez *1975* by Clayton K. S. Chun, © Osprey Publishing, part of Bloomsbury Publishing Plc.

Tang Island: Situation 4:00 p.m., May 15, 1975

Adapted from *The Last Battle: The* Mayaguez *Incident and the End of the Vietnam War* by Ralph F. Wetterhahn

Chapter 5

Operations against SS Mayaguez and Koh Tang

Adapted from *The Last Boarding Party: The USMC and the SS* Mayaguez *1975* by Clayton K. S. Chun, © Osprey Publishing, part of Bloomsbury Publishing Plc.

Index

Abramowitz, Morton I., 106, 127
Aerospace Rescue and Recovery Service, 106
affective concepts, 154
Air Force, US (USAF)
    40th Aerospace Rescue and Recovery
        Squadron, 43
    56th Security Police Squadron, 27
    locations US air bases in Thailand, 20
    operations planning, 38–39
    See also Commander of US Support Activi-
        ties Group and Seventh Air Force
Airborne Command Post, 94
aircraft, fixed-wing
    A-6 Intruder, 54, 55
    A-7 Corsair, 28, 31, 54, 55, 59, 61
    AC-130 Spectre gunship, 31, 46, 48, 59, 61
    OV-10 Bronco forward air control aircraft,
        60–61, 106
    B-52 Stratofortress
        considerations of mainland strikes,
            91–92
        debate concerning use of, 14, 15, 33,
            36–37, 73
        opposition to use of, 15, 33, 36, 165
    C-130 Hercules, 62
    EC-130 airborne command and control air-
        craft, 38
    F-4 Phantom, 19, 21, 30, 59, 61
    U-21 Ute, 45, 124
airstrikes
    first wave, 51
    second wave, 54
    third wave, 55, 57
    armed reconnaissance mission, 93
    cancellation of, 50–51, 60, 94
    Coral Sea TACAIR assignments, 51, 54–55, 57

debate concerning use of, 14, 15, 33, 36, 73
Ford's reaction to cancellation
planning of, 38–39, 41
resumption of, 51, 54
use of riot control agents, 31
Albert, Congressman Carl B., 43
Allison, Graham T., 137
armed reconnaissance
    definition of, 93
Army, US (USA)
    and *Mayaguez* operations, 43, 45
Austin, Lieutenant Colonel Randall W., USMC,
        45–48, 57–59, 61–65, 124–25

Bay of Pigs, 105–6
belief system model, 116–17, 151–60
belief systems, decision makers'
    as guide to evaluating decision makers'
            postcrisis explanations, 116–19,
            134–35
    major themes of, 151–60
    Ford
        concern with US prestige, 118
        on use of force, 153
    Kissinger
        concern with American prestige, 155,
            259–60n80
        concern with North Korea, 178–79
        on lessons of Vietnam, 152, 155
        on use of force, 154–55
        view of EC-121 crisis, 154–55
    Schlesinger
        on American credibility, 155
        on disproportionate force, 72, 143, 155,
            157–58

belief systems, decision makers' (*continued*)
Scowcroft
on *Pueblo* analogy, 156
similarities with Kissinger, 153–54
BLU-82 bomb, 39, 62–63
Brown, General George S., USAF, 95, 98–100
Brzezinski, Zbigniew, 179, 200, 264n46
Buchen, Philip W., 33, 40–41, 93, 144, 209
Bucher, Captain Lloyd M., 14, 209, 211
Bureau of Intelligence and Research (INR), 11, 22, 35, 52
bureaucratic politics model, 142–51
Burns, Lieutenant General John L., USAF
authorization requirements, 26
communication to resume airstrikes, 51, 96
impact of faulty intelligence, 125–26
operations planning, 38–39
orders to isolate Tang Island, 20–21
use of BLU-82, 39, 62
Bush, George H. W., 175, 222n14, 252n139
Byrd, Senator Robert C., 24

Cambodia
attacks by, 23, 43, 45–48
broadcast announcing release of *Mayaguez*, 48–49
communication with China, 15, 27
communication with United States, 48
considerations of mainland strikes, 91–101
defense of Tang Island, 45–48
estimates of defenders on Tang Island, 32, 41
indications of possible diplomatic resolution to crisis, 22–23, 35
NSC members' opinion on motivation for behavior, 12–13
opinions on ultimatum to, 23, 24–25, 40–41, 74–80
overview of crisis, 1–7
resistance to Marine withdrawal
See also Khmer Rouge
Carter, Jimmy, 179
case studies
configurative-idiosyncratic, 137–38
disciplined-configurative, 137, 138
Cassidy, Captain Barry, 59
casualties
expectations of, 41

number of, 27, 48, 65, 240n2
prevention of higher numbers of, 105, 106
Central Intelligence Agency (CIA)
Colby's opinion on motivation for Cambodian behavior, 12
Foreign Broadcast Information Service, 49, 51, 96
chain of command, 199
Chen, Huang, 134, 175
China, People's Republic of (PRC)
communication with Cambodia, 15, 27
communication with United States, 48, 226n3
Ingersoll's communication from, 15
reaction to US behavior in crisis, 174–76
report of use of influence in crisis, 35
CIA. *See* Central Intelligence Agency
Cicere, Second Lieutenant Michael A., USMC, 48, 59, 61
CINCPAC. *See* commander in chief, Pacific Command
civil-military relations, 1–7, 203–6
Clements, William P., Jr., 13, 33, 41, 72, 144–45, 227n16, 243n40, 256n33
Clifford, Clark M., 14
Colby, William E.
briefing to NSC meeting, 23, 39
considerations of mainland strikes, 91
estimate of Cambodian strength, 41
impact of faulty intelligence, 123, 127
misperception of crisis, 129
on motivation for Cambodian behavior, 12
North Korean concern, 133
on timing of military operations, 32
commander in chief, Pacific Command (CINCPAC)
chain of command, 199
military operations planning, 15–16
Commander of US Support Activities Group and Seventh Air Force, 26
communications map, 38
COMUSSAG/7AF. *See* Commander of US Support Activities Group and Seventh Air Force
configurative-ideographic approach, 137–38
configurative-idiosyncratic approach, 137
Congress
Ford's briefing to, 42–43

investigation of *Mayaguez* crisis, 111–12
    reaction to handling of crisis, 110–12
Coogan, Rear Admiral R. P., 64–65
Coral Sea, USS
    cancellation of airstrikes, 50–51, 60, 94
    debate concerning use of aircraft, 33, 36
    opinions on redirecting carrier, 13–14
    redirection of, 15
    resumption of airstrikes, 51, 54–55, 57
Coulter, Lieutenant (junior grade) R. T., 64–65
Cuban missile crisis, 137
Cushman, General Robert E., Jr., USMC, 37

Daniel, Congressman Dan, 195
Davis, Captain James H., 63–65
decision-making models
    belief system model, 116–17, 151–60
    bureaucratic politics model, 142–51
    information requirements, 160–62
    rational actor model, 139–42
Defense Intelligence Agency (DIA)
    draft ultimatum to Cambodia, 24–25, 77
    estimate of Cambodian strength on Tang
        Island, 32
    impact of faulty intelligence, 124, 127, 162–63
    indications of possible diplomatic resolu-
        tion to crisis, 22–23
defense reform, 195–97
Deng Xiaoping, 27, 175–76
Department of Defense (DoD)
    ultimatum consideration, 76
    on use of force, 22
Department of State
    Bureau of Intelligence and Research, 11, 22,
        35, 52
    Kissinger's control of staff, 77–78
DIA. *See* Defense Intelligence Agency
diplomacy
    communication efforts with China and
        Cambodia, 48
    efforts of, 42–43
    Kissinger's reluctance to seek diplomatic
        resolution, 36, 74–79
disciplined-configurative approach, 137, 138
DoD. *See* Department of Defense
domestic politics, 34, 108, 109, 110–14, 122, 168, 213
domino theory, 153

Dunford, General Joseph F., USMC, 196–97

Eagleton, Senator Thomas F., 111–12
Eastland, Senator James O., 110
EC-121 crisis, 70, 71, 87, 154–55

FBIS. *See* Foreign Broadcast Information Service
fishing boat
    decisions concerning use of riot control
        agents, 30–32
    release of *Mayaguez* crew to, 53
    sighted, 28, 53
Fisk, Technical Sergeant Wayne L., USAF, 64,
        219n3
Ford, President Gerald R.
    adjustments to the description of crisis
        behaviors, 101–3
    anger toward Schlesinger, 144–50, 166–67
    announcement of recovery of ship and
        crew, 59
    belief system, 156–59
    briefing to Congress, 42–43
    communication with Schlesinger, 19–20,
        21, 27, 54–55
    communication with Scowcroft, 19, 27–28
    concerns regarding inaccurate informa-
        tion, 23
    considerations of mainland strikes, 91–101
    decision-making process, 115–22
    decision to resume airstrikes, 51
    declaration of incident as act of piracy, 15
    desire to handle crisis, 11
    domestic political concerns, 110–14
    firing of Schlesinger, 166–67
    on Khmer Rouge, 30, 129
    misperception of crisis, 128–31
    on operating US forces out of Thailand,
        21–22
    order to sink patrol boats, 32
    overview of handling of crisis, 1–7
    on *Pueblo* crisis, 14
    quarantine of Tang Island, 24
    questions concerning US motivation and
        behaviors, 1–7
    reaction to Cambodian broadcast, 50–51
    reaction to news of crisis, 11

Ford, President Gerald R. (*continued*)
    reaction to news that crew had been released, 54
    response to Cambodian broadcast, 51
    on timing of military operations, 25–26, 33, 86–89
    on ultimatum to Cambodia, 24–25
    on use of force, 73, 80–82, 153
    on use of riot control agents, 31
    on War Powers Act, 111
Foreign Broadcast Information Service (FBIS), 49, 51, 96

Gallup poll, 14
GAO. *See* US General Accounting Office
Gayler, Admiral Noel A. M., 15–16, 50, 55, 62, 94–99
General Accounting Office. *See* US General Accounting Office
Gleysteen, William H., Jr., 174
Goldwater-Nichols Act, 195–96
Guilmartin, John F., 105–6, 107, 119–20, 133, 181

Habib, Philip C., 1, 49
Hall, Gary L., 64
Hancock, USS, 69, 79, 85
Hargrove, Joseph N., 64
Harold E. Holt, USS, 39, 44–45, 63, 85, 86, 147
Hartmann, Robert T., 59, 207
helicopters
    CH-53 Sea Stallion, 43, 106
    HH-53 "Super Jolly Green Giant," 43, 106
Henry B. Wilson, USS, 39, 48, 53, 61, 64, 97
Holloway, Admiral James L., III, 40, 41, 93, 95, 99, 195–96
Holsti, Ole, 137–38
Holtzman, Congresswoman Elizabeth, 111
Houghton, David P., 168
Hunt, Major General Ira A. "Jim," 126
Hutto, Representative Earl D., 195
Hyland, William G., 11, 114

Ingersoll, Robert S., 15, 49, 79
INR. *See* Bureau of Intelligence and Research

intelligence estimates
    impact of faulty intelligence, 122–28, 162–63
IPAC. *See* Pacific Command's intelligence center

Japan, 172–73
JCS. *See* Joint Chiefs of Staff
Jervis, Robert, 168–69
Johnson, Colonel John M., USMC, 183, 241n15, 266n81
Johnson, Lyndon B., 112
Joint Chiefs of Staff (JCS)
    chain of command, 199
    draft ultimatum to Cambodia, 24–25
    and *Mayaguez* operations, 50, 55, 119
Jones, General David C., USAF
    considerations of mainland strikes, 93, 96
    defense reform and, 196
    impact of faulty intelligence, 124, 126–27
    military operations planning, 15–16
    opinion of mainland bombings, 39–40, 41
    on quarantine orders, 23
    on timing of military operations, 33, 86–90
    on ultimatum to Cambodia, 40, 77
    on use of airstrikes, 36
    on use of force, 73, 80–82, 146

Keith, First Lieutenant James D., "Dick," USMC, 47, 48, 59
Kennerly, David H., 54, 128, 129
Khmer Rouge
    China influence in crisis, 35
    defensive positions on Tang Island, 45
    reports of attacks, 23
Kim Il Sung, 133, 135, 172–74. *See also* North Korea
Kissinger, Henry A.
    actions following Cambodian broadcast, 49–51
    belief system, 157–60
    communication with Scowcroft, 178–79
    communication with Sisco, 36, 49, 52–53, 78–79
    concerns related to EC-121 crisis, 70, 71, 154–55
    considerations of mainland strikes, 91–101
    discussion of military options with Schlesinger, 14–15

on domino theory, 153
impact of faulty intelligence, 123, 126
misperception of crisis, 130
on National Security Council microman-
	agement, 198–200
North Korean concern, 132, 134, 178–79
notification of US allies, 42
on operating US forces out of Thailand,
	21–22, 25, 78–79
overview of handling of crisis, 1–7
on priorities during crisis, 70, 74
reaction to news of crisis, 11, 114
reaction to news that crew had been
	released, 54
relationship with Schlesinger, 143–51
reluctance to seek diplomatic resolution to
	crisis, 36, 74–79
response to Cambodian broadcast, 51–53
State Department staff control, 77–78
on timing of military operations, 32–33,
	86–89
on ultimatum to Cambodia, 24–25, 40–41, 77
on use of force, 13–14, 32–34, 37–39, 55,
	72–73, 83, 154–55
on use of riot control agents, 30–31
on withdrawal from Vietnam, 152–53, 155
Koh Tang. See Tang Island
Kompong Som (Sihanoukville), 13, 14, 16, 19, 21,
	26, 29, 38, 39, 40 43, 50, 55, 80, 83,
	87, 91, 93, 94, 99
Korea. See North Korea; South Korea
Kraft, Joseph, 123

Laird, Melvin R., 200
Laitin, Joseph, 38, 145
Lucas, First Lieutenant John P., USAF, 61

M-60 machine gun, 61, 64
Mahoney, Robert J., 120–22, 133
Mansfield, Senator Michael J., 111
maps
	command and control communications, 38
	Khmer Rouge defensive positions on Tang
		Island, 45
	local area, 12
	locations US air bases in Thailand, 20

mainland Southeast Asia, 3
Marine forces on Tang Island after first
	wave, 58
operations against SS Mayaguez and Tang
	Island, 81
planned Tang Island and Mayaguez
	actions, 44
Tang Island assault, 47
Tang Island evacuation efforts, 62
Marine Corps, US (USMC)
	assault on Tang Island, 2, 22, 45–48
	boarding of Mayaguez, 43–45
	close air support of, 39, 59, 60–61, 95, 96
	commandant of, 37
	evacuation efforts, 60–65
	forces on Tang Island after first wave, 58
	improvised radio relay system, 59
	missing Marines on Tang Island, 64–65
	moved from Okinawa to Thailand, 25, 26
	operations planning, 38–39
	orders to deploy, 26
	personnel left on Tang Island, 64–65
	reaction to BLU-82, 62–63
	reaction to cessation of operations, 60
	second wave sent to Tang Island, 57
	transport of forces, 43
	units
		1st Battalion, 4th Marines, 43
		1st Battalion, 9th Marines, 107, 185
		2nd Battalion, 9th Marines, 43
	withdrawal order, 60
Marlantes, Karl, 203
Marsh, John O., Jr., 32, 74
Marshall, Danny G., 64
Mayaguez, SS
	operations against, 81
	quarantine of, 19–20, 80–85
	release of crew, 53
Mayaguez crisis
	adjustments to description of crisis behav-
		iors, 101–3
	day one of debate and decision making,
		11–17
	day two of debate and decision making,
		19–34
	day three of debate and decision making,
		35–55
	day four of debate and decision making, 57–65

Mayaguez crisis (*continued*)
    diplomacy efforts, 42–43, 74–80
    efficacy of force, 169–79
    evacuation efforts, 60–65
    execution of critical decisions, 74–101
    Ford's declaration as act of piracy, 15
    impact of faulty intelligence, 122–28
    international implications of, 26, 171–79
    key events and decisions, 75
    leaflets drop consideration, 65
    micromanagement, 179–95
    misperception of, 128–31
    mission command, 179–95
    morality of force, 206–11
    motives for US response, 108–36, 213–17
    operational and tactical issues, 106–8
    overview of handling of crisis, 1–7
    priorities of critical decision-makers, 69–74
    questions concerning US motivation and behaviors, 1–7
    as rescue operation, 138
    riot control gas use, 30–32, 44
    timing of operations, 25–26, 85–91
The Mayaguez Incident (Mahoney), 120–22, 133
McDaniel, Second Lieutenant James, USMC, 47
McFarlane, Major Robert C. "Bud," USMC
    communication to resume airstrikes, 51
    communication with Scowcroft, 16
    considerations of mainland strike, 95
    informing Ford and aides on return of crew, 54
    on need for situation reports, 36
McGovern, Senator George S., 111
McNemar, Gunnery Sergeant Lester, USMC, 65
micromanagement concept, 179–95
military chain of command, 199
military operations, US
    adjustments to description of crisis behaviors, 101–3
    assault on Tang Island, 43–45
    beginning of crisis, 11–17
    chain of command, 199
    confusion concerning, 38–39
    considerations of mainland strikes, 91–101
    Coral Sea TACAIR assignments, 51, 54–55, 57
    efficacy of force, 169–79
    execution of critical decisions, 74–101
    international implications of, 26
    key events and decisions, 75

    loss of helicopters, 46–48
    micromanagement, 179–95
    mission command, 179–95
    misunderstandings between Pentagon and the White House, 16
    morality of force, 206–11
    operational and tactical issues, 106–8
    options for, 14–15
    overview of handling of crisis, 1–7
    planning of, 15–16, 39–40
    priorities of critical decision-makers, 69–74
    questions concerning US motivation and behaviors, 1–7
    riot control gas use, 30–32, 44
    timing of, 25–26, 85–91
    transport of forces, 43
    withdrawal order, 60
Miller, Captain Charles T.
    description of US pilots' efforts to turn around fishing boat, 31
    stalling tactics, 19
    on use of riot control gas, 31
mission command concept, 179–95
morality of force, 206–11

Nakhon Phanom, 20
National Military Command Center (NMCC), 11, 26, 36, 51, 54
National Security Agency (NSA), 23, 51–52
National Security Council (NSC)
    first meeting, 12–14, 113
    second meeting, 23–24, 75, 76, 80
    third meeting, 30–34, 72, 75, 78, 86
    fourth meeting, 39–42, 77, 79, 113, 147
    fifth meeting, 147–48
    indications of possible diplomatic resolution to crisis, 35
    reform, 197–203
Navy, US (USN)
    cancellation of TACAIR strikes, 50
    EC-121 crisis, 70, 71
    operations planning, 38–39
    use of SEALs, 64–65
    See also Coral Sea, USS; *Hancock*, USS; *Harold E. Holt*, USS; *Henry B. Wilson*, USS; *Okinawa*, USS
Nelson, Senator Gaylord A., III, 111

Nessen, Ronald H. "Ron"
    Ford's informing of crisis, 12
    news media questioning on crisis, 37–38
    on response to Cambodian broadcast, 52
    White House photo with Ford and celebratory advisors, 54
news media
    explanations for US response to crisis, 108–9, 115–22
    questioning of military operations during crisis, 112
    reports on crisis, 37
Newsweek, 109, 131–32
Nixon, Richard M., 109, 144
NMCC. *See* National Military Command Center
North Korea
    EC-121 crisis, 70, 71
    Pueblo crisis, 14
    US decision maker's concern with, 108–9, 131–36
NSA. *See* National Security Agency
NSC. *See* National Security Council

Okinawa, USS, 79
O'Neill, Congressman Thomas P., 43, 110
Operation Eagle Claw, 195
Osborne, John F., 112

Pacific Command's intelligence center (IPAC)
    considerations of mainland strike, 94–95
    estimates of Cambodian strength, 32
    impact of faulty intelligence, 124, 127, 162–63
Pahlavi, Ashraf, 175
Pahlavi, Mohammad Reza, shah of Iran, 52, 131, 152, 172, 226n3, 229n40, 229n42
Park Chung Hee, 133, 178
Pauly, Lieutenant General John W., USAF, 27, 28–30, 84
Perilous Options (Vandenbroucke), 118–19, 133
Phnom Penh, 55, 129–30
Pol Pot, 253–54n13
Poulo Wai, island of, 12, 16, 22, 81, 130
Powell, Colin L., 200
Pramoj, Kukrit, 25

public opinion
    and decision makers' concern over strategic bombings, 114
    divided by Vietnam War, 112
    expectations in hostage crises, 115
    likely reaction to failure in crisis, 72
    and *Mayaguez* crisis, 36, 136
    monitored by White House, 110
    and Pueblo crisis, 70
    sensitivity to public opinion on use of B-52s, 114
Pueblo analogy
    different interpretations of explanatory importance possible, 246n9
    Ford's concern with, 246n79, 248n103
    and Kissinger, 156, 246n79, 253n7
    military's concern with, 70
    Scowcroft's concern with, 156, 246n79
    significance of, 246n79, 248n103
Pueblo crisis, 13, 14, 70, 128, 156

Qiao Guanhua, 175

Rabin, Yitzhak, 171–72
Radio Phnom Penh, 51, 96
rational actor model, 139–42
Reagan, Ronald W., 168
Ream, 39, 54, 55, 83, 140
riot control agents
    airstrikes, 31–32
    discussion on use of, 30–31
    use on *Mayaguez*, 44
Rockefeller, David, 134
Rockefeller, Vice President Nelson A.
    concerns regarding inaccurate information, 23
    opinion on redirecting USS Coral Sea, 14
    on priorities during crisis, 70
    reaction to news of crisis, 114–15
    on risks of island assault, 23–24
    on significance of *Mayaguez* crisis handling, 13
    on timing of military action, 85–86
    on use of force, 33, 80
Rumsfeld, Donald H.
    impact of faulty intelligence, 123

Rumsfeld, Donald H. (*continued*)
    reaction to news that crew had been
        released, 54
    on timing of military operations, 88–89
    on ultimatum to Cambodia, 77
    on use of airstrikes, 33, 35–36

Scali, John A., 37, 53, 78
Schlesinger, James R.
    cancellation of fourth airstrike, 60
    communication with Ford, 19–20, 21, 54–55
    concern of collateral damage, 37
    considerations of mainland strikes, 91–93,
        96–97, 100
    discussion of military options with
        Kissinger, 14–15
    on domino theory, 154
    estimates of Cambodian strength, 32, 41
    firing of, 166–67
    impact of faulty intelligence, 123–24, 127
    misperception of crisis, 130
    on motivation for Cambodian behavior,
        12–13
    North Korean concern, 132
    on operating US forces out of Thailand,
        21–22
    opposition to B-52 use, 15, 33, 36, 165
    orders to Burns to isolate Tang Island, 20–21
    outline of military options for president, 13
    on priorities during crisis, 70
    reaction to Cambodian broadcast, 51
    relationship with Ford, 144–50, 166–67
    relationship with Kissinger, 143–51
    on risks of island assault, 24
    sensitivity to public opinion on use of B-52s, 73
    on timing of military operations, 33, 86–87,
        89–90
    on ultimatum to Cambodia, 23, 40, 77
    on use of force, 22, 72–73, 80–85, 206–7
    on use of riot control agents, 30–31
    view on operations in Vietnam, 155–56
Scowcroft, Lieutenant General Brent, USAF
    actions following Cambodian broadcast,
        49–51
    on advisability of bombings, 36
    on attempt to disable fishing boat, 27–30
    belief system, 157–59

    communication with Ford, 19, 27–28
    communication with Kissinger, 178–79
    communication with McFarlane, 16
    communication with Wickham, 16–17, 19,
        27–30
    considerations of mainland strikes, 91–101
    on domino theory, 153–54
    misunderstandings with Pentagon on mili-
        tary options planning, 16
    North Korean concern, 133
    orders to sink patrol boats, 32
    on priorities during crisis, 69–70
    Pueblo crisis views, 156
    reaction to news of crisis, 11
    reaction to news that crew had been
        released, 54
    on risks of island assault, 24
    on timing of military operations, 25–26, 86
    on use of force, 73, 80–82
    on use of riot control agents, 30–31
SEALs, 64–65
Senate Foreign Relations Committee, 38
Seventh Air Force. *See* Commander of US
    Support Activities Group and
    Seventh Air Force
Shultz, George P., 200
Singlaub, Major General John K., USA, 182–83, 194
Sisco, Joseph J.
    communication with Kissinger, 36, 49,
        52–53, 78–79
    diplomatic initiatives of, 36, 37, 49
    interruption of NSC meeting for guidance, 42
    on Kissinger's relationship with Ford,
        261n99
    notification of US allies, 42
    role in NSC meeting, 75
Sitton, Lieutenant General Ray B., USAF, 222n15
South Korea, 108, 132–36
Southeast Asia
    map of, 3
Special Operations Command reforms, 196
Special Operations Squadron, 21st, 43
Spectre-61, 31, 46, 48, 59, 61
State Department. *See* Department of State
Stearman, William Lloyd, 51, 55, 94, 134–35
Steele, Vice Admiral George P., 89
Swift, Elizabeth Ann, 210

Ta Mok, 130

TACAIR. *See* tactical air

tactical air
  armed reconnaissance mission, 93
  cancellation of use, 50–51, 60, 94
  debate concerning use of, 14, 15, 33, 36, 73
  planning of use, 38–39, 41
  resumption of strikes, 51, 54–55, 57
  use of riot control agents, 31

Talbott, Strobe, 25

Tang Island
  assault of, 43–48
  Cambodian defense of, 45–48
  evacuation efforts, 60–65
  insertion of Marines, 43–48
  Khmer Rouge defensive positions, 45
  map of, 12
  Marine forces on island after first wave, 58
  Marines left on, 64–65
  operations against, 81
  quarantine of, 24

tear gas. *See* riot control agents

Thailand
  anger concerning US forces operating out of Thailand, 25
  captive fishermen, 31
  locations of US air bases, 20
  opinions concerning operating US forces out of Thailand, 21–22, 79

Tonkin Gulf Resolution, 112

UN. *See* United Nations

Undorf, Major Robert W., USAF, 60–61

United Nations (UN), 37, 48, 78, 136

United States
  communication with Cambodia, 48
  communication with People's Republic of China, 48
  efficacy of use of force, 25, 93, 99, 148
  Ford administration's threat against Korea, 108–9, 131–32, 134
  Kissinger on use of force, 13–14, 32–34, 37–39, 55, 72–73, 83
  location of military forces, 20, 81
  military forces due on scene, 14, 37, 74, 77, 79, 123, 128, 191
  military objective of ship and crew recovery, 99, 117
  proportionate versus disproportionate use of force, 33, 72, 114, 139, 143, 155–58, 193
  Schlesinger on use of force, 22, 72–73, 80–85, 206–7
  US military on proportionate and discriminate use of force, 73, 100, 150, 155, 157, 205, 259n69
  use of force in hostage incidents, 13, 23
  warnings to international shipping, 25, 93, 99, 148
  See also Austin, Lieutenant Colonel Randall W., USMC; Brown, General George S., USAF; Joint Chiefs of Staff; Military operations, US; US Support Activities Group

US General Accounting Office (GAO), 111–12, 116

US Support Activities Group (USSAG)
  chain of command, 199
  Nakhon Phanom location of, 20

USSAG. *See* US Support Activities Group

Uyl, Johannes del, 37, 49, 53

Vance, Cyrus R., 200

Vandegeer, Second Lieutenant Richard, USMC, 46

Vandenbroucke, Lucien S., 118–19, 133, 184

A Very Short War (Guilmartin), 119–20, 133

Vietnam
  dispute with Cambodia over islands, 12–13, 128–29, 221n6
  fall of Saigon, 1, 168, 173
  Ford's willingness to bomb, 260n81
  impact on US behavior in crisis, 121, 152
  Kissinger on US involvement in, 152–53, 155
  lessons of, 112, 132–33, 152, 188
  Schlesinger on aid to, 154
  Scowcroft on US withdrawal from, 145

Vietnam War, 1, 112, 152, 204, 216, 220n1

Waggoner, Joseph D. "Joe," 24

Waldheim, Kurt J.
  communication with China, 48
  contact with Cambodians, 48

Waldheim, Kurt J. (*continued*)
  US communications with, 37
War Powers Act, 6, 22, 43, 111, 113
Watergate, 112
Weikel, First Lieutenant Gary L., USAF, 195, 196
Weinberger, Caspar W., 200
Wetterhahn, Ralph, 187–88
Whitehead, Clay T., 144
Wickham, Major General John A., Jr., USA
  on attempt to disable fishing boat, 28–30
  communication on timing of military operations, 25–26
  communication to resume airstrikes, 51
  communication with Scowcroft, 16–17, 19, 27–30
  relationship with Schlesinger, 167
  on use of military force, 36–37, 83–84
Wilson, Captain Gregory, 63
Word, Brigadier General Charles E., USAF, 94–96
Wyatt, Staff Sergeant J., USMC, 61

Xiannian, Li, 174

Ybarra, Lance Corporal A. Louis, USMC, 61

A US Air Force surveillance photograph shows two Cambodian gunboats alongside the SS *Mayaguez* dead in the water off the island of Poulo Wai. Official US Air Force photo

Above: On the morning of May 12, 1975, President Gerald R. Ford (*right*) listens in the Oval Office as National Security Advisor and Secretary of State Henry A. Kissinger argues the significance of the *Mayaguez* seizure. Courtesy of the Gerald R. Ford Presidential Library

Left: In the Cabinet Room at the White House, Deputy Secretary of State Robert S. Ingersoll (*left*), President Ford, and Secretary of Defense James R. Schlesinger (*second from right*) during the first National Security Council meeting. White House Chief of Staff Donald H. Rumsfeld looks at an enlarged photo in the background. Courtesy of the Gerald R. Ford Presidential Library

Bottom left: Henry Kissinger (*left*), Vice President Nelson A. Rockefeller, and Deputy National Security Advisor Brent Scowcroft (*in background*) during the first National Security Council meeting. Courtesy of the Gerald R. Ford Presidential Library

Top left: The director of the Central Intelligence Agency, William E. Colby, advises the National Security Council on the *Mayaguez* situation on the evening of May 13, 1975. Courtesy of the Gerald R. Ford Presidential Library

Left: Air Force Security Police from Nakhon Phanom, Thailand, volunteered to retake the *Mayaguez* but one of the CH-53s crashed, killing all eighteen policemen as well as the five-man helicopter crew. Official US Air Force photo

Bottom: The acting chairman of the Joint Chiefs of Staff, Air Force General David C. Jones (*standing*), briefs the National Security Council on possible military options during the second meeting on the *Mayaguez* crisis. Courtesy of the Gerald R. Ford Presidential Library

Top left: Henry Kissinger emphasizes a point during the third National Security Council meeting, where the fate of the boat with crew members on the bow was discussed. Courtesy of the Gerald R. Ford Presidential Library

Left: President Ford (*right*) and William Colby examine a map of Cambodia during the third National Security Council meeting. Courtesy of the Gerald R. Ford Presidential Library

Bottom: *From left*, Donald Rumsfeld, Henry Kissinger, Brent Scowcroft, and Nelson Rockefeller hold an impromptu meeting following the third National Security Council meeting. Courtesy of the Gerald R. Ford Presidential Library

Above: On May 14, 1975, General David Jones—the acting chairman of the Joint Chiefs of Staff—shows aerial photographs of Cambodia next to a chart displaying arrival times for US forces during the fourth National Security Council meeting. Courtesy of the Gerald R. Ford Presidential Library

Left: Using visual aids, General David Jones explains the Joint Chiefs of Staff's recommendations for military operations during the fourth National Security Council meeting on the *Mayaguez*. Courtesy of the Gerald R. Ford Presidential Library

Bottom left: James Schlesinger in the Cabinet Room at the White House during the fourth National Security Council meeting. Courtesy of the Gerald R. Ford Presidential Library

Above: Admiral James L. Holloway III—the chief of naval operations—makes a point during the fourth National Security Council meeting. Courtesy of the Gerald R. Ford Presidential Library

Left: White House Counsel Philip W. Buchen (*left*) and Donald Rumsfeld at the fourth National Security Council meeting on the *Mayaguez.* Courtesy of the Gerald R. Ford Presidential Library

Bottom left: Henry Kissinger (*right*) and Donald Rumsfeld during the fourth National Security Council meeting. Courtesy of the Gerald R. Ford Presidential Library

Above: Henry Kissinger in the Oval Office after the fourth National Security Council meeting, advising President Ford on his upcoming meeting with members of Congress. Courtesy of the Gerald R. Ford Presidential Library

Left: Henry Kissinger (*left*) and James Schlesinger talking prior to a May 14 meeting with bipartisan congressional leadership regarding the seizure of the SS *Mayaguez*. Courtesy of the Gerald R. Ford Presidential Library

Bottom left: Representative Carl B. Albert, D-OK; President Ford (*center*); and Senator Mike J. Mansfield, D-MT, during the May 14 meeting with bipartisan congressional leadership. Courtesy of the Gerald R. Ford Presidential Library

Left: Gerald Ford and Henry Kissinger simultaneously gesture toward a map of the Cambodian coastline during their May 14 meeting with members of Congress in the Cabinet Room at the White House. Courtesy of the Gerald R. Ford Presidential Library

Bottom: Senator John C. Stennis, D-MS, (*left*) pokes his finger into Gerald Ford's chest following the May 14 meeting with bipartisan congressional leadership on the *Mayaguez.* Stennis urged Ford publicly to "be as severe as necessary." Brent Scowcroft is in the background. Courtesy of the Gerald R. Ford Presidential Library

Top left: A US Air Force aerial surveillance photo from May 14, 1975, showing both the east and west beaches on Tang Island, Cambodia. Official US Air Force photo

Bottom: A US Air Force surveillance image shows Knife-23 (*left*) and Knife-31, destroyed CH-53C Sea Stallion helicopters, on east beach on Tang Island. Official US Air Force photo

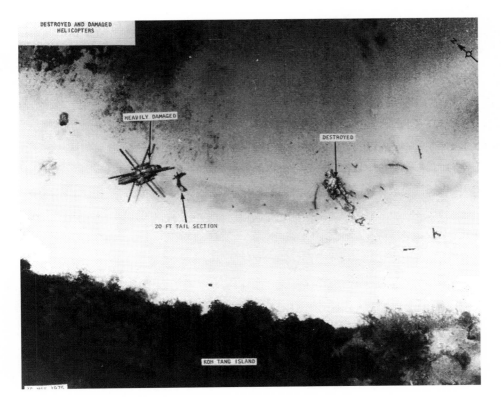

DESTROYED AND DAMAGED HELICOPTERS

HEAVILY DAMAGED

DESTROYED

20 FT TAIL SECTION

KOH TANG ISLAND

Right: A port view of the USS *Harold E. Holt* in the Gulf of Thailand during rescue operations of the merchant vessel *Mayaguez*. The small landing pad is visible. National Museum of the United States Air Force

Below: US Marines from the USS *Harold E. Holt* storm aboard the merchant ship *Mayaguez* to recapture the ship and rescue the crewmen being held captive. No one was found aboard the ship. Official US Marine Corps photo

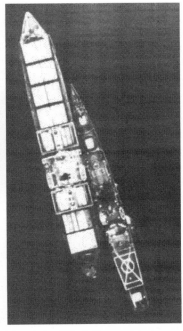

Above: A US Air Force aerial surveillance photo shows the US Navy ship USS *Holt* (*right*) as it pulls alongside the container ship *Mayaguez* to allow the Marine boarding party to board. Official US Air Force photo

Top left: The Marines stormed the *Mayaguez* to recover the ship captured by the Cambodians. No one was aboard, but the crewmen were returned later by a fishing boat. Official US Marine Corps photo

Left: USS *Holt* tows the *Mayaguez* away from Tang Island. National Museum of the United States Air Force

Below left: Merchant mariners from SS *Greenville Victory* discuss with Commander Robert A. Peter-son (*center*), commanding officer of USS *Holt*, how they will prepare *Mayaguez* for a tow. Official US Navy photo

Left: US Marines abandon their damaged CH-53 helicopter, Knife-22, after an emergency landing in Trat Province, Thailand, during the *Mayaguez* operation. Official US Air Force photo

Bottom left: The sunken Cambodian patrol boat with .50-caliber machine guns off Tang Island that bedeviled U.S. helicopters; it was spotted by Nail-68 and destroyed by the USS *Wilson*'s 5-inch gun. Official US Air Force photo

Below: Smoke rounds fired by *Henry B. Wilson* on the eastern side of Tang and riot control agents delivered by A-7s drift out to sea. The *Wilson* expended 176 5-inch shells in support of the Marines that were instrumental in the evacuation from the eastern side of the island. Naval History and Heritage Command Vietnam Collection

Below: US Air Force OV-10 Bron-cos such as this one provided crit-ical battle management and close air support during the combat operations on Tang. Official US Air Force photo

Top left: In the national security advisor's office on May 14, 1975, Robert C. "Bud" McFarlane, Scowcroft's assistant, talks with the National Military Command Center, passing instructions to the Pentagon on airstrikes. Counselor to the President John O. Marsh stands nearby. Courtesy of the Gerald R. Ford Presidential Library

Bottom left: Smoke rises from a warehouse in the Cambodian port of Kompong Som (formerly Sihanoukville), bombed by aircraft from the carrier *Coral Sea*. Naval History and Heritage Command Vietnam Collection

Bottom right: Henry Kissinger and Brent Scowcroft (*foreground*) on the phones in Kissinger's West Wing office discussing the *Mayaguez* operations, having stepped away from the after-dinner coffee with Prime Minister Uyl of the Netherlands. Courtesy of the Gerald R. Ford Presidential Library

Top left: Secretary Schlesinger talks on the telephone in Kissinger's West Wing office just before 9:00 p.m. on May 14, ensuring airstrikes were turned back on. President Ford is seated in the background, having briefly stepped away from the dinner with Prime Minister Uyl. Courtesy of the Gerald R. Ford Presidential Library

Below: In the national security advisor's office at the White House, Brent Scowcroft (*back to camera*), Henry Kissinger, and National Security Council staff discuss the contents of a US response to the Cambodian broadcast with White House Press Secretary Ron Nessen (*center*) on May 14. Courtesy of the Gerald R. Ford Presidential Library

From left: on May 14, Brent Scowcroft, Scowcroft's assistant Bud McFarlane, Henry Kissinger, and Gerald Ford in conversation in the Oval Office. McFarlane is informing the group that the *Mayaguez* crew has been recovered. Courtesy of the Gerald R. Ford Presidential Library

Above: President Ford (*right*) and Henry Kissinger shake hands just after receiving news of the safe return of the *Mayaguez* crew on May 14, 1975. Courtesy of the Gerald R. Ford Presidential Library

Left: Donald Rumsfeld (*left*) offers his congratulations to the president after hearing of the *Mayaguez* crew's safe return. Henry Kissinger stands in the background. Courtesy of the Gerald R. Ford Presidential Library

Clockwise from left: Bud McFarlane, Donald Rumsfeld, Henry Kissinger, Gerald Ford, and Brent Scowcroft comment on Secretary Schlesinger's phone call informing the president of the *Mayaguez* crew's release and recovery. Courtesy of the Gerald R. Ford Presidential Library

In the White House Briefing Room on May 15, 1975, President Ford makes a statement to the media following the recapture of the SS *Mayaguez*. Courtesy of the Gerald R. Ford Presidential Library

Above: AC-130 gunships such as this one provided fire support for Marines being extracted from Tang Island in the dark. Department of Defense photo

Made in the USA
Middletown, DE
23 July 2020

13346314R00196